THE TREATY NAVY

The Story of the U.S. Naval Service Between the World Wars

James W. Hammond, Jr.

WESLEY PRESS

Co-published with Wesley Press

National Library of Canada Cataloguing in Publication Data

Hammond, James W.
  The Treaty navy
  ISBN 1-55212-876-8
  1. United States. Navy--History. I. Title.
VA58.H35 2001   359'.00973   C2001-911194-0

TRAFFORD

This book was published *on-demand* in cooperation with Trafford Publishing.
On-demand publishing is a unique process and service of making a book available for retail sale to the public taking advantage of on-demand manufacturing and Internet marketing.
On-demand publishing includes promotions, retail sales, manufacturing, order fulfilment, accounting and collecting royalties on behalf of the author.

Suite 6E, 2333 Government St., Victoria, B.C. V8T 4P4, CANADA

Phone	250-383-6864	Toll-free	1-888-232-4444 (Canada & US)
Fax	250-383-6804	E-mail	sales@trafford.com
Web site	www.trafford.com	TRAFFORD PUBLISHING IS A DIVISION OF TRAFFORD HOLDINGS LTD.	
Trafford Catalogue #01-0278	www.trafford.com/robots/01-0278.html		

10   9   8   7   6   5   4   3   2   1

CONTENTS

DEDICATION

To Donna
My Bride for more than 40 years;
Severest Friend and Dearest Critic

PREFACE

How the Navy won the sea war against Japan from 1941 to 1945 has been told so many times it would seem that was all the Navy ever did or was. But that's not true. The wartime Navy grew from a small and proficient Naval Service of the previous two decades. Unfortunately the deeds of that Navy and Marine Corps of the '20s and '30s have been overshadowed by their deeds of the early '40s. Those deeds of World War II had their roots in the prewar Navy. It was that Navy, despite treaty limits, low pay, slow promotions, congressional under-funding and apathy, public opposition and pacifist attacks, that was the foundation of the fleet which beat Japan in the Pacific. Because of treaties limiting navies and the U.S. Navy in particular, the prewar naval service was "The Treaty Navy."

This is the story of The Treaty Navy. It is the men and ships between the two World Wars. Strictly speaking, the era of The Treaty Navy began at 10:39 a.m. on Sat., Nov. 12, 1921, when Secretary of State (SecState) Charles Evans Hughes addressed delegates of nine powers in Washington, D.C. They were there to discuss naval limitations and other matters concerning the Pacific and Far East. The Treaty Navy could have ended abruptly just before 8 a.m. local time, on Sun., Dec. 7, 1941, when the first Japanese bombs fell on Pearl Harbor, Territory of Hawaii (T.H.) The era lived on, however, in the men, ships and spirit that fought across the Pacific to ride victoriously at anchor in Tokyo Bay on Sept. 2, 1945.

In reality, The Treaty Navy began before Hughes' proposal for scrapping what would have been the most powerful navy afloat. And concomitantly, its legal end preceded that first American defeat of World War II.

The era goes back to the struggle for supremacy at sea by the belligerents in World War I before U.S. entry in 1917. Its roots are found in the accusations by the U.S. against both Germany and Great Britain of violating international law by interfering with neutral American ships a sea. The difference that led to American entry on the side of the Allies was that while the British were seizing and searching U.S. ships, the Germans were sinking ships and killing Americans with unrestricted submarine warfare.

The legal end of The Treaty Navy can probably be set at Mar. 31, 1938, when SecState Cordell Hull notified the remaining parties to the Washington Treaty and two later London treaties that the U.S. was invoking the "escalator clause" because of Japan's non-adherence. Thus, the U.S., with a genuine fear of Japanese supremacy in the Pacific, was releasing herself from agreements to keep her Navy within treaty limits.

The. U.S. was finally admitting what a few far-sighted naval officers had been saying for more than a generation – Japan was the potential enemy. It wasn't always so stated. There was a dichotomy of assessment among naval officers. The older, more senior, who were at the helm until about 1930, viewed Britain as the traditional naval rival. She was more of a threat than Japan. Younger officers, many of them disciples of RAdm. William S. Sims, a protégé of

Theodore Roosevelt, envisioned a different type of war with a different enemy than one speaking the same tongue.

One of the disciples of Sims was a Marine who had attended the Naval War College with him in 1911. Maj. Earl H. "Pete" Ellis had served in France as a lieutenant colonel but reverted to his permanent rank. RAdm. Sims (who had reverted from four stars) returned to be President of the Naval War College. Ellis was there temporarily. He went on to the Planning Section of Headquarters, Marine Corps (HQMC) and produced a document that was the Marine version of Sims' Naval War College scenario. Significantly, it opened, "In order to impose our will upon Japan, it will be necessary for us to project our fleet and land forces across the Pacific and wage war in Japanese waters." It was approved by MajGen. Commandant (MGC) John A. Lejeune on Jul. 23, 1921. Ellis was dead less than two years later while on "leave" in the Japanese Mandates. His mysterious death has never been adequately explained.

It was the dichotomies of conviction that provided the background for The Treaty Navy. The older traditionalists, reared under the influence of Capt. Alfred T. Mahan USN, stood for the supremacy of the battleline in a major sea engagement to eliminate the enemy's main force, permitting subsequent destruction of his defenseless sea trade. Loss of commerce would force an enemy to sue for peace. The Sims' school saw the efficacy of the new weapons growing out of World War I. The submarine and airplane posed significant threats to the unarmored bottoms and unprotected decks of battleships. Torpedoes exploding under the keel or bombs plunging from above practically doomed battleships. Costly modification would come at the expense of performance. Moreover, the submarine and airplane could possibly skip the showdown battle and go right to the heart of the matter – destruction of the enemy's commerce. Thus evolved the myth of "battleship admirals" and "carrier admirals" that dominated the pens of every pseudo-military "expert" who wrote during the '40s. The real rivalry was not based on traditional versus newer weapons as much as it was based on who would be the enemy and where would be the arena. "Battleship admirals" saw Britain as the yardstick of naval power. If you could defeat the Royal Navy (RN), you could defeat anybody. That was the essence of Plan RED, the possible war at sea against Great Britain. The "carrier admirals" (with the submariners) saw the enemy as ORANGE, *viz.,* Japan. To them it would be a long-range war across the Pacific, a Pacific, after 1919 dotted with islands (north of the equator) mandated to Japan by the League of Nations. At first, it required U.S. defense of positions, fortified bases were banned by treaty, in the Western Pacific, *viz.* Guam and the Philippines, while the fleet moved to a position to interdict Japanese trade routes from the Home Islands south. Battleships were needed as a deterrent to Japanese battleships, not necessarily as a means of forcing a decisive engagement. Submarines and aircraft operating from bases or carriers, astride the Japanese trade routes would strangle her economy. Such a strategy required a long, arduous trek across the Central Pacific. In subsequent ORANGE Plan evaluations, it was determined that the Philippines would have to be recaptured because they could not be held.

The path to the Japanese north-south trade routes led west through the Japanese Mandates. The Ellis plan was the blueprint for the drive across the Central Pacific that *was executed in 1944.*

The dichotomy of opinion lasted until about 1930. Up to then the traditionalists had prevailed. They had influenced ship construction and fleet size. They even influenced the Fleet Problems that were the annual exercises when the Scouting Fleet (Atlantic-based) joined with the Battle Fleet (West Coast-based). In regard to construction, differences led to another conference on limitations. The Geneva Conference of 1927 foundered on the demands of Britain for additional smaller cruisers while President Coolidge had asked for the conference to reduce the numbers of such "combat auxiliaries." An amusing sidelight of that conference was the claim by a charming charlatan and self-styled "naval expert" to having wrecked it at the behest of American shipbuilders. The watershed year for the Navy was 1931. After that things began to improve. Several things happened. The new carriers began to demonstrate their worth with the fleet. The Democrats gained control of the House and a landlubber lover of the Navy from Georgia became Chairman of the House Naval Affairs Committee. Carl Vinson later allied with the Navy-minded President Franklin D. Roosevelt, was to use the treaties as a legal upper limit to which to build the Navy. Also, a new Chief of Naval Operations was announced. Adm. William V. Pratt was a Sims man from the days of the Atlantic Torpedo Flotilla where Sims, its commander, had trained a breed of cocky, innovative destroyer skippers. After 1931, things got better in the fleet – but not rapidly. Vinson and Roosevelt put into operation a construction plan that had been advocated by former (1924-29) Secretary of the Navy (SecNav) Curtis D. Wilbur since 1925. Unfortunately, Wilbur, the first Naval Academy graduate to be SecNav, had fought a stingy Congress and lost. Still, it was the ships of Wilbur, created by the ingenuity of Vinson and Roosevelt, which were available to stem the Japanese tide in 1942.

This is why I set the informal end of The Treaty Navy at Dec. 7, 1941. Ships, even destroyers, take time to build, especially in the business-as-usual attitude of peace. All the ships in commission on that "date of infamy" were either legacies from World War I or recent construction of The Treaty Navy, i.e., authorized between 1916 and 1938 and completed before 1941. They were built under the restrictions of the treaties. They were The Treaty Navy. It was these ships, manned by officers and men who were mostly regulars (it takes longer to train good seamen than it does to build ships) of the period between the wars, who kept the United States from defeat in 1942. It was, of course, the ships and men of the post-1942 era which reinforced the remnants of The Treaty Navy to "impose our will on Japan."

Those are some of the facts and reflections that are paraded on the following pages. Even with a deep love for my subject, however, I realize that any dry recitation of events can be dull. The story of the past is a narrative of events. It is also the story of personalities. To be readable to more than desiccated academics it must be replete with personalities and their actions.

That is the story I bring to the reader – The Treaty Navy with its yarns, anecdotes, and sea stories, the tale with the tragedies and personal triumphs, with the opponents and the heroes, but most of all with the ordinary guys and their long-suffering families. It was the officers and men who manned such ships with the affectionately bestowed nicknames of *Arky,* and *Okie,* of *Prune Barge* and *Blue Goose,* of *Lady Lex* and *Sara* and even *Swayback* and *WeeVee* who made The Treaty Navy real.

It is a story of contrasts and contradictions. There were many ironic turns of evens. In 1921, the Naval Academy Class of 1881 were guests of their Classmate, Adm. Uriu Baron Sotokichi, in Japan. Two years later, men and ships of the U.S. Navy won the admiration of the Japanese people by bringing humanitarian relief during the great earthquake. (The same year that Pete Ellis died mysteriously in the Mandates.) In 1938, the heavy cruiser, *Astoria,* returned the ashes of the Japanese ambassador to a sincere welcome in Japan. Four years later, she succumbed to the guns and torpedoes of the Imperial Japanese Navy (IJN) off Savo Island.

Other personalities abound. There is the epic of a turret explosion and the young turret officer with his dead hand on the magazine flooding valve that saved the battleship. The stump of the charred arm was identified from his Naval Academy Class Ring. Or there is the tragic drama of the faint tapping from the after torpedo room of a rammed submarine on the bottom off New England. As rescuers were thwarted by a violent storm, they promised the entombed men they would be back. They were but it was too late. On the brighter side is the tale of Cdr. John Rodgers, scion of a Navy family reaching back to the Revolution, being overdue on the first San Francisco-Honolulu flight. His seaplane crew rigged sail and paddled to Kauai to compete the mission. We look at the Wardrooms of the '20s and '30s to see some of the major characters of World War II as young men who enjoyed a bit of horseplay to break the routine of life at sea.

The mores of the period are recalled in perspective. The episode of Marine BGen. Smedley D. Butler (son of the Chairman of the House Naval Affairs Committee) court-martialing his host, a colonel for drinking (not illegal) during Prohibition is an example. We see Marines guarding the mails with orders to shoot to kill. They did and the robberies ceased. The same Marines spent a half dozen years being bushwhacked by *sandinistas* (a term not new but more than 75 years old) while other Marines mounted two major expeditions to protect American lives and property in China.

Technical innovations, e.g., dive-bombing, spotting of aircraft on carrier decks for rapid turnaround, refueling underway, amphibious operations with naval gunfire support, advance mobile bases and more, all came about during this era. These were to revolutionize naval warfare in the Pacific. By the time war came, these were well-defined evolutions in the Navy.

There is a nostalgic side as well. Hollywood discovered the Navy. Wallace Berry was great in *Hell Divers.* Likewise, Pat O'Brien, George Brent and Wayne Morris (to be a Navy fighter ace with seven kills during the war) demonstrated modern submarine rescue techniques in *Submarine D-1* while Americas followed the real drama of snatching part of the crew from the sunken submarine *Squalus*. The Naval Academy was the scene of several movies. One, with the singing of Dick Powell and dancing of Ruby Keeler, *Shipmates Forever* (a William Randolph Hearst production), drew storms of protest from those who deemed it warmongering. Less troublesome was *Navy Blue and Gold* with Jimmy Stewart, Robert Young, Tom Brown, Lionel Barrymore and Florence Rice (daughter of noted sports writer, Grantland). We look at several other Navy films of the '30s.

Sports were part of the period too. Twice, Marine Corps teams appeared in the Rose Bowl. So did a Naval Academy team in 1923. Three years later, undefeated Navy met once-defeated Army for the national champion ship. More than 102,000 watched the struggle in Soldiers' Field, Chicago, as a Navy field goal tied it 21-21 to secure the title by default. Navy's tailback on that team, incidentally, swam away from burning *Arizona* at Pearl Harbor and survived to command a Marine regiment on Okinawa and retire as a lieutenant general.

Magazines from Sunday supplements to *Scientific American* and *National Geographic* featured stories of the Navy and its men. *Saturday Evening Post* and *Colliers* sang the praises of the Navy. *Life* devoted several photo essays to life in the fleet.

Not all Americans were favorably disposed to a Navy that was expensive and not of immediate use. (They were glad it was there when needed, however.) Naval appropriations had strong opponents. Some said ship money might be better spent for relief (welfare) as the nation emerged from the Great Depression.

The story of The Treaty Navy is the story of an era that we shall see no more. Social, economic and political changes since the watershed of 1941-45 have confined it to the past forever. Yet, we can vicariously relive those days of the peacetime naval service as it prepared for a war it wished would never come but that it knew would. That is my purpose in writing its story – to give the reader a taste of what things were like in a small but efficient (necessarily because of a paucity of appropriations) Navy and Marine Corps.

If the reader chooses to make comparisons with events of today, so be it. All I ask is that the reader have just as good a time reading it as I have had in telling it. To this end I have avoided notes and citations. I want this story to be read and enjoyed and not be the basis for academic niceties. Readers wishing to know more specifics about such events are invited to the annual *The New York Times Index* and other readings outlined in the Bibliographical Essay. Incidentally, I found that *The New York Times* was a more informative source about the Senate investigation of Mr. William B. Shearer and his "wrecking" of the Geneva Conference of 1927 than the 735-page official report of the investigation. The latter omitted much testimony by direction of the chairman to "strike that from the record" while the newspaper included all.

This is usually the place where an author acknowledges the help and assistance of many. Much of the material, particularly that of personalities and little known events, which would be sidebars in a news story, are the result of conversations over the years with those involved. These run from cocktail party conversations to sea stories oft retold, to reminiscences of members of The Treaty Navy most of whom are long since gone. During my tenure as editor of *Shipmate,* the Naval Academy Alumni Association magazine, I had many old salts and even some of their ladies share their memories of The Treaty Navy with me. To dignify a conversation with say, Adm. Jerauld Wright while "killing a few snakes" (his term for a libation) at the Alibi Club as an "interview" would be a bit pompous on my part. Likewise, a monologue at a Wardroom table or a discussion among senior officers in the mess about their days in Nicaragua could hardly qualify as the basis for a citation. Much of the personal material herein is *tradition* in the ecclesiastical sense. I am providing heritage not history. Thus, my thanks and gratitude is extended to all those who served in and made The Treaty Navy what it was and what it did for the nation.

My only moralizing is in the Epilogue. There the message is that if we hadn't had The Treaty Navy, which was partially preserved after World War I and created in the '20s and '30s, some fat *samuari* would be affecting an Al Capone attitude and demanding, "Whom are you buying your *saki* from?" Now, at least we have a choice between Zenith and Sony or between Buick and Toyota. The question is "For how long?"

Special Appreciations

I have had the benefit of the memories and sea stories of many distinguished members of the Naval Service who lived in the era of The Treaty Navy. I met them over the years. They knew of my interest in the era and were happy to share their experiences with me. All of them have since retired from or left active duty. Most of them are deceased. Perforce, there are some inadvertent omissions but I am grateful to the shared memories of the following: Adm. Arleigh A. Burke, Mrs. Jean Carlson, Adm. Robert B. "Mick Carney, Jr., RAdm. Joshua W. Cooper. RAdm. John. G. Crommelin, Maj. Donald Dixon, VAdm. George C. Dyer, RAdm. Henry C. Eccles, RAdm. E.M. "Judge" Eller, RAdm. William F. "Dolly" Fitzgerald, RAdm. Francis D. Foley, Cox. Joseph A. Glacken (my uncle and coxswain of Capt. E.J. King's gig), Capt. Paul H. "Growler" Grouleff USN, Col. Robert D. Heinl, Jr., MGen. Sam Jack, VAdm. Frederick N. "Nappy" Kivette, MGen. Francis M. McAlister, RAdm. A.B. Metsger, RAdm. Harold B. "Min" Miller, Capt. Elias B. "Benny" Mott USN, RAdm. Joseph H. Nevins, Jr., RAdm. Schuyler N. Pyne, RAdm. Paul H. Ramsey, Capt. Paul R. Schratz USN, Capt. William B. Short USN, Gen. David M. Shoup (I was his aide-de-camp), LtGen. Julian C. Smith, Capt. Roy C. Smith, III USN, Capt. John D. Spangler USN, Mr. John A. "Tex" Underwood (a Classmate of Tom Massie) RAdm. Harvey T. Walsh and Adm. Jerauld Wright.

J.W.H., Jr.
Reno, Nevada

PART I

Before 1924

Chapter I

Prologue

The Navy declined rapidly after the Civil War because the government refused to spend for upkeep of relics that emerged from the victorious blockade of the South. More serious was the disinclination to move into the modern era of fighting ships. The naval art of the Civil War ironclads had moved on to armored ships of steel. The Navy remained a sail-driven, albeit augmented with steam, motley collection of wooden vessels. Steam was available but captains disdained its use since soot soiled the weather decks. Further, Congress was unwilling to spend on coal when the wind was free.

In the 1880s, naval revival began. Four modern ships were ordered (armored cruisers: *Atlanta, Boston* and *Chicago* plus the dispatch boat, *Dolphin.*) These "ABCDs" were followed by more as the writings of Capt. Alfred T. Mahan and his mentors at the Naval War College were heeded. By 1898 there was a modicum of a modern Navy with battleships and combat auxiliaries (the term applied to combatants lesser than battleships) to fight the war with Spain. That war brought two significant victories of the Navy over the obsolete Spanish ships but they were hardly professionally done.

Como. George Dewey took his squadron into Manila Bay and engaged an inferior Spanish squadron riding at anchor. Fighting was intense but brief. The Spanish were annihilated but Navy marksmanship was meager. The percentage of hits to rounds fired was pathetic. Likewise at Santiago on the south coast of Cuba, the Spanish ships sortied one-by-one into the guns of massed American battleships. Shooting was spotty again but what hits were made ignited the decorative interior woodwork of the enemy ships and they burned and beached or sank.

The teachings of Mahan were revisited. The Cuban victory had been the result of massing all the available U.S. battleships. Even *Oregon* had made the dash from the West Coast around the tip of South America to reinforce the Atlantic Squadron. Mahan had preached concentration of naval power *vice* diffusion. A canal through Central America was needed to allow rapid concentration of ships from one coast to the other.

There was another major development in warship design. Till then, battleships carried guns of mixed size as main batteries, e.g., 8-in., 10-in., and 12-in. Not all guns were mounted along the centerline (which would give the same broadside to either side), and some even had the smaller, e.g., 8-in. in pairs in a gun house, superimposed over pairs of 10-in. or 12-in. guns in a turret. The ranges of the larger guns were rarely used effectively since fire control and spotting were primitive.

In 1906, Adm. Lord John "Jackie" Fisher RN made all older battleships obsolete with *HMS Dreadnought*. She had all 12-in. guns mounted in pairs in five turrets. Three turrets were along the centerline; the other two were on either side. Thus, she had a broadside of eight all 12-in. guns to either side She revolutionized the concept of the capital ship and started a scramble in every navy to modernize with "dreadnoughts."

Theodore Roosevelt, a navy- and imperial-minded leader was in the White House. While at Harvard he had written and published *The Naval War of 1812* on the supremacy of gunnery. As Assistant SecNav, he had connived with Dewey to send the Navy to Manila Bay in 1898. Although, he was navy-minded, he realized that he lacked the nautical experience to serve in the Navy during the Spanish war. He led the way in organizing the "Rough Riders" of voluntary cavalry. He led them to fame at San Juan Hill and then rode that fame to the governor's mansion in Albany and then the vice presidency with McKinley. The ballot returned McKinley to office but an assassin's bullet put "Teddy" in the White House. He led a nation that had just acquired overseas responsibilities by annexation (Hawaii 1898); conquest (Guam, the Philippines, Puerto Rico); and [Roosevelt] Corollary, i.e., the United States would guarantee the collection of Latin American debts to foreign nations by controlling the Latin American customs houses. Along the way in 1903, T.R. aided the overthrow of the government of Colombia in Panama. The new government granted a canal right-of-way across the isthmus. His administration boded well for the Navy.

T.R. pushed for a building program of at least a pair of battleships every year. His goal was a fleet of 48 battleships. One of his most vocal opponent to naval expansion was Senator Eugene Hale (R-Maine). Still more than a dozen battleships were laid down during the T.R. administration. An interesting insight into the pervading looseness with facts of the anti-naval and military factions over the years can be found in a later writer who pushed his case against naval armaments citing the "uselessness" of T.R.'s 48 battleship goal. Such ships (with one exception) were named for states. This "scholar" shrugged off T.R.'s program as being nothing more "than wanting to have a battleship named for every state." Had he done his homework he would have found that there weren't 48 states until three years after T.R. left office. Such were the arguments that proponents of The Treaty Navy had to endure.

Several major events with overtones for The Treaty Navy occurred during the Roosevelt administration. The first was the Russo-Japanese War of 1904-05. The President used his "good offices" to bring about the Treaty of Portsmouth ending the war and bringing him the Nobel Peace Prize. Japan gained territory and influence on the East Asian mainland but not the indemnity from Russia she sought and needed to compensate for war costs. The resultant enmity toward the U.S. is not as important to The Treaty Navy as the two major naval actions fought. We've already noted the poor gunnery at Manila Bay and Santiago. The Japanese, although victors, did no better. In the initial attack on Port Arthur, misses greatly exceeded hits. When the ill-fated Russian Baltic Fleet arrived off Tsushima after a seven-month voyage east from Europe to be sunk by Adm. Togo, the IJN got poor marks for accuracy.

Accuracy was difficult with prevailing methods of fire and direction. In addition, a mix of gun sizes diluted the effort causing engagements to occur at the range of the smallest gun. High speeds complicated the matter with rapid rates of change of range, an acceleration not a linear function.

Enter LCdr. William S. Sims USN. Sims was what would later be called a "Young Turk" as far as the Navy was concerned. Standing slightly below the middle of the Academy Class of 1880, he was a thinker and a doer. Further, he was dissatisfied with the *status quo* if he saw something better. He had been ship's intelligence officer on the China Station during the Sino-Japanese War of 1894-95; there he made deep analysis of the battles, the effect of gunnery and the armor of those battleships. His reports filed with the Office of Naval Intelligence (ONI) drew high praise not only from his superiors but also from Assistant SecNav Roosevelt. Evidently, Sims was aware of the latter. After duty as Naval Attaché in Paris and St. Petersburg (where he met one of the U.S. Ambassador's daughters), Sims was off to the Asiatic Station again. There he became professionally acquainted with Capt. Percy Scott RN. Scott was deep in the reform off British gunnery. One of his devices was the Morris tube. It let gunners go through all the motions of aiming and firing but using a sub-caliber gun inside the tube of the big gun. Familiarity could be obtained on a daily basis without excessive wear on the bore and at a lesser expense than full-sized ammunition. Pointers and trainers could practice at will. The second device was an electrical interlock. When the gun pointer (aimer) was on the target, he depressed the firing key. The gun did not fire if the breech was open even though the key was depressed. Closing the breech completed the circuit and the gun fired. Accuracy and speed increased since it was a simultaneous procedure not one of load, aim and fire. Aiming was constant during loading. The RN was getting 80 to 85 per cent hits to the best the USN had to offer of 13 per cent. Sims duly reported these new procedures and successes through channels where they lay buried in the files in Washington.

In the summer of 1901, the North Atlantic Fleet had made a deplorable showing at target practice. When the news reached the China Station, Sims took a fateful step. He went out of channels and could have been accused on insubordination. But like most "doers" he realized that "forgiveness is easier to get than permission!" He wrote to the new president in November 1901. His topic, *inter alia,* was the poor gunnery and his remedies for it. Roosevelt read it and snapped, "Get me those reports!" He ordered another target practice and the gunners were on their mettle but still hit less than 15 per cent of the time. "Cable to China for that young man to come home at once," was T.R.'s next order to the Navy. "Give him entire charge of target practice for eighteen months; do exactly as he says. If he does not accomplish something in that time, cut off his head and try somebody else."

3

Sims came back as Inspector of Naval Target Practice for most of the next eight years. He taught the Navy to shoot and hit. In addition to the two devices of Percy Scott, Sims incorporated the invention for fire control and range measurement of Capt. Bradley Fiske USN. Optically obtained ranges were read electrically. Firing was more accurate at greater ranges and – more importantly – the data could be transmitted quicker., thus adjusting for the rapid rates of change of range while ships were maneuvering.

In 1907, Sims was promoted to commander and Naval Aide to the President probably as a reward for giving T.R. his "big stick" While in Washington; Sims married Anne Hitchcock, daughter of Roosevelt's Secretary of the Interior (SecInt), Ethan Hitchcock, and late Ambassador to St. Petersburg.

In 1902, probably fearing the rise of American naval power in the Pacific, Great Britain had made an alliance with Japan for mutual assistance if either of them went to war with a third party. The North Sea and Mediterranean-based RN gained a surrogate in the Far East against an American fleet able to shift oceans upon the completion of the Panama Canal. Such a canal would allow the Navy to adhere to the Mahan *dictum* of keeping forces concentrated *vice* spread thin over the oceans.

Then there were two more events with overtones for the later Treaty Navy.

The U.S. Pribilof Islands were a nesting and breeding ground for vast herds of seals. Seal hunting was lucrative and the U, S, had failed in its attempt to get an international ban on pelagic hunting of the herds. Still, she could enforce anti-hunting laws within her own territory. American poachers were seized, tried in U.S. courts, and their ships confiscated. Poachers of other nations were undeterred by U.S. law. Force was used to prevent poaching. In 1906, poachers were shot and killed on U.S. territory. They were not Canadian, British, Russian or other Caucasians. They were Japanese.

About the same time, the San Francisco School Board decided that schools were overcrowded after the 1906 earthquake and fire. A solution was to segregate Oriental children into their own school. Many Oriental grade schoolers were actually in their teens and American parents feared having their youngsters in classrooms with older "children." Mostly however, the reason was economic. Orientals, especially the recent wave of Japanese had made a "broken voyage" via Hawaii then abandoned the older labor opportunities there for those on the mainland. They worked longer and harder for less money than Americans or European immigrants.

The Japanese government urged on by a jingoistic press, protested vigorously. Roosevelt was in a quandary – a municipal government's action was threatening foreign affairs. He was never a man to yield to pressure, foreign or domestic, when it threatened his policies. He forced a settlement of the school issue on the Californians. The settlement was officially satisfactory to Japan but it left a legacy of distaste in Japanese-American relations. Japanese resented the implication of racial inferiority, an issue that was to recur later in the ratios of the naval limitation treaties.

4

As usual in any international crisis, a coterie of "experts" arose to prognosticate what lay ahead. Prophecies almost became self-fulfilling. They aggravated the situation. A Russian said the United States must fight Japan or submit. A Briton saw that war was inevitable. A German naval analyst also predicted war seeing the United States as an obstacle to Japan's ambitions in Asia and the Pacific. Reports (reliability unknown) stating that through the Anglo-Japanese Alliance, Japan would extend agreements to Germany, France and Russia were received at the White House. Thus, Japan would be free to take the Philippines and Hawaii with future possibilities of Alaska and California. Japan's naval building program was said to be not against Russia but against the U.S. Japan saw America as the natural enemy because she refused to recognize Japanese as equals. T.R.'s failure to provide an indemnity at the Treaty of Portsmouth was a further irritant.

His ambassador to Germany informed him that the highest German military and naval experts thought that Japan's motive was "the contest for supremacy in the Pacific Ocean." They didn't think Japan wanted the West Coast but only Hawaii and the Philippines. They also felt the Japanese would strike from Mexico or Peru to destroy the Panama Canal before completion.

Roosevelt assessed the situation soberly. Because of its large Japanese population, Hawaii would be in peril, commercially and militarily, if war came. The Philippines were of great concern and he wrote Secretary of War (SecWar) William H. Taft, "The Philippines are our heel of Achilles. They are all that makes the present situation dangerous ... I would rather see this nation fight all her life than give them up to Japan or any other nation under duress." He was optimistic, nonetheless. He told SecState Elihu Root that he did not trust the Japanese. He did not trust his opposition at home either. He wrote his ambassador in London, "My chief concern in foreign affairs is over the Japanese situation .... Should we fear the California mob and San Francisco yellow journals [Hearst?]?... or ... the downright cowardice as well as shortsighted lack of patriotism of men like Senator Hale in trying to keep the navy weak. This invites war."

His optimism was based on faith in himself and something else as well. He told Root, "In France, England and Germany the best information is that we shall be beaten. My own judgment is that the only thing that will prevent war is the Japanese feeling that we shall not be beaten and that feeling can only arise by keeping and making our navy efficient in the highest degree."

Sims had given the Navy the efficiency of being able to shoot, the *sine qua non* of combat at sea. The kernel of the later written expression of Pete Ellis was formed. T.R. was going to impose his will upon Japan by projecting his fleet across the Pacific to Japanese waters. One problem was the lack of bases for ships west of Hawaii. The island groups were devoid of facilities for succoring warships. More significantly they belonged to a third power and a neutral - Germany

There were two routes to the Far East (as the Brits called it) or the Western Pacific as our orientation sees it. They only differed by a few thousand miles if

Japan was the goal. An American fleet could sail south along South America, transit the Straits of Magellan and then go north to the West Coast. west to Hawaii and cross the Pacific. The other route was across the Atlantic, through the Mediterranean and Suez Canal across the Indian Ocean and up the Asian littoral to Japan. This was essentially the route of the ill-fated Russians in 1904-05. The logistics of either route were enormous. Coal alone made it a nightmare and refueling had to be scheduled beforehand. Weather was another problem. The Strait of Magellan in the South American winter (our summer) was a difficult passage.

Roosevelt announced that he was sending the battleships (with suitable escorts) to the West Coast. The nay-sayers in Congress were up in arms. They held that there weren't sufficient coal appropriations to get the ships back to their bases in the Atlantic. T.R. took the cavalier attitude that he was sending the ships and it was the problem of Congress to get them back.

On Dec. 16, 1907, T.R. in top hat and frock coat stood on the bridge of the Presidential Yacht, *Mayflower,* in Hampton Roads as the Great White Fleet (the battleships had been repainted for the cruise. Were there racial overtones?) stood out to sea. Beside in full dress and sword stood his naval aide, Cdr. Sims. Which one had concocted the scheme is moot. Suffice it to say that Sims was to live to be the link to the future and what developed into the group of thinkers who held that a naval war would be with Japan in the Pacific not Britain around the world.

The President was sending the fleet to the West Coast via the Strait of Magellan in the South American summer and then around the world. It was taking both routes to the Far East, albeit, one in reverse. He was reconnoitering both routes. The fruits of victory were apparent when during the leg "down under" to Australia; Japan issued an invitation for the Great White Fleet to visit the Japanese home islands.

The big stick had been used successfully to cool down a situation, which could have led to war. As it was, war in the Pacific was delayed for almost 35 years until another generation of Japanese jingoes forgot the lessons of the Great White Fleet to take on another Roosevelt and lose.

Theodore Roosevelt demonstrated that the real purpose of military and naval readiness is the avoidance of war by convincing the other fellow that he cannot win. This bit of wisdom was later lost on the politicians who framed the naval disarmament treaties in 1921-22 and later. The weak do not inherit the earth *nor* the sea.

T.R. left office less than a month after the Great White Fleet returned to Hampton Roads in February 1909. Sims went to command the battleship, *Minnesota,* as a commander in a captain's billet. He subsequently commanded the Atlantic Torpedo Flotilla, which in addition to developing aggressive tactics for employing the new type of vessel –destroyers, produced a cadre of future commanders for the Navy of World War II. These were cocky, aggressive but deep-thinking professionals of war at sea.

In the meantime war clouds were gathering in Europe. The Anglo-German naval race was just a portent of things to come. In 1911 the Anglo-Japanese

Alliance was renewed for another ten years. The Panama Canal was formally opened on Aug. 14, 1914. Two weeks before, Germany had declared war on Russia and then France and executed a modified Schlieffen Plan to sweep across Belgium and south of Paris to encircle the French army from its left flank. The violation of Belgium brought Britain into the war against Germany. Most of the cast was in the play. A few others would follow.

The events on land, except for the Dardanelles disaster, had little bearing on The Treaty Navy until after 1917.

At sea, it was different. Three weeks after Britain declared war on Germany, Japan joined her ally in declaring war. Japanese landing forces immediately occupied German's Marshall, Mariana, Palau and Caroline Island groups. In any future war in the Pacific the American way to Japan was no longer through the area of a third party neutral. The stepping-stones were seize able. The German China Squadron crossed the Pacific to Chile. A British squadron hunting them unfortunately found them at Coronel. The victorious Germans then headed for the Atlantic with the intention of raiding the Falklands in the South Atlantic en route home. They were out-gunned and sunk by heavy capital ships sent from England to accomplish that objective.

German submarines sank three British cruisers off the Dutch coast and made an unsuccessful raid on the base at Scapa Flow in the Orkneys. The Grand Fleet temporarily retreated to Rosyth on the Scottish coast while its base at Scapa was fitted with submarine nets. The British in true Mahan doctrine were keeping the Grand Fleet concentrated as a fleet-in-being at Scapa while the German High Seas Fleet was bottled up in the Jade and Kiel. In spite of a few surface raiders that eluded the blockade or were at sea before the war, Germany's flag had practically been swept from the seas. Allied shipping was uninterrupted. Germany, however, was beginning to feel the pinch of the naval blockade. She now focused on the only force left to her on the high seas – the submarine.

A body of International Law (civilized custom) developed after the Middle Ages. The purpose was to define usage for belligerents and protect the rights of neutrals at sea. There were rules for land warfare but those don't concern us. Search and seizure of enemy vessels were allowable. Since many belligerents used false flags, the stopping of neutrals for search before allowing them to proceed when ship's papers were found to be in order was routine. In the case of an enemy merchantman, she was stopped; boarded; and when identified was either captured or sunk. If the former a prize crew went aboard to take her to the nearest port of the captor for disposal by a Prize Court. If sunk, the crew and passengers were taken off and provided for by the captor as prisoners. The safety of civilians at sea was a cardinal rule of International Law.

Submarines had been in the world's navies since the turn of the century, they were initially crude and cramped but as with any new weapon, they evolved rapidly. German boats were able to operate on the high seas with an adequate crew and a good supply of torpedoes, self-propelled missiles with a large warhead that could be launched either afloat or when submerged. A submerged submarine could elude the blockade. She could fire at blocking vessels without warning. That was fair. Firing at merchantmen without warning, however, was against the rules. German submarines initially observed International Law when engaged in commerce raiding (the final objective phase of Mahan's *dicta*.) There were certain impossibilities, however. Once a submarine stopped a ship, it was difficult to see to the safety of the crew. Submarines were too small to take them aboard. A prize crew could not be spared; thus the ship must be sunk. Early in the war, the British began to arm their merchantmen and often they were more than a match for the gun of a surfaced submarine. Another trick was the Q-ship, which capitalized on the vulnerability of the submarine observing International Law. The Q-ship was a heavily armed decoy posing as an innocent unarmed merchantman. Once the U-boat (*Uterseeboot)* was lured into the trap she was done for. A desperate Germany resorted to unrestricted submarine warfare, sinking without warning all ships in a proscribed ocean area.

But before that occurred in earnest in 1917, there were two events, which were to have an effect on the future Treaty Navy. The stalemate of trench warfare which afflicted the war in France as well as the Russian predicament on the German eastern front caused the Allies to look for ways to relieve both pressure points and sweep to victory over a surrounded and blockaded Germany. First Lord of the Admiralty Winston S. Churchill favored providing supplies and reinforcement to Russia. The route through the Baltic was impassable while the High Seas Fleet was intact. The alternative was through the Mediterranean, Dardanelles and into the Black Sea. Turkey, a less than formidable partner of Germany and Austria-Hungary, controlled the Dardanelles. The RN, reinforced by French units, bombarded the Turkish forts to force a passage and take Constantinople. Older battleships were used in the bombardment. Despite losses to mines, the bombardment was on the verge of success when the British admiral called it off to defer to an amphibious landing behind the Turkish guns at Gallipoli. That fiasco nearly doomed forever the concept of amphibious war. Suffice it to say, Gallipoli was a study in "what not to do and how not to do it" From studies of Gallipoli emerged the U.S. Marine Corps doctrine of amphibious warfare in the '30s to *be executed in the '40s.*

The other event occurred late in the afternoon at the end of May 1916. The High Seas Fleet sortied from the Jade. It bumped into the British battle cruiser squadron and later the Grand Fleet, which was making a sweep of the North Sea on learning that the High Seas Fleet was out. It looked like it was going to be the classic Mahan clash of battlelines. The German ships were better handled, shot better and had better compartmentation and damage control. At that time of year in those latitudes darkness comes late but the High Seas Fleet was able to escape under cover of darkness (before radar) after forcing the Grand Fleet to turn away from a covering torpedo spread. The Grand Fleet was the strategic victor despite losing three battle cruisers, three cruisers, eight destroyers and 6,784 men. The tactical victor lost one old battleship, a battle cruiser, four light cruisers, and five destroyers and had 3,039 casualties but was able to reach the safety of its minefields. The lessons of Jutland for The Treaty Navy were that better armor and compartmentaion and damage control were needed in future capital ships. Henceforth, capital ships were either pre-Jutland or post-Jutland designs.

The sinking without warning in May 1915 of RMS *Lusitania* en route from New York to England by a U-boat brought such a protest from the U.S. that Germany suspended unrestricted submarine warfare for a while.

Britain, as is the wont of a dominant sea power, was enforcing her blockade on all ships bound for Europe. Contraband, heretofore regarded as munitions and other material of war, came to be considered anything, including foodstuffs, usable by the enemy. British ships stopped and searched all vessels on the high seas, including American. Some were remandered to England for determination by prize courts. To the U.S., this was clear violation of neutral rights and freedom of the seas, keystones of an American policy. Britain, using the excuse of the needs of war got away with it because she was dominant at sea.

Between German's unrestricted sinkings and British flaunting of her sea power to flout neutral rights, the U.S. took steps to enlarge her Navy.

Almost three months to the day after Jutland, President Woodrow Wilson signed into law, "An Increase in the Navy" on Aug. 29, 1916. It authorized, "Ten first-class battleships carrying as heavy armor and as powerful armament as any vessels of their class, to have the highest practicable speed and greatest desirable radius of action ... four of these to be begun as soon as practicable." The law authorized him to undertake other construction prior to Jul. 1, 1919. These were six battleships, four to be begun as soon as practical; ten scout cruisers, four to be laid down right away; 50 torpedo boat destroyers; 20 to be started immediately; nine fleet submarines, 58 submarines, 27 to be built soonest; three fuel ships, a repair ship, a transport, a hospital ship, two destroyer tenders, a submarine tender, two ammunition ships and two gunboats. The appropriation was $139,345,287. Subsequent ones (annual or special) would fund the balance of the program.

SecNav was authorized to improve and equip navy yards at Puget Sound, Philadelphia, Norfolk, New York, Boston, Portsmouth, Charleston and New Orleans for the construction.

But the law contained a clause that was more political than legislative and as it turned out was prophetic:

It is hereby declared to be the policy of the United States to adjust and settle its International disputes through mediation or arbitration, to the end that war may be honorably avoided. It looks with apprehension and disfavor upon a general increase of armament throughout the world. but it realizes that no single nation can disarm, and that without a common cause agreement upon the subject every must maintain a relative standing in military strength.

In view of the premises, the President is authorized and requested to invite, at an appropriate time, not later than the close of the war in Europe, all the great Governments of the world to send representatives to a conference which shall be charged with the duty of forming a court of arbitration ...to which disputed

Questions between nations shall be referred for adjudication and peaceful settlement

If at any time before the construction authorized by this Act shall have been contracted for there shall have been established with the cooperation of the United States of America, an international tribunal ... competent to secure Peaceful determination of all international disputes, and which shall render Unnecessary the maintenance of competitive armaments, than and in such Case naval expenditures as might be inconsistent with the engagements of Such tribunal ... may be suspended, when so ordered by the President of The United States.

Although the British Orders in Council which offended American concepts of freedom of the seas were an annoyance, it was Germany's second unleashing of her submarines that is traditionally cited as the cause of U.S. entry into the war as an associate power of the Allies. Whatever the cause it had a distinct on American naval construction and the subsequent Treaty Navy.

If the U.S. wanted to help her associates in battle, she had to get an Army to Europe. The U-boat menace was a real as ever. They plied the Atlantic and even sank ships off the American coast. The best warship to fight the U-boat was the former "torpedo boat destroyer" now just known as a destroyer. The 1916 law had authorized 50 and funded 20. The law of Mar. 4, 1917 (before declaration of war) appropriated money for 15 more. These were still not enough. More destroyers were needed and an emergency act of Oct. 6, 1917 authorized the President to build as many as he deemed necessary and appropriated unlimited money to do so. Wilson had a blank check for destroyer construction and he used it. Except for those already building under the 1916 Act, no more were charged against that authorization. There was a shortage of building ways so Wilson was authorized to suspend the construction of the major units of the 1916 program to make room for emergency destroyer construction. Destroyers were vital to protect convoys of troopships to France. They were turned out in record time, many of them ready before the Armistice in 1918 and most commissioned soon after.

The Navy wanted to get into action immediately. Marines were also eager. In at November 1917, four coal-burning battleships departed Lynnhaven Roads, Virginia, for Scapa Flow to become the Sixth Battle Squadron of the Grand Fleet, *Delaware, Florida, Wyoming* and *New York* were coal burners supplemented by oil. The shortage of oil and the abundance of coal in the British Isles dictated that the older rather than the newer all-oil ships be sent. In early 1918, *Texas* joined the Squadron and later *Arkansas* replaced *Delaware*

The real challenge and key to U.S. Navy participation was to get destroyers to Europe to combat the U–boats. One of the first officers sent to England was our old friend, now RAdm. W.S. Sims. After commanding the new battleship, *Nevada,* which under him was known as "The Cheer Up Ship" he attained flag rank. His first flag assignment was President of the Naval War College at Newport. One of the officers on his faculty was Maj. Ellis. When war was declared, a liaison officer was needed in London to work with the RN. The billet at the War College was not critical operationally and Sims was tagged to go. He and an aide departed under aliases in civilian clothes. The British welcomed him initially with open arms (He had been censured earlier by President Taft for a London speech saying that if war came America would support Britain.) His welcome was short-lived when he began criticizing the British for their lack of convoying thus losing ships to U-boats. The British pointed out to him that there were a high percentage of unescorted ships arriving at British ports safely. He turned the tables by analyzing the traffic and finding that they were using apples and oranges to get the wrong answer. The unattacked coastal shipping between British ports inflated the success figure while the percentage of overseas arrivals was miserable. U-boats were taking their toll of vital import shipping. The convoy system was reluctantly adopted by the RN abetted by the U.S.

A base for U.S. destroyers was built on the RN facilities at Queenstown in County Cork then, now and always Cobh to the Irish, in southwestern Ireland (not yet a Free State or a Republic). It remained to get the short-legged destroyers "across the pond." Refueling them at sea en route was the answer.

A requirement to fuel destroyers at sea had been anticipated. *USS Maumee,* a Navy tanker had experimented with refueling destroyers underway, albeit in calm seas. The basis for further development was there. In essence the tanker (now known as oilers) towed the destroyer alongside and it became the "riding abeam" or later "broadside" method. The first destroyers across were larger and had sufficient range to make it to Queenstown without refueling. That division under Cdr. Joseph K. Taussig (his son, Ens, Joseph K. Taussig, Jr. lost a leg getting *Nevada* underway at Pearl Harbor) endeared itself to the RN. A month after declaration of war, Taussig's division arrived. RAdm. Bayly RN anticipating a period of upkeep after the arduous passage inquired of Taussig as to when he would be ready for sea. The reply was classic, "We are ready now, sir, that is as soon as we finish fueling." Subsequently, *Maumee* took position in mid-Atlantic to refuel east-bound ships. By mid-summer 1917, she had serviced 34 destroyers on the way to Queenstown. Her executive officer was cited for his role in devising the method used. LCdr. Chester W. Nimitz would later play a significant role in reviving refueling at sea when he was a flag officer. For a while the "run scared" attitude of The Treaty Navy had let it fall into disuse.

The Navy successfully convoyed more than 2,000,000 troops to France without a single casualty. Troopships were lost to submarines but on the empty voyage home. In addition to destroyers at Queenstown, there were bases at Saint Nazaire, Brest and in the Mediterranean.

Marines also got to war and earned a reputation which was the bane of Gen. John J. Pershing, the American Expeditionary Force (AEF) commander. SecNav, early after the declaration of war offered a Marine regiment to SecWar. This was later increased to another regiment and a machine gun battalion. The Fifth Marines (Marine regiments are known by a written number followed by "Marines" much as Army units are designated 165th Infantry, 15th Artillery etc.) sailed first while the Sixth Marines formed at Quantico, Va. They and the 6th Machine Gun Battalion joined the Fifth Marines and became the 4th Marine Brigade. With the 3rd Infantry Brigade (9th and 23rd Infantry) plus an artillery brigade and engineers and other support units they became the 2nd Infantry Division (Regular Army). Initially, a Marine brigadier general commanded the Marines but when he was invalided home, Pershing promoted his Chief of Staff from lieutenant colonel to brigadier general and gave him the Marine Brigade. Meanwhile, BGen. J.A. Lejeune had escaped from his billet as Assistant Commandant at HQMC and was in the new base at Quantico preparing units for action in France. At his side was his alter ego, LtCol. Pete Ellis. While they were at sea en route to France, Marines were in action in Belleau Wood under BGen. James Harbord AUS.

Pershing had resisted Allied efforts to feed American troops into British and French divisions as replacements. He held out for forming his own divisions and using them in a separate U.S. sector. The German's desperate drive after the collapse of Russia which had released troops from the eastern front changed Pershing's plans slightly. The German drive began in the spring of 1918 to split the British and French fronts and win the war before the weight of American manpower could be brought to bear. Thus, Pershing released the divisions of the AEF temporarily to serve intact in French and British corps. The 2nd Infantry Division found itself moving east toward Chateau-Thierry along the Paris-Metz Road. When the Germans invested Belleau, the nearest unit available was ordered to defend the position south of it as the defeated French withdrew. The Sixth Marines deployed and stopped the advancing *Strumtruppen* cold. The Fifth Marines deployed on their left. With the 6th Machine Guns in the line the 4th Marine Brigade was ready for battle for that insignificant bit of terrain. But there was great significance to Belleau Wood both for the war and the AEF.

It effect upon the war was realized by a German division commander who said: "American success along our front, even if only temporary, may have the most unfavorable Influence on the attitude of the Allies and the duration of the war. In the coming battles, therefore, It is not a question of possession or non-possession of this or that village or woods, insignificant in itself; it is a question whether the Anglo-American claim that the American Army is the equal or even the superior of the German Army is to be made good."

In a month of furious fighting with enormous Marine casualties, the claim of American superiority was made good when Harbord received the message, "Woods now U.S. Marine Corps entirely." Gen. Degroutte, commanding the French Sixth Army renamed Belleau Wood, *"Bois de la Brigade de Marine."*

The last and the fact that Marines were identified in the press, a Pershing no-no, since he rigidly controlled which units, if any, were mentioned did not endear Marines to "Black Jack" Pershing or the rest of the AEF. Lejeune landed in France and reported to Pershing for duty. Harbord had been promoted and given command of the 2nd Infantry Division, He recommended that his old friend from the Philippines be his relief in the Brigade. BGen. Lejeune accompanied by his operational planner, LtCol. Ellis took command. Lejeune commanded the Brigade for less than a week when Harbord was reassigned by Pershing to command the Services of Supply (SOS) and "straighten out that mess!" Harbord recommended that Lejeune command the 2nd Division. The

Marine Corps did not have a selection system for officer promotion (the Navy had adopted one in 1916); neither did it have the freewheeling spot promotion system of the Army. There had been another major general slot created for the Marines that had not been filled. If Lejeune could be promoted before Pershing assigned another Army officer to command the division, he could get the command. Ellis cabled Sims, now wearing four stars in London and commanding U.S. Naval Force in Europe. Within days MajGen. Lejeune was commanding an Army division. Marine officers commanded Army battalions and regiments and some Army officers served in the Marine Brigade.

Under Lejeune the 2nd Division went on to bloody victories at Soissons and St. Mihiel. The penultimate endeavor was when it was detached from the American First Army for relief of the French in the Champagne sector. Blanc Mont had been a salient in the French front for four years. The 2nd Division was ordered to reduce the position. When Lejeune looked at the plan his French superior had drawn up for him, he sent for Ellis. His officers advised him that LtCol. Ellis was "resting." Lejeune ordered, "Get him! Ellis drunk is still better than anyone else sober." He was. In a week the 2nd Division did what the French had been unable to do for four years. They broke the German line and advanced to the railroad forcing the Germans to retreat 40 miles. The Division returned to the First Army for the final fight of the Meuse-Argonne and a year of occupation in Germany before a victory parade in New York City and then disbanding. The 4th Marine Brigade provided the nucleus of combat-trained Marines who were to make up the small Corps of The Treaty Navy and high command in World War II.

Another Marne Brigade, the 5th served in France. It was assigned to the SOS as security troops. Its commander was BGen. Smedley D. Butler, a two-time Medal of Honor winner. Another famous member was Gene Tunney who was to defeat Jack Dempsey for the world heavyweight title in 1927. In addition, Harbord kept releasing Marines from the SOS to go forward as replacements for "his Marines." Replacements were necessary. Casualties in the Marine Brigade were nearly twice those in other brigades.

Navy big guns got into action but not at sea. Five 14-in. naval guns arrived in France in late summer 1918 under RAdm. Charles P. Plunkett. They were on railroad mounts. Crewed by sailors they were in action from September to the end of the war along the American front near Verdun.

Naval aviators were not to be denied. There was a tremendous expansion of naval aviation for the war. The appropriations Act of Apr. 17, 1917 added $3,000,000 to the $3,500,000 of the previous year. Before the end of 1917 an additional $56,000,000 was provided to be used at the discretion of the President or SecNav. These were shots in the arm for an almost non-existing force. A Naval Aircraft Factory was constructed a Philadelphia to build flying boats. The terror struck in London by the German rigid airship bombing caused attention to be given to that type. In addition, non-rigid lighter-than-air craft (initially known "limps") were experimented with. There were two experimental models, the A and the B. The latter was found to be the better and the B-limp was born.

13

Aviation abroad grew to more than 7.000 officers and men. There were hundreds of aircraft operating in France, the Adriatic and Azores. They did scouting, bombing and anti-submarine patrolling. Aircraft were both seaplanes and land planes. Operation of the latter was to spark a conflict with the Army that existed through World War II.

Another major feat with implications for The Treaty Navy was the Great North Sea Mine Barrage. Its objective was to destroy the submerged U-boats transiting the North Sea. It was not completed before the Armistice but thousands had been laid. These had to be swept after the end of hostilities. A legacy to The Treaty Navy was "Bird" class minesweepers. There were 54 840-ton vessels produced in late 1918 and 1919 to sweep the mine barrage. During the '20s and '30s these bottoms were available for other duties. Some were converted to salvage ships, submarine rescue vessels and even seaplane tenders. A frugal Navy could not afford to waste a single ship.

Three new concepts affecting war at sea emerged from World War I. One was that the submarine posed a threat to surface ships no matter how heavily armed or armored. Second was that aircraft could be carried on; flown off; and landed upon ships especially built to do so as the RN had successfully done at the close of the war. The third was that rigid airships had the potential to span oceans. The last was to absorb a lot of time, money and lives before it was abandoned. The U.S. Navy's aircraft in France were either of European manufacture or arrived in crates. Even seaplanes were shipped rather than flown.

In 1919, the Navy was ready to fly the Atlantic. Toward the end of 1917, designs for a long-range seaplane were on the drawing boards. Glenn Curtiss, an aviation pioneer who had taught the first Naval Aviators to fly, was asked to design a plane to be built by the Navy The first, NC-1, was ready at Rockaway Air Station on Long Island in October 1918. (Naval aircraft used to be designated by type, manufacturer and the sequence of types built by a manufacturer {See Appendix 7}. It was a unique system and for logistics purposes was effective, Alas, it was beyond the ken of McNamara's "whiz kids" in the '60s and they put all aircraft under the USAF system and started over from number one. In the case of NC-1, N stood for Navy, the maker, and C for Curtiss, the designer.) NC-1 was 68+ feet long with a 126- foot wingspan. Her three Liberty engines lifted 25,000 pounds. When NC-2 with four engines lifted 28,000, NC-1 was retrofitted with four engines. A gale and a fire damaged NC-1 and NC-4. They were repaired by turning NC-2 into a "hangar queen" for parts. On May 2, 1919, Seaplane Division One was commissioned with NC-1, NC-3 and NC-4, LCdr John Towers, commanding in NC-3. Towers would command the Pacific Oceans Area after Adm. Chester Nimitz in 1946. Other famous names in the division were Pat Bellinger and Marc Mitscher in NC-1. LCDR A.C. Read commanded NC-4.

They planned to fly from Long Island to Trepassey, Newfoundland, thence to the Azores, Lisbon and London. The three seaplanes left Rockaway heading north on May 8, 1919. Mechanical trouble forced NC-4 down off Cape Cod but she "taxied" to the air station at Chatham. The others made it and awaited NC-4 in Newfoundland. Bad weather delayed he start on the 14th and NC-4 joined and was the first off on the 16th. Sixty-eight destroyers at 400-mile intervals had been strung across the route as marker buoys using smoke by day and searchlights by night. NC-4 reversing her bad luck sped ahead. NC-1 alit in a fog and was damaged. A Greek freighter picked up her crew but she sank under tow. NC-3 also had troubles and didn't get beyond Flores. Read took NC-4 all the way to Plymouth.

The flight yielded valuable data on long-distance flying, ship-to-air communications, radio direction finding, navigational instruments and the need for more meteorological data. It also boosted the confidence of the Naval Aviators in the fleet. It did nothing, however, to make Congress provide more money for naval aviation.

Now, advocates of a new American naval policy appeared. Park Benjamin, a Naval Academy graduate of 1867 who resigned after two years, had acquired the credentials of "naval expert" by his writings in *The Independent* and *Scientific American* during the naval revival of the '80s and '90s. He was a patent attorney and writer. He had a sarcastic and vitriolic pen. From 1914 until 1921 his writing had been dormant. He resurfaced. On Apr. 23, 1921, his last article (at age 71), "David and Goliath" appeared in *The Independent* The editor noted that Benjamin "had played not an inconsiderable part in the upbuilding of the American Navy." Park Benjamin was again a zealot for an idea, which was opposed by many.

Harking back to his theme that a torpedo that could strike below the armor of a battleship could sink her just as easily as any other vessel, he built his case. Heretofore, the problem had been getting close enough to launch a torpedo and obtain a hit. Technology had solved that problem. The war had shown submarines and torpedoes to be potent weapons. Aircraft would both launch torpedoes (thanks to another invention of RAdm. Bradley Fiske USN) and dive toward he decks of battleships, climbing back to the safety of the sky after releasing a bomb. His key argument was that the battleship only moved in one plane, which was the surface of the sea. Aircraft moved in the three-dimensional attitude, which was the sky. Submarines did the same thing in the sea. Both were capable of destroying the floating fortresses and therefore rendered them less than the backbone of sea power. The new backbones would be aircraft and submarines. The Navy should consist of submarines to sweep the seas of enemy commerce; and of aircraft on carriers to project what formerly had been limited by the term itself – sea power. The term was now more correctly national power, and it should be projected to the homeland of any enemy.

Another iconoclast to break into print, mostly about not by him, was now again RAdm. Sims. After the war he returned to the Naval War College but he was not silent. He spoke out against what he considered to be mismanagement of the Navy during the war by SecNav Josephus Daniels and Chief of Naval Operations (CNO) Adm. William S. Benson. As a sign of protest, Sims refused to accept the medals and honors from the Navy Department for his wartime achievements. Having piqued the public interest he unleashed accusations about the Navy's supposed inability to fight a strong enemy. A Congressional investigation reached no firm conclusions but ripped the Navy apart and created a bitter Daniels-Sims feud.

Sims retired from the Navy in 1922 but continued his insurgent views in articles and speeches. He championed naval aviation as the way of the future. During his last years at the War College, War Plan ORANGE became a mainstay of instruction there. Briefly on the faculty immediately after the war was Maj. Pete Ellis. No doubt, he adopted a Marine version of ORANGE in his *Advanced Base Operations in Micronesia* (see Chapter II), which was approved by his other mentor, now MGC John A. Lejeune.

As noted, the wartime need for destroyers postponed the completion of the ships of the 1916 Naval Expansion Act. After the Armistice, construction was resumed as the need for destroyers to fight the U-boats had passed. In 1919, the Navy had a fleet of 297 destroyers with 43 building. These had flaws. Basically, all were the same design. No improvements had been incorporated as the result of underway experience. All had been built within two years so they were the same age. Block obsolescence was a future but major problem to be faced. In addition, quality was not uniform. Some were of inferior construction as was their machinery.

Mention has been made of War Plan ORANGE, a major obsession of the years of The Treaty Navy. It was a contingency plan for war in the Pacific with Japan. American military and naval contingency plans were given color code names to distinguish the enemy (singular). BLACK was Germany; GREEN was Mexico; RED was Britain (her Empire had variations of the color, e.g., Canada was CRIMSON), The U.S. was always BLUE except that domestic emergency was WHITE. (See Appendix 1.)

ORANGE, which varied over the years, initially had the projection of American sea power across the Pacific to relieve the Philippines. Later revisions had the Philippines being recaptured after the move across the Central Pacific. Before 1914, the possession of the Central Pacific island groups by a third neutral power posed a problem inasmuch as such islands would be required as intermediate advanced bases en route. The capture of them by Japan and their retention under League of Nations mandate made this a non-problem. They were ORANGE territory subject to taking.

Let us close this chapter by looking at the legacy of SecNav. Josephus Daniels was a crusading temperance editor from North Carolina. During his stewardship the Naval Expansion Act of 1916 was passed. Subsequent emergency wartime acts that produced the huge destroyer fleet were also passed. The General Board (see Chapter II for discussion of the General Board function) rather than SecNav was the driving force in such endeavors. Daniels was more interested in social reforms within the Navy. According to Park Benjamin in his final article the so-called "accomplishments of which Daniels boasted had a negative effect on the Navy." These were, *inter alia,* making officers specialists in lecturing, teaching and exploring *vice* being naval professionals; elimination of the officers' wine mess and banning soft drinks aboard ship for enlisted; making ships floating schools for the formal education of enlisted men; having men write their grievances directly to SecNav; and the protection of the men without due process. Daniels according to Benjamin (or some naval officers for whom he spoke) said SecNav refused to take advice. His barb said, "… he 'means well but don't know;'." Benjamin criticized an advisory board of 22 experts on inventions headed by Thomas A. Edison. Benjamin wondered why there were no shipbuilders or aviation experts on the board. He speculated that the purpose of the board was to sell its inventions to the Navy after the board had accepted them even when they were not needed. It was a bureaucratic monster, which was an example of Daniels' "peculiar brand of socialism."

Daniels left office when the Wilson Administration did in 1921. So did his able assistant. Franklin D. Roosevelt had been the worker and doer in the Department of the Navy. The naval education of F.D.R. may have been Josephus Daniels' most significant contribution to The Treaty Navy.

Chapter II

After the War

War ended with an armistice on Nov. 11, 1918. The formal ending was the subject of the series of treaties over the next few years. These legal niceties decreed the end just as the start had been declared.

We noted in the previous chapter, that the U.S. returned to the 1916 building program, which would make her supreme at sea by 1924. Her fleet of battleships and battlecruisers would be superior to either Japan or Britain even if they started building on a greater scale. It would take them years to catch up because of lead-time required in designing, gathering material and building capital ships. A question mark in the sea power equation was the disposition of the German High Seas Fleet. It had surrendered to the Grand Fleet and its American Squadron. It was interned in Scapa Flow. The other potential sea powers, France and Italy neglected their navies during the war in favor of land armaments.

The Navy had entered the war with 23 predreadnoughts: *Indiana, Massachusetts, Oregon, Iowa, Kearsarge, Kentucky, Illinois, Alabama, Wisconsin, Maine, Missouri, Ohio, Virginia, Nebraska, Georgia, New Jersey, Rhode Island, Connecticut, Louisiana, Vermont, Kansas, Minnesota* (BBs 1-22 although the BB designation for battleship hulls did not come in until 1921. (See Appendix 2.) and *New Hampshire* (BB-25) Two unsatisfactory ships, *Mississippi* and *Idaho* (ex *post facto* BBs 23 & 24) had been sold to Greece in 1914. All these coal-burners were built before 1906 and many had gone around the world.

There were 14 dreadnoughts in commission in 1917. They were *South Carolina* (BB-26) and *Michigan* (BB-27), 16,000 tons with eight 12-in. guns; *Delaware* (BB-28) and *North Dakota* (BB-29), 20,000 tons with ten 12-in. guns; *Florida* (BB-30) and *Utah* (BB-31), 21,825 tons with ten 12-in. guns; *Wyoming* (BB-32) and *Arkansas* (BB-33), 26,100 tons with twelve 12-in guns; *New York* (BB-34) and *Texas* (BB-35), 27,000 tons with ten 14-in. guns; *Nevada* (BB-36) and *Oklahoma* (BB-37), 29,000 tons with ten 14-in. guns; *Pennsylvania* (BB-38) and *Arizona* (BB-39), 33,100 tons with twelve 14-in. guns. Three ordered in 1914 had had their keels laid: *New Mexico* (BB-40), *Mississippi* (BB-41) and *Idaho* (BB-42) but were launched in 1917. *Idaho* was not commissioned until 1919. They were 34,000 tons with twelve 14-in. guns. Two other pre-1916 Act ships were ordered at the end of 1915 and their keels laid but would not be launched until 1919. *Tennessee* (BB-43) and *California* (BB-44) were 32,000 tons with twelve 14-in. guns.

The naval revival of the 1880s started with construction of three protected cruises, the "ABCs" and the aviso, *Dolphin.* Then two fine armored cruisers, *New York* (ACR-2) and *Brooklyn* (ACR-3) were built and saw service against Spain along with a series of protected cruisers of varying size and armaments built before that war but still around for World War I. Initially, armored cruisers

18

had the mission of raiding enemy commerce or protecting their own. But as battleships increased in size and power there came a change in the cruiser mission. They were fleet units for scouting and screening the battleships.

Between 1900 and 1908, ten large armored cruisers were built. Initially named for states but when that designation was given to battleships their names were changed to a city within that state. These were the 13,700 ton, *Pittsburgh*, (CA-4), *Huntington* (CA-5), *San Diego* (CA-6) lost to a U-boat mine in 1918, *Pueblo* (CA-7), *Frederick* (CA-8) and *Huron* (CA-9). They had a battery of four 8-in. and 14 6-in. guns. The other four were *Memphis* (CA-10) lost off Santo Domingo in 1916, *Seattle* (CA-11), *Charlotte* (CA-12) and *Missoula* (CA-13). They were 14,500 tons with four 10-in. and 15 6-in. guns. Battlecruisers made these ships obsolete and no more were built but many of them were around until 1930. Their roomy accommodations made then desirable flagships on foreign stations. During the war they had contributed to naval aviation by providing the platforms for launching seaplanes.

Scout cruisers were another category built after the Spanish War. There were two classes of these. The *Denver*s were 3,200 tons with ten 5-in. guns. They were *Denver* (CL-14), *Des Moines* (CL-15), *Chattanooga* (CL-16), *Galveston* (CL-17), *Tacoma* (CL-18) and *Cleveland* (CL-19) The *St. Louis*s were 9,700 tons with 14 6-in. guns. These were *St. Louis* (CL-20), *Milwaukee* (CL-21) wrecked off Eureka, California, on Jan. 13, 1917 and *Charleston* (CL-22). Three experimental–design scouts were 3,750 tonners of 1907. They had two 5-in. and six 3-in. guns They were the last cruisers to be built or ordered before the Act of 1916.

The end of the war left the Navy with more than 300 destroyers. There was a modicum of submarines. Originally they had names but later just a letter and a number. There were seven in he A-class of 145-ton surfaced/173 tons submerged. Three in the B-class of 145/173 tons; five in the C-class of 238/275 tons; two of the four F-class were lost. F-1 sank after a collision off Point Loma in December 1917 with F-3 and F-4 foundered in Honolulu on 1915. Four G-class, there was one of 288/337 while the others were 400/516 tons. The nine H-class were 358/467 tons; eight K-class of 392/521 tons; eleven L-class of 450/525 tons; one M-class of 488/676 tons. There were three AA-class of 1,107/1,482 tons which were the first real fleet bats. Seven N-class were 340/415 tons. Sixteen O-class were of 521/629 or 491/566 tons. These were the last ordered before the 1916 Act. Next came the R-boats. Thee were 27 of then and they were of two displacements: 530/690 tons and 510/680 tons.

The S-type ("old S boats") of which there would be 51 were part of the 1916 Expansion Act. These were of four different types depending on the builder. They became the mainstay of the submarine fleet after their commissioning in the early '20s.

The immediate post war Navy had the usual complement of auxiliaries (the term we use today to be distinguished from the combat auxiliary definition.) These included repair ships, tenders by category, e.g., destroyer, submarine, seaplane etc., oilers (tanker), collier (rigged to replenish alongside in a sheltered harbor), transports (the Army also operated it own), store ships, mine ships, sub chasers and tugs, salvage vessels etc. A new type with much potential was the aircraft carrier; *Langley* (CV-1) converted from the collier, *Jupiter* (AC-3) in 1920. She was the platform, which trained the Navy's fledging carrier pilots.

At the beginning of Fiscal Year (FY) 1920, the Fleet Organization (See Appendix 3 for selected subsequent Organizations.) was:

ATLANTIC FLEET
Battle Squadron Two
Connecticut F   *Louisiana   New Hampshire*
Kansas   Minnesota   South Carolina   Michigan
Battle Squadron Three
Utah F   *Delaware   North Dakota   Pennsylvania* FF
Oklahoma   Nevada   Arizona
Cruiser Squadron One
Huntington F   *Wheeling   Topeka   Castine*

PACIFIC FLEET
Battle Squadron One
Virginia F   *New Jersey   Rhode Island*
Georgia   Nebraska   Vermont
Battle Squadron Four
Wyoming F   *Arkansas   New York   New Mexico* FF
Texas   Tennessee   Idaho   Mississippi
Cruiser Squadron Two
Seattle F   *Cleveland   Denver   Tacoma*
Marblehead   Machis   Vicksburg

U.S. Naval Forces, Europe
Pittsburgh F   *Galveston   Chattanooga*
De Moines   Sacramento   Olympia

Asiatic Fleet
Pueblo F   *Brooklyn   New Orleans*
Albany   Helena   Wilmington

Reserve
Maine   Missouri   Ohio   Frederick
Montana   North Carolina
South Dakota   Charleston   St. Louis

F = Flagship   FF = Fleet Flagship

The number in reserve indicates the personnel situation after the war. With more than 300 destroyers in commission, it was difficult to man other ships as well. Suffice it to say that the destroyers and attendant auxiliaries were assigned to the various fleets *supra,* but many were rotated between active and reserve.

The resumed construction was for four battleships of approximately 32,600 tons with eight 16-in. guns; and a second and more powerful class of six ships of 43,500 tons with twelve 16-in. guns in four triple turrets. Those were the ten "first-class battleships" enumerated in the Act of 1916. The four to be begun "as soon as practicable" were ordered before the declaration of war in April 1917.

Maryland (BB-46) who was to give her name to the class was ordered from Newport News Shipbuilding Co. on Dec. 15, 1916. On the same day two sisters were ordered. *Washington* (BB-47) from New York Shipbuilding in Camden, N.J., and *West Virginia* (BB-48) from Newport News Shipbuilding. A month later, on Jan.17, the order for *Colorado* (BB-45) was placed with New York Shipbuilding. Thus, two different civilian yards were assembling material and preparing to build four *Maryland*s when war was declared. None of the keels were laid, except for *Maryland*, until almost a year after the Armistice. Her keel was laid less than three weeks after the declaration of war. She was not launched for three years because work was deferred to the vital destroyers,

Of the six other battleships authorized to be constructed before Jul. 1, 1919 four were ordered on Jul. 2, 1918 while the other two were ordered more than a year later, The first four were: *South Dakota* (BB-49) who gave her name to the class, from New York Navy Yard (Brooklyn), *Indiana* (BB-50) also from Brooklyn, *Montana* (BB-51) from Mare Island Navy Yard, and *North Carolina* (BB-52) from Norfolk Navy Yard. *Iowa* (BB-53) was ordered on Oct. 27, 1919 from Newport News Shipbuilding and *Massachusetts* (BB-54) on Nov. 15, 1919 from Bethlehem Shipbuilding, Quincy, Mass.

Six other battleships were to be constructed prior to Jul. 1, 1919. Again, "four to be begun as soon as practicable." These turned out to be battlecruisers. Initially, the Navy had not been enthusiastic about battlecruisers. another favorite of the First Sea Lord "Jackie" Fisher who had brought them into the RN. Such ships were as powerfully armed as battleships but with greater speed. The theory was their speed would enable them to maneuver into favorable position over the slower battleships and thus "cross the T" of the opposing battleline (A word picture of a maneuver wherein one battleline crosses the course of the other perpendicularly and the capping fleet brings all its broadsides to bear while the capped line can only aim its forward turrets.) Speed had not always been a primary factor in American naval thinking. But inasmuch as other possible enemies, e.g., Britain, Germany, Japan and France had them, the U.S. Navy felt it should have battlecruisers. But the laws of physics are unforgiving. Speed *requires* a larger propulsion plant and it must push less weight through the water to attain the increased speed. The swap for speed is armor. An advantage of speed is the ability to run away to fight another day. Unfortunately, the poorly compartmented British battlecruisers (and poorly handled by Beatty) at Jutland could not absorb the hits from the better German gunners and three blew up and sank.

Feeling that the lessons of Jutland, i.e., better protection within turrets, better compartmentation and better damage control, could make battlecruisers viable in the Navy, plans were drawn for a battlecruiser design. These were for a ship of 43,500 tons with eight 16-in. guns in four turrets and making a speed of 33.5 knots. These six took the class name from the lead ship, *Lexington* (CC-1).

The first ordered was *Constitution* (CC-5) from the Philadelphia Navy Yard on Mar. 17, 1917. Next *Lexington* was ordered on Apr. 17, 1917 from the Fore River Shipbuilding Co in Quincy, Mass. The order for *Saratoga* (CC-3) was placed with New York Shipbuilding at Camden on May 5, 1917. Two more orders were placed n May 24, 1917 for *Constellation* (CC-2) and *Ranger* CC-4) with Newport News Shipbuilding. The last ship in the class, *United States* (CC-6) was ordered from the Philadelphia Navy Yard on Jul 2, 1918.

Battlecruisers were named for famous American battles or for famous American ships, which had won battles. As we shall see, two of these ships were saved to be aircraft carriers. Hence, up until the end of World War II when President Truman renamed the intended *Coral Sea* for the late President Roosevelt, carriers were so-named. Exceptions were the two *Langely*s (CV-1 and CVL-27) and *Shangri La* (CV-38.)

But for *Maryland* no keels were laid for the capital ships of the !916 Act until after the Armistice. The Act also authorized other ships. There were ten scout cruisers, 50 destroyers, nine fleet submarines, 58 submarines, three fuel ships, a repair ship, a transport, a hospital ship, two destroyer tenders, a submarine tender, two ammunition ships and two gunboats. The emergency destroyer program crowded most of these off the ways. Some of the destroyers under the 1916 Act were begun and finished under the Act but not all. The blank check for destroyers after declaration of war was applied leaving unused some of the 1916 Act destroyer authorizations. These were to be critical in the early '30s. Also, the fleet submarines authorized went unbuilt. The "old S-boats" were to be built between 1919 and 1923.

The first cruisers to be constructed since 1906 were the new scouts authorized in 1916. They took their class name from *Omaha* (CL-4) ordered from Todd Shipbuilding and Drydock in Tacoma on Dec. 26, 1916. They were 7,050 tons with twelve 6-in. guns. The guns were an unusual arrangement. There were twins in gun houses, fore and aft, on the centerline. Forward and aft there were casemates on either side mounted one above the other. These could only bear to either side and the effective broadside was eight. They also had torpedo tubes mounted on deck. There were seaplane catapults aft of the fourth stack, on each side.

The next order was on Jul. 30, 1917 from Wm. Cramp & Sons, Philadelphia for *Richmond* (CL-9) and *Concord* (CL-10). *Raleigh* (CL-7) and *Detroit* (CL-8) were ordered from Bethlehem, Quincy, on Aug. 21, 1917. Todd, Tacoma, received orders for two more, *Milwaukee* (CL-5) and *Cincinnati* (CL-6), on Aug.27, 1917. The final three were ordered from Cramp on Jan. 24, 1919. They were *Trenton* (CL-11), *Marblehead* (CL-12) and *Memphis* (CL-13).

Three of the names were taken from older cruisers stricken or lost between 1917 and 1919. These were *Detroit, Marblehead* and *Milwaukee.*

The ships of the 1916 Act and emergency legislation were not all commissioned, as we shall see in the next chapter. They were not limited by size or armament by the Limitation Treaties so strictly speaking they were not *of* The Treaty Navy but since they were vital units of the fleet between the wars they were *in* The Treaty Navy and shall be so treated on these pages.

But ordering and building ships were not the only activities of the post-war Navy. Turkey, the former "sick man of Europe" was in the throes of revolution and chaos. Thousands of varied ethnic refugees were seeking asylum and escape. Newly promoted RAdm. Mark L. Bristol USN was named commander of a naval detachment in the eastern Mediterranean in January 1919. He flew his flag in *Scorpion* (PY-3) a converted yacht dignified with the classification of patrol boat. Her accommodations, however, were suitable for his tasks. He became the point of contact with the Ottoman Empire. Formal relations had been broken by the U.S. in 1917. In August 1919, Bristol was appointed High Commissioner in Turkey. He operated from his flagship based in Constantinople but was mobile enough to supervise the destroyers rotating in and out of his command. For eight years he maintained American presence and interests through the turbulence of the dissolution of the Ottoman Empire and the founding of modern Turkey under Kemal Ataturk. Bristol directed American relief operations among Greek and Armenian refugees, Turkish Christians, White Russians and other groups. He made himself a most respected figure to both sides. Formal relations were reestablished with Turkey in 1927 and the mission dissolved.

The Marine Corps was most active after the war. The MGC during the war was George Barnett. He had been appointed in 1914 for a four-year term. In early 1918, that term was coming to an end. Barnett, capping a distinguished 40-year career had performed the duties as Commandant well. Under his leadership at HQMC, the Corps had expanded; sent two brigades to France; formed an aviation contingent; continued its numerous expeditions to the Caribbean; and basked in the glory of fighting in France. Thus, with high praise, SecNav Daniels announced in February 1918 Barnett's reappointment to a second term. He did not state, however, that he had asked Barnett to sign an undated request for retirement to be invoked at the pleasure of SecNav. When Barnett bridled at such an affront, Daniels demurred. In June, a Naval Personnel Bill with a provision to make the Commandant a lieutenant general and add second stars to three staff billets was discussed in Congress. Daniels was mute on his support for the bill. It came up for action in the House on Jun. 18, 1918, just as Marines were fighting in Belleau Wood and gathering glory,

It was assumed by Barnett and the others affected, as well as most Marines that it would pass. They were surprised when Rep. Thomas Butler (R-Penn.) arose with blistering wrath to oppose the promotions. The father of two-time Medal of Honor winner, temporary BGen. Smedley D. Butler, who was then struggling to leave his post in Haiti for France, called Barnett and his HQMC colleagues "rocking chair warriors" and "swivel chair heroes." He noted that SecNav had declined endorsement of the promotions. The bill failed.

Exactly two years later, Daniels sent a sealed note to Barnett saying that the latter was to be relieved one day next week suitable to him and before the end of working hours to indicate his desire to retire immediately or as the law allowed to remain on active duty as a brigadier general.

Barnett opted to command the Department of the Pacific, relic of the days of poorer communications when it served as a West Coast HQMC. He went as a brigadier general. His socialite lady remained in Washington to vilify Daniels.

The furor, which flowed in a Republican Congress over a Democratic appointee relieving Barnett, was mollified by the announcement that his successor would be MajGen. Lejeune triumphantly returned from France and commanding at Quantico. Later, Daniels said the relief of Barnett had been decided by Wilson to reward officers who had distinguished themselves in the European war. Since Wilson was incapacitated from a stroke and unable to confirm or deny, the explanation was weak. It was generally acknowledged that Barnett and Wilson had been on the closest professional terms since 1914.

Lejeune became the 13th Commandant on Jun. 30, 1920. His protégé, Pete Ellis, reported to a special planning section in HQMC.

Barnett presided over the rapid demobilization of the war-expanded Corps. Its fivefold expansion from 1917 abruptly contracted to 17,400 in 1919 as the 4th and 5th Brigades were disbanded at Quantico and Norfolk. Unfortunately, the *cacos* in Haiti and their counterparts in Santo Domingo had not demobilized, The 17,400 Marines (down from a wartime peak of 75,000) weren't enough for all the jobs they were called upon to do. In 1920, Congress authorized a Corps of 1,093 officers and 27,400 enlisted men. But only appropriated for 20,000.

Officer ranks had grown greatly for the war. Initially, college graduates augmented the annual input from the Naval Academy but SecNav Daniels put a crimp in the latter (much to the joy of many anti-Marine Navy officers) when he decreed that all officers would be commissioned from the ranks. Officers then came from college men enlisting and from experienced Non-Commissioned Officers (NCOs) "fleeting up." Barnett had convened a board to select officers for retention to determine in what ranks retainees would serve (reverting was the order of the day) and relative seniority within final ranks. The last was vital in a Corps without a selection system for officer promotion (the Navy had one since 1916 for commanders and above) and vacancies for promotion only occurred by death, resignation or retirement. Captains of lower precedence could serve decades in that rank.

The Russell Board (headed by Col. John H. Russell, who had commanded in Haiti and Santo Domingo and hadn't gotten to France) formed under Barnett's direction created bitterness, Its criteria ignored wartime exploits for more of the "social graces." The fighters from France felt betrayed. Lejeune convened another board under BGen. Wendell Neville. "Buck" Neville had a penchant for succeeding Lejeune whenever the latter was promoted to a higher billet. Buck, who wore a Medal of Honor for Vera Cruz, had distinguished himself in France by commanding a regiment and then the 4th Marine Brigade. His board came up with a complicated "formula" for determining the same things the Russell Board had been asked to do. Parameters were, *inter alia,* length of service in rank, combat, decorations, wounds, age, total length of service, reports of fitness and several other criteria. The results overturned those of the Russell Board. Both boards showed that no such proceedings could please everyone. It set a pattern, for better or worse, of personal and professional rivalry into the future.

In the meantime, Pete Ellis was putting in long days and nights. He produced Operation Plan 712 "Advanced Base Operations in Micronesia." It was more of a concept of operations than a detailed operation plan. It laid out the requirement for the seizure, by amphibious assault, of advanced bases in the Japanese Mandates for use by a fleet advancing across the Pacific to do war in Japanese waters. He opening sentence was "In order to impose our will upon Japan, it will be necessary for us to project our fleet and land forces across the Pacific and wage war in Japanese waters." It did go into some detail on the logistics involved but it did not spell out a scheme-of-maneuver. Mobilization planning assembled Marines from various barracks as well as their equipment. Diagrams depicting this with timetables and choke points on critical paths presaged the management "invention" of the '50s called PERT (Program Evaluation and Review Technique). All of this from a mud Marine who had never been to Harvard Business School. For the seizure of Eniwetok, the estimate of Ellis in 1921 was just 50 Marines shy of those who seized it in 1944.

MGC Lejeune approved Operation Plan 712 on Jul. 23, 1921. It was a concept for the future of the Marine Corps. In the old sailing Navy the mission of the Marines was to man the "fighting tops" and fire down on enemy ships and at "Away Boarders!" come to grips with them on their own decks. Steam and the advent of long-range, breech-loading guns, obviated that mission. There were no longer "fighting tops" and ships no longer came close enough to board. Many of the anti-Marine Navy officers tried to seize on this to eliminate Marines. But steam brought another requirement. Bases were needed to refuel and service ships. They must be defended if we owned them. If not, they must be seized and defended. The Corps moved into the 20th Century.

"Advanced Bases Operations in Micronesia" was both Pete Ellis's monument and epitaph. He departed on "leave." His supposed destination was Europe but he turned up in Japan. He had been trying to get to the Mandates from Australia. He used the cover of employment by Hughes Trading Company (Owned by retired a retired lieutenant colonel. "Johnny-the- Hard" Hughes had commanded a battalion at Belleau Wood and had been physically retired.) Ellis had been in a hospital in Sydney and later in the U.S. Naval Hospital in Yokosuka. Drinking? He had been in cable contact with officers in HQMC and had obtained an extension of his leave. He left the hospital without release and on May 21, 1923, the Embassy in Tokyo cabled the State Department that the Governor General of the Japanese South Sea Islands had informed them that R.H. [*sic*] Ellis, representative of Hughes Trading Company had died at Parao, Caroline Islands, on May 12. The story broke in a speculative press and ran for a while saying that Ellis had not been on leave but had been a spy to determine the extent. if any, of Japanese fortifying the Mandates. The 1923 Earthquake in Japan preempted the story after it had been milked. To this day, what was his mission, if he had one, who authorized it and how he died remain mysteries.

The Marine Corps was not really part of the Navy. From a legal and organizational sense it was in the Department of the Navy, a Cabinet level office. The Navy Department, which included the active sea-going Navy and the Bureaux, was the other part of the Department of the Navy.

The operating forces, the sea-going part, were under the CNO. He reported to the President via SecNav. He ran the Navy, if you consider only the operations of ships and aircraft as the Navy. He was helped but more often hindered in his work by the Chiefs of the Bureaux who were autonomous in their own spheres and did not come under him. CNO had been created to fill a need before the war. RAdm. Bradley Fiske, the operational deputy, had been the advocate for the creation of the post to provide centralized direction much as the Elihu Root (SecWar August 1899-January 1904) Army reforms of 1903 had created a Chief of Staff (to the Commander-in-Chief) of the Army *vice* a Commanding General. To his great disappointment, Fiske did not become the first CNO since Josephus Daniels preferred the more pliant William S. Benson. In October 1919, Adm. Robert E. Coontz succeeded Benson as CNO.

In 1919, and until the creation of the Bureau of Aeronautics (BuAer) on Jul. 12, 1921, there were seven bureaux. Not all titles are indicative of their function. The Bureau of Navigation (BuNav) was concerned, *inter alia,* with personnel matters although it handled operational matters as well, mainly as to charts and navigational instruments but its main function was assignments. The Chaplain Corps (ChC) also came under BuNav. The Bureau of Ordnance (BuOrd) had to do with weapons and fire control including instruments. It was responsible for guns but not really gunnery. The Bureau of Steam Engineering (BuEng) looked after the propulsion plants of ships and their attendant auxiliary machinery. The Bureau of Construction and Repair (BuC&R) handled most things to do with plans for construction, repairs, major and minor alterations of ships and had its own group of officers called Naval Constructors. These were usually among the top graduates of the Naval Academy and rode the larger ships as advisers on ship alterations and made sure that "ShipAlts tantamount to modification" were not performed by over-zealous skippers or their crews. They, not a ship's skipper, were responsible for the dry-docking of vessels in a Navy Yard. The Bureau of Yards and Docks (BuY&D) work, including construction, approved or recommended by BuC&R, was done in the Navy Yards. From this Bureau was to come the SeaBees of World War II. Many officers in this Bureau were of the Civil Engineer Corps (CEC). The Bureau of Supplies and Accounts ((BuSandA) were the "bean counters." The Supply Corps (SC) was in BuSandA. Because of the cuff device worn by SC officers and its resemblance to a pork chop, SC officers were referred to, usually not to their faces, as "pork chops." The Bureau of Medicine and Surgery (BuMed) was responsible for the health of the Navy. It administered the officers and enlisted men of the Medical Corps (MC), and the officers of the Dental Corps (DC) and the Nurse Corps (NC). All of the last were women, the only women in the Navy at that time. Hospitals and dispensaries were run by BuMed. Officers and men of the MC and DC served with Marines.

Although nurses were the only women *in* The Treaty Navy, there were others *of* The Treaty Navy. These were the wives of the officers and men who put up with the hardships, constant moves to follow the fleet, poor housing, low pay, long separations and other inconveniences of being a Navy wife. They listened to the problems of their spouses; endured the uncertainties of transfers or missed promotions; had their husbands' bachelor messmates over for a home-cooked meal; paid the bills during long absences; reared the children; and made a significant contribution to the success of The Treaty Navy. They were as much a part of The Treaty Navy as the men, ships and aircraft. They could rightfully be proud of their roles.

The other major factor in the Navy Department was the General Board. It had been formed in 1900 by SecNav John D. Long who felt his own lack of naval experience required that he have seasoned body of senior flag officers to advise and guide him. (Probably after his assistant, T.R., had sent Dewey to Manila Bay while Davis was at lunch.) A long-time President of the General Board who remained on active duty long after statutory retirement age was Admiral of the Navy George Dewey. He was President of the Board until his death in 1917. The functions of the Board were not codified nor written into law, but it was in Navy Regs. It was a collegium of Navy elder statesmen who defined its own sphere of Navy policy depending on the strength and weakness of the incumbents in the offices of SecNav and CNO. The Board usually concerned itself with ship types, recommending capabilities and desired characteristics rather than specific designs. Designs were the functions of the various Bureaux. The General Board, however, reserved he right of review to ensure that their wishes had been carried out by the various "mechanics" of the Bureaux. The Board, although usually populated by officers who were no longer eligible for commands, wielded considerable influence on The Treaty Navy. Sometimes, a young maverick was assigned temporarily to the Board awaiting an opening for command equal to his potential.

Before turning to the Washington Conference of 1921-22, which initiated The Treaty Navy and the events leading up to, the Conference, we must look at the competition. Who were the other naval powers and what were their fleets?

The German High Seas Fleet was riding at anchor in Scapa Flow. On Jun. 21, 1919, Adm. Von Reuther eliminated his warships from the question of post-war use. He signaled his captains to open the seacocks and scuttle their ships. There was no more viable German navy.

Austria who had had a fairly respectable fleet in the Adriatic before and during the war was no longer a naval power having lost her access to the sea with the dissolution of the Austria-Hungary Empire and loss of territories to Italy and the creation of Yugoslavia. Russia was fighting an internal war and much of her fleet had mutinied. This left the potentially major players at sea as Great Britain, Japan, France, Italy and the U.S., the last about to be the most powerful on completion of her building program in 1924.

In 1921, Great Britain had 21 battleships, seven battlecruisers with one, *Hood,* completed after the war but not totally incorporating the lessons of Jutland. Two more ordered in April 1916 had been cancelled in March 1917. The material assembled for their construction was saved for ships built later. Four other battlecruisers had been ordered in late 1921 and would introduce the 16-in. gun to the RN. In addition, preliminary sketches had been drawn for more battleships in 1921 but the work was suspended in November. The RN also had seven carriers, one as large as 28,800 tons and one as small as 3,300 tons. Carriers were still in the development stage and with the establishment of the Air Ministry and of the Royal Air Force (RAF) as the single air arm, albeit with a confused place in the structure for naval air, the development of the Fleet Air Arm was inhibited.

The RN was strong in cruisers, which she felt she needed for defending her far-flung sea-lanes and worldwide system of bases as well as for regular fleet work. There were 57 cruisers mostly between 5,000 and 6,000 tons with guns smaller than 6-in. although three were more than 12,000 tons with 7.5-in. guns. In destroyers, including flotilla leaders, she had 196 ships. Including six assigned to the Royal Australian Navy (RAN) there were 80 submarines

The French Navy had a predeadnought and ten dreadnoughts launched between 1909 and 1913. Work on four battleships had been suspended when war broke out and the factories and shipyards were used for land armaments. Four others were ordered in 1913 and launched but the work was suspended on these as well. One was eventually completed n 1924 as a carrier (*Bèarn*). There were 14 French armored cruisers, four built in the '90s and the rest between 1900 and 1908. Of the five light cruisers, three had been built between 1911 and 1915. France's destroyers and submarines were about equal in numbers. There were 49 destroyers including nine acquired from the Germans. Of the 47 submarines, eleven were former U-boats.

The Italians had ten battleships. Four were predreadnoughts. One battleship had been ordered in 1914 and launched late in that year. Work was suspended in March 1916 but resumed in October 1919. She was launched in December 1920 to clear the ways. Sold to a steamship company for completion as a high-speed cargo ship she was scrapped in 1921 as uneconomical. Three others had been ordered in 1914 but were cancelled in early 1916. One Hungarian had been allotted to Italy but never served under the Italian flag and was scrapped n 1924.

There were 14 Italian-built cruisers of various categories in the Italian navy. Five were armored cruisers; four were protected cruisers and scouts or torpedo cruisers. In addition, two former Austrian and three former German light cruisers served in the Italian fleet, Italy had 67 destroyers of which, ten, three ex-German and seven ex-Austrian were spoils of war. Her submarines were of a mixed breed. Six were classified as ocean going; four as sea going and 32 were coastal. The last had surface displacements of between 250 and 397 tons.

The new kid on the block as a naval power was Japan. After purchasing capital ships from British, American and German shipyards, Japan began building capital ships in her own yards. The last foreign-built capital ship for Japan was *Kongo,* a battlecruiser built in England in 1911-13. She had three identical sisters built in three different Japanese yards from 1911 to 1915. Japan also received two old German battleships and an ex-German predeadnought, which was then Turkish, as war reparations. These ships were not taken over by Japan, however, and were stricken or demilitarized.

Thus, in 1921, Japan had nine coast defense ships five of which were prizes or raised enemy ships of the Russo-Japanese War. She had one 21,000-ton semi-dreadnought and six dreadnoughts displacing from 30,600 tons to 39,900 tons. The latest ship, *Matsu,* had been completed on Nov. 22, 1921, ten days after the start of the Washington Conference. Two newer battleships, *Kaga* and *Tosa* of 44,200 tons with ten 16-in. guns launched in November and December of 1921 were incomplete. There were four battlecruisers of the 27,500-ton *Kongo* class in commission. Four battlecruisers had been ordered in 1920 and 1921 and were on the ways but not launched In addition four others were contemplated but no work had been started in 1921. All were part of the Japanese three- year "eight and eight" program. This post-war announced program was for a total of eight battleships and eight battlecruisers to be built over a three- year period to give Japan 16 new capital ships about the same time the U.S. completed her building program in 1924. An interesting sidelight to the "eight and eight" program was the misinterpretation by some writers at the time that it was 16 ships each year for three years. This was obviously beyond Japan's resources or shipyard capacity. Still, I have come across more recent "scholars" who have accepted this distorted figure and refer to it as fact. *Praelector emptor!*

In the cruiser category, Japan had 11 armored cruisers only two of which were less than 12 years old. There were seven others, of which three were less than ten years old. There were ten light cruisers built during the war, with six more in the water fitting out. Japan divided her destroyers into third class (older and less than 400 tons), second class (newer and 600-800 tons), and first class (newest and about 1,300 tones.) Of the third class there were 31 from ten to 15 years old. Of the second class there were 37 with eleven building. First class had 16 in commission with another 17 building or ordered. Submarines were either third class or second class, i.e., coast defense and not ocean-going. There were ten of the former of about 300 tons surface displacement. The latter ranged from a low of about 750 tons to some more than 850 tons. There were 26 of these and ten building.

Although those were the naval strengths of the principal players that was not the sum total of world capital ships. (Capital ships are cited because as we'll see in the next chapter, rightly or wrongly, that was the yardstick of naval power used at the Washington Conference.) Other nations had capital ships of varying ages, armament and seaworthiness according to the state of training of their navies.

Germany still had eight predreadnoughts. The Soviet Union had four dreadnoughts and four relics of the previous century. Sweden had 14 coastal battleships ranging from 3,000 to 7,900 tons. Norway had four similar coastal craft of about 3,500 tons. Denmark's five coastal battleships were about 3,700 tons. The Netherlands had a larger type of 5,000 tons which she called coast defense ships. Spain had one predeadnought and three 15,450-ton battleships. Greece still had the two old unsatisfactory predreadnoughts purchased from the U.S. Turkey had a battlecruiser of 22,390 tons. Brazil had two predreadnoughts and two 19,200-ton battleships. Argentina had two 27,000-ton battleships of 1911 vintage. There was one modern 28,000 to battleship in the Chilean navy.

Thus, as the major sea powers prepared to discuss naval limitations in November 1921, there were 17 ships that could be considered capital ships scattered among the rest of the world. Many of the existing capital ships were about to face a fate for which their owners were not prepared. Up to that time less than a dozen capital ships had been sunk in combat. Friendly action on a grander scale was going to do what enemy action had not.

Chapter III

The Washington Conference November 12, 1921 – February 1, 1922

The Wilson Era ended in 1921 when Republican Warren G. Harding was inaugurated. Wilson's Fourteen Points had not been accepted *in toto* particularly those of freedom of the sea and neutral rights. The League of Nations had been formed from the Treaty of Versailles but the U.S. Senate refused its consent and the U.S. was party to neither Treaty nor League. A separate peace was made with Germany. France was still paranoid about a revival of German militarism and feared armaments but felt she must keep strong. By 1924, the U.S. Navy would be the world's most powerful as its 1916 Program was completed. Japan was also building and the speculation was against whom? The Anglo-Japanese Alliance would automatically renew unless abrogated. The world was war weary, economically drained by armaments and entering a recession.

At an Imperial Conference in London, the Dominions raised the question of renewal of the Japanese alliance. They, especially Canada, opposed renewal because it could conceivably be invoked against the U.S. There was fear of Japanese-American friction. If it led to war, Britain would be obligated to aid Japan. Canada would be defenseless against a neighbor with whom she was unwittingly at war. Another Empire concern was the cost of armaments. Keeping in commission the ships she had was expensive for Britain. Sustaining Britannia's supremacy would mean building to compete with the wealthier U.S. A limitation on naval armaments would solve both problems because it would make the Japanese alliance unnecessary under the changed conditions.

There were other international questions. One was the new situation in the Pacific. Japan's acquisition of the German islands as Mandates and of concessions in China was a concern to the U.S. and Britain. The former wondered about the Open Door and the cable through Japanese-controlled Yap. Britain feared trade competition.

In 1920, the Navy had proposed another building program that included 38 ships: four capital ships, 30 light cruisers (a category of controversy throughout the decade) and four others. Britain was stimulated to compete and proposed her own program. Meanwhile, American feeling was strong for retrenchment in military spending. Labor, church and women's groups, supported by influential editors clamored for congressional disapproval of the new Navy program and for a general reduction of arms. Before Harding was in office, Sen. William E. Borah (R-Idaho) who had led the fight against the League and Versailles introduced a resolution. He asked, "... if not incompatible with the public interest [the President] advise the governments of Great Britain and Japan respectively, that this government will at once take up directly with [them] ... and without waiting on the action of any other nation the question of disarmament... with a view of quickly coming to an understanding by which the naval building programs of each … shall be reduced annually during the next five years by fifty percent of the present estimates..."

Harding took office realizing Americans favored naval limits and reductions. The. U.S. and Britain felt each other out on the subject in preliminary exchanges. The latter wanted discussions to reach an understanding before any conference. She also wanted a broader agenda than navies. Lest it cause suspicion and mistrust among other parties the U.S. declined bilateral contacts.

After assurances of acceptance by preliminary query, Harding had SecState Charles Evans Hughes formally invite Britain, France, Italy and Japan to meet in Washington on Nov. 11, 1921. They were to confer on limitations of armaments whose "… enormous disbursements … constitute the greater part of the encumbrance upon enterprise and national prosperity: … is a constant menace to the peace of the world rather than an assurance of its preservation." Other items were to be discussed as well: "… it may be possible to find a solution of Pacific and Far Eastern problems, of unquestioned importance at this time," The broadened scope opened the way for others who were not major naval powers. China was invited, as were those with Pacific and Far Eastern interests, *viz.,* Belgium, Portugal, the Netherlands. Unrecognized U.S.S.R. was ignored.

In September, Hughes proposed the tentative agenda:

Limitation of Armament
I   Limitations of Naval Armament, under which shall be discussed:
   A) Basis of limitation
   B) Extent
II. Rules for control of new agencies of warfare
III. Limitations of land armament

Pacific and Far East Questions
I.   Questions relating to China
     1.   Principles to be applied
     2.   Application
     3 . Subjects
         (a) Territorial integrity
         (b) Administrative integrity
         (c) Open Door - equality of commercial and industrial opportunity
         (d) Concessions, monopolies of preferential economic privileges
         (e) Development of railways, including Chinese Eastern Railway
         (f) Status of existing commitments
II. Siberia (similar headings)
III. Mandated Islands (Unless questions earlier settled)
IV. Electrical Communications in the Pacific.

Under the head of "status of existing commitments" it was expected that opportunity would be afforded to consider and to reach an understanding with respect to unsettled questions involving the nature and scope of commitments under claims of rights would there after be asserted.

The Conference convened on Saturday morning, Nov. 12, 1921 in Memorial Continental Hall, D.C. As host, Hughes presided over the first session.

The American Delegation, Advisory Committee and Technical Staff were impressive. Delegates were: Hughes, Senators Henry Cabot Lodge and Oscar R. Underwood (Harding avoided Wilson's omission of senators at Versailles when they were needed for Senate consent) and former SecWar and SecState Elihu Root. Three women were on the Advisory Committee as were labor leaders, Samuel Gompers and John L. Lewis. Others were General of the Armies John J. Pershing and Secretary of Commerce (SecCom) Herbert Hoover.

The large technical staff included the controversial aviator BGen. William Mitchell. SecNav Edwin Denby was not a member but his assistant, Theodore Roosevelt, Jr., was. RAdm. W. A. Moffett and Capt. W.V. Pratt were the naval experts.

Prime Minister Lloyd George led the Empire delegation aided by Arthur J. Balfour and First Lord of the Admiralty, Baron Lee Fareham. Chief naval advisor was the First Sea Lord, the controversial commander of the ill-fated battlecruisers at Jutland, Admiral of the Fleet David Beatty.

Arsiste Briand, Minister of Foreign Affairs, headed the four-man French delegation. Italy was led by a Senator of the Kingdom, Carlo Schanzer, assisted by a senator famed for his three-volume treatise on the origins of the previous war, Luigi Albertini. Japan was represented by her Navy Minister, Adm. Baron T. Kato with Prince Iyesato Tskugawa, President of the House of Peers. Other delegations were similarly represented but were not there for naval discussions.

After an opening prayer, Harding welcomed them and departed. Balfour with the concurrence of the others asked Hughes to be chairman. Hughes accepted. Then the Chairman set the tone for the conference by proposing reductions and limitations. He addressed the plurality of questions without assigning relative importance to any but implying that naval limitations was the key to the others and should be addressed first. Other questions could be considered concurrently by subcommittees. He then placed his "bombshell" before the delegates. He gave the core of the problem as "... competition in naval programs ..." because, "One program inevitably leads to another, and if competition continues, its regulation is impractical." After applause, he said the solution was to end competition immediately.

It could not be accomplished without sacrifices and no power should be expected to sacrifice alone. Amid more cheers, he called for fair but reasonable sacrifices from all. Then he introduced a key but controversial factor by stating, "... the American delegates are advised by their naval experts that the tonnage of capital ships may be taken to measure the relative strength of navies, as the provision for combat auxiliary craft should sustain a reasonable relation to capital ships tonnage allowed."

To more applause, he proposed a ten-year "holiday" in capital ship construction. He was authorized by the President to go further and offer, "... a concrete proposition for an agreement for the limitation of naval armament." Mainly, it concerned three naval powers, Britain, Japan and the U.S. since the

33

war had not left France or Italy relatively as strong. Their situations could be discussed after agreement had been reached among the big three. His proposal was: 1- all capital ship building programs, actual and projected, be abandoned; 2- older ships should be scrapped, reducing fleets; 3- in general, regard should be given to the existing strengths of the concerned powers; and 4- capital ship tonnage should be the standard measurement with proportionate allowance of combat auxiliaries.

He addressed the specific situations of the three navies. American completion of the 1916 program would add ten battleships and six battlecruisers by 1924. *Maryland* was completed. The other 15 were in various stages of construction with more than $333,000,000 expended. He would scrap all 15, twelve still on the ways and *Colorado, Washington* and *West Virginia* in the water. This represented 618,000 tons of ships. He would also scrap 227,740 tons in 15 older battleships.

The other two powers were asked to take commensurate actions. Britain was asked to stop work on four new *Hood* –class battlecruisers not yet laid down but subject to some expenditure. This was a potential of 172,000 tons. Also, she was asked to scrap 19 predreadnoughts, second-line and older first-line battleships for another 411,375 tons.

Japan was asked to abandon her "eight-and-eight" program. She was to scrap three battleships – *Matsu* launched but not yet completed (see below for the closeness of this assertion), *Tosa* and *Kaga* on the ways. Four battlecruisers, *Amagi, Akagi, Atago* and *Takao* were to be scrapped. This was seven ships for 289,100 tons. Another 159,828 tons of predreadnoughts and second-line battleships were to go to the breakers.

At one stroke, Hughes was destroying 60 capital ships of the three leading sea powers for a total of 1,878,043 tons. He was reducing the U.S. Navy to 18 capital ships of 500,650 tons; the RN to 22 of 604,450 tons and the IJN to ten ships of 299,7000 tons. Replacements were not to exceed 35,000 tons each. As ships were replaced, the three nations would bring themselves into a total tonnage of capital ships of U.S. –500,000 tons; Great Britain- 500,000 tons; and Japan – 300,000 tons. Thus was established the principle of Anglo-American parity and the 5:5:3 ratio which became hateful to Japan.

There were provisions for limiting combat auxiliaries – carriers, cruisers and destroyers. Hughes gave copies of his proposal to the delegates and after minor debate and professions of "agreement in principle" they adjourned. Counter-proposals were saved for private sessions.

Private sessions of heads of delegations, committee meetings of advisors and technical experts plus plenary sessions went on for almost three months before a compromise on naval limitations was signed. Other treaties emerged and were signed at the same time. Two minor treaties were done in a month.

Hughes had played his ace, potential American mastery of the sea by 1924, on the first day. Japan questioned the size of the generosity by contesting his accuracy of calculations. These had included the tonnage of unfinished ships as a percentage of their designed tonnage on the basis of work completed. Japan held that only completed ships given up represented sacrifice. Hughes countered that a partially built ship could be rushed to completion in war long before a new one could be laid down and finished. Japan yielded.

But there was one point on which she was unyielding. Hughes had referred to *Matsu* as not yet completed and designated her for scrapping. Evidentially, she had been rushed to completion after the preliminary conference proposal because Baron Kato announced she was in commission and at sea (actually commissioned on Nov. 22 but could have been on builder's trials before with a full crew.) Her scrapping would be unacceptable to the Japanese people. Compromise was required. In return for keeping *Matsu* the ratio would be maintained by the U.S. scrapping two older battleships scheduled to be spared and completing two of the *Maryland* class (*West Virginia* and *Colorado* eventually, although initial plans had *Washington* saved and *West Virginia* scrapped) which were launched. Since they were larger than the older ones scrapped, total American tonnage increased. Japan was satisfied but Britain was not. Britain's capital ship building had lagged since Jutland (where lessons were learned about vulnerability.) Only *Hood,* a 41,000-ton battlecruiser, had been completed since 1916. The British argued that *Matsu* gave Japan two post-Jutland ships and the compromise gave the U.S. three. *Hood* was a partially post-Jutland ship incorporating only some battle lessons. The acceptable British solution was to be allowed to build. She had plans for 43,000-ton ships and had assembled some material. She wanted to proceed with two of these. Thus, she was allowed to build two 35,000-ton (treaty limit) ships. *Nelson* and *Rodney,* laid down in 1922 were commissioned in 1927. The "naval holiday" was not completely intact.

The question of calculation of tonnage arose. Navies used different standards. The RN used full-load displacement; the French used metric and the Japanese a third method. American proposals were in standard displacement tonnage. This was the compromise inserted in the eventual treaty. Displacement was that of the complete ship, fully manned, engined and equipped for sea, including armament, ammunition and equipment, provisions (including fresh water for the crew), all stores but not fuel or reserve feed water on board. Allowance was made for non-chargeable displacement of 3,000 tons per ship for modernization by adding torpedo "blisters" on the hull and for deck armor as protection against aerial bombs.

As a larger sea power, Britain favored abolishing submarines. France, a smaller sea power, favored retaining them in the world's navies. Japan wanted submarines for coastal defense of her home islands. The U.S. favored anything reducing armaments while Italy straddled the fence on the issue. Discussion of combat auxiliaries, especially cruisers and destroyers, was linked to the existence and numbers of submarines.

Submarines became part of a separate treaty. It required them to conform to International Law in stopping and searching merchant ships during war. Since this was recognized as nearly impossible, the Parties, in effect, outlawed unrestricted submarine warfare. The same treaty also outlawed poison gas. All

35

signed and the U.S. Senate gave its consent but the treaty never came into effect because France refused ratification of the submarine provisions. Throughout the conference, France sought to bargain for a bigger slice of combat auxiliaries and submarines, generated by fear of Italy in the Mediterranean. France rejected the premise that the capital ship was the measure of naval strength. Discussion of combat auxiliary limitations broke down on the issues of global (total) tonnage versus limiting tonnages within categories, e.g., capital ships, cruisers, and destroyers. The French favored global tonnage, which would have fixed the amount allowed and left the choice of allocation to each nation. France could disdain capital ships and build cruisers instead. With one exception quantitative limits on combat auxiliaries did not come to pass at Washington.

The exception was the aircraft carrier. It was prophetic that the type, which would supercede the capital ship as a measure of naval power, was included from the beginning of naval limitations. Carriers were a new development. The U.S. had made the initial experiments in launching and landing aircraft from shipboard platforms. The British constructed (converted) the first ship capable of carrying, launching and recovering aircraft that were not seaplanes. Still, there was little data available for determining limitations on size. All were suspicious that carriers would be converted to capital (gun) ships in time of war. The debates concerned allowable displacement and size and number of guns. Britain and Japan had carriers. The. U.S. was converting a collier, *Jupiter,* (AC-3) into her first carrier, *Langley,* (CV-1). Neither France nor Italy had carriers.

It was agreed to limit carrier tonnage in the 5:5:3 ratio and when the capital ship ratio for France and Italy was initially set at 1.75, it followed that their carrier ratio should be the same. Hughes proposed to save two of the U.S. battlecruisers for conversion to carriers as an economy move. He presented his plan. The ships designed for 43,000 tons would be 33,000-ton carriers. He proposed that the others do the same. Agreement had been reached setting total carrier tonnage at 135,000 for Britain and the U.S. and 81,000 tons for Japan. Maximum size of each ship was set at 27,000 tons. Since the burden on taxpayers was a key element of the conference, Hughes emphasized the economy of the proposal. Lacking carriers, the U.S. would have to build to reach parity and treaty limits. Conversions would be cheaper than construction. Balfour was initially opposed. Japan leaned toward the proposal because she had two ships available for conversion. Hughes said that each nation should be allowed no more than two 33,000-ton carriers chargeable against total carrier tonnage. Britain had no ships to convert and would need to build, hardly a saving. France and Italy pointed out that within a 1.75 ratio, they had only 42,750 tons and could not build more than one vessel. At least two were needed because one would be useless when in overhaul. Britain held firm and Hughes revealed the honesty of his position when he said he desired to serve the taxpayers but he desired more to give them a treaty. The *impasse* broke when it was pointed out that the U.S. had yielded to Britain on the two post-Jutland battleships with an increase in overall tonnage. In the compromise, Italy and France were increased in carrier tonnage to 60,000 tons each or a 2.2 ratio. The

36

U.S. saved *Lexington* (CV-2) and *Saratoga* (CV-3) as 33,000 carriers. Japan saved *Akagi* and *Amagi* (damaged beyond repair on the ways in the 1923 earthquake and replaced by scrap-bound *Kaga.*)

The biggest obstacle was the ratio, Baron Kato bargained in good faith and his apparent sincerity is what got the treaty through. He feared the lesser tonnage would be unacceptable to his government and people. A superior American or British fleet operating from bases near his home islands would be a more formidable force than the smaller Japanese fleet. Britain disavowed any hostile intent but recognized the concern. She proposed maintaining the *status quo* on Pacific bases other than those in the Japanese home islands, Hawaii and the Panama Canal Zone, plus Australia and New Zealand. Japan was spared the threat of nearby foreign bases at Hong Kong, Guam or the Philippines. Of course Japan was not to fortify her new Mandates. When the question of the base under construction at Singapore arose, the classic British rejoinder was, "That's *Inja,* not Pacific Ocean, old boy!" (Equivalent of the later Japanese, "So solly!") Freezing of base building paved the way for acceptance of the ratios and removed the last obstacle.

Other treaties emerged as well. A four-power treaty among the U.S., Britain, France and Japan signed on Dec. 13, 1921, concerned insular positions in the Pacific. For ten years there was to be consultation among the Parties when disputes over rights in the Pacific arose. A Nine-Power Treaty protected the territorial integrity of China; allowed China the opportunity for self-improvement; guaranteed the principles of the Open Door; pledged the Parties against taking advantage of conditions in China to further their own self-interest in the Far East. It was this pact, which Japan violated in the "China Incident" of 1937 ultimately leading to war involving the U.S. with China against Japan. Another treaty assured the Pacific cable through Yap. And, of course, there was the aforementioned stillborn submarine and poison gas treaty.

The treaty, which gave its identity to our era, was the Treaty to Limit Naval Armaments (known as the Washington Treaty of 1922, although there were several treaties of that place and time.) It was signed by five powers (U.S., Britain, Japan, France and Italy) and came into effect upon ratification by all on Aug. 17, 1923. Major provisions were:

- Nations could retain those capital ships specified by name. Tonnages approximated the final ratios and the numbers allowed each nation a specific quantity. Differences in numbers and variances in tonnages from the ratio were based on slight qualitative evaluations of age, size and guns.
- The U.S. could complete two ships under construction but must dispose of two older (named) ships when the new ones were completed. Britain could construct two new ships but must dispose of four (named) ships upon completion. (Appendix 4)
- No new capital ships were to be built for ten years except to replace accidental losses.

37

- The goal for eventual tonnage as new ships replaced older ones in the future was for the U.S. and Britain to be on a par of 500,000 tons, all others in the ratio of 5:5:3:1.67:1.67. [The upward compromise downgraded France and Italy.]
- Replacement capital ships were not to exceed 35,000 tons or have guns greater than 16-in.
- Aircraft carriers were not to exceed 27,000 tons with the exception that each nation could have, within allotted tonnage, two of 33,000 tons. Carrier guns could not exceed 8-in. Existing carriers were experimental and not chargeable against allowances of U.S. and Britain – 135,000 tons each; Japan – 81,000 tons; France and Italy – 60,000 tons each. Carriers less than 10,000 tons did not count against the allowance.
- No other warships exceeding 10,000 tons or having a gun larger than 8-in. could be laid down. Capital ships were those more than 10,000 tons. [This led to the category known as "Treaty Cruisers" – 10,000 tons with 8-in. guns.]
- Preparations could not be made to convert merchant ships except for strengthening decks to mount guns [6-in or less]
- Subterfuge of transferring doomed capital ships to friendly nations or constructing capital ships for them or other ways of hiding tonnage was banned.
- The *status quo* on fortifications and naval facilities was to be maintained in the Parties' insular possessions.
- Capital ships, carriers and standard displacement were defined.
- Reconstruction or modernization was allowed to provide protection against air or torpedo attack but displacement could not be increased more than 3,000 tons per ship. No alterations could be made in side armor or in gun size or mounting. An escape clause provided for consultation if the national security of a Party was threatened by a non-Party or if technical developments altered the situation. Engagement in war might give a Party the right to notify the others of the suspension of the Treaty during hostilities.
- The Treaty was to remain in effect until Dec. 31, 1936. If no one had notified his intention to terminate two years before that date, the Treaty continued in force until two years from the first notice to terminate.
- The powers were to reconvene within eight years [Aug. 17, 1931] of the Treaty coming into force. A conference was to be held within a year of anyone's signifying intent to cancel.

The immediate effect was cessation of capital ship construction. Taxpayers and pacifist groups were pleased. Shipyard workers and those in related industries were not. Exceptions were those retained to break up ships n the ways. Anglophobes spoke of knuckling under to Britain. One, William B. Shearer, whom we'll meet later, unsuccessfully sued SecNav to prevent destruction of a capital ship. Feelings were mixed and emotions ran high. But Harding and Hughes had succeeded in what they had set out to do. They had the nations agree to limits and on paper; they had capital ship parity with Britain. Indirectly, they had renounced the policies of neutral rights and freedom of the seas. Insistence on freedom of the seas had led to war with Germany, although it could have just as easily led to war with Britain in 1917 as it had in 1812. Almost 15 years later under F.D. Roosevelt, Congress formally abandoned the policies by several neutrality acts.

Another immediate effect was to set a limit on the size of cruisers. A new class of 10,000 tons with 8-in. guns but without numerical limits or total tonnage began to be constructed by he world's navies. The U.S. was not among those building a fleet of the new "Treaty Cruisers." This was a problem for the initial years of The Treaty Navy.

It came as no surprise that the officers of the U.S. Navy were not happy with the situation with which they were going to have to live over the next two decades. Expectations of a modern fleet able to control the seas by 1924 were dashed. Likewise the clause on non-fortification beyond Hawaii doomed the Philippines and hampered any effort of the Navy to range across the broad reaches of the Pacific. A reduced navy meant slower advancements and for some officers - discharges.

Thus, entered the era of The Treaty Navy. It was to endure until about 1938 when world conditions made the Navy once more the pride of the American people. Meanwhile, it remained the pride of those who served in it.

Chapter IV

The Denby Years 1921-1924

On Mar. 10, 1924, there was a ceremony in SecNav's office. The Marine Band played as MGC Lejeune swore in Edwin Denby as a Marine Reserve major. Denby, a Michigan attorney who had been a football star at University of Michigan before the Spanish War had enlisted in the Marines at age 47. The three-term (1904-11) Congressman made it through "boot camp" and was commissioned. When Warren G. Harding and the Republicans were elected in 1920, he chose Denby for the Cabinet post of SecNav. He was sworn in on Mar. 4, 1921.

When Harding died in August 1923, his successor, Calvin Coolidge, retained most of Harding's Cabinet including Denby. Now, Denby was resigning. He had become an embarrassment to the Administration and Congress had pressured Coolidge to request his resignation. The ceremony marked his last day in office.

The three years of Denby's incumbency were benchmarks for The Treaty Navy. They included not only the Washington Conference which gave us the Treaty but also changes in the way the government did business fiscally. The latter was significant to The Treaty Navy until the watershed years of Vinson and F.D.R.

One of Denby's first acts was to assure the apprehensive MGC that he was being retained for a full term. Lejeune had been appointed abruptly in the summer of 1920 to succeed MajGen. Barnett. Lejeune, who saw himself as a "lame duck" until reappointment, was able to guide the post-war Marine Corps with confidence.

The Budget Accounting Act of 1921 vested power of the purse in the Bureau of the Budget. All executive branches were affected but we are only concerned with the Naval Service. There were two major changes in the way the Navy's business was done. No longer was new construction authorized and its appropriations made in the same enactment. Now authorizations were made allowing for construction but money came piecemeal in annual increments. Such procedures put construction at the mercy of the annual belt-tightening and caprice of Congress. It was inefficient because it did not allow for adequate estimating or planning.

Previously, the Bureaux had gone directly to Congress with their requests with SecNav merely setting the stage and allowing Bureau Chiefs to argue their cases. Now, SecNav had to draft a Department-wide budget; submit it and defend it to the Bureau of the Budget and receive approval for a whittled down amount which had less relation to hard requirements than what the Budget Director allowed as a total amount. This then had to be submitted to and defended before Congress as sums retranslated into line-item requirements. Often, this eliminated entire categories or curtailed requirements making them more expensive in the future. As upkeep and repairs were delayed or neglected they were more expensive. Appropriations for alterations and repairs dropped from $44 million in fiscal year (FY) 1921 to $23.6 million in FY 1922 and to less than $17 million the next FY.

Where the cuts were felt most keenly was in personnel. The 1916 Act had "authorized" a peacetime maximum strength of 137,500 enlisted and 5,000 commissioned line and staff officers. While the number of ships in commission might be assumed as fixed, this was not true. Ships were a function of crews to man them.

For FY 1923, the Navy needed 106.000 enlisted men as the minimum to keep 18 battleships, ten new scout cruisers (and a modicum of the older types), 103 destroyers (many were in reserve status laid up in the backwater on both coasts but periodically rotated to active status) and 84 submarines at authorized manning level (not war-time strength but minimums required for reduced operation.) To do so would mean inactivating trade protection squadrons in the Caribbean, on the Yangtze and South China Sea. Yet the request was only for 96,000 enlisted and 4,160 officers. The House Naval Affairs and Appropriations Committees wanted to know what would be the effect on the fleet of appropriations for 65,000 enlisted. The answer was a drastic cut of the number of ships in commission.

A harbinger of things to come occurred in FY 1924, when in January 1923, the appropriations for appointments to the Naval Academy for each Senator and Representative was reduced from five to three (not the annual number but the number one appointer could have in the Academy at any time.) However, authorizations remained at five. The Class of 1928, still styles itself as "The Biggest Little Class" since it graduated 173 versus the previous five-year average of 483 annually.

Another deficiency was fuel. It was expensive and to keep from burning too much, ships were reduced to "swinging on the hook" *vice* training and operating. The annual winter maneuvers for 1922 were cancelled because of lack of funds for fuel. Fewer funds also cut down on the amount of ammunition. Gunnery training suffered. In short, it appeared that the Navy and naval policy were being run by a new and powerful bureaucracy of the budget over which Congress had no control. Still, Congress had the constitutional responsibility "To provide and maintain a navy."

The Washington Conference and resulting limitation treaty occurred during this time. SecNav Denby was not a member of the U.S. delegation. There was also a paucity of Navy representation except on the technical staffs. This was the direct result of SecState Hughes's conviction that the conference was too important to be left to naval officers of the world. He wanted it to be a conference of diplomats and civilians responsible for world peace. Britain and Japan did not strictly adhere to this criterion in their delegations but the U.S. did. Denby's assistant, Theodore Roosevelt, Jr., acted as liaison between the Navy Department and the conferees. It was the "striped-pants-and-cut-away-coat-crowd" who produced the Treaty. Navy officers were appalled at the "give-away" of the right to fortify bases in the Pacific.

41

After the Conference but before the Treaty took legal effect, CNO Coontz reorganized the fleet structure. He did basically what his predecessor, Adm. Benson had done on paper in January 1919. Benson had established a U.S. Fleet by abolishing the Atlantic Feet as a separate entity and making a single command. The enigmatic Josephus Daniels reverted to two fleets. Atlantic and Pacific, within six months. In December 1922, Coontz therefore made one of his major contributions as CNO to The Treaty Navy. Actually, he had done it surreptitiously earlier.

SecNav Denby in April 1921 had told SecState Hughes that it was about time (the European war was over) that the Navy became acquainted with the Pacific and the navy yards and bases on the West Coast. In a May 31, 1921 reply, Hughes had no objection in principle but wanted to wait to until the end of the coming Washington Conference. Rather than waiting and with the approval of Denby, Coontz reorganized the heretofore Atlantic and Pacific Fleets into the U.S. Fleet. In the summer of 1921, VAdm. Hilary P. Jones commanded the Atlantic Fleet and VAdm. Edward E. Eberle the Pacific Fleet, Secretly, VAdm. John D. McDonald was privately ordered to take command of the Atlantic Fleet while Jones added a fourth star to be Commander-in-Chief U.S. Fleet (CINCUS). Thus, he had both fleets plus the Fleet Base Force and the Control Force (submarines.) See Appendix 3 for the two Fleet Organizations of 1923.

On Dec. 6, 1922, General Order No. 94 was issued. It provided for a U.S. Fleet under Jones with components of a Battle force under Eberle and a Scouting Force under McDonald. Thus, there were four major commands in the U.S. Fleet. The Battle Fleet had 12 of the most modern battleships. It and the Fleet Base Force would be West Coast-based. The Scouting Force with six of the older battleships and the Control Force would be Atlantic-based. Other commands operating separately were the Asiatic Fleet, Naval Forces Europe, the Special Service Squadron (Caribbean) and Naval Transportation Service. Coontz also created type commands, i.e., administrative commands of the same type ships. They were responsible for the administration and logistics, including upkeep and repair, plus manning of such vessels. Type commands were to be a controversy in The Treaty Navy.

Coontz had become CNO in November 1919 at age 55. In 1923, he was still short of statutory retirement age and the usual course was to drop back to the permanent rank of two-stars and command one of the Naval Districts. Denby surprised Coontz by offering him the CINCUS billet. Coontz was doubly delighted to accept. He was getting out of Washington and back to sea. He was also going to exercise the fleet and determine its capabilities and weaknesses. He did so during the winter maneuvers of 1923-24 in the Caribbean. He turned the CNO reins over to Adm. Eberle.

With the creation of the U.S. Fleet, annual operations fell into a routine. The Battle Fleet on the West Coast made its home in several ports. The destroyers and submarines were at San Diego where facilities were adequate for smaller ships. As yet there was no major cruiser force inasmuch as the older cruisers in commission did not operate with the fleet. The battleships anchored off Long

Beach and San Pedro near Los Angeles. The two smaller cities became bedroom communities to the families of married offices and men. (Far fewer married men in proportion to now. Callings of career combined with low pay made postponement of marriage a fact of life.) In the winter, the Battle Fleet headed south, transited the Canal and conducted operations, usually a Fleet Problem (See Appendix 5) with the Scouting Fleet. Then both fleets made their way north along the coast showing the flag, holding open house (ships) for public approval of their Navy. After returning to its West Coast bases for the summer, the Battle Fleet would cruise to Bremerton for dry-docking and upkeep. Tactical operations would be done en route south with good will stops at San Francisco and smaller ships going to other ports. Fleet Week in San Francisco was an annual gala occasion in the life of The Treaty Navy. Part of the Scouting Fleet spent the summer as the Midshipmen Training Squadron visiting Europe or South America.

The winter maneuvers of 1923-24 took place after two major mishaps in September 1923. (These are covered in Chapter V since they were legacies for the next SecNav.) Fleet Problems II and III concerned the Panama Canal. Coontz with an eye to obtaining support for the Navy by making the public aware of fleet deficiencies brought about by budget restrictions and congressional apathy, played to the press. Newsmen were on board most battleships and received regular briefings on happenings. A senior officer in command was made available to lecture newsmen during maneuvers. His efforts were successful. The "Coontz Report" after the exercises stirred up a hornet's nest in he press and eventually in Congress. A version of the formal report to SecNav had been prepared and released to the journalists.

The gist of the report was that deficiencies had reduced the effectiveness of the Navy, which should have been supreme at sea in 1924, to a fraction of that of the RN, not parity. There were several problems. The old armored cruisers were inadequate as flagships but they had to be used. The battleships of the Battle and Scouting Fleet could not operate together. This lack of homogeneity was critical. The Scouting Fleet's older coal-burners were slower and lacked the cruising radius of the newer ships. Some were in such poor shape with bad boilers that they were tantamount to cripples. Further, the mix of 12-in. (two ships had older mounted 14-in.) guns made them incompatible with the newer 14-in. and 16-in. guns of the Battle Fleet. The older guns and newer guns lacked a common maximum range. The older ships lacked the armor protection to let them stand with the newer ships in a battleline. An absolute necessity was more scout cruisers. The interim use of destroyers in that role was unsatisfactory. Lastly, the submarines were a disgrace. They were too slow, badly ventilated and leaked oil, not only a fire hazard but also a give-away of location when submerged.

The oil leaks were one thing. The press leak was another and it was to have the desired effect on the public and Congress in the immediate future, albeit, *pro tem* It was oil, however, which was Denby's undoing.

During the administrations of Taft and Wilson, two oil reserves had been set aside for future use of the Navy, which was then shifting from coal. These were at Elk Hills, Calif., and Teapot Dome, Wyo. (It is interesting to note that about the same time Britain was taking similar action but on a grander scale. First Lord of the Admiralty Winston S, Churchill persuaded Chancellor of the Exchequer Lloyd George to finance RN purchase of 51 percent of what became the Anglo-Persian Oil Company.) In early 1921, President Harding at the urging of SecInt Albert B. Fall, a former senator, and with the approval of SecNav Denby, transferred to the Interior Dept., administration of the naval oil reserves at Teapot Dome and Elk Hills. Then on Apr. 7, 1922, Fall secretly leased the Teapot Dome reserves to Harry Sinclair, owner of Mammoth Oil Company. A few weeks later, the Elk Hills fields were leased to Edward L. Doheny, owner of Pan-American Petroleum Company. A purported *quid pro quo* for the Navy was vouchers for refined oil for the fleet *vice* oil in the ground. Not the intended purpose of *reserves*! In addition, Sinclair was to build storage tanks in Hawaii and on the West Coast for the Navy. These were built but their acceptance was tied up in litigation for years. The tank farm at Pearl Harbor was the one ignored by Japanese bombers on Dec. 7, 1941. These tanks provided the fuel used by the survivors of The Treaty Navy to operate during early 1942, a fatal omission by the Japanese.

The "Teapot Dome" scandal broke in 1924, the year after Harding's death. A Senate Committee found that before leasing the reserves, Doheny had lent Fall $100,000 without benefit of interest or collateral and further after Fall left the Cabinet, he had received a "loan" of $25,000 from Sinclair. The Supreme Court later declared (1927) the leases invalid. Fall was indicted for bribery and conspiracy; convicted of bribery and sentenced to year in prison and a $100,000 fine. Sinclair and Doheny were acquitted of bribery. Sinclair was sentenced to nine months in prison and fined $1,000 for contempt of court.

Evidently, neither Harding nor Denby were aware of Fall's bribes for the release of the oil. But the politics of the day required a scalp. Harding was dead. The other "party" was Denby whose only crime was probably being loyal to Harding and refusing to believe that such venality could exist in a former senator and Cabinet Officer. On Feb. 11, 1924, the Senate resolved 47 to 36 to ask Coolidge to request Denby's resignation. That led to the ceremony on Mar. 10.

None of Denby's subordinates believed him culpable in criminal activity. Coontz felt Denby had been good for the Navy. RAdm. J.K. Robinson, Chief BuEng, to whom Denby had transferred management of oil reserves from CNO, had encouraged the transfer. He believed that strained relations with Japan generated a need for oil tanks in the Pacific *vice* crude underground.

Although Denby left office at the nadir of his tenure, his term was not all that bad. He presided over the initial post-treaty Navy and saw the beginning of the scrapping of what would have been the most powerful force afloat at the time he left. While the ships were being scrapped, not all their machinery or equipment was lost. Boilers of the uncompleted ships were available for installation in the old battleships whose power plants were deemed deficient in the Coontz Report. This was done later. Other machinery went to replace equipment in the fleet.

The 16-in guns ordered but never installed in the scrapped ships found their way to Army shore fortifications as coast artillery. (The emplacements, not the guns, can still be visited, *inter situs,* on the Marin side of the Golden Gate.) There was a unique monument to the uncompleted ships. Steel girders from the scrapped ships built Thompson Stadium at the Naval Academy, football field until erection of the Navy-Marine Corps Stadium *circa* 1959. At Quantico, the Commanding General (CG) was the irrepressible BGen. Smedley Butler also decided to build a stadium. MGC Lejeune had urged competitive athletics in the post-war Corps to boost morale and keep the Corps in the public eye. Butler decided on a do-it-yourself stadium at Quantico. It involved all hands regardless of rank, including the CG himself, in the manual labor. Butler Stadium still serves Marines..

Among other Denby accomplishments was the retention of Lejeune as MGC. That was to make a significant impact on The Treaty Navy. Likewise, pushing the completion of the ten *Omaha* scout cruisers was a plus. Approval of the Coontz fleet reorganization played a major role in the future of The Treaty Navy. Denby's successor was to be another lawyer and former football star. He was also the first Naval Academy graduate to be SecNav.

The Naval Academy was also the locale of another scandal of the Denby era. Again, he was a bystander. It concerns the incident of "The Perforated Page" in the 1922 *Lucky Bag* (Academy yearbook.) It has been depicted as a case of anti-Semitism and over the years, Adm. Hyman Rickover, a Jew who became an Episcopalian, let it be inferred that he was the victim. He was not. The incident was the climax of a four-year rivalry for the top spot in the Class between Jerauld L. Olmstead and Leonard Kaplan. The former was most popular among his Classmates. The latter was incidentally Jewish but obnoxiously brilliant. Olmstead was Regimental Commander and stood first. Kaplan stood second. But Olmstead was editor of the *Lucky Bag*. With or without approval of his senior officers, the editor had Kaplan's photo and unflattering biography put on a perforated page to facilitate removal.

Olmstead, whose brother was First Captain and stood number two the same year at West Point, died a year after graduation as an Ensign. The Class dedicated a plaque to him. Kaplan went on to a career as a Naval Constructor, retiring in 1949 as a Capitan. He had the last laugh.

The Naval Academy Alumni Association gives a monetary award to the graduate standing first. When Kaplan died in 1983, in his will he left a monetary prize exactly twice the amount of that of the Alumni Association's award. It was to go to the graduate *standing second!*

PART II

The Wilbur Era and Beyond

Chapter V

1924-1927

Coolidge's Cabinet was in turmoil. His Navy Secretary had resigned under pressure. His Attorney General was in trouble. Curtis D. Wilbur, a Naval Academy graduate and Chief Justice of the California Supreme Court, was mentioned for the Justice Dept. Another Naval Academy graduate, John W. Weeks, was Coolidge's SecWar.

Coolidge didn't want a hasty appointment. He desired a man of good administrative ability, able to handle the work of the Navy but also the problems of the oil leases then in litigation. Several candidates were considered but each wanted the "more prestigious" job of Attorney General. Sen. S.W. Shortridge (R-Calif.) suggested Wilbur. The senator pointed out Wilbur's fine judicial record, interest in military and naval affairs and distinguished family – a brother, Dr. Ray Lyman Wilbur (to be Hoover's SecInt) was chancellor of Stanford.

Three days after Denby's resignation, Coolidge wired Wilbur, "You seem to be the man I need for the Navy. Am drafting you today. Please answer." Ten minutes later, the new Secretary replied, "I will accept the appointment and will come to Washington as soon after confirmation as possible." Thus began Wilbur's five dynamic years at the helm of what looked like a sinking ship. He was to guide its rebirth into the true Treaty Navy.

He led the Navy through the perilous '20s when Congress was tight-fisted; the Navy was being attacked by outside interests and pacifists; and when it was saddened by death and disasters. He stood his ground against criticism; argued for funds and ships; solved inherited problems; and when he departed in 1929, there was a naval policy and building program which was to revive the Navy and set the table for the Vinson-Trammel construction of the New Deal. His efforts provided the cruisers that bore the brunt of the fighting in the early days of 1942.

Wilbur was born in Boonesboro, Iowa, on May 10, 1867 and reared in Dakota Territory. Entering the Naval Academy in 1884, he was an excellent athlete. He was a tackle on the football team; ran track and set a world record for the hitch-kick (still stands as the event no longer exists.) of 9-feet-1-inch. He stood 6-foot-3 in height and third in the Class on graduation in 1888. (Lejeune stood 13th in the Class and two others we'll meet later in this chapter, Charles F. Hughes and Henry A. Wiley stood 20th and 34th, respectively, out of 35 graduates.) With few commissions to go around, Wilbur resigned and went to California. He taught school; studied law and was admitted to the bar in 1890. He progressed from Deputy District Attorney to judge of the Superior Court and finally Chief Justice.

In 1924, the Navy should have been the most powerful in the world. We have seen what negated that. Wilbur inherited a Navy at a low ebb in everything from money to morale. There were 4,785 line officers. With 1,976 Midshipmen at the Naval Academy, the new Plebe Class would be the smallest in years because of cuts in appointments. Limited by money appropriated for pay, there were 86,000 enlisted men. The Marine Corps had 1,158 commissioned and 16,175 enlisted Marines. The U.S. Fleet (Battle Fleet, Scouting Fleet, Control Force and Base Force), Asiatic Fleet, Special Services Squadron and Naval Forces Europe operated at vastly reduced manning levels, 18 battleships, seven second-line cruisers, eight first-line scout cruisers, an experimental aircraft carrier, 103 destroyers, 81 coastal submarines and 108 auxiliaries. Unmanned but maintained with limited funding and personnel were more than 100 decommissioned destroyers at Philadelphia and San Diego. Tight budgets that did not provide enough training to maintain proficiency at sea hurt. The hurt was often serious. The results were often tragic. Wilbur inherited the results of some disasters and had some of his own.

Six months before Wilbur assumed office, the destroyer squadrons (DesRon) were in San Francisco at the end of Fleet Week. The Commander of DesRon-11 called his skippers together for a conference on *Melville* (AD-2). He had good news for those assembled. He had three destroyer divisions (DesDiv) of six ships each and flew his pennant (he was a captain not a flag officer) in *Delphy* (DD-261). Not all 19 skippers were present to get the good news. Five were missing because of engineering breakdowns and in one case a collision. Such incidents were normal in those days. But to the others, the good news was a destroyer man's dream. After a year of economy operating, they had been approved for a 20-knot speed run home to San Diego. ComDesRon-11 wanted to sortie the Golden Gate before Colors (8 a.m.) on Saturday, Sept. 8, 1923. He was anxious to get the jump on rival DesRon-12 also cleared for the same run.

The 14 ships cleared the Bay in column astern of *Delphy*. Navigators got a visual fix on Pigeon Point before noon. It was their last. Unlike ComDesRon-12 who opted for a course farther off shore, ComDesRon-11 was hugging the coast to the Santa Barbara Channel where he would make his turn east and follow the coast to San Diego. Fog rolled in but the ships continued in column at 20 knots navigating by dead reckoning and radio bearings from stations along the coast. To avoid saturating the radio net, only *Delphy* requested bearings. It was determined that the column should turn into the Channel at 9 p.m. Actually, they still were almost 20 miles north of the Channel. *Delphy* struck the rocks off Honda Point (misnamed in the press from the sign on a railroad shack above the bluff but it gave its name to history.) *S.P. Lee* (DD-310), *Young* (DD-312), *Woodbury* (DD-309), *Nicholas* (DD-316), *Fuller* (DD-297) , *Chauncey* (DD-296), *Somers* (DD-301) and *Farragut* (DD-300) followed. The last two struck bottom but had enough warning from the whistles of leading ships that they were able to back off. The others were scattered among the rocky reefs and even at the foot of the 50-foot bluff. *Delphy* broke in two. *Young* turned on her side; *S.P. Lee* was broadside to the bluff on the rocks; *Nicholas* struck farther out and was turned seaward but breaking up. Seven American destroyers were total wrecks.

The immediate sequel was one of bravery and devotion. Of the 750 crewmen only 23 were lost, 20 from capsized *Young* and three from *Delphy*. Some swam through the surf with lifelines to guide others ashore. In the morning local fishermen took off many of the crews. The locals responded with blankets and relief supplies. The next morning a special train took the survivors to San Diego.

Speculation as to the cause of the disaster varied from tidal effects of the recent Japanese earthquake to reciprocal radio bearings. None were excuses.

The officer named to conduct the investigation was RAdm. W.V. Pratt, then ComBat 4. He had cut his teeth in destroyers in the "Band of Brothers" of Sim's Torpedo Flotilla. Pratt thought it was the worst job he ever had. Most of these men were his friends. He was a destroyer man and a friend of the organization. He had to do what was best for the Navy. Pratt balked at the requirement for an open hearing because he distrusted the press. SecNav Denby knew an open hearing would be the best and it was. All parties cooperated and waived their right to remain silent. ComDesRon-11, Capt. E.H. Watson, took responsibility but Pratt recommended all parties (skippers and navigators) be court-martialled and they were. Three were found guilty of "culpable inefficiency and negligence" and sentenced to loss of considerable numbers on the lineal list ending their career aspirations. Two skippers went on to retire as captains. Two made flag. Cdr. W.S. Pye, ComDesDiv-31 retired as a vice-admiral. CO *Young,* Cdr. W. L. Calhoun retired with four stars. A host of junior officer made flag during World War II. Could that happen in today's Navy when minor mishaps can devastate a career?

The finding of guilty for CO *Nicholas* was set aside leaving only ComDesRon-11 and CO *Delphy* guilty. Political Washington, including Coolidge and Denby, thought the sentences "lenient." They were reminded that naval courts martial are more concerned with justice than law.

Three weeks later, submarine O-5 was rammed off Panama by a freighter and sank. In January 1924, the old cruiser, *Tacoma,* ran aground off Vera Cruz and her skipper was drowned in the wreck. In February, the new scout cruiser, *Cincinnati,* stuck a reef off the coast of Chile. She was damaged but saved. These were the disasters that preceded Wilbur's oath of office. He was to have his own.

His first was more of a tragic-comedy but it did make headlines which were unfavorable to the Navy. After the Fleet Problem in the Caribbean in early 1924, the Battle Fleet steamed north for visits in various East Coast ports. *Arizona* (BB-39) visited New York and anchored in the Hudson River. Her crew had liberty ashore the first week in March 1924. She then headed back toward the Canal. On Apr. 12, she was preparing to leave Balboa for San Pedro when a stowaway was discovered. A chief radioman reported that he had seen a woman in sailor's dungarees. The search was on and a 19-year-old hooker was found.

She had been on board a month. The question was whether she was the only one. She was. While in New York, some of the crew had become friendly with "Blackie" (the name they gave to the perky brunette) and concocted a scheme to allow her to ply her trade and mix it with a little adventure. They got her aboard disguised in a sailor's liberty uniform with the collar of a pea jacket turned up to cover her now-bobbed hair and stashed her in a generator room. She set up shop there and some cooks shared in her profits by charging her ten bucks a day for food. After her capture. the senior petty officers held a kangaroo court that night in their mess They got all the details and the names of the culprits. Twenty-three of the plotters were later tried, found guilty and sentenced to terms of up to ten years in "The Castle" (Naval Prison, Portsmouth, N.H.) Blackie was put ashore but was still brash. She convinced the Grace line agent in Panama that thee Navy would pay her first-class passage back to New York and sailed home in style. When the Navy Department got the bill they sent it to the CO *Arizona.* There is no record of his reaction but it was another episode of The Treaty Navy.

SecNav Wilbur was firmly on board and his first action was to take personal charge of the oil reserves and not release any oil until litigation was over. He refused to take possession of the oil tanks at Pearl Harbor. He said that the oil reserves were "... an important national insurance ... there is estimated to be but 20 years of supply within the limits of the United States. When this is exhausted w will be dependent upon foreign sources for supply."

The next day, Apr. 11, William B. Shearer, a self-styled "naval expert" challenged the oil estimate. Shearer was a violent Anglophobe. He said that the Navy didn't have enough oil to get to the Far East while Britain controlled the oil in ports around the world. Asst. SecNav Theodore Roosevelt, Jr. publicly refuted Shearer, Shearer came back with charges in the press that the Navy was covering up the Coontz report on deficiencies. He also charged hat the Navy was inferior to Britain's and that Britain was not adhering to the 5:5:3 ratio.

At the Naval Academy on May 2, Wilbur replied. He said that the purpose of the exercise (Fleet Problems II and III) was to detect weaknesses. They were found and he Navy needed money to correct them. A few days later, Wilbur spoke on related topics. He opposed service unification and supported the views of naval aviators against a single air service. The Navy existed for national defense and execution of national policy. He favored another arms conference to cover those categories omitted from the Washington Treaty. Then he held a little "school-of-the-boat." He urged a continuous peacetime building program, adequate funding for personnel and a Navy on a par with the strongest afloat. The London *Daily Mail* called him a militarist and said the policy of the U.S. was to build to superiority and then call a conference on limitations to keep competitors inferior. Wilbur remarked that there were many who called him a pacifist. He carried his crusade to Congress and placed responsibility for fleet deficiencies on them. He charged that they were neglecting the Navy in appropriations. He stated that because of this the actual ratio was 5:4:3 and this did not take into consideration the lack of bases in the Western Pacific that were forbidden. Retired RAdm. Bradley Fiske wrote to Wilbur that he had not gone far enough. The Navy was actually inferior to the IJN and could not project itself beyond Hawaii was Fiske's observation.

The new Secretary started a campaign that was to be the theme of every day of his tenure. At a surprise speech to he national YMCA, he stated that the Navy needed more men; more combat auxiliaries; to convert four battleships from coal to oil; and required at least eight new cruisers.

Wilbur was attending the Republican National Convention in Cleveland on June 12, 1924 when tragedy struck. Three ships, *Arizona, Mississippi* and *Idaho* of Bat Div 4 were in column conducting live-fire exercises at sea. *Mississippi* was firing straight ahead simulating a chase. With two salvos left to go, Turret 2 exuded a wisp of smoke from the hatch, trained slowly to port and locked at maximum train aft. Warning lights in the fire control center indicated that the magazines had been flooded and the ship was in no danger. It was deduced that firing into the relative wind from forward had negated the compressed air evacuation system of the gun and that the gun captain had failed to note burning fragments from the powder bags still in the breech when the next powder bag was rammed home. The result was a flareback through an open breech into the turret. Three officers and 44 men died. The last act of the Turret Officer, Lt. (j.g.) T.E. Zellars was identified from the Class Ring ('21) on the charred stump gripping the flooding valve lever saving the ship.

On June 17, the Battle Fleet had a memorial service for its dead on Trona Field in San Pedro. Officers in full-dress and crews from all the ships formed a hollow square around the 47 caskets hidden by flowers. Families and friends by the thousands reinforced the square. RAdm. Pratt, ComBatDiv 4 gave the eulogy. His immediate boss, VAdm. H.A. Wiley, ComBatFlt, described the funeral address as, "full of feeling, full of the traditional spirit of the service." The next day Pratt receive a scathing letter from a clergyman who held that a naval officer had no business taking part in a funeral service. Such were the moods and attitudes toward The Treaty Navy.

After the tragedy it was back to business for the determined new Secretary. There was a bill pending in Congress to authorize eight cruisers (10,000-ton "Treaty cruisers") with 8-in. guns; modernize the coal-burning battleships; build six river gunboats for Chinese waters; and one point of contention – increase the main battery elevations of the older battleships. The last was held by many to violate the Treaty. Wilbur referred it to SecState and the guns remained unaltered.

The Secretary then embarked on a controversial course that he would follow for the next five years. He left on a West Coast vacation making speeches supporting Coolidge (for the party) and urging an adequate Navy (for his conscience.) Coolidge asked him to return to Washington. The given reason was to confer on restoring Budget Bureau cuts. Naval aviation was threatened by the loss. The opposition, however, said that Wilbur was recalled because he was taking stands, e.g., anti-Japanese, anti- Prohibition and pro-Navy detrimental to Coolidge's election. For the next five years, Wilbur was the prime target of the Democrats. Despite rumors to the contrary, he was one of the few Cabinet members retained after March 1925. To his enemies (British, pacifists and Democrats) he now added Japanese and Drys. He made friends in the fleet, however, especially after he rescinded part of Josephus Daniels's fiat and restored soft drinks aboard ship.

On Oct. 24, 1924 there was another turret tragedy. A new scout cruiser, *Trenton,* firing for the first time had two powder bags explode in a hoist. The death toll was 13 men and an officer. That officer, Ens. H.C. Drexler, not six months out of the Academy, was awarded the Medal of Honor for dumping flaming powder bags over the side.

On Navy Day (Oct. 27) Wilbur carried his crusade forward. He pointed out that the Navy was below the 135,000 allowed tons in carriers, that she had fallen behind in cruisers and that money was needed for battleship modernization. He noted that the bill for all he asked had been thwarted in the Senate by filibuster.

As Secretary, Wilbur had the responsibility to carry out the terms of the Treaty. The hull of uncompleted *Washington* was to give her life for the Navy. Tests of the effects of underwater explosions on a modern battleship hull were her fate. On Nov. 10, 1924, Shearer was again on the scene. (A full coverage of Shearer's infamous deeds appears in Chapter VIII,) He challenged the legality of the Treaty; argued that the British were not living up to it; and had a court order keeping SecNav from sinking *Washington.* It was overruled and she went to her grave off the Virginia Capes with honor. Shearer admitted that in gathering information about the Navy for two senators, King (R-Utah) and Pittman (D-Nev.) who led the filibuster, he had the cooperation of disgruntled naval officers who provided information on the perfidy of Britain regarding the Treaty.

Wilbur stuck to his guns and asked for new construction and more appropriations. He said that previous cuts had made the Navy unsatisfactory materially. To avoid over-spending, he had to order all improvements stopped. He cited the need for new ships saying it would help navy yards and provide employment. He asked for 22 new cruisers and 60,000 tons of submarines. He got authorization for eight cruisers, six river gunboats and modernization of six battleships. Having authorizations, he asked for money. He wanted an orderly building program and outlined one costing $110 million a year for the next 20 years. Congress gave him a moderate appropriation and only two of the authorized cruisers could be laid down the next year, *Salt Lake City* (CA-24) and *Pensacola* (CA-25).

Tests on *Washington* and previous Army Air Corps sinking of old ships encouraged air advocates against battleships and other surface craft. The leader was ex-BGen. "Billy" Mitchell. He had been admonished and demoted but still was loud in 1925. His target in a quest for a single air service was the Navy. Wilbur supported by Naval Aviators opposed a single air service. He advocated aviators who were familiar with ships and naval tactics. Mitchell trained his sights on Wilbur and accused him of neglecting aviation in the Navy. Mitchell hinted that there was a plot of shipbuilders to suppress aviation. Meanwhile, Wilbur directed that aviation be put in the Naval Academy curriculum. Mitchell ridiculed that as tokenism since not all Midshipmen could qualify to fly.

Wilbur's indirect reply (never dignifying the attacks by debate) came in a speech stating that aircraft alone could not suffice in national defense. A navy was required to protect America's shores as well as her citizens abroad. The summer was quiet as Wilbur cruised with the Midshipman Practice Squadron on the West Coast. At the same time Coontz took the Battle Fleet "Down Under." Australia and New Zealand were visited by 45 ships and 23,000 men in a visit that threw light on the security of the Pacific basin.

After attacks by Mitchell, naval aviation was out to prove its mettle as part of the Navy. Three seaplanes were to make a non-stop flight from the West Coast to Hawaii. Two got off but one had to ditch 300 miles out and be towed back to San Francisco. The other was overdue on Sept. 2, 1925. Wilbur suspended the third flight until Cdr. John Rodgers and his crew was found. In the meantime, a rigid airship, *Shenandoah*, on a planned operational flight from Lakehurst, N.J., to the Midwest, was wrecked in a storm over Ohio. LCdr. Zachary Lansdowne and several of his crew died. Mitchell charged Wilbur and the Navy with "gross negligence" in their aviation policy. Sen. Claude Swanson (D-Va.), later to be SecNav, criticized the Navy for taking unnecessary risks. Mitchell's attack led to two events bearing on aviation history. The first was his court-martial for insubordination by the Army for his attacks n the Navy. The other was the select committee on aviation, military and civil headed by Dwight Morrow (Morrow Board). Some of the familiar faces on the board were MajGen, James G. Harbord USA and Rep. Carl Vinson (D-Ga.). Their findings supported naval aviation. It caused Congress to enact three laws in 1926. One related to civil aviation and another largely to the Army. The act of Jun. 2, 1926 authorized a five-year program for the navy to build 1,000 planes with definite numbers to be built each year. Two new dirigibles were authorized.

In late September 1925, Wilbur had good news and bad news. Rodgers and his crew were safe. The scion of a Navy family dating back to the Revolution, Rodgers had used the fabric from his lower wings to rig a sail and proceed to Hawaii. But on the night of Sept. 26, the submarine S-51 was rammed by *SS City of Rome* off Block Island. Of the six officers and 31 men in S-51, three survived. Heavy seas hampered the sub's recovery that took several months under the direction of Capt. E.J. King USN

The twin tragedies, *Shenandoah* and S-51, aroused public indignation, ably abetted by anti-administration newspapers and the Mitchell accusations. Wilbur weathered the storm and continued to plead for funds to keep the ships and planes safe; the officers and crews adequately trained; and ships properly manned. He said that the only 100 percent safe place of aircraft was in their hangars and for ships in drydock " ... for ships have sunk alongside the dock." He advocated training at sea and in the air and the funds to do it. "We... accept all hazards to reasonable activity. [The Navy] must function daily in time of peace as in time of war or be useless in either. This involves danger." He felt it criminal to require American boys to accept hazards from inadequate equipment or lack of training because of under-funding.

Still, his enemies wanted his scalp. At the end of November, the California governor offered his old job back as Chief Justice. Wilbur replied, "I appreciate more than I can tell you your offer to appoint me ....However, I feel that my post of duty is here..." He closed out the year citing that the disasters were unfortunate but few compared to the extent of operations. He urged Congress and the people to support our boys. He cited the extensive steaming of the fleet (finally) during the year, including exercises off Hawaii and the visit "Down Under." Navy morale was high as desertions were down from 3,161 in 1924 to 991; there were fewer sick; reenlistments were up from 50 percent to 72 percent. A final boast was that 99 out of the 100 enlisted appointments to the Naval Academy were filled. This was a direct result of using that method of accessions to offset the cut in Congressional appointments. Wilbur also boasted that his pet project of having school children contribute to saving "Old Ironsides" (*USS Constitution*) was successful.

Although there were no funds for new ships and the remaining six cruisers authorized were not laid down, 1926 was serene through the summer. Then on Jul. 10, all hell broke loose when the Naval Ammunition Depot at Lake Denmark, N.J., was struck by lightning and exploded. There were more fireworks before the year was out. Retired RAdm. Fiske sued Wilbur and others for not protecting his "invention" of the torpedo plane. Then in the "Teapot Dome" trials of December, the defense accused Wilbur of muzzling the officer who had signed the oil leases, now-Capt. J.K. Robinson, former flag officer-in-charge of construction. Wilbur had instructed him not to reveal any classified information acquired on active duty. Robinson complied but one of the defendants did not. He stated that Robinson had told him that the Navy would be helpless without fuel in Hawaii. This was purportedly in 1921 when the Navy was said to have had a secret report alleging that the Japanese were about o go to war. This "Pacific Peril" report, according to the defendant, prompted him to build the oil tanks at Pearl Harbor in return for favored treatment on the oil leases. He said that Robinson's instruction came from Denby. Wilbur maintained his dignified silence on the "Pacific Peril" papers.

In 1927, the Navy had fallen behind in cruisers. It had ten of the 7,050-ton *Omaha*s with 6-in. guns while two of the authorized "Treaty Cruisers," *Pensacola* (CA-24) and *Salt Lake City* (CA-25) had been laid down. Larger cruisers with greater bunker capacity were needed since the Treaty had forbidden base improvement in the Western Pacific. The General Board favored the longer ranged 8-n. gun even though its shell weighed too much to be manhandled like the 6-in. shell. The trade-off was range for rate of fire. There had been qualitative but not quantitative limits on combat auxiliaries except for carriers. Other nations were using the loophole to build cruisers. Coolidge was against competition in navies for reasons of security and economy. (His apocryphal quip in reply to an Army request for more aircraft, "Buy one and let them take turns flying it," is indicative of his alleged attitude.) Still, Wilbur did get Congress to approve money for the six remaining cruisers of the 1924 program. *Northampton* (CA-26), *Chester* (CA-27), *Houston* (CA-30) and

Augusta (CA-31) were ordered in June 1927 while *Louisville* (CA-28) and *Chicago* (CA-29) had been ordered two months earlier. There was a bit of chicanery in naming the ship, which gave her name to the class. Northampton, Mass., was Coolidge's hometown.

Coolidge arranged for another conference of the Washington Treaty Parties. That will be covered in the following chapter. Before that, however, we'll look at the Marine Corps of the early Wilbur years. We'll see how a Corps smaller than the New York City Police Dept. fulfilled nation- and world-wide commitments

Lejeune had been appointed by Daniels; retained and reappointed by Denby; and when his Classmate, Wilbur, became SecNav, he was assured of a friendly ear for development of his "new Marine Corps." This was the Corps of readiness *vice* expeditions. The latter had been a mission since after the Spanish war. It was unique to the Marine Corps because the function of the small standing Army was routine garrison, at home and abroad, e.g., Philippines and Canal Zone, and maintaining a cadre for wartime expansion. Both countries on the island of Hispanola were the scenes of Marine expeditions and prolonged occupation during pacification of rebels who were mere bandits. The occupation of the Dominican Republic ended on Sept. 16, 1924, when the last Marines departed. They left behind a national constabulary renamed *Policia Nacional Dominicana* from *Guardia Nacional de Dominicana* to signify the police function not that of a banana army.

Lejeune had turned-to and worked hard to keep the standards of the Corps high and maintain morale. Prevention of idleness was a key to the latter. The principle under which Lejeune operated was simple. "The good of the Corps, combined with the just treatment of all officers and men, was paramount and therefore took precedence over all other considerations." From this flowed many things. Officers' military education was essential. Schools were established: at Philadelphia for second lieutenants; at Quantico, one for company grade (lieutenant and captain) and one for field grade (major to colonel.) The Marine Corps Institute (MCI) helped many Marines get the high school diploma they lacked. Athletics, especially baseball and football were stressed. Marine teams played in two Rose Bowls. They provided exposure that recruited the Marines he wanted. The minimum age was raised to 21 and physical standards were rigid. Recruits flocked in and Lejeune, supported by his Classmate, Wilbur, opposed a senator who wanted to end recruiting. Enlisted Marines finally became eligible for the Academy. One of the first was Lofton Henderson, who as a major sacrificed his life by diving his stricken dive bomber onto the deck of a Jap cruiser at Midway. He was immortalized in Henderson Field, the key to Guadalcanal n 1942.

Lejeune organized an annual reenactment of Civil War battles in the northern Virginia area. Marines from Quantico would march to the sites and encamp. Lejeune joined these encampments and often was accompanied by SecNav and President Coolidge. Whenever in the presence of Coolidge, Lejeune did not waste the opportunity and talked about the needs and capabilities of his Corps.

Marines had already begun taking steps toward an amphibious capability despite the nay-sayers who regarded Gallipoli as the graveyard of such operations. In 1922, landing exercises were held on Culebra, P.R.; in 1923 in Panama. These were preludes to ones on a broader scale. A brigade was in the 1924 fleet exercises. Marines were developing doctrine.

It was not all development and training. In his 1923 annual report, Lejeune noted that for the first time Marines did not have an expedition abroad. At the behest of the CG there, BGen Smedley Butler, Lejeune asked to purchase the town of Quantico. It was surrounded on three sides by the Marine base and on the fourth by the Potomac River. It was deemed a menace to morale as an abode for bootleggers and other undesirables. He was refused.

Mention has been made of the Marines guarding the mails in the Denby incumbency. Lejeune reported to Congress that that success had cost the services of 53 officers and 2,200 men and $416,780. In October 1926 mail robberies reoccurred. In keeping with Marine experience that if you do a good job they hand you another, the Post Master General asked for 2,500 Marines to assist. With the same order "to shot to kill" Marines were promptly provided. The robberies ceased just as promptly.

The Marines Corps was to obtain some other notoriety of mixed value.

In early 1924, BGen. Butler, at the request of the mayor and citizens of Philadelphia, was granted a leave of absence by Lejeune. Butler was to be the Commissioner of Public Safety (Police Commissioner) with the mandate to clean up crime, corruption, vice and especially enforcing violations of Prohibition. The XVIII Amendment prohibited sale, manufacture and transportation of liquor. It did not prohibit consumption. Although a Quaker, Butler was not then a teetotaler but was a temperate drinker. He entered into his new duties with a zeal that made for quick success. He made enemies among the purveyors of alcohol, i.e., the big hotels and restaurants as well as the illegal makers and distributors. He castigated the last as "hyphenated Americans" a slur on ethnic groups in the bootlegging business. Lejeune reluctantly agreed to a year's extension of Butler's stay in Philadelphia but when he refused another, Butler resigned from the Marine Corps to remain as police chief. Unfortunately, he failed to consult with the mayor who was "happy with an active duty Marine but did not want a resigned Marine." After several vituperate allusions to the mayor in the press, Butler withdrew his resignation and returned to the Marine Corps.

That was the preamble to his taking command of the Marine Corps Base in San Diego in March 1926. That brigadier general's billet had been filled for two years by Col. Alexander Williams, also CO Fourth Marines. In addition to being "an old drinking buddy" of Butler, Williams was the son of a New York City police captain who gave the title "Tenderloin" to the red light and gambling districts of big cities. When "Clubber" Williams was told of his new precinct assignment, he was eating dinner. He looked at the hamburger on his plate and said, "Once I get up there, it will be nothing but tenderloin!" He subsequently was forced off the police force by the reforming Commissioner, Teddy

Roosevelt, who disbelieved that Williams had accumulated his fortune "speculating in Japanese real estate." Whatever the foibles of the father, they were not found in the son. Col. Williams had a distinguished record and had followed Butler as Chief of the *Gendarmerie d' Haiti* when Butler succeeded in getting to France in 1918.

On Mar. 6, 1926, the officers of the Fourth Marines and their ladies were invited to a buffet supper at the quarters of Col. And Mrs. Alexander Williams in Coronado. It was in honor of BGen. and Mrs. Butler. When the general arrived he noted several officers drinking what he found to be alcohol when a serving girl offered him one. He refused it, now being a teetotaler after his Philadelphia experience. Two days later after consultation with RAdm. Ashley Robertson, Commandant of the Naval District (ND) Butler preferred charges against his host, Col. Williams. Public reaction was immediate but mixed. Some thought Butler was "out for more headlines." Another thought that he was properly starting to "rule with an iron hand." Col. Williams was thought foolish for offering drinks without "knowing his guests." *The New York Times* had an editorial on Prohibition and the laws of hospitality. It speculated that Butler would, "never be invited to dinner again." It held that there was a "higher law" of looking the other way discreetly and ignoring incidents. Many opposing Butler cited his tactics in Philadelphia allowing police to beat drunks with clubs. "Clubber" would have understood, however.

Before the end of March, Wilbur named members of a general court-martial to try Williams. RAdm. Robertson acknowledged urging Butler to bring charges. The Drys in Congress backed Butler. These included his father. During the trial, a defense counsel, Capt. Clifton Cates, later to be Commandant (1948-52), and an attendee at the party, said that Butler had tried to coerce witnesses by calling them in and saying, "You boys know what is wanted. Now go back and write new statements." Despite such allegations, Williams was convicted and sentenced to loss of four numbers on he colonel's list of 35 and transferred to the Dept. of the Pacific in San Francisco. A year later, on a ferry crossing San Francisco Bay to Sausalito, his car rolled forward into the Bay carrying Williams to death by drowning.

In the meantime, Butler had "cleaned up" the base and the parties had stopped or moved to Tiajuana where one could host a party safely and cheaply.

The next year, Butler led the Marine Expeditionary Brigade including the Fourth Marines to China. The watchword was, "Smedley Butler has arrived in China. The war will go in but the parties will stop!" That episode as well as the campaign in Nicaragua at the same time is told in Chapter VII.

Chapter VI

The Geneva Naval Conference of 1927

Total world disarmament was a goal of the League of Nations. The U.S. was not a member and while not as concerned as much with land as with naval armaments supported the disarmament principle. The League was sponsoring a disarmament conference at its headquarters in Geneva starting in 1927. Members plus the U.S. were invited to Preparatory Commission discussion before the conference.

On Feb. 19, 1927, Coolidge told Congress that he had asked his Ambassadors in London, Paris, Rome and Tokyo to ask those governments to empower delegates to the Preparatory Commission to negotiate a treaty supplementing the Washington Treaty and limiting categories not covered there. He felt that the Treaty was incomplete and that competition was beginning in cruisers. He observed that some had a basis to combine limiting air, land and naval arms but saw that as too big a question. Since a naval limitation treaty existed, the precedent was set. His logic was to solve the naval part of the problem and leave the rest to continental powers concerned with the air and land limitations.

Replies varied. France and Italy declined couching the reason in diplomatic prose. British and Japanese acceptances stated preliminary positions dooming the conference from the start.

Japan, albeit flowery phrased, came right to the point. Since she regarded it of utmost importance, she would need to augment the Geneva group with experts and requested a delay until June. She welcomed the proposal since it was not to be a conference of rigid ratios.

Britain clearly stated that her geographic position, i.e., vast empire, long lines of sea communications, necessity of protecting the food supply of the United Kingdom (UK) and other special conditions, had to be considered. Still, she was ready to discuss how Washington principles could be extended to ratios in other categories.

The conference opened in League-furnished facilities on Monday, Jun. 27, 1927. U.S. Ambassador to Belgium, Hugh Gibson, presided and his chairmanship was confirmed by the other delegates. The other U.S. delegate was RAdm. H.P. Jones, Chairman of the General Board. The eight naval advisers were two flag officers, four captains and two lieutenant commanders. Allen W. Dulles future CIA head, was legal adviser. Wilbur was not a member.

Britain designated all of her group including those of the Dominions as delegates. First Lord of the Admiralty W.C. Bridgeman headed the 18-man delegation assisted by Viscount Cecil of Chelwood. The Admiralty was heavily represented but the First Sea Lord Earl David Beatty was not there. Twenty additional delegates represented Canada, Australia, New Zealand, the Union of South Africa, the Irish Free State and India. Beatty's absence may have been caused by the presence of the Governor-General of New Zealand, Admiral of the Fleet Earl Jellicoe of Scapa (and Jutland ???)

Japan had two delegates and a large staff of 15 naval advisers. The head was Adm. Viscount Makoto Saito, Governor-General of Korea. Her Ambassador to France, Viscount Kikujiro Ishii was the other.

After procedural preliminaries, Gibson opened confident of agreement on four points. These were in the interest of international understanding there would be no competitive building among the three; each navy should be maintained at the lowest level consistent with national security and never of a size to be suspect of aggressive intent; wise economy dictated keeping building at a minimum; and the principles and methods of Washington were practical and effective and should be extended to other categories. He reminded them of the huge sacrifice made by the U.S. in 1922. The U.S. kept naval forces for adequate defense and had no aggressive intent.

Gibson made suggestions for limits. He felt the Washington ratios should be applied to cruisers, destroyers and submarines. The expiration date of the Washington Treaty should apply. Combat auxiliaries should be considered in four categories: cruisers (3,000 to 10,000 tons); destroyers (600 to 3,000 tons), faster than 17 knots; submarines (regardless of size) and an unrestricted class of vessels of negligible combat value.

After discussion of peculiar national requirement with adjustments applicable to all, tonnage would be discussed. He suggested for openers:
Cruisers: U.S. and British Empire - 250,000 to 300,000 tons each; Japan - 150,000 to 180,000 tons.
Destroyers: U.S. and British Empire – 200,000 to 250,000 tons each; Japan - 120,000 to 150,000 tons.
Submarines: U.S. and British Empire – 60,000 to 90,000 tons each; Japan – 36,000 to 54,000 tons.

Age limits before replacement was 20 years for cruisers, 15 to 17 years for destroyers and 12 to 13 for submarines, In the transition period, the total tonnage for destroyers and cruisers would be combined and the over-age factor ignored. Scrapping of individual ships was determined by each nation.

Bridgeman stated that they had anticipated and welcomed Coolidge's invitation, He sounded off on the peculiar position of the UK and her absolute dependence on imports to survive; the lengths of the British sea-lanes; and the great coastlines of the Empire. He proposed increasing the life of capital ships from 20 to 26 years; fixing the life of 8-in. cruisers at 24 years, destroyers at 20 and submarines at 15; reducing the size of future capital ships from 35,000 to less than 30,000 tons; reducing the size of guns from 16-in to 13.5-in.; limiting carriers to 25,000 *vice* 27,000 tons; reducing carrier guns from 8-in. to 6-in; accepting the 5:5:3 ratio for 10,000-ton, 8-in. cruisers; all future cruisers (after decision on numbers of 8-in. cruisers) to be limited to 7,500 tons and 6-in. guns. Destroyer leaders were to be limited to 1,750 tons and destroyers to 1,500 tons with 5-in. guns; and if submarines were not abolished there should be two sizes – up to 1,600 tons and less than 600 tons.

His position was that limits on combat auxiliaries was insufficient for the conference. Revision downward of the Washington Treaty should also be considered.

Saito said Japan was desirous of any reasonable plan effectively limiting competition. He hedged, however, that the uses of ships were many and according to the needs of each nation. Needs were reflected in present strengths and programs and should be thus considered. Since capital ships and carriers were already covered, he did not include them in his proposal. No one should adopt new building programs or increase present strength. Present strength, he considered, was ships built, building or authorized up to the spring programs of 1927 for Japan and the U.S. and that of 1925 for Britain. By June of 1927, the U.S. had ordered the last six cruisers authorized n 1924. Japan had a formula: A = under-age ship tonnage; B = building tonnage; C = ships authorized but not laid down and D = tonnage of ships going over-age (replaced ships). In cruisers, e.g., the U.S. had A of 70,500 tons; B of 20,000 tons; C of 60,000 tons and D of zero. (Japan did not count the old coal burners). The formula was A+B+C-D or for the U.S. 70,500+20,000+60,000-0 or 150,500 tons. The totals for Japan were much higher. Depending on the age limit for destroyers and the end date for the agreement, the U.S. would not fare well there. She had a large A, no B or C, and block obsolescence for a large D.

After presentation of the three proposals the plenary session adjourned to leave the experts to handle technical aspects. These discussions were long and detailed and broke into three major positions as would be expected.

Japan's was the simplest. She wanted to take home the principle of parity even if she did not build to it. She wanted unlimited small coastal submarines. The size she considered small was larger than the others wanted to concede but Japan argued that these were the smallest seaworthy in her home waters.

The adamant British position was for a large increase in cruisers, restrictions on gun size and a number of smaller cruisers with 6-in. guns. She said smaller ships were cheaper to build – true on an individual basis. A 10,000-ton ship costs more than a 7,500-tonner to build and maintain but in a 30,000-ton limit, three 10,000 tonners are less expensive overall than four 7,500-ton ships. Crews for three larger ships were fewer than those for four smaller ships.

In her drive to revise the Washington Treaty provision on capital ships, carriers and cruiser qualitative upper limits Britain held that agreement of all three parties present would not be a violation of the Treaty. SecState Frank B. Kellogg in a note to Coolidge felt a change would be a violation.

Yet it was not a difference over capital ship provisions that caused the conference to founder. It was the cruiser question. It stemmed from fundamental differences in concepts of employment; from differences in geography; as well as a poorly –veiled British attempt to get something for nothing. Britain had 15 cruisers of about 10,000 tons with 8-in. guns. She intended to keep them. She also wanted 60 smaller cruisers of about 7,500 tons with 6-in. guns. Her total cruiser tonnage would be 465,000 tons. To the U.S. this was not a reduction. The key British proposal was elimination of the 8-in. cruiser that out-ranged the

6-in. ship. If there were no 8-in. cruisers to engage in commerce raiding, 6-in. cruisers could protect convoys. The weight of a 6-in. shell let it be manhandled while the 8-in. required a turret infrastructure. Fast merchantmen, in which Britain abounded, could be converted into auxiliary cruisers by putting pedestal mounted 6-in. guns on strengthened decks. These could convoy merchantmen and not worry about being out-ranged by enemy cruisers. If the British scheme were adopted, she would get something for nothing.

A subtle point concerned when cruisers were over-age. The British wanted 24 years based on experience that a ship could be refitted every eight-and-a-half years. After two major refits, the hull was worn out. When the conference settled on 20 years for over-age cruisers, Britain asked for a compromise based on "peculiar requirement" for Parties to retain 25 percent of authorized strength in over-age ships. Based on the "need" for 450,000 tons of under-age ships that would add 112,5000 tons for a total of 562,500 tons of cruisers. Adm. Jellicoe stated the rationale for so many cruisers. It was accepted that for fleet work, five were needed for each three capital ships. With 15 capital ships allowed by Washington, fleet work required 25 cruisers. This left 45 of the 70 claimed to be needed. Twelve could be expected to be refitting at any time, leaving 33 to cover 8, 000 miles of sea-lanes. When he commanded the Grand Fleet, his 114 cruisers were insufficient for all tasks. The British position was based on *absolute* needs.

American proposals were based on *relative* needs, modified by the requirements for larger ships with greater radius of action. Surrendering the right to bases in the Western Pacific made the larger ship necessary. The U.S. was not going to agree to a ship that was useless to her. She opposed the small cruiser concept. She wanted a cruiser tonnage limit and let anyone build, within Washington limits, the size wanted as long as total tonnage was not exceeded. Choice was not restricted. Britain countered that the upper limit of the Treaty became the standard and what nations would build. Her tonnage requirements would increase because of her absolute requirement in numbers.

The New York Times of Jul. 11, 1926 carried an article by its reporter, Wythe Williams, that Britain had been cheating on adherence to capital ship limits. This was unusual since *The Times* was not Anglophobe like the Hearst and McCormick papers. Purportedly, the genesis of the article came from a similar one in a Boston (Irish) newspaper of January 1927. The author was the ubiquitous, William B. Shearer, now at Geneva as an observer for American shipbuilders.

The British decided to appeal to world public opinion via a plenary session. They alleged that American shipbuilders were attempting to wreck the conference. The reason was that the shipbuilders wanted assurance for their contracts of the recently ordered six cruisers. They didn't want cancellation. Bridgeman pleaded his case to the public and Jellicoe made his aforementioned statement on absolute needs.

The conference dragged on for another three weeks but it was already dead. Failure to agree on cruisers, i.e., types, sizes, total tonnage and national requirements had doomed it. At the third plenary session on Aug. 4, after pleading and platitudes from the Parties, Gibson adjourned it and formally notified Coolidge of its failure.

In a message to Congress on Dec. 6, 1927, Coolidge addressed, *inter alia,* national defense. Speaking of land and air forces, he generalized on the requirement for moderate forces there. He devoted the bulk of his speech on defense to the purpose of the Navy and events at Geneva. "Our Navy is a weapon of defense..." He spoke of foreign commerce and outlying territories as well as continental coasts. "To meet these responsibilities we need a substantial sea armament ... We can plan for the future and begin a moderate building program .... This country has put away the Old World policy of competitive armaments. It can never be relieved of the responsibility of adequate national defense ... one treaty was secured by an unreasonable attitude of generosity on our part ... recently we made every effort to secure a three-power treaty to the same end ... much cooperation by Japan, but we were unable to come to an agreement with Great Britain ... We know that no agreement can be reached ... inconsistent with a considerable building program on our part ... any future treaty of limitations will call on us for more ships ... We should enter on no competition. We should refrain from no needful program ... Where there is no treaty limitation, the size of the navy which America is to have will be solely for America to determine."

Thus Coolidge closed out to Congress the high hopes he had broached to them at the beginning of the year. Failing on agreement, he was prepared to proceed with a program to add new under-age cruisers to the fleet in order to reach parity with Britain and avoid inferiority with Japan.

The year 1928 brought two events which paved the war for substantial discussion and agreement on limitation of combat auxiliaries. The first was an increased American naval program. The second was an international agreement on war as an instrument of national policy. An interesting sidelight occurred during the following year, during preliminary talks on the next conference when the Senate investigated the alleged influence William B. Shearer and the shipbuilding lobby had had on the failure at Geneva. That is covered in Chapter VIII. Next we return to events in the final two years of SecNav Wilbur's term.

Chapter VII

After Geneva

The failure at Geneva was an opening for SecNav Wilbur to push for an adequate Navy and a "balanced fleet." He had a plan. The Navy was short of cruisers; it was below allowed tonnage in carriers, even with *Lexington* and *Saratoga* in commission (November and December 1927); destroyers were many but were old and faced block obsolescence; there weren't enough submarines and more aircraft were needed. The shipbuilding industry had atrophied. Ships took time to build and delay in starting combat auxiliaries would bump into the resumption of capital ship replacement allowable in 1932.

The remaining six 8-in. cruisers authorized in 1924 were ordered before Geneva and would be laid down during 1928. They were about 9,300 tons and incorporated lessons learned from the first two. In December 1927, Wilbur presented his program. He asked for a five-year program of $1 billion. The Navy should build for "its own needs" and these were 71 ships – 25 cruisers, five carriers, 32 submarines and nine destroyer leaders, In addition four battleship replacements were asked for 1932. It hit Congress like a bombshell.

Just before Christmas, tragedy struck again. The submarine S-4 running submerged in the operating area off Provincetown was struck by *USCG Paulding* (a destroyer turned over to the Coast Guard.) *Paulding* was chasing rumrunners who were using the submarine operating area as a sanctuary. S-4 went down with her crew inside. When Navy divers located S-4, all but six of her crew had suffocated on the cold ocean bottom. Tapping was heard from the after torpedo room. Desperate attempts to get an air hose into the sub were thwarted by the weather and almost cost one diver his life when he was trapped on the hulk. A heroic effort of a fellow diver who exceeded his allowable daily dives to rescue him was the only bright spot in the event as rescue operations were suspended because of violent storms. When the rescuers returned, the tapping had ceased and it was no longer a rescue but a salvage operation. The team that raised S-51 was reassembled for S-4. Edward Ellsberg, a Naval Constructor, who had resigned after working on S-51, demanded that his Naval Reserve status be invoked and dove on S–4.

On the day S-4 went down, Congress in a rebuff to Coolidge voted 15 to 1 in the House Naval Affairs Committee to reject presidential control of construction. Wilbur had included a clause allowing the President to suspend building in the event of an arms limitation conference. This was standard and in every program since 1916. Since they had little faith in naval arms reduction, Congress would force the President to build. During his testimony before the House Naval Affairs Committee, Wilbur had been asked by a minority member, Carl Vinson (D-Ga.), if the Navy was a first-class one. Wilbur replied, "No!"

As if the S-4 disaster wasn't enough, two days after Christmas, an explosion on *Langley* had killed one man and injured seven. Meanwhile headlines were criticizing Wilbur and the Navy because an amateur aviatrix was lost on a flight to Newfoundland from Long Island. Wilbur replied by saying that the Navy responds to the law of the sea regarding ship and air wrecks but could not be responsible for actions of those seeking suicide and not informing authorities of their flight or plans.

Not all of Congress thought like the House Naval Affairs Committee. Sen. Borah who had urged the resolution on Harding to press for a naval conference in 1920 lashed out at "Big Navy" advocates vowing to fight construction in the Senate. Sentiment and emotion ran high. Retired RAdm. C.P. Plunkett, who had commanded the railroad guns in France, made a speech saying the enemy was Britain and we should build to beat her.

The unkindest cut came from Rep. L.M. Black, Jr. (D-N.Y.) declaring that the Navy's efficiency had declined under an "economy" administration and that Wilbur had failed to obtain financial support from Congress. That did it! Curtis Dwight Wilbur, a gentleman throughout, decided he was no longer "Mr. Nice Guy" in dealing with Congress. He had a well-conceived plan for construction over the next 20 years and he was going to see it started before he left office.

First he took on pacifist Sen. King. To King's assertion that the naval bill was a revival of militaristic spirit, competition in arms and unwarranted expense, Wilbur replied that after the abortive Geneva try, there was no alternative but to go with the General Board's building program. He cited the system of authorization then acceptances of budget estimates and finally annual funding as awkward. He stressed that the Navy's needs were not internationally competitive. He told how cruisers and destroyers supported the battleline. It was vital to create a modern balanced fleet and keep it modern by continuing replacements. We needed larger cruisers because other nations with bases could leave part of the weight, i.e., fuel, stores, ashore and we could not. He advocated an orderly and steady program that would not run into replacement building allowed by the Treaty. Finally, it was a "crime to send men to sea in inferior ships." That was round one.

In his budget message of January 1928, Coolidge said he would build ships as fast as possible as long as the Treasury could afford it and conditions warranted it. He wanted the first major program since 1916 to be orderly.

Debates continued on the number of ships; the need for them; and the economics of building them. Should they be built in government or private yards? Women's groups protested construction and Coolidge vacillated. He came out for cruisers but other portions of the program were rejected. CNO Adm. Hughes calculated "absolute needs" as Jellicoe had cited for the RN. With a strength of 18 battleships, he found that to keep scouts across a 250-mile swath of sea with 25 miles between ships required 10 cruisers. To detect what the first scouting line might miss in the dark took another eight cruisers. To maintain a cordon around a battle fleet of 30 miles diameter with a cruiser every 12 miles took eight. To protect six convoys (the number needed in order to have two always at sea) – six cruisers. Protection of American ports took nine cruisers and two were needed as flagships for destroyer squadrons. The total was 43. There were 18 built or authorized (ten of 1916 and eight of 1924) so 25 more were needed.

In late January, Wilbur started round two and took his case to the people. "We should either scrap our Navy or maintain modern ships in a high state of efficiency." After Coolidge wavered under pressure from his initial support of building, the House approved a diluted authorization of 15 cruisers and one carrier to be built within eight years.

Wilbur continued to answer critics. He said that they would rob the fleet of its eyes (cruisers) and imperil our sailors. As to cost, he cited that the entire program cost less than that spent annually for candy or by ladies for cosmetics, "... there are times when gunpowder is more valuable than face powder."

He lashed out at those who denied preparedness prevents war. He felt there were sincere pacifists who through lack of understanding were asking Congress to betray its oath of office and leave Americans at the mercy of potential enemies. On Mar. 16, 1928, he made a final speech for the entire program. He and the Navy carried the fight for the 71-ship program; it was now up to Congress and the people. He challenged them with, "... we have performed our duty." He finished by attacking the opposition. "If there is one churchman who can tell me off hand within 200, the number of craft in the Navy today, I will concede him the right to question whether we need 71 new ships."

The bill had been reduced to 16 ships. Rep Fiorello La Guardia (R-N.Y.) said, "There is not the remotest chance for war in the lifetime of the ships we are asked to authorize today." It required Wilbur's presence on the floor of the House to get it through.

Also in 1928, while ship authorizations were a matter of debate and argument, there was, "an idea whose time had come." The world mood after the World War was weariness of conflict, exasperation with the economic burdens of war and a sincere search for peaceful ways to settle differences between nations without resort to war. The U.S. and France, traditional friends since the American Revolution, had a general treaty of arbitration due to expire or be renewed in 1928. In 1927, Aristre Briand, Minister of Foreign Affairs whom we met as Head of the French Delegation to Washington in 1921-22, suggested the two nations pledge a treaty of perpetual friendship, never to go to war with each other under any circumstances. This implied that either nation must remain neutral whenever the other was at war with a third party. To avoid any embarrassing overtones, SecState Frank Kellogg thought it would be agreeable if the treaty were open to general membership. Thus was born a pact wherein the multiple signatories, including all major powers, condemned recourse to war for solving international problems and renounced it as an instrument of national policy. They pledged to settle international controversy among themselves by peaceful means. It was agreed to by the Senate and ratified by more than 60 other countries. The Kellogg-Briand Peace Pact was a milestone, if it worked. It didn't.

After passage in the House of his "cruiser bill" Wilbur continued the fight through the spring knowing that it faced rough going in the Senate. He spoke around the country. He stressed that good ships were needed as good homes for the men – clean and shipshape for good service. He also stressed that money was needed for constant training. Men must be trained; they must use their ships. Use means wear and tear, fuel and upkeep, "... as housekeeping in the home." He noted that ships were more costly because of American prosperity. Ships could be purchased abroad cheaper but we should build in America and pay Americans. He pointed out that 80 percent of costs went for labor. An orderly building and replacement plan kept the yards and related industries operating. He began to get support from patriotic organizations and some women's groups. He boldly walked the halls of the senate to secure votes against the actions of the small group who vowed to, "talk the bill to death." Congress adjourned for an election summer without Senate action. When it returned for a "lame duck session" the Senate had the Kellogg-Briand Peace Pact and a farm bill as priority items. Wilbur's whittled down "cruiser bill" looked doomed. The Navy had a few friends in both houses and they came to Wilbur's aid. It was not as great as Wilbur had striven for, but it was a start. Fifteen new cruisers and an aircraft carrier of "about 15,000 tons" were authorized. From it came *Ranger* (CV-4) ordered in 1930 and heavy cruisers (a term not coined until the 1930 London Conference): *New Orleans* (CA-32), *Portland* (CA-33), *Astoria* (CA-34), *Indianapolis* (CA-35) and *Minneapolis* (CA-36) all ordered in 1929. Heavy cruisers *Tuscaloosa* (CA-37), *San Francisco* (CA-38), *Quincy* (CA-39), *Vincennes* (CA-44) and *Wichita* (CA-45) were ordered between 1931 and 1934. The remaining five were light cruisers, a category of 10,000 tons with 6-in. guns created by the London Treaty. These were ordered in 1934 and 1935 – *Phoenix* (CL-46), *Boise* (CL-47), *Honolulu* (CL-48), *St. Louis* (CL-49) and *Helena* (CL-50). All were in commission by 1939. After the battleline sank to the mud of Pearl Harbor, these were the ships that had joined the carriers of other programs to hold the line against Japan in the early days of the war. Except for the ten aged 7,050 cruisers of the 1916 program and four light cruisers of Roosevelt's N.R.A. public works, *Brooklyn* (CL-40), *Philadelphia* (CL-41), *Savannah* (CL-42) and *Nashville* (CL-43), the entire cruiser strength of the Navy in1941 was the result of Wilbur's dedication. Wilbur's cruisers were at Pearl Harbor, Java Sea, Coral Sea, Midway and the waters off Guadalcanal in the fall of 1942. Where would the country have been if Wilbur had not insisted on cruiser construction? The reaction of the mayor of New York City in 1941-42 to the existence of the cruisers "which would never see war in their life time" as the salvation of the nation is not recorded. Mayor La Guardia was engaged in chasing fire engines and reading the Sunday comics over the radio.

But all the conflict was not in the halls of Congress or in the press. Marines and Bluejackets were fighting and dying in far off places in 1927-29.

The six river gunboats of the 1924 authorization had been built in Shanghai in 1927 and 1928 from American material. They were on the waters of China's rivers to protect U.S. interests in the interior. They were shallow draft for the rivers but had enough power to climb the Yangtze's rapids. They were *Wake* (formerly *Guam*), *Tutuila, Panay, Oahu, Luzon* and *Mindanao.* The last was attached to the South China Patrol while the others formed the Yangtze Patrol up river at Hankow. In the ebb and flow of Chinese warlord politics, they were frequently fired upon by bandits as the boats patrolled the river. They replaced old coal-burner prizes from the Spanish War.

Problems arose in Nicaragua in 1925. There had been a Legation Guard of four officers and 101 men at the capital, Manuaga, since 1913. It was withdrawn in August 1925 at the behest of the State Dept. Whether it was a condition of cause and effect is moot but three months later the Conservative forces seized the heights commanding Managua and purged the government of its Liberal opponents. In May 1926, the Liberals struck back. Revolt flared along the east coast of Nicaragua. There were Americans in Bluefields as well as U.S. and foreign property there. The old cruiser *Cleveland* (CL-15) landed her Marines to maintain order in May 1926. They withdrew in a month but by August it had to be done all over again. Marines from the old cruiser *Galveston* (CL-17) landed. The situation grew too big for Marines from ship's detachments to handle and a battalion from Guantanamo Bay, Cuba, was ordered in. This grew quickly to a brigade and the campaign was on. Counting Marines from ships of the Scouting Force, *Texas, Florida* and *Arkansas*, there were 2,000 distributed among 14 towns. It was another expedition.

The U.S. had vital interests in the Caribbean. Foremost was the Canal in Panama. Threats there were serious. Second was the Monroe Doctrine to prevent Europe from pursuing her own debt collection among defaulting nations as reaffirmed by its Roosevelt Corollary. Coolidge asked former SecWar (1911-13) Henry L. Stimson to mediate the mess. He did so successfully and with the backing of Marines there was some sort of order. A local constabulary, officered by Marines was set up. The *Guadia Nacional de Nicaragua* was fashioned along the same lines as previous organizations in Haiti and the Dominican Republic. Still the situation called for every Marine who could be sent. The concomitant commitment to China n 1927, strained Marine resources. Despite that a brigade with aviation (to become a Marine trademark) was fielded. For a while things were tranquil – then enter Augusto Sandino.

A wild young man, Sandino shot a man in their hometown in northern Nicaragua in 1916. Sandino fled to Mexico and worked in the Tampico oil fields. Purportedly, he made revolutionary contacts that helped him in his misdeeds later. Despite speculation, over the years, of his leftist leanings and the financial support he received from suspected Red groups there is nothing to prove that he was politically motivated. He was a mean little *bandito* with a large ego never sated even by the darkest of deeds. He enjoyed robbing, killing and the subjugation of the natives. He was a despot.

A mixed garrison of Marines and *guardias* occupied Ocotal as a patrol base in Sandino's home province. Hearing that Sandino was in the area on Jul. 1, 1927, Capt. Gilbert Hatfield sent word that the bandit should cease his depredations and surrender. During the night of Jul. 16, Sandino came but not to surrender. He attacked with dynamite bombs, machine guns and rifles. Some of his band carried extra weapons and ammunition for any sympathizers in the village. They also had orders to destroy aircraft on the small Marine strip but it was devoid of planes. The Marines were besieged by Sandino who had proclaimed as his objective to "drink *Yanqui* blood!" Hatfield declined Sandino's demand for "dignified" surrender. As the siege developed into a standoff in the afternoon, Marine aircraft on routine patrol checked the garrison since the wires were down and they had not reported. They returned to their base at Managua and reported the situation. Slightly after noon, Maj. "Rusty" Rowell CO Observation Squadron One (VMO-1) took off with all his five DH-4s. (Rowell had been a guest at the infamous buffet in San Diego at the quarters of Col. Williams.) Each aircraft carried four 25-lb. bombs and ample machine gun ammo. Two hours later they saw the situation in Ocotal plainly. Rowell led the attack by diving from 1,500 feet and pulling out at 600. The next attack was from 1,000 feet with a pull out at 300. It was the first combat dive-bombing and it was a sensational success. The *sandinistas* (a term to be coined much later) fled in groups and the horses panicked. Rowell and his wingmen had a field day. The garrison moped up the stragglers. About 300 bandits and sympathizers were killed, mostly from air. One Marine was killed and four Marines and *guardias* wounded.

The war had escalated and it was now a bandit chase of ground and air patrols through the hills for the rest of the campaign. Marine annals still catalog the cruelty of the man and his band who would "drink *Yanqui* blood." A pilot and his observer crashed but survived the accident. They were deep in enemy territory but able to move with the help of some hired guides. These led the Marines into Sandino's hands. The mutilated bodies were hanged and photographed by the bandits. The photos were published in Honduran and Mexican newspapers after being distributed by Sandino.

In December, a Marine column was ambushed and *Guardia Teniete* Thomas Bruce (1st Sgt. USMC) was killed. The bandits dragged off his body, stripped it, mutilated it and Sandino later boasted that he had drunk *Yanqui* blood. The column with it casualties fell back on Quilali. They had 30 wounded of which eleven would never have survived evacuation by mule. They were surrounded. Maj. Rowell determined that if some shacks were leveled, the "main" street of the village could serve as a rough airstrip. 1st Lt. Christian Schilt stepped forward. He would attempt the mission. During Jan. 6-8 1929, Schilt made ten trips into and out of Quilali under fire. He brought in a relief commander, Capt. Roger Peard, emergency medical supplies, ammo and provisions. Outbound he took the wounded. Schilt was awarded the Medal of Honor for heroism at Quilali. He served in World War II; commanded the Air Wing in Korea and retired as a lieutenant general.

The campaign known as "Second Nicaragua" dragged on until 1933. The Marine leaders of World War II learned the trade of war in this episode of The Treaty Navy. One of them, Capt. Merritt A. ("Red Mike") Edson led a long and productive patrol on the Co Co River. He was to receive a Medal of Honor on Guadalcanal and retire as a major general. Another patrol leader was 1st Lt.

Lewis B. "Chesty" Puller. His exploits occurred in 1932 and we will come back to them and the fate of Augusto Sandino in a later chapter.

While Marines were busy in Nicaragua, things were popping in China. The civil war there appeared to be taking on the aspects of another Boxer Rebellion. (The 1900 disturbance in China which was a distinct threat to foreigners there.)

In February 1927, troops under the rising Chiang Kai-shek threatened Shanghai. A provisional battalion gathered from Guam, the Philippines and Marine Detachments from the Asiatic Fleet landed at Shanghai. A call for help went out and two weeks later, the Fourth Marines arrived from San Diego. Disorder and attacks on foreigners continued. Lejeune ordered another regiment and brigade headquarters under Smedley Butler to China. The Sixth Marines had been disbanded in late 1925 but they were hastily put together from Marine Barracks at navy yards and other sources. The mail guards remained on duty diluting the numbers available for expeditionary duty since there were already Marines in Nicaragua. The ships of the Asiatic Fleet, particularly the four-piper destroyers of the World War Emergency Program were active in Chinese ports protecting Americans and their property.

Butler arrived and brought an aviation unit. When the trouble moved north, Butler left the Fourth Marines at Shanghai and moved to Tienstin with the Sixth Marines and aviators. They settled down to routine duty. Butler kept them busy with "spit and polish" and showing the flag. By early 1929, the situation was quiet enough for the 3rd Brigade to return to the States leaving the Fourth Marines in Shanghai until they were evacuated to the Philippines as war clouds gathered in November 1941.

Unlike Nicaragua where a Second Nicaragua Campaign Medal was awarded, no special campaign medal was awarded for China. Participating Marines were awarded the USMC Expeditionary Medal that covered expeditions not meriting a special medal. One of the recipients was 2nd Lt. David M. Shoup pulled from class at The Basic School in Philadelphia to lead a platoon in the Sixth Marines. He was to win the Medal of Honor at Tarawa in 1943 and become the 22nd Commandant (1960-63) with four stars. He referred to the China Expedition as "The China Exhibition." He may have been right.

The Wilbur Years came to a close in 1929 as Coolidge left office. There was speculation that the incoming Hoover might keep him on as SecNav. Instead, Hoover appointed him to the federal court in San Francisco. Conventional wisdom thought Hoover feared Wilbur as "Big Navy-minded." Wilbur retired from the bench in 1945 and lived in Los Altos until he died in Palo Alto on Sept. 8, 1954 at 87.

His accomplishments in office are noteworthy for The Treaty Navy. He left a Navy whose morale and efficiency were by a greater magnitude than when he arrived. He cleaned up the oil scandal; fought the Navy's battles for money and ships; argued with pacifists who would eliminate the Navy; and succeeded in getting major construction to rebuild the post-war Navy. He organized school children to save "Old Ironsides;" championed naval aviation and put it in the curriculum of the Naval Academy. On Oct. 6, 1928, he approved the first naval policy since 1922. It called for a Navy of Treaty strength that was later written into law by the Vinson-Trammel Act of 1934. He set the plate for the emergence of The Treaty Navy from the nadir of the '20s. His departure also brought the close of an era. Since 1927, the top echelon of the Naval Service had been filled by Alumni of the Naval Academy Class of 1888. They were SecNav Wilbur, CNO Adm. C.F. Hughes, CINCUS Adm. H.A. Wiley and MGC John A. Lejeune. The odds on that happening again are extraordinary.

Before The Treaty Navy emerged into the sunlight of the Vinson and F.D. Roosevelt era, it had to pass through the darkness of the Hoover interregnum and the beginnings of the Great Depression.

Chapter VIII

The Interregnum

Herbert Hoover was elected in November 1928. His acceptance speech supported a strong Navy. This was immediately attacked by Dr. Nicholas Murray Butler of Columbia University. Butler, a leader among pacifist thinkers felt the president-elect was off base on the place of a navy in world peace. One of the first to come to Hoover's defense was William B. Shearer, styled by the press since after the war, as a "naval expert." His activities and notoriety had gained an interview with Coolidge. He had also earned he enmity of SecNav Wilbur. If he was trying to ingratiate himself with Hoover, it turned out opposite.

After his lop-sided win over Al Smith, Hoover opted for a tour of South American before inauguration. Coolidge placed *Maryland* at Hoover's disposal. ComBatFlt Adm. W.V. Pratt went out of his way extending every courtesy to the president-elect. Hoover went from his home in Palo Alto to San Pedro. Pratt met him at Pier 5 in his barge. Escorted by ComBatFlt to *Maryland,* Hoover found the rails manned on every ship in the anchorage; received a 21-gun salute and the ruffles and flourishes due a sitting president. The only item absent was the President's official blue flag flying on *Maryland.* The gesture had mixed reaction among press, public and the Navy. Many in the Navy thought it a breach of protocol and an effort by Pratt to ingratiate himself with Hoover. If so, it worked better than Shearer's ploy. After Hoover took office, Pratt became CINCUS and in September 1930, he became CNO.

Hoover's nomination for SecNav was Charles F. Adams from Massachusetts. A member of a distinguished New England family, he provided geographical balance to the Cabinet. He also brought managerial talent. Like all of the Adams family he had been graduated from Harvard, incidentally the same year Wilbur had at the Naval Academy. He too was a lawyer but had earned his reputation as treasurer of the Harvard Corporation increasing the endowment of the university eight-fold. He served as a director on various corporate boards. An avid yachtsman, he had skippered *Resolute* to victory in the 1920 *America*'s Cup.

On of the first major events of The Treaty Navy in 1929 was a comic opera episode. Rep. Fiorello La Guardia (R-N.Y.), a bit of comic opera himself, described the principal player in the drama as an asset to peace and disarmament, whose, "… blundering stupidity has done more for peace than anything else." La Guardia wondered how practical men of industry would have been so gullible as to be duped by our old friend, W.B. Shearer. They were; and they were not alone.

The drama was set in motion by Senate Resolution 114 of 1929. "… to investigate the alleged activities of William B. Shearer in behalf of certain shipbuilding companies at the Geneva Conference…"

Shearer had been at Geneva attending the League of Nations preliminary conference on arms limitations, declaring, "What bunk disarmament is!" He was also at the abortive naval conference that followed. He had press credentials, and a spacious rented apartment, where he entertained lavishly and distributed accurate technical information to the press. His wife and teenage daughter acted as hostess and typist. He was amply bankrolled but queries as to the source were "nobody's business." He was friendly with most of the American delegation except Amb. Gibson and RAdm. Jones. Drew Pearson, a reporter, alleged that RAdm. Reeves had told Shearer that he hoped the conference would fail. Pearson also stated that RAdm. F.H. Schofield and commanders H.H. Frost and H.C. Train frequently dined at Shearer's apartment.

Some of the antics of Shearer during the '20s as he built his credentials as a "naval expert" and advocate have been recounted. A more detailed discussion of his character is now appropriate. In 1920, Shearer was feted by military, naval and political dignitaries, including New York's mayor, at the launching of his "invention," a four-man torpedo boat built for the Navy. After the war the contract had been cancelled and Shearer abandoned her at the wharf for lack of funds. Four years later, Shearer was "amazed" to find his 58-foot, bullet-proof vessel which he had left in Bayonne seized in Mystic, Conn., by the Coast Guard as a rumrunner.

We have seen Shearer's futile attempt to save *Washington*. In December 1924, he spoke to the National Security League. He said the General Board had leaked to him that Japan planned war and the Naval War College had a war scenario against Japan (Plan ORANGE?) He said that there was an American spy aboard ship in the RN. Attendees who agreed with him were several active duty naval officers and retired RAdm. Bradley Fiske.

Investigation showed Shearer's source as personal letters between two friends. Capt. Hugo Osterhous of the Naval War College wrote Capt. William Berry in New York. Berry gave the letters to Shearer. Wilbur declined to prosecute on a legal technicality. Shearer was persuasive in playing on the emotions of many.

Later on the West Coast, working for Sen. King of the Naval Affairs Committee, Shearer held the Navy was not on a par with Britain. The U.S. was third in the world. In December 1926, after alleging that the British were violating the Washington Treaty, he spoke to the Government Club. He said there was little difference among British, Japanese, pacifists and Bolsheviks. All had the same objective, "It is to weaken America."

When the conference in Geneva had broken up in the summer of 1927, a Geneva newspaper ran a profile on him – "The Man Who Wrecked the Conference."

Whether he wrecked the conference is moot. But in the late summer of 1929, he tried to capitalize on the accusation. Just before Britain's new Labour Prime Minister, Ramsay MacDonald, was due to talk to Hoover in Washington on naval matters, Shearer sued several shipbuilders for back pay.

Before that in July, speaking at the Kiwanis Club in New York, Shearer's theme was that British propaganda in the U.S. was for our debt cancellation and to get the U.S. to join the World Court. He challenged Labour's sincerity on naval disarmament citing its retention of North American and Caribbean bases. He warned against the coming Hoover-MacDonald talks. Was he pouting because Hoover did not give him an interview?

The suit which Shearer filed in New York in August led to the investigation by the Senate and set the mood for the '30s "merchants of death" inquiries. He sued three shipbuilders for $257,655. He said the money was owed for publicity, services and expenses from Dec. 10, 1926 to Mar. 27, 1929. He had been retained and partially paid to represent them in New York, Washington and Geneva. He had been their "observer" in Geneva in 1927.

Reaction came in a fortnight. Sen. Borah howled for an investigation saying, "Those familiar with the history of the Geneva Conference know something of the propaganda there, and something of Mr. Shearer's connection." He alleged that Shearer had been active in Washington during the "cruiser bill" debates in 1928.

Hoover was incensed over the charges and referred to the shipbuilders as an "insidious lobby." He challenged them to defend themselves against claims they had worked against cuts in the Navy. Borah said that if Shearer's part had been known in 1928, the "cruiser bill" would not have passed.

On the railroad platform in his home, Stamford, Conn., Shearer gave an impromptu interview (his forte.) He was a "patriot." He had worked for high Navy officials and the shipbuilders. The Navy had given him data for the fight and he had used it at Geneva. State Dept. pressure forced his firing by the shipbuilders. He was a "practical electrician" and had been a gunner's mate in the Spanish War and a theater manager in London. He had "nursed along" the title of "naval expert." In 1919, he had, lobbied, successfully, for higher military pay. He had attacked the leader in pacifism and disarmament, Dr. Butler. for having criticized Hoover's speech endorsing the Navy.

He had been smeared by British delegates and press at Geneva. High-ranking naval officers had solicited his services at a Union League dinner in 1924. He had been to lunch aboard *California* with admirals S.S. Robinson and Henry A. Wiley plus rear admirals, W.V. Pratt and Plunkett. He had worked for Sen. King without pay until hired by the shipbuilders in 1926. He ended, "I believe in my country ... in Washington's warning, 'no foreign entanglements' ... in the Monroe Doctrine ... in late President Roosevelt's appeal to 'keep up the fight for Americanism.' I am against all internationalism."

The Navy denied helping him. Hoover defended RAdm. Jones. King said Shearer's work was administrative only. Sen. Allen, Republican National Chairman, said Shearer had made a speech for the party in Boston. SecNav Adams held Shearer had no Navy connection and his "inside" information came from press releases available to all. Eugene E. Grace of Bethlehem Shipbuilding assured Hoover that Shearer was merely an observer" a Geneva for $25,000 and had been terminated for cause. Pratt disclaimed any connection. He remembered, however, the 1924 meeting and had had Shearer to lunch aboard his flagship, *West Virginia*. Although no help was asked or given by either party, Pratt believed Shearer to be 100 percent American.

Sen. Shortridge (R-Calif.) chaired the inquiry and opened it on Sept. 20, 1929. Sen. Allen was also a member as was Sen. J.T. Robinson. Shearer acted as if he was on friendly personal terms with all three. He bandied back and forth with abandon often interjecting asides into witnesses' testimony. Several times the Chairman asked Shearer's lawyer, Judge Daniel J. Cohalan, to remind his client to keep order. This was especially true when he referred to Allen having sent him to Boston to speak for the Republican Party to "those simple Irish."

The shipbuilders, including Chares Schwab of Bethlehem Steel, the corporate parent of the shipbuilding company, conceded that Shearer had been hired. He was to be their eyes and ears. If the conference was to cause cancellation of their contracts as provided in the law, it was advantageous to know that as soon as possible. Likewise, if it appeared that the conference would not cause cancellation, they needed to know. Advance knowledge provided for sound business decisions about ordering or canceling steel or hiring or laying off labor. Shearer's information would be worth more than the $25,000 paid him. He was there to report not to influence the outcome.

Homer Ferguson, a former Naval Constructor who was graduated from the Naval Academy in 1892, was head of Newport News Shipbuilding. As a witness he mentioned that Shearer had referred to a "secret British document which had swayed a senator to vote 'yea' on the "cruiser bill."

Shearer was called on Sept. 30. When sworn he was asked to identify himself. He bellowed, "William Baldwin Shearer, American, Christian, Protestant, Nationalist!" Shortridge struck all but the name from the record. Shearer refuted the Scotland Yard dossier in the press as well as the statement of the New Rochelle police chief. The latter said Shearer was one of 15 arrested in "one of the biggest liquor hauls" in memory from a rumrunner docked with $100,000 of booze.

Shearer said he enlisted in the Navy in 1898; later built veterans' barracks in California and New Mexico; operated a mine in Nevada; managed boxers; operated a cabaret and managed a theater in London. He was a journalist, Florida real estate operator, naval expert, inventor, actor, artist, and writer and had run a racetrack operation in England. He excused allusion to some activities as misunderstandings like forfeiting bail in New Rochelle while trying to buy some illegal Scotch. There was a misunderstanding over a forged check taken from the "Baron" in London. The Baron was his betting agent. ("Gentlemen don't wager personally.") The false arrest in Ostend, Belgium, over a jewel theft from a German princess in 1913 with his alleged accomplice, Kid McCoy, who was getting ready to fight Georges Carpentier, was a canard. He denied the aliases attributed to him by Scotland Yard.

He tried to sway his listeners with charm and rhetoric; that failing, he bullied them. He evaded facts of previous witnesses. He was glib and patronizing. He joked with the senators. Sprinkled through the transcript was the Chairman's, "Mr. Shearer, will you please be responsive to the question?"

When he had finished, Shearer gave the committee his "secret British document." It was *The Reconquest of America*. Shearer had gotten it on the West Coast when there to interest his "good friend," W.R. Hearst in the "Big Navy" movement. Shearer said the document had been written in 1919 by Sir William Wise, head of the British military intelligence in the U.S. It was an outline of methods to regain her lost colonies. It included such devious methods as inculcation of American youth via the British-founded Boy Scouts and infiltration of Wall Street to make financial institutions dependent on repayment of British war loans. Hearings adjourned to keep the press from embarrassing Hoover during MacDonald's visit. The press thought a document a hoax.

The inquiry reconvened in January. Dr. William J. Maloney, a physician living in New York was called. He was born in Ireland, educated at the University of Edinburgh and emigrated to the U.S. He returned for service with the Irish Guards and was invalided out after Gallipoli. In 1919, as a member of an Irish patriotic organization, he wrote *The Reconquest of America* as satire. It was widely distributed until banned by the Espionage Act. Its purpose was to thwart American entry into the League and World Court. Irish-Americans thought such moves counter to the best interests of their new country and would lead to British domination. The Chair asked Dr. Maloney who was the head of the Irish patriotic organization in 1919 when he wrote the pamphlet. He pointed to Judge Cohalan, Shearer's attorney. ("Simple Irish" indeed!) The inquiry adjourned.

On June 11, 1930, Shortridge reported. They had found no evidence that Shearer had been sent to Geneva to defeat the plans of the government.

The importance of the episode is how close a charlatan came to wrecking prospects for resurgence of The Treaty Navy. Shearer had been given information by well-meaning but naïve naval officers. He had duped shipbuilders, but probably not at the highest corporate level, into believing he could wreck Geneva and save the cruiser contracts. It was probably the lower ranking advocates who pushed the venture, with visions of advancement up the corporate ladder, if successful. Fortunately, it backfired and did not severely damage the efforts of sincere Navy advocates to build an adequate fleet.

The comic opera interlude has faded to a footnote to history. It could have been more tragic than comic. It is significant that some naval officers with a valid case for an adequate Navy felt they had to resort to chicanery to get it.

The Treaty Navy was alive and well outside Washington. Marines were still fighting Sandino in Nicaragua. The new carriers, *Lexington* and *Saratoga* had joined the fleet. They were assigned to the Battle Force. Naval Aviators were ecstatic with the new ships. The flight decks were more than ample after postage stamp-sized *Langley*. Commander Aircraft Squadrons Battle Fleet (ComAirRons) was RAdm. J. M. Reeves. He believed the carriers enormously enhanced the fleet's combat power. It was demonstrated in the Fleet Problem in January 1929. CINCUS, Adm. Wiley, had set up a scenario once again around the defense of the Panama Canal.

In January 1929, BLUE forces including *Lexington* defended the Pacific side of the Canal from hostile BLACK forces. Pratt as ComBatFlt commanded the

Black force which included *Langley* and *Saratoga*. It was an opportunity for Pratt to show his command ability and for Reeves to demonstrate that his faith in carriers as the future capital ships was justified. *Saratoga* with O*maha* as plane guard, instead of a smaller and slower destroyer, made a long arc sweeping to the south and launched a long-range air strike against the defenders. The latter were caught napping at dawn. The idea of carrier task forces as offensive striking forces was born. From then on, task forces, built around carriers with escorts of fast cruisers, became the standard experimental maneuver element in the succession of Fleet Problems of the '30.

There is a revealing sidelight to the Shearer hearing involving aircraft carriers which is little known. A group of shipbuilders wanted to build a fleet of fast merchant ships convertible into carriers during war. At the time of the hearing, Shearer was a paid lobbyist for the group headed by the former president of American Brown Boveri, a maker of heavy electrical equipment and owner of New York Shipbuilding. The shipyard had been bought with the idea of using it for electrical manufacturing. The Camden yard had built *Saratoga*. R. Wilder, formerly of American Brown Boveri was an advocate of the merchant marine. He formed a consortium of shipbuilders to build six "four-day liners" for the North Atlantic run. They would embody the design lessons of *Saratoga* and travel between North America and Europe in four days carrying passengers and high priority cargo. High-speed mail service (under government subsidy and a change to the postal laws) was to be a special feature. Mail and passengers, if they desired, would be flown off (and landed on) the flight deck which ran the length of the ship. Control stations were offset to starboard just as on a Navy carrier. Wilder did not see this as a violation of the Washington Treaty even though his ships were almost exact duplicates of the *Lexington* design. He held, "These are ships built for commerce. Airplanes and airports are not military units whether ashore or afloat."

The question was one of attitude and good faith. After the British insistence on limiting cruisers to 6-in. guns which could (although never stated) be used to create auxiliary cruisers from fast merchantmen, how could the Wilder scheme by viewed by parties to the Treaty? It became a non-problem. Wilder was having trouble finding financing for his enterprise. After the Shearer hearing ended, the Wall Street "crash" set in motion the Great Depression. The quasi-carriers were stillborn.

The new carriers were still a novelty both to the Navy and the public at the end of the decade. The Pacific Northwest was experiencing a drought in the fall and early winter of 1929. The people were depressed and it wasn't because of the stock market crash. The lack of rain had dropped water levels in the reservoirs. Hydroelectric generating capacity was down. There was an energy crisis. While it affected the entire region, political and corporate in fighting between public utilities caused Tacoma to suffer particularly hard.

While the Navy came to the rescue, it did so reluctantly and after much debate and telegrams. It took a personal appeal to President Hoover by the city of Tacoma.

The star of the Navy's role in the drama was *Lexington.* She had been commissioned two years before but she had been laid down eight years earlier. She had joined the Battle Fleet in early 1928 and participated in the fleet routine of operating from San Pedro during the week, winter exercises in the Caribbean and good will cruises north along the West Coast. Calls at Bremerton were necessary for docking. The dry docks were the only ones on the West Coast able to take the 888-foot long, 106-foot beam vessels. Both carriers were in Bremerton prior to winter exercises when the drought became acute. *Saratoga* was in overhaul and expected to rejoin the fleet in January 1930. *Lexington* had arrived in September for routine overhaul and new arresting gear. She was to conduct trials after leaving the yard. Although in commission for two years, her turbines and generators had yet to be accepted from General Electric (GE). Trials would determine if modifications during overhaul were satisfactory.

The two carriers were the most powerful-engined ships afloat. *Lexington's* 16 Yarrow boilers were fired by oil. Four GE turbines were coupled to four three-phase generators of 40,000 kva each. These supplied electrical power at 5,000 volts to eight 16,500 kwa electric motors. The motors were connected to each of four shafts. Designed for 180,000 s.h.p. she actually developed 210,000 s.h.p. on her trials and the propellers on the four shafts sped her through the water at 34.2 knots. The tremendous electrical power in the ship was known to the people of the Northwest.

Lexington was scheduled to leave Bremerton at the end of November. On Nov. 18, Seattle and Tacoma having cut back on municipal power, wired the Navy Department for use of *Lexington* as an emergency power station. The shipyard commander was skeptical. He didn't think the situation was critical. He wasn't sure there was water deep enough near any pier to prevent fouling of the ship's turbines. GE, the owner of the turbines, would have to give permission. Tacoma's request included the rationale that it supplied power to the Army at Fort Lewis.

The wires buzzed with telegrams. *Lexington* did not sail on schedule but swung on the hook awaiting a decision. Tacoma's officials deemed that the water off Baker Dock on the waterfront met the requirement of 50 feet or 23 feet under her keel. Navy divers checked the site and moorings to the dock were installed. Cables could be rigged ashore.

Tacoma went to the public in the appeal. They said that the great ship should be used both for peace and for war. The power that gave her great speed in action had industrial value. She could light a city of 800,000; they asked for but a fraction.

Hoover overruled the fears of SecNav Adams and the Navy staff. On Friday, Dec. 13, *Lexington* stood in toward Tacoma. It started to rain.

To supply 35,000 kwh, *Lex* had to use six boilers to drive one generator. They burned 2,500 barrels of oil a day. The "black gang" kept three watches of 60 men each dedicated to the city's power. Ship's power was extra. Tacoma was charged for the fuel (Navy contract price), dockage for 30 days and the approximate labor costs of the dedicated portion of the crew. This was about

$150 an hour or $0.185 pr kwh. Tacoma paid $6,000 in advance for the first week.

The Navy pointed out that this was an inefficient and expensive way to provide power as well as a misuse of a powerful unit of the fleet. She had 92 officers and 1,000 men. The payroll of the "power plant" was $128,000 a month. The crew ate $22,000 worth of food in that time and the cost of maintenance and upkeep was $202,000 for 30 days. Navy ships were not inexpensive toys.

Despite initial reluctance, the feat was a huge good-will success. The people of Tacoma were grateful for the lights being back on and industry operating. Christmas wasn't as bleak as expected. The rain and snow that came with the carrier on Friday the 13th was a good omen. The citizens responded with hospitality. Golf courses welcomed the ship's officers. Many of the crew had Christmas dinner in private homes. Tours were arranged. There were 30 days of great liberty. *Lexington* welcomed visitors on board. More than 500 Boy Scouts had a day's outing and were thrilled as the Marine Detachment drilled.

When her 30 days were up, *Lexington* left Puget Sound for her delayed trials and return to the fleet. She left at 10 a.m. on Thursday, Jan. 16, 1930. Tacoma paid $95,000 for her use and $20,000 for the dock. For that it received 4,000,000 kwh of Navy electricity.

Lexington came back to Bremerton often but never to Tacoma. She lived out the '30s in The Treaty Navy and was at sea delivering aircraft to Midway when Pearl Harbor was bombed. She gave a good account of herself in the first five months of the war as the center of a carrier task force taking the war to the Japanese in the South Pacific. In May, she participated in the first battle between carriers who never came in sight of each other. She was lost May 8, 1942 in the Coral Sea.

A new *Essex*-class carrier building at Fore River, Quincy, her birthplace, was renamed *Lexington* (CV-16). Ironically, she too participated in an episode which *"Let there be light."* On Jun. 20, 1944, U.S. carrier planes were returning in the dark from locating and destroying Japanese carriers in the Marianas. The task force commander was VAdm. Marc Mitscher, whom we met in NC-1. He flew his flag in *Lexington*. The planes were low on gas and the pilots not adept at night landings. Mitscher's concern was his pilots. His command, "Turn on the lights!" was an epic in Navy annals. The people of Tacoma probably did not even know of Marc Mitscher's order. They were content to know that when needed n 1929, it was another *Lexington* who turned on their streetlights. The Treaty Navy was the people's Navy.

The combination of a worldwide depression and the good feeling generated internationally by the Kellogg-Briand Peace Pact paved the way for another try at limiting combat auxiliaries. After some preliminaries, a conference met in London in accordance with the Washington Treaty provisions for one within eight years of its coming into effect.

Chapter IX

The London Naval Conference of 1930

The two years after Geneva brought many changes. The world financial situation left little money for maintaining large military establishments. British naval spending dropped nine percent from 1927 to 1930 but U.S. spending rose with the start of three of the 15 "cruiser bill" ships. Labour was back in power in Britain and the Republicans were still in the White House but under the Quaker-oriented Hoover. His SecState was H.L. Stimson, former SecWar for Taft. At the initiative of Hoover, Stimson had the ambassador to the Court of St. James, Charles G. Dawes, sound out the Labour Government on bilateral preliminary talks before the next conference required by the Washington Treaty. Talks were held between Dawes and MacDonald in London. Other Parties were informed lest they suspect collusion. The rationale was that if the U.S.-British cruiser differences were worked out, other questions could be solved by all Parties. This led to the Hoover-MacDonald talks in Washington (and at a fishing lodge on the Rappanhannock). On Oct. 7, 1929, Britain invited all Washington Treaty Parties to a conference in London in January 1930.

Three days later, Hoover and MacDonald issued a public statement revealing that talks on a naval agreement had been held during the summer; that the Paris Peace Pact put the arms question in a new light; that war between the English-speaking nations was out of the question; and that views on naval limits were so close that former obstacles were removed. "In view of the security afforded by the Peace Pact, we have been able to end, we trust forever, all competitive building between ourselves with the risk of war, and the waste of pubic money involved by agreeing to a parity of fleets by category." Again the cards were face up.

France and Italy who disdained participation at Geneva accepted because of technical advances in the past eight years. As it turned out, they would not adhere to a limit on combat auxiliaries. That would be a three-party pact.

SecState Stimson led a seven-man delegation. SecNav Adams was a delegate. There were two senators and three active ambassadors Dawes (Britain), Gibson (Belgium) who had headed Geneva, and Dwight Morrow (Mexico) who had headed the aviation board. Eight advisers included RAdm. Hilary P. Jones who had been at Geneva and CINCUS, Adm. W.V. Pratt, who had been at Washington as a captain.

MacDonald headed the British delegation of four plus those from the Dominions. The Japanese had four delegates. Among her advisers was RAdm. Isoroku Yamamoto, to be the architect of Pearl Harbor and the loser at Midway a decade later. The eight French included Aristre Briand now with a lesser portfolio and another World War II name, RAdm. Jean F. Darlan. Italy weighted her delegation with naval officers.

The U.S. position was unchanged – parity with Britain in all categories; tonnage as the proper measure of limits; and that "absolute needs" led to competitive building. She held that reduction should include actual ships, built or building as well as potential ships, i.e., (arms race) if there was no agreement. She still needed the larger cruiser, preferably with 8-in. guns, for greater radius. With fewer cruisers than the RN, the U.S. must build to parity.

Size was still a British concern. Her worldwide bases could replenish and fuel smaller cruisers but bases and sea-lanes required protection. Her ships had to be at sea in all climates so she needed habitability found only in ships larger than destroyers. The argument that if the 8-in. gun were the maximum, it would be standard persisted. But the Anglo-American antagonism of the '20s no longer existed; there were other potential enemies.

Japan wanted the ratio stigma removed. Ratios announced to the world she was inferior. American sources heard that Japan would compromise on 10:10:7 if pressed. She considered that the least for security from attack by a U.S. knockout blow in the event of war. She also wanted parity in submarines.

France wanted submarines; strength based on global tonnage; and superiority over Italy. She also wanted guarantees of security in case of continental attack. Italy would agree with any limits as long as she had parity with France.

King George V opened the conference on Tuesday, Jan. 21, 1930. Stimson nominated MacDonald for chairman. A basic agenda was adopted to consider technical questions of tonnage, gun size, ship size, etc. of categories not covered quantitatively by Washington. The Washington categories would also be addressed.

Gibson asked for limits by category and for all to keep the others informed of building programs. Not all had the open legislation of authorization and appropriations of the U.S. The Italians reminded that the conference was political not technical. Nations were restricting their sovereign right of self-defense.

The U.S. and Britain came closer on the cruiser issue when Stimson asked if she could create a "police vessel" to show the flag yet not be a cruiser. In agreeing to consider it, Britain countered with a cruiser size fixed at 10,000 tons regardless of gun size and that numbers of 8-in. cruisers be limited. Cruisers would be "heavy" or "light" by gun size not displacement. When the U.S. accepted, the *impasse* of Geneva was broken. Britain fell off the need for many cruisers.

Other problems still remained – peculiar to each of the other nations. Japan wanted a change in ratios. France wanted submarines, global tonnage and security assurances. Italy just wanted parity with France.

A "big navy" group in Japan opposed the principle of limits. Thy were critical of U.S. "non-concessions." But an election in Japan during the conference returned the incumbents and thus endorsed the conference.

The submarine question was the most complex. Britain wanted abolition holding that they were not defensive and could only be used effectively by violating International Law. It was really a question of economics and real disarmament since submarines were the most expensive warships per ton to build and operate. Further, they had a direct influence on the number of destroyers built by the world's navies. France disagreed. She felt a submarine was like any warship. It was defensive, needed by all and could be regulated like any other weapon. Nations had a legal right to derive protection from technical advances. There was a sovereign right of defense and the submarine was the way small nations could ensure freedom of the sea.

French insistence on continental guarantees and argument that her divided coastline caused her to need a larger navy ran into Italian insistence on parity with France. It began to look like a three-power agreement was the best to be had. The conference was breaking into an agreement on combat auxiliaries among the U.S., Britain and Japan. Italy and France were balking at extending the Washington ratios to additional categories but still involved in modification of Washington. The London Treaty of 1930 eventually became a two-part agreement.

The significant modifications of the five-power part were: "... carry forward the work begun by the Washington Naval Conference of 1922." Replacement of capital ships was postponed until after 1936. Ships (U.S. –10, Britain –10, Japan –6, France –3 and Italy –3) to be built between 1931 and 1936 would not. Italy and France could build two ships under rights not exercised since 1922. Specific ships were to be scrapped by the U.S. (3), Britain (5) and Japan (1). The three were to reduce capital ship tonnage to Treaty limits immediately and not wait until 1936. These were 15 ships (453,500 tons), 15 ships (472,550 tons) and nine ships (266,070 tons) respectively. Each could retain a target ship and a demilitarized ship for training. Others must be disposed of as per the Treaty. (See Appendix 4.)

Aircraft carriers were any warships fitted exclusively for launching and landing aircraft. Other warships having aircraft incidentally, e.g., catapulted seaplanes, were not carriers.

Submarines could not exceed 2,000 tons nor have a gun larger than 5.1-in. Each could retain three submarines of 2,800 tons with 6.1-in. guns. France kept her 2,880-ton *Surcouf* with an 8-in. gun.

Smaller ships and auxiliary vessels were not regulated. Age limits before eligibility for replacement were added for ships not covered by Washington. It had set capital ships and carriers as over-age 20 years after completion. New ages were set for others. Between 3,000 and 10,000 tons (cruisers) there was division by date of keel laying. After 1920, they were over-age in 20 years; before 1920, it was 16. The dividing date for ships less than 3,000 tons (destroyers) was 1921. If laid down before then, their life was 12 years; after that it a 16. All submarines were over-age at 13 years. When a replacement was laid down, all had to be advised of the nature of the construction within a month.

All agreed that submarines were bound by International Law regarding merchant ships. Before she sank one, the crew, passengers and papers must be put in a place of safety. Ship's boats were not a place of safety. The new Treaty would remain in force for the life of the Washington Treaty (Dec. 31, 1936) but the submarine observation of international law was indefinite in duration.

France and Italy abstained from Part III of the London Treaty and it applied only to the U.S., Britain and Japan. This defined cruisers as warships between 1,850 and 10,000 tons with guns greater than 5.1-in. There were two categories. Category A (heavy) had a gun greater than 6.1-in but up to 8-in.; B had guns between 5.1-in. and 6.1-in. Destroyers were less than 1,850 tons with 5.1-in. guns or smaller.

Completed tonnage on Dec 31, 1936 to be at or below:

	U.S.	British/Commonwealth	Japan
Cruisers			
A (Heavy)	180,000 tons	146,000 tons	108,400 tons
B (Light)	143,500 tons	192,200 tons	100,430 tons
Destroyers	150,000 tons	150,000 tons	105,500 tons
Submarines	52,700 tons	52,700 tons	52,700 tons

Any ships causing total tonnage to be exceeded were to be gradually disposed of before Dec. 1, 1936. Heavy cruisers were limited by nation: U.S. – 18, British Commonwealth – 15, Japan – 12. Not more than 16 percent of destroyers could exceed 1,500 tons. Not more than 25 percent of cruisers could be fitted with decks (not catapults) for aircraft. Transfer of not more than ten percent of tonnage could be made between destroyers and light cruisers. There was an option for the U.S. in the Anglo-American cruiser compromise; parity was calculated not by total tonnage but by considering the parameters of size, guns and category. Thus in heavies the ratio was 10:8:6 by tonnage and 10:8.3:6.7 by ships. This allowed the U.S. 15 heavies that were contemplated by 1935 (eight of the 1924 program completed and seven of 1929 ordered). The other three could be laid down one a year starting in 1933 taking three years to build. If the U.S. opted not to construct them, she could convert their 10,000 tonnages into 15,166 tons of light cruisers. If this option were used for all three, total U.S. tonnage (33,998) would be tons less than Britain for ratios of 5:5:3. Under the Treaty, heavy cruiser ratios were 10:8.1:6; light cruiser ratios were 10:13.3:7. In total cruisers they were 10:10.4:6. Destroyer ratios were 10:10:7; submarines were parity and the total non-capital ship (less carriers) ratio was 10:10:7.

It is popular to refer to the Washington ratio as 5:5:3:1.75:1.75 but the Italians pointed out at London when the compromise was made after the *Matsu* matter raising the tonnage of the three larger powers by 25,000, 25,000 and 15,000 respectively, no adjustment was made in the 175,000 tons given to France and Italy. Their real ratio was 1.67. While the popular press of the day and some later historians cite the London ratio as 10:10:7 in cruisers they don't calculate correctly. The 10:10:7 is seen as a Japanese success while in reality the cruiser ratios were closer to the capital ship ratios. This rankled many Japanese.

The three powers to the combat auxiliary limits at London protected themselves from construction programs of others. If a Party felt, "... materially affected by new construction ... [of a non-Party] will notify the other Parties ... as to the increase required ... and shall be entitled to make such increase ... the

81

other Parties ... shall be entitled to make a proportionate increase..." This "escalator clause" would maintain the ratio but allow construction and not penalize a threatened Party.

It was signed on Apr. 22, 1930 but the preliminary work had ensured success. The three powers ratified their part; the others did not. President Hoover commented on the successful conclusion. He compared it to what would have come out of Geneva if concession had been made to Britain's demands. It was a better agreement and meant building competition ceased. Nine battleships were scrapped (230,000 tons) and 16 deferred for six years. Various navies would reduce 300,000 or more tons over the next few years. "...but some categories of them must be increased in order to come up to the standards set." Hoover said that Geneva failed because of the British demand for a navy of 1,500,000 tons leaving the U.S. no choice but to embark on a huge building program or be perpetually inferior. It would have cost the U.S. from $1,400,000,000 to $1,750,000,000 for new ships and replacements plus annual maintenance costs. Parity was about 1,136,000 tons, much less than the Geneva demands. Hoover estimated that it would cost the U.S. about $550,000,000 to $650,000,000 during the next six years for new construction, much less than the Geneva terms. American savings over the six years would be up to $1,000,000,000. Adding that of Britain and Japan, the world savings from arms competition would be $2,500,000,000. "This sum devoted to reproductive enterprise will be a great stimulus to world prosperity."

The London Treaty doomed three U.S. battleships. *Florida* was scrapped; her sister, *Utah,* became a target ship and was mistaken at Pearl Harbor for a carrier by the Japanese. She capsized. *Wyoming* was demilitarized into a gunnery training ship plying the Chesapeake during the war.

Five old armored cruisers, nine old protected cruisers and three pre-war scout cruisers went to the breakers. Fifty-four destroyers were disposed of. Most having defective machinery (Yarrow boilers) were scrapped. A few were demilitarized or sold. Several were converted to minelayers, minesweepers or seaplane tenders. This was legal since alteration stripped them of destroyer capabilities. Forty over-age submarines, including some of the 1916 program were stricken.

The year 1930 brought some changes. For the first time since the days of Wilson, the Democrats gained control of the House. Carl Vinson (D-Ga.), an advocate of an adequate Navy, became the Chairman of the Naval Affairs Committee. A new age was approaching for The Treaty Navy.

Five of the cruisers authorized in 1929 were on the ways and the carrier, *Ranger,* had been ordered. One submarine, *Dolphin,* was under construction. *Barracuda, Bass* and *Bonita* ordered in 1920 were commissioned in 1924,1925 and 1926 respectively. *Argonaut,* a minelayer, ordered in 1924 was commissioned in 1928. She was America's largest submarine at the time. Two, *Narwhal* and *Nautilus,* were ordered in 1925 and commissioned in 1930. The last three each carried two 6-in. guns keeping with the concept of surfacing to stop and sink merchantmen under international law.

The Navy was committed to the new classes of cruisers and the terms "heavy" and "light" were immediately coined. No new destroyers had been built since the emergency program of the war. Chairman Vinson was considering a building program to bring the Navy to Treaty strength since he considered the Treaty to be the law of the land. A crash program with its block obsolescence, which was about to occur, was to be avoided this time. Vinson was a disciple of Wilbur who in turn was one of the General Board's for orderly construction.

There were obstacles to a major building plan, however. A depressed economy and depleted Treasury could not finance a major program. It had been several years since the U.S. had built destroyers, therefore technical improvements had to be tested at sea. It was decided that 12 destroyers authorized in 1916 had not been laid down prior to the blanket destroyer authorization in 1917. Therefore, new authorization was not needed, just appropriations. The "cruiser bill" had authorized 15 cruisers and only five were building. London limits could be met from that authorization. Two could be laid down immediately, if funded, and one in each of the years 1933, 1934 and 1935. The remaining five could be the new category of light cruiser.

Hoover attempted to revive the economy by using federal funds to prime the pump. Congress authorized public works construction programs at military and naval facilities to aid the destitute economy. Vinson observed and waited.

As the ink on the London Treaty dried, the world drifted deeper into an international depression. Events within the next three years would make for drastic changes on the international scene.

Meanwhile The Treaty Navy continued in its routine and with significant incidents along the way.

`Chapter X

The Watershed

For The Treaty Navy, 1930 through the end of 1932 was a watershed. The Treaty Navy evolved into Mr. Vinson's Navy. But there were important events in those two years. In addition to changes in Congress and eventually in the White House, there was a significant change in the Navy. This was not only a swing from the "old guard" of Mahanism to the philosophies of Sims. It was also a change from Anglo-American antagonism to a tacit acknowledgement that Japan was going to be the enemy. Although this latter thought had been foremost in the thinking of many officers it was not until the vestiges of fear of inferiority to the RN were shed that The Treaty Navy could move forward in the direction of the new concept of war at sea. This was appreciation of the power of aircraft at sea which the U.S. recognized and developed while the RN, hindered by dominance of the RAF, failed to foster. The RN despite tonnage parity declined while the U.S. grew stronger. Unfortunately, so did its likely opponent – the IJN.

Hoover was sworn in as President on Mar. 4, 1929. On Mar. 20, SecNav Adams wrote to Adm. W.V. Pratt that on May 21, he would be relieved and detached as ComBatFlt and proceed and report "to Commander in Chief, United States Fleet for duty as his relief." Pratt was relieving H.A. Wiley, the penultimate member of the quartet from the Class of 1888 who had held the helm from 1927 through 1929. SecNav Wilbur and MGC Lejeune had left in March 1929. CNO Adm. C.F. Hughes was scheduled to retire in 1931.

Even though it was usual for prominent offices to "climb the ladder" in a *pro forma* manner, i.e., battleship command, battleship division command, battleship force command, battle fleet command and U.S. fleet command, many in the Navy thought Pratt was riding the wave set in motion when he first rendered shipboard honors to the President-elect in San Pedro in November 1928. Pratt had his enemies in the Navy. Most of them were the "old guard" who were Mahanites and who identified Pratt as one of the Sims upstarts. During the war, when Capt. Pratt was assistant to CNO Benson, he regularly corresponded with Sims, his old mentor, in London keeping him informed of Washington events and decisions being made. This was done "back channel" rather than by standard Navy communications. It was no secret that Hughes did not favor Pratt as his relief as CNO. Neither had Wiley wanted Pratt to be his CINCUS relief but he was.

When Pratt was sent to London for the Conference, the other Navy adviser of rank was retired RAdm. H.P. Jones. They were of opposite schools and convictions.

Jones was of the old battleline school that held that the RN was the yardstick to be beat. If you could stand up to Britain, you cold enforce freedom of the seas and neutral rights. Strength measured by capital ship tonnage was the key. These were the principles given by the General Board to SecState Hughes in 1921. These were the principles which set the ratios for Washington and which were found wanting as the cruiser competition began in the mid '20s. Many of these officers had commanded ships attached to the Grand Fleet in Scapa Flow during the war. Officers such as Hughes, Wiley, Jones *et al* had put up with the subtle British insults about the American Navy. It is fair to assume that the "old guard" was basically Anglophobe, it not openly then covertly.

Pratt was an Anglophile who believed most of the world's problems were solvable by a united effort of the U.S. and Britain and their not going in opposite directions. He had an open mind and was able to adjust to changing circumstances. Better still he was able to recognize such circumstances before they were apparent to others. He was a follower of the Sims school of naval thought. Although, there is no evidence of direct influence on Pratt by his mentor who retired in 1922, Sims was still active in writing on naval matters. If the group who thought Japan was the likely enemy had a titular leader, it was the still-living Sims The other school lacked a leader or real spokesman other than the tenets of the long-dead Mahan.

If the "old guard" needed a spokesman at this time the mantel would fall on Jones. His influence at the abortive Geneva Conference was his being adamant about the 8-in. gun cruiser. He was later abetted by CNO Hughes's outline of U.S. absolute needs in 8-in. cruisers to rebut Jellicoe's similar needs for the RN. At London, Jones's lack of influence was noteworthy. It was at London, under Adm. Pratt that the other faction came to the fore.

As a captain, Pratt had been an adviser at the Washington Conference. He had been appalled when other advisers, those of the General Board's persuasion, had banned submarines and given away the right to fortify bases in the Western Pacific. Fortunately, for the U.S., France declined to ratify the submarine ban and it never came into effect. At London, Pratt realized that insistence on the 8-in. cruiser that had wrecked the Geneva Conference was of little importance. It mattered not whether the British had many smaller cruisers. They were not going to be an enemy. What mattered was what size, in terms of tonnage, cruiser the U.S. was allowed. By keeping the 10,000 ship with 6-in. guns, Pratt was able to obtain a treaty that limited further Japanese construction of cruisers and provided for American ships with an operating radius to be effective in the Pacific. Pratt returned from London and less than six months later "fleeted up" to CNO.

It is interesting to note that during the '20s which was the period of Anglo-American antagonism, Navy relations with the IJN were outwardly cordial. In 1921, Baron Admiral Uriu Sotokichi of the IJN invited his Classmates from the Naval Academy Class of 1881 to celebrate their 40th Reunion as his guests in Tokyo. All survivors except SecWar Weeks attended. They sailed in a Navy transport. During the Japanese earthquake in 1923, U.S. warship mercy missions were appreciated by the Japanese. But in 1924, the Immigration Act ("Oriental Exclusion Act") fueled the fires of hatred of Japan's anti-Treaty faction who resented the ratios. Still, during Geneva the Japanese tried to play the role of honest broker as the U.S. and Britain haggled over cruisers.

Prior to his meeting with Ramsay MacDonald in 1929, Hoover and the General Board disagreed on the cruiser question. Six days later Pratt was asked to the White House. Stimson was there. After being questioned on his position on cruisers, Pratt stated his rationale for a 6-in., 10,000-ton ship. Hoover decided that Pratt would go to London as an adviser with retired RAdm. Jones and others. With that Pratt's relations with CNO hit a low.

Things were in low ebb throughout the country in the summer of 1930. Pratt inspected the Battle Fleet and enjoyed Fleet Week in San Francisco. Hoover's response to the Great Depression was cost cutting in government with a view toward tax cuts to encourage industrial production and keep men on the payroll. Not all cost cutting affected the Navy evenly. Spending for ship modernization and small construction funding kept shipyards going and workers employed. The other side of the coin (no pun intended) was cuts in operations. Ships were to be laid up, personnel reduced, exercises and cruising curtailed to save fuel and upkeep costs and the final blow, a 15 percent pay cut in the Navy, Army and for all government employees. Soldiers and sailors were now "employees," The officers and men of The Treaty Navy found themselves treated like hired hands instead of professionals. RN pay cuts of 1931 had led to the Invergordon Mutiny. American sailors evidently felt more loyalty to The Treaty Navy and to their pride in being part of it.

The pressure fell on CNO Hughes whose health, he was 64, was not good. In early September, SecNav Adams inquired of CINCUS Pratt as to his priorities in operational cuts to meet budget allotments. CNO received a copy at the same time the Budget Director, with Hoover's approval, told him to reduce the authorized spending for FY 1931 by $20,000,000 later a cut of $30,000,000. Pratt had not been given a dollar goal just been told to recommend reductions. Pratt's list of priorities in cuts retained battleships, carriers, cruisers, destroyers and submarines but they would be impotent or inoperative. His priorities began with decommissioning the old battleships of the Scouting Fleet, now three after London, next submarine divisions; crews and air personnel of *Lexington* and *Saratoga;* squadrons would fly ashore to be decommissioned; mine squadrons would go; crews of the Battle Fleet would be reduced and then destroyer squadrons (loyal to the end to his destroyers) would be decommissioned.

On Sept. 9, 1930, Pratt was ordered to temporary duty in the Office of CNO with the *caveat* of being prepared to stay in Washington. Adm. Hughes saw the handwriting on the bulkhead and in mid-September he offered the President his resignation as CNO. Although, he could have sniveled with claims of ill health, he told the President that he felt it was for the best inasmuch as a successor must face the important problems and decisions of the immediate future that would influence the next several years. He felt that these should be made by the officer who was to execute them.

The unpretentious change of command took place in the CNO's office on Sept. 17, 1930. The press was courteous to Hughes's feelings and handled it as a matter of "ill health." He died four years later.

Pratt was to set the course for the rebirth of The Treaty Navy that came to fruition under the Roosevelt-Vinson coalition. Pratt was followed as CNO by officers of the anti-Japanese group who believed in the efficacy of the submarine and carrier over the capital ship. They influenced naval policy and thus the nation's capability to have a foreign policy that dealt from strength. Not immediately apparent but always a belief of Pratt was that the Navy would not fight the IJN alone, the RN would assist.

A year after Pratt became CNO, an incident occurred which illustrated the cultural isolation of The Treaty Navy but even more important, the solidity of his members. It happened in Honolulu on Sept. 21, 1931 but it started before then.

Lt. (j.g.) Tom Massie and his young wife attended a party on Saturday night at the Ala Wai Inn in Honolulu. It was Sept. 21, 1931. Massie had been graduated from the Naval Academy in 1927; gone to sea; and then submarine school in New London. He was in a submarine at the Submarine Base at Pearl Harbor to qualify for his dolphin insignia as a *bona fide* submariner. Among the officers and wives in Honolulu, the Massies were a different couple.

Thalia Fortescue was the younger daughter of Grace and "Major" Fortescue of Washington, D.C. The father was not on active duty and though American hung on to his military title in the British manner long after being mustered out. He was an indifferent parent and husband. Grace was overbearing and pushy. They lived like aristocrats but could barely afford it. After the crash of 1929, things got worse. Before that, however, 16-year–old Thalia ran away to new Ens. Massie. Marriage seemed a solution for both. Thalia escaped her mother, and Tom, the country boy from Kentucky, had entrance into the Washington social scene. Four years later they were in Hawaii. Their marriage was a gossip item among the wives. The Massies were not the ideal devoted couple although there was no hint of infidelity by either.

At the party they went their separate ways and Thalia wandered off supposedly to go home. Missing her when the party broke up, Tom assumed she had gone on with friends to their house to continue the party. When he failed to find her there he called home. She answered and told him to come home at once since something terrible had happened. Within minutes he found her bruised, bleeding and hysterical. She said she had been raped by several natives. He called the police and reported that his wife had been "assaulted." To the lackadaisical Hawaiian police, "assault" was a usual Saturday night occurrence and *"No big ting, brudda."* When three police arrived much later and the rape charge was made, they reacted differently. The rape of a white woman by natives was touchy in the Territory of Hawaii. When she couldn't respond to interrogation she was taken to the hospital for examination. She had a broken jaw.

Thalia managed to give a license number of an auto. A suspect was picked up and tentatively identified by Thalia. He had been driving his sister's car and was present at another assault that night but denied the Massie attack. Under questioning he gave the names of his four companions and they were picked up. Thalia identified one of them as an attacker. Two of the others had criminal records and were professional boxers. One was Joe Kahahawai.

Massie had cabled his mother-in-law of the attack but not of the sexual aspect. Grace Fortescue and her other daughter arrived in Honolulu. The "major" was tied up by business and was not with them. While Thalia was difficult for Tom to handle, her mother was impossible. The defendants went to trial and Honolulu was split on the incident. To the Navy it was a clear case of natives out of hand. Others thought the five defendants would be railroaded by Navy pressure and racial prejudice. Their trial lasted three weeks and after 97 hours the jury could not reach a verdict. Under territorial law a witness other than the victim was needed to verify the crime. The hung jury meant they could be tied again. RAdm. Yates Stirling, Jr., commander in Honolulu, felt the jury had divided on racial lines and, "the defendants were not men who might be given the benefit of a reasonable doubt." In Navy circles feeling ran high. One of the defendants was tracked down and beaten by sailors. The Navy was "taking care of its own." More care was about to be needed.

Mrs. Fortescue concocted a scheme to get one of the defendants to testify against the others. She singled out Joe Kahahawai. She had rented a beach cottage and a car for her stay in Honolulu. The thought that her daughter's word was doubted as opposed to five natives was unthinkable. It fanned her rage and hindered her judgment. The mood spread to Tom Massie, now quite docile in face of his militant mother-in-law. Kahahawai was required to report to the courthouse every morning because of his criminal record. Massie mentioned the plot to some sailors around the base seeking physical help in her scheme. Two sailors loyal to the Navy volunteered to assist. Both were members of the boxing team that Massie coached.

On a pretext the two sailors lured Kahahawai into the car. Massie was at the wheel and he drove to Mrs. Fortescue's beach cottage. A bailiff had seen the abduction and reported the license. A few hours later the car was stopped and searched. There were four in the car. Tom Massie, Mrs. Fortescue, one sailor and bundled in the rear, the body of Joe Kahahawai. He had a .32 caliber bullet hole in his chest. A search of the cottage nabbed the other sailor and found blood stains and pieces of rope. It was assumed that in trying to intimidate him someone had "accidentally" fired a gun. Under territorial law, no matter who fired the shot, all were chargeable with first-degree murder.

The feeling ran even higher than during the original trial and subsequent hung jury. Fearing riots during the funeral, the Navy confined all sailors to the base. Many of Grace's friends thought she had served the end of justice and that her actions were planned and justified. Congratulations and support poured in from the mainland. The prisoners were confined on board the receiving ship in Pearl Harbor.

A first class defense lawyer was sought for the new defendants. In his prime, Clarence Darrow had been the best. Now he was 75, hadn't defended a case in several years but he was also broke. Navy friends suggested Darrow and the hat was passed in Honolulu, in wardrooms around the fleet and among the Naval Academy Class of 1927. It wasn't Darrow's usual fee but since he had never enjoyed a trip to Hawaii, he accepted.

He didn't have much of a case and speculation was why was the champion of liberal causes taking the other side in a case with racial overtones? The trial started in the spring of 1932. When Massie took the stand, the prosecutor asked him if he was aware of a statement attributed to CNO Pratt which strongly suggested he condoned or even encouraged American men to take immediate reprisal without waiting for sanctions of law against natives who rape American women. Tom had not heard the alleged remark.

The verdict was guilty of manslaughter. In Hawaii, except in the Navy, the verdict was considered just. The Navy voices were even more indignant when on May 6, 1932; the judge sentenced the defendants to ten years hard labor. The question now became political. The cry in the Navy and on the Mainland was for immediate pardon. The governor was anxious to rid the islands of the upheaval of trials and possible retrial of the four surviving native defendants. Assured that there would be no retrial, the Governor commuted the sentences to one hour in the judge's chambers before they were whisked off the island. Tom Massie went to a battleship on the West Coast and never served in submarines again. He retired as a lieutenant in 1940 and died at age 82 in 1987. Thalia was to be hard from again.

The incident points up two things about The Treaty Navy. It was a culture unto itself. Further, the members were intensely loyal to that culture and those in it. The readiness of the two sailors to help their officer(s) and the raising of the defense attorney's fee illustrate that. The Treaty Navy took care of its own.

While the Massie trials were going on, Carl Vinson was busy as the new Chairman of the House Naval Affairs Committee. Using Hoover's opening for construction to keep shipyards running and labor employed, Vinson secured funding for eight destroyers authorized by the Naval Expansion Act of 1916 but never ordered. They were ordered in 1931-32 and laid down in 1932. These 1,375-ton ships of the *Farragut* class carried five dual-purpose (surface and air where the old four pipers had only four 4-in. single purpose guns) and eight 21-in. torpedo tubes in quadruple mounts.

Farragut , Dewey, Hull, MacDonough, Worden. Dale, Monaghan and *Alywin* (DD-348 to 355, respectively) were the first of 382 new destroyers to join The Treaty Navy before 1941. There were eleven different classes, each one benefiting from the sea experience of the previous class. Mr. Vinson was building his Navy.

PART III

Mr. Vinson's Navy

Chapter XI

The Beginnings

It was a changing world after the Crash and Depression. Europe was gripped in political turmoil and the Old Order was changing. Russia had succumbed to communism in 1917 and the Bolsheviks had ruthlessly consolidated their grip on the vast multi-ethnic population in the Union Of Soviet Socialist Republics (U.S.S.R.) in the 1920s. The new masters were attempting to forge an industrial economy from an agrarian base by a succession of Five-Year Plans.

The Italian monarchy still held the throne but since 1922, a comic opera albeit ruthless dictator, Benito Mussolini, had pulled the strings with his fascist government. Styling himself, *Il Duce,* he boasted of bringing order out of chaos with the epigram of having "made the trains run on time!"

France was flirting with a succession of faltering regimes, heavy debt, and a paranoid fear of revival of German militarism on the continent or an Italian naval challenge in the Mediterranean cutting the metropolitan area off from Algeria.

The dissolution of the Austro-Hungarian Empire and the Ottoman Empire after the war brought new political entities and ethnic political problems to the Eurasian heartland and part of its periphery. Problems in what the British called the Middle East abounded. There was the age-old problem of Arab against Jew, helped by Britain's forked-tongue pronouncements. The realization that the area was rich in oil gave a new dimension to the situation(s) and the struggle for spheres of influence was on. Britain and France backed their national oil companies' interests. The U.S. only half-heartedly supported her oil companies in the race for riches.

Great Britain was hardly still great. The war had depleted her Exchequer leaving her deep in debt (mostly to U.S. bankers). She had lost the flower of her manhood in four years of futile trench assaults. The RN was no longer undisputed Mistresses of the Seas. The reason was simple – money. Keeping a major fleet equal to the combination of any other two (the prewar stated standard) was impossible for the impoverished isles. The Naval Treaties had limited her battleline to mostly pre-Jutland capital ships although she was building cruisers to maintain her supremacy in that category. All Ireland, save six of Ulster's nine counties, had broken away to form an Irish Free State with tenuous ties to the United Kingdom. Although pledged in the treaty establishing the Free State, access to anti-submarine bases in the south that commanded the Western Approaches was doubtful in time of war. Fear that the Irish precedent would awaken rebellion in India kept British troops committed to that subcontinent. The other Dominions were beginning to show signs of interests that didn't coincide with the major interests of the Mother Country. It has been seen how the intended base at Singapore was spared the non-fortification restrictions of the Washington Treaty. This was a sop to Australia and New Zealand who saw Japan as a rising threat. It was also a strategic ploy to provide an impregnable bastion in the region on which to base a powerful fleet. Naval treaties and financial restrictions negated the building of that fleet. The base itself was an on-and-off proposition for a generation as political parties took or relinquished power in Commons. When Labour came in, work stopped. When Labour left, work was resumed. So it went for almost 20 years.

The U.S. ebb and flow of naval fortunes and the internal political factors that dictated them have been noted on previous pages. External factors were about to make the '30s different from the '20s and bring on the climatic '40s.

Three events ushered in the '30s. Japan became a rising dominant force in the Western Pacific (Far East to the Brits). In the U.S. the Democratic Party ousted a Republican Congress in the mid-term elections of 1930 and in 1932 elected a Democratic president. Two months before Franklin Delano Roosevelt was inaugurated in March 1933, German President Paul von Hindenburg, after a succession of inept governments, asked Adolph Hitler and his Nazi Party to form a government. The world would never be the same.

Before that, however, Japan was feeling her oats in the Pacific and on the Asian mainland. Although China had thrown off the Manchus in 1911 and rallied behind Sun Yat-Sen, she was hardly united. The Japanese had seized and retained the German concessions and sphere on the Shantung Peninsula at the outbreak of World War I. At the same time they had seized the German archipelagos in Micronesia. At Versailles, Japan was awarded those north of the Equator as Mandates, a euphemism for possessions, albeit, supposedly administered for the League of Nations. With the earlier take-over of Korea in 1908, Japan had a foothold on the Asian mainland of Shantung and Chosen (her name for Korea.) The real wealth, mostly in minerals but also in potential water power lay in Manchuria, a Chinese province in the north abutting Siberian Russia (U.S.S.R.) A Sino-Russian clash over Manchuria in 1928 signified two things. Nationalist China was showing signs of resurgence and the U.S.S.R. had a vested interest in the northern part of the province. Japan had investments in the southern part.

An explosion in the night damaged the Japanese-controlled South Manchurian railroad. It was Sept. 18, 1931. The speed with which Japan retaliated and overran key Chinese positions in Manchuria was indicative of a previously well-planned operation giving rise to the accusation that the explosion had been a deliberate act by the Japanese Army to provide a *casus belli*. By October Japanese arms were in control of the south of Manchuria and the province was late proclaimed the "independent" state of Manchuko with the last heir of the Manchus as a Japanese puppet emperor. Japan's military action was branded aggression by the rest of the world. It was clearly a violation of the League Covenant, the Nine-Power Pact (One of the Washington Treaties of 1922 guaranteeing the territorial integrity of China), and the recent Kellogg-Briand Peace Pact.

Sanctions including an embargo of Japan were proposed but SecState Stimson declined to go along with the League saying that the Navy "probably" would not interfere with a League embargo. No embargo was forthcoming. The U.S. responded with the Stimson (sometimes Hoover-Stimson) Doctrine of non-recognition of gains obtained by force. The answer from Japan, supposedly to counter boycotts stemming from the "Manchurian Incident" was an assault and bombardment of Shanghai. Revulsion swept the U.S. but Hoover demurred on taking overt action. Harbinger of things to come, the U.S. Fleet was moved to Hawaiian waters where it was believed to be so situated as to have a sobering effect on Japan. A year later, in March 1933, Japan gave her two-year notice of withdrawal from the League as her delegates walked out.

Concomitant U.S. events on the naval front occurred. The ordering of the first new destroyers since 1919 under Carl Vinson House Naval Affairs Chairmanship was mentioned in the last chapter. More significant but less publicized was the changing of the guard in the Navy. The Anglophobes exited.

Flag officers such as Hughes and Wiley who as battleship captains in Scapa Flow had been subjected to caustic RN remarks denigrating the U.S. Navy were retired. Likewise, Plunkett, whose Irish heritage had no room for "limey loving" departed after a blistering anti-British speech in New York.

A new phase of Anglo-American affinity in naval thinking emerged. The new CNO, Adm. Pratt, was the American leader. He still had no opposite number in affinity in the RN, however. The titular American leader can assumed to be retired RAdm. W.S. Sims who was occasionally writing on naval affairs. He had influenced a group of young destroyer captains in his Atlantic Torpedo Flotilla before World War I. Pratt had been his second in command but there were young skippers, not all of whom were Anglophiles like Sims and Pratt, who were to hold high command in World War II and to demonstrate that they adhered to the Sims philosophy of innovation. The only real Anglophile among them was Harold Stark, who as CNO in 1941 was to take the lead for the Navy in advocating "Germany first" in the two-front war. He finished the war in London as senior Navy representative. Two others heeding Sims's advocacy of the place of air in the Navy went to flight training in their fifties. One, W.F. "Bill" (his father was "Bull" because of his strong command voice) Halsey, Jr. who was to conduct the early carrier raids in 1942; win the waters around Guadalcanal; and sail into Tokyo Bay. His feelings about the Brits were ambivalent. The other Naval Aviator was the wartime CNO (relieved Stark) and COMINCH (after Pearl Harbor CINCUS had a bad pronunciation). E.J. King was hardly a "limey lover" but he was a "Jap hater" and that's what counted even in the '30s.

While not admitted by its members, the RN was no longer the once-potent force it had been. Besides lacking ships incorporating the lessons of Jutland on damage control and compartmentation, it hadn't recognized the threat from the air. Her ships had little anti-aircraft armament. Their decks were not armored against bombs but worst of all control over the Fleet Air Arm was virtually vested in the Air Ministry not the Admiralty. Hence, the RAF had priority in aircraft procurement and the Fleet Air Arm had to do with the dregs. While there were relatively quite a few carriers in the RN they were small and carried fewer aircraft than the U.S. or IJN carriers. There was no first line fighter; dive-bombing did not really exist and the torpedo bombers were old, slow biplanes. As later shown off Norway, Crete, Malta, Malaya and Ceylon, the RN was naked to air attack.

Likewise, anti-submarine defense was left to diplomacy to outlaw the submarine rather than face the problem and solve it.

Like many in the U.S. Navy, the RN still foresaw another Jutland-like engagement of battlelines for all the marbles. When it was over, the victorious fleet could sweep the enemy's commerce from the seas just as Mahan had maintained. While Mahan was a pseudo-historian, his principles of sweeping enemy commerce from the seas and strangling her were sound. His methods bore examination. Yet, Jutland was still studied and war-gamed on the checkerboard decks of the Naval War College.

Enter the new generation of innovators! In his time, Alfred Thayer Mahan was a pseudo-innovator. His analysis embodied in his opus, *The Influence of Sea Power Upon History 1660-1783,* which he copyrighted in 1890, codified some principles of naval warfare and the wealth and power to be derived from supremacy at sea. His innovation was the recognition and codification of those principles. These principles still held or at least the ultimate one did – the destruction of the commerce of an enemy dependent on sea trade for her existence. Were the new innovators to rewrite Mahan, they would entitle it *The Influence of Geography Upon Sea Power.* There were only two powerful or potentially powerful island kingdoms in the world. Both were dependent on imports from food to raw materials, including oil, to survive. Thus they were vulnerable to interdiction of their sea trade. The new innovators only saw one of these island nations as a potential enemy – Japan. They also saw the great differences in geography between the Atlantic and the Pacific. Long-ranged fleet submarines could attrite Japanese commerce. Aircraft carriers, protected by a balance of surface units could project sea power across the Pacific and defeat insular Japan. Mobility combined with the increasing ranges of carrier-based aircraft could defeat Japan without the rival battlelines coming in contact.

With the new carriers, *Lexington* and *Saratoga* coming on line, the early pilots who had qualified on the small, experimental deck of *Langley* were in Seventh Heaven. These carriers were large, fast, carried more than 90 planes in a squadron mix of fighters, scout, dive- and torpedo-bombers. In addition to developing the tactics of projecting air power from their decks to destroy the enemy, the all important techniques of fueling, arming and rapidly launching aircraft then recovering them, refueling and rearming them for relaunching were improved with practice. The choreography of flight deck operations was a significant evolution in the projection of American sea power across he Pacific. Also, experience showed the distinct advantage of having multiple carriers available in a single fleet formation. It became a geometric progression of power.

Aviation became more of a specialty with fewer Naval Aviators returning to surface duties as they became immersed in flying. Still, they were naval officers and stood deck watches on carriers or if attached to the aviation unit of a battleship or cruiser on those ships. Sea-going skills had to be maintained for the law required that carriers be commanded by Naval Aviators (or earlier in the period, Naval Aviation Observers). Likewise the Executive Officer (XO) of a carrier had to be qualified in aviation. Things had come a long way since Naval Aviator Number 1, "Spud" Ellyson, had qualified in 1911 yet commanded a destroyer in World War I.

The submariners had a different problem. Submarines had demonstrated their value in the U-boat attacks against Britain that almost brought her to her knees in 1917. The combined Poison Gas-Submarine ban treaty of 1922 at Washington had not come into effect because France refused. But the 1930 London Treaty among, Great Britain, Japan and the U.S. stated in Part IV, Article that "The following are accepted as established rules of International Law:" It then held that with regard to merchant ships, submarines must obey the rules incumbent upon surface ships. Further, except for a merchant ship refusing to heave to for search or actively resisting a search, a submarine may not sink her without placing passengers, crew and ship's papers in a place of safety. Ship's boats were not considered a place of safety unless in proximity to land or another surface ship. But the Treaty went further. Part V, Article 23 said, "The present Treaty shall remain in force until the 31st December 1936, subject to the following exceptions: (1) **Part IV shall remain in force without limit of time;**" [Emphasis supplied.]

Despite the restrictions of the London Treaty, the new innovators were designing submarines with the ability to cross the pacific and "wage war in Japanese home waters." They were preparing to attack Japanese sea commerce without waiting for the elimination of its battleline by surface or air action. They were ready to go to the heart of the matter as defined by Mahan. They were gambling that Japan would do so and the U.S. would have the power of retaliation instantly at hand.

Interestingly, while Japanese submarines were effective against American fleet units during the war, commerce raiding was not one of their strong suits. American unrestricted submarine warfare against Japan could be justified despite the Treaty because Japan's Axis partner, Germany, initiated it in September 1939. *Rebus sic stantibus* is implicit in any treaty.

With Japan as the "undeclared" but obvious enemy, the Navy planners directed their attentions to the problems of the Pacific. The Fleet Problems assumed new scenarios. Defense of the Panama Canal still figured in such exercises but defense of Hawaii became a scenario. Likewise, the seizure and defense of advanced bases received new attention. American possessions west of Hawaii, still restricted from being fortified (not just guns but facilities to base ships and aircraft) received attention. Midway and Wake plus the outlying islands of Johnston, Palmayra, Canton and Samoa increased in potential importance. An unexpected windfall came in the form of American commercial aviation. Pan-American, a South American and Caribbean-based airline wished to expand to the Pacific. Using multi-engined Boeing seaplanes styled "Clippers" Pan-Am inaugurated a regular service to the Orient from the West Coast via Hawaii, Midway and the U.S. islands west. Facilities short of fortifications were built on the islands.

But Japan had the majority of islands west of Hawaii and east of the Philippines and Guam thanks to the League of Nation mandates of the former German possessions north of the equator. These could be stepping stones to or from Hawaii depending on who was advancing. Since Japan maintained the utmost secrecy about her activities in the Mandates, even barring foreigners or at least inhibiting their entry to the point of total discouragement, the question arose as to whether Japan was violating the Treaty and fortifying them. Speculation remained that "Pete" Ellis was on a spy mission to determine if the Mandates were being fortified when he died mysteriously in 1923. Since such suspicions were a fixation with him, some speculate that when he found no evidence of fortifications (in 1923) he turned to drinking in frustration and drank himself to death. Who knows? The question was not what was going on in the '20s but what was happening in the '30s since Japan was rattling her sword in Asia.

The vast distances of the Pacific required a Navy different from that of Britain. The RN could range around the world from England refueling at a series of bases from Portsmouth to Gibraltar, across the Mediterranean and Indian Ocean or via Africa to Singapore and Hong Kong. Significantly, such bases were almost the same distance apart, i.e., the fuel bunker capacity of her ships.

The new U.S. ships, carriers, cruisers, destroyers, submarines and auxiliaries needed characteristics that would let them carry out continuous combat missions at extended ranges. The distances across the Pacific were vast. Even had they been fortified, the Philippines and Guam would be difficult to hold if war with Japan came. The long supply line across the Pacific through the Mandates would make support of American possessions in the Western pacific an enormous undertaking. The American merchant shipping to do so did not exist in sufficient numbers. Likewise, the Navy had insufficient auxiliaries, particularly oilers, to sustain a fleet that far from home.

The question arose about how to finance a program even as relatively modest as the whittled down version of the Wilbur program authorized under Coolidge. Lack of annual appropriations of the Hoover administration was delaying the completion of even those few ships, mostly heavy cruisers with a lone small carrier.

Carriers and the new concepts required aircraft and aviators. How the latter were furnished will be covered in later chapters. The question of aircraft was manifold. The initial concept of aircraft had been one of scouting ahead of the battleline and locating the enemy. Scouting was still a primary mission. Now there was the mission of attacking the enemy's ships to sink or damage them so that they were no longer a threat. The Marines, all Naval Aviators trained by the Navy, had initiated dive-bombing against the *sandinistas* in Nicaragua. Its potential use at sea wherein a single bomb could be accurately dropped on the deck of an enemy ship (or close enough to do structural damage) was quickly realized. Dive-bombing became another carrier mission. Dive-bombing never really took hold in the Army Air Corps. It was more concerned with the development of a long-range heavy bomber to carry war to the enemy's industrial base. Retired RAdm. Bradley Fiske had "invented" an aerial-launched torpedo before World War I. It had been improved over the years. Torpedo-bombing was another carrier mission. Antiaircraft guns alone could not suffice to protect ships from enemy air attack. Fighters were required to do this. Concomitantly, attack aircraft had to be protected from enemy fighters. The fighter mission was dual. Thus, carrier air had three missions: scouting, bombing or attacking from above (dive-bomber) or along the surface (torpedo-bombers) and providing fighter protection against enemy attackers.

Naval Aviation was more than just carrier-borne, however. The *Omaha* class scout cruisers had been built with catapults for launching floatplane scouts. The aircraft were carried on deck on the catapults. The first of the "Treaty Cruisers" *Salt Lake City* and *Pensacola* had similar arrangements for floatplanes. The subsequent cruisers were built with a hangar for the floatplanes. Earlier classes had the hangar and the catapults amidships while later ones had the hangar aft below the main deck on the fantail. Hangars for floatplanes were a trademark of U.S. cruisers.

Patrolling the coastlines and from insular possessions required aircraft with longer range and in most cases multi-engines. Offshore patrols were a navy mission. Naval Aviators were trained for long-range navigation over water; Army aviators were not. Hence, two types of aircraft were used. For a long time because of the preoccupation with rigid airships by ChBuAer, RAdm. W. Moffett, a lot of time and money were wasted on rigid airships. Several lives were lost including Moffett's in the futile attempt to develop a combat-capable dirigible. The solution to long-range patrolling lay elsewhere and was finally found in multi-engined seaplanes of great endurance. Although these were designated patrol bombers, their main capability was ocean scouting and patrolling. A unique advantage was that with a tender they could be based on many of the barren atolls dotting the Pacific.

Each of the potential naval antagonists in the Pacific had unique vulnerabilities. All were geographical. The U.S. had the unfortified Philippines and Guam plus the almost barren islands of Midway, Wake, Canton, Palmayra, *et al.* Hawaii, Alaska and the Panama Canal also required defending. Japan was dependent on imports via the sea. She had an army on the Asian mainland to support. Her Mandates could be either an asset or a liability. As the former, when occupied or fortified like the bastion of Truk they were a formidable bar to enemy passage across the Pacific. As the latter, they were a drain on assets if each one had to be manned and defended.

Thus, we close this chapter with an examination of the dichotomy among naval thinkers. The Mahan school held for the "fleet in being" of capital ships concentrated and prepared for the showdown battle for control of the sea. The new school of innovators sought to exercise control of the seas by the new weaponry of air and submarines providing flexibility and mobile striking power. The latter allowed concentration at successive locations and defeat of the enemy piecemeal and in detail. A balanced fleet of various categories, including amphibious troops to seize and hold advanced bases, could maximize friendly potential and attrite enemy power.

Writers of the era erroneously categorized this as a fight between the "battleship admirals" and the "carrier admirals." It was not a struggle between the "gun club" and the "Airedales." The real question was: "Who is to be the enemy?" (Or where is the potential arena –Atlantic or Pacific?) If the enemy was to be the RN, battleships and big guns were the answers. If it were to be Japan, than battleships would play a lesser role because of their lack of speed and thus mobility. Carriers could project air power and submarines could attrite the enemy commerce. The latter was to start immediately on the outset of war and maintain pressure until victory.

The question was ultimately straddled. Big, faster battleships were ordered. But fortunately, so were carriers, cruisers, destroyers, submarines and auxiliaries. The concept of a balanced fleet for a war of mobility prevailed.

Chapter XII

The Pre-New Deal Years

Under Harding, Coolidge and Hoover, the party successors to "Big Navy" advocate, Theodore Roosevelt, few warships were programmed. In fact only SecNav Wilbur's urging of Coolidge spurred a new program just as Coolidge was about to leave the White House. The "cruiser bill" authorized construction of 15 cruisers over a period extending past the mid '30s. A carrier was also authorized. She was to be the first designed from the keel up, her predecessors being conversions. There had been austere authorizations since the emergency destroyer programs of 1917-18. While some of the authorizations of the 1916 Naval Expansion Act had been completed after the war, there had been minimal authorizations.

All of the post-war authorizations had been concentrated on "Treaty Cruisers" and an aircraft carrier. This was not unusual since the emergency programs of 1917-18 concentrated on destroyers for convoys and gave the U.S. the largest destroyer fleet in the world. By 1930, these destroyers, all of almost identical design, were approaching simultaneous obsolescence. The useful life of a destroyer built before 1920 was less than 20 years. The Navy faced an over-age destroyer fleet in less than a decade. It being unwise to replace all ships as they suddenly became over-age, there was an urgent requirement to plan an orderly replacement program to put new ships in the fleet as the destroyers of the emergency programs began to reach the end of their useful lives. Some of them, poorly built, had already done so. An orderly program would let designers profit by experience with each incremental class as it entered service. Spreading construction over several years it would mean full employment in shipyards and 144 related industries. Ships could be a way of employing workers in at least 44 states.

This method of providing employment was not lost on Hoover and contrary to popular belief he saw naval shipbuilding as public works to get shipyards and related industry busy. Unfortunately, his Republicans hesitated in such remedies and as seen in the next chapter, it was the new administration that successfully took up the Republican lead.

Submarines had been authorized in the 1916 Act and thence came the multitude of coastal boats of the R and "old S" classes. Smaller than foreign boats they were ineffective for fleet work as revealed in the Coontz Report of 1922. Nine boats authorized in 1916 had not yet been funded. (There was a "Neff experimental type as well.) During the early '20s, six V-boats of fleet sized submarines were built and charged against the earlier authorization. Thus they only had to undergo the single jeopardy of appropriation debates not the double of authorization and funding hassles.

The first (V-1 through V-3) were ordered in 1920 and entered service in 1925-26 and known as B1, B-2 and B-3. In 1931, names of marine life were given to the larger submarines and they became *Barracuda* (SS-163), *Bass* (SS-164) and *Bonito* (SS-165). They were 2,000 tons. In 1924, V-4, originally A-1 but later *Argonaut* (SM-1/SS-166) was ordered as a minelayer. At 2,740 tons with two 6-in. guns she was in overall length and submerged displacement second only in size to the French *Surcouf*.

Two more V-type fleet boats were ordered in 1925. N-1 and N-2 became *Narwhal* (SS-167) and *Nautilus* (SS-168). At 2,730 tons they mounted two 6-in. guns and six 21-in. torpedo tubes. Until 1929, when V-7 was ordered as D-1 (see Chapter XVII for the movie of the same name) there was no new construction of subs. *Dolphin* (SS-169) at 1,540 tons with a 4-in. gun and six tubes was smaller than the boats of 1924-25. The two remaining under the 1916 authorization were ordered in 1931 and will be described later.

The aging destroyers were recognized as a problem during the debates on the "cruiser bill" in 1928. At that time, Thomas S. Butler, Chairman of the House Naval Affairs Committee declined to recommend authorization for new destroyers, "... because the Act of August 28, 1916, authorized 12 such vessels, ... for the construction of which no appropriations have yet been made. Your committee regard this authorization as sufficient authority for the appropriation of funds to build needed destroyer leaders."

Nothing came of the funding for destroyer for destroyer leaders in the "cruiser bill." Destroyer leaders were not then a category in the Navy but were a necessity for controlling the tactical maneuvers of destroyer squadrons.

The midterm elections of 1930 gave the Democrats their first majority in the House in more than a decade. By this victory, a long-time member of the House Naval Affairs Committee succeeded to the chairmanship. Carl Vinson (D-Ga.) replaced the Republican Fred A. Britten who had succeeded the late Thomas S. Butler a few months before.

Vinson was born in Baldwin County, Georgia, in November 1883. He attended Georgia Military School. In 1903, he earned a L.L.B. from Mercer University and became a country lawyer. He was a county judge for two years before he was elected to fill the vacancy left when T.W. Harwich resigned from Congress. From 1914 until he retired in October 1964, he was returned for 26 terms in Congress. In 1917, Vinson was appointed to the House Naval Affairs Committee and became a spokesman for naval preparedness.

"Uncle Carl" as he was known among naval officers of the '30s lost no time in asserting his advocacy of a strong Navy. Capitalizing on the authorizations of the 1916 Act, he introduced a bill in early 1931 for the construction of the 12 destroyers previously authorized. He wanted funding to prevent the American destroyer fleet's approaching obsolescence. At the time many destroyers of the war emergency programs were gong to the breakers as a result of the London Treaty of 1930. To Vinson, the new treaty was a blessing in disguise, as will be seen later. Suffice it to say, as the Democratic naval advocate, he was doing his best to initiate a construction program under a parsimonious administration as well as in the face of many of his own party's anti-Navy partisans.

He succeeded in getting initial funding for 12 destroyers. These were of two classes. Eight were of the *Farragut* class. Less than the treaty limit of 1,500 tons, they were still at 1,375 tons a third larger than the "four pipers." They had five 5-in.dual -purpose (surface and air) guns and eight 21-in. torpedo tubes in two banks along the centerline. They were powerful fleet additions. The others were destroyer leaders at the 1,800-tn London Treaty limit. The first four of the *Porter* class mounted eight 5-in (surface only) guns in four doubled gun houses. Like the *Farragut*s they had eight 21-in. torpedo tubes in two banks on the centerline.

Funding soon ran aground in the administration's economy moves. The cutback allowed only five ships in 1931. *Farragut* (DD-348), *Dewey* (DD-349), *Hull* (DD-350), *MacDonough* (DD-351) and *Worden* (DD-352) were ordered. In 1932, Vinson managed to get money for the remaining three and *Dale* (DD-353), *Monaghan* (DD-354) and *Alywin* (DD-355) were ordered before the Republicans left the White House. Funds for the *Porter*s, however, had to come from another source. Two submarines were funded in 1931-32. These were C-1 or *Cachalot* (SS-170) and C-2 or *Cuttlefish* (SS-171). They were 1,100-ton boats with a 3-in. deck gun and six 21-in tubes.

At this point the fortune of the Navy changed. A former Assistant SecNav with a proud naval name was elected president. He was of the same party as the Chairman of the House Naval Affairs Committee and the two had been acquainted during World War I.

Thus, when Franklin D. Roosevelt was elected in 1932, he came with the credentials of a friend of the Navy. Naval officers looked to him for support in building the Navy to meet the threat they foresaw. First, it seemed he might not.

F.D.R. inherited some economy measures from his predecessors that had serious effects on service morale. A 15 percent pay cut had been ordained for all federal employees, including the armed services. Resentment among officers and enlisted was two-fold. The loss of money hurt but being reduced to the status of "employees" was a severe blow to the pride of men dedicated to serve. A pay slash in the RN which discriminated against older ratings versus newer ones resulted in a mutiny on board vessels at Invergordon. American sailors had too much pride in their Navy and themselves to mutiny. They took the pay cut; the decreed one-month leave without pay; and continued to serve. When the Naval Academy Class of 1930 made lieutenant, junior grade (Lt. j.g.), in 1933, they sewed the extra half stripe above the ensign full stripe but instead of the increased pay of the new rank they took a 15 percent cut in their ensign's pay.

Most of the officers and men stayed despite the slap in the face because things were worse outside the Navy. At least, they still had a paycheck and a career. Many of the rest of the nation's manhood were unemployed. While new enlistments were subject to a waiting list, reenlistments, although competitive, were high.

Not all were allowed to remain in the Navy, however. A little known fact was that Midshipmen at the Naval Academy were in the Navy since Midshipman was a rank between Chief Warrant Officer and ensign. Cadets at West Point were not in the Army. F.D.R. inherited another problem that went back to his days as Assistant SecNav.

In 1916, sitting in for SecNav, F.D.R. was a member of the board which reformed personnel procedures including an officer selection system which did away with lock-step promotion based on mere seniority. Henceforth, officers competed among themselves for promotion *vice* waiting until death, retirement or resignation (rare in the upper ranks) made a vacancy. The Navy had a selection system while the Marines had to wait another generation for one. Part of that personnel law set the number of officers on active duty at a fixed percentage of the number of enlisted. As appropriations were slashed for the number of sailors in the fleet, the number of commissions for active duty officers declined.

Concomitant with the 15 percent pay cut, a movement started in Congress to commission only half of the Naval Academy Class of 1931. the chief source of commissioned officers. At the eleventh hour the motion was defeated but it was tried again, unsuccessfully, with the Class of 1932.

In the winter of 1932-33, Congress finally passed a bill that not only denied commissions to two-thirds of the Class of 1933 upon graduation but also placed two major restrictions on those commissioned. The first provided that commissions were to be probationary for two years after graduation. Ensigns and second lieutenants whose Fitness Reports indicated below average performance could be discharged at the end of two years. The second restriction forbade marriage during the probationary period. This was rescinded but later reapplied to Classes who were graduated when war broke out in Europe, only to be rescinded again after the U.S. entered the war.

The Navy Department added another unfair requirement. At the end of the probationary period, ensigns would take professional examinations for permanent commissions. On the surface, this was logical and reasonable. But it was unfair in the fact that post-graduation duty varied. Those in larger ships with fewer duties could be formally tutored by senior officers. (Captains would take pride in a high percentage of their ensigns qualifying.) Ensigns in destroyers, although probably better qualified by duties, were too overworked as were their seniors for formal schooling for the exams. A similar "enlightenment" occurred in the later '90s when Sen. Nunn (D-Ga.), Chairman of the Senate Armed Services Committee, abetted by Sen. Glenn (D-Ohio), a retired Marine who started as a NavCad, pushed a bill through denying Service Academy graduates regular commissions until several years after graduation.

The Class of 1933 at the Naval Academy was basically split into three parts (A case could be made that there were up to eight but for our purposes there were three segments determined by Class standing at graduation), '33-A was commissioned and went to the Fleet or Marine Corps. '33-B received Reserve commissions and went home to await the "pleasure of the President." '33-C were discharged with a diploma. Incidentally, 1933 was the first year that the *Grand Poobahs of Academia* consented to recognize the Naval Academy as an accredited degree-granting institution and all graduates henceforth received a Bachelor of Science degree.

There are several legends as to what happened to bring '33-B back on active duty. Two that I like are presented here and you can take your choice.

One has an ensign serving in the Presidential yacht telling the plight of his Classmates to F.D.R. Supposedly, F.D.R. made an immediate investigation and '33-B were given regular commissions.

The other has F.D.R. presenting diplomas on Jun. 1, 1933 and recognizing the son of a neighbor from the Warm Springs "White House" in Georgia. Short time later, at Warm Springs, F.D.R. met the young man again and inquired as to why he was not at sea. The lad gave the sad story of his being in '33-B.

Whatever the impetus, legend has F.D.R. taking action and getting '33-B commissioned as Regulars with dates of rank of May 29, 1934 maintaining their relative seniority over the Class of 1934 which was graduated two days later. Legend also has it that someone in '33-C found a legal clause stating that anyone involuntarily given an honorable discharge before the end of normal service was due a year's severance pay. The suit probably dragged on in court for years.

Many of those in '33-C came on active duty for World War II. Of the 432 graduates, 73 achieved flag rank and six were Marine general officers. Two members of '33-B were awarded the Medal of Honor. John D. Bulkeley got his for his deeds in the early days in the Philippines and David McCampbell for 35 kills as a fighter pilot. So much for economy!

When Roosevelt took office in March of 1933, it was the nadir of the Depression. The 1929 Crash was worldwide but it hit the U.S. hardest. Prosperity had been taken for granted since recovery from a slight recession in 1921. When the Depression hit, unemployment rose as industry shut down. There was a ripple effect throughout the economy. Shipbuilding is a typical example. It had allied industries that depended on it for orders and employment. About 125 trades and professions were involved in ship construction. Steel companies, electrical manufacturers, boiler producers and the instrument industry had a stake in shipbuilding. Material came from almost every state in the nation. During the debates after the "cruiser bill," William Green of the American Federation of Labor (AFL), urged Hoover to accelerate construction of the ships in order to put the shipyards back to work and relieve unemployment.

None of this was lost on Vinson.

When he was sworn in, F.D.R. viewed his major task as restoring confidence. In late 1932, the President-elect and Vinson conferred. Since the beginning of the year Vinson, perhaps sensing a Democratic victory in November and recognizing that it would be F.D.R., a "Big Navy" man, had been pushing for building. He introduced a ten-year naval construction program. As the election neared in September, he grew bolder and sought an allocation of $8.8 million to fund ships already authorized. At this time he had not asked for more authorizations. Facing a hostile administration, there was a possibility that a veto would have spelled defeat for future moves.

Thus, it came as a surprise to Vinson, when on Nov. 30, 1932, the President-elect indicated that he might favor cuts in government spending. Two days later, after talks with Vinson, F.D.R. came out in support of a strong fleet.

Still words are not actions and Roosevelt was to become known for his variance between each. The final acts of the Hoover administration in February were to initiate five percent cuts in naval appropriation, which were promptly opposed by Vinson. Then the new administration began to concentrate on traditional methods to reduce expenditures, to balance the budget and to get the country going again. Reduced spending hurt the Navy; caused cuts in its manpower; and it looked like F.D.R. was reneging on his word to Vinson and the Navy.

Then, Roosevelt underwent a fundamental change (or at least manifested it) that bode well for the country, for rearmament and for the Navy. Shipbuilding became a vital cog in recovery. It could be a dual solution for problems, both foreign and domestic. With high employment it could be a spur to many allied industries and put money in the hands of the average working man. About 85 percent of money spent for shipbuilding went for labor, either directly or indirectly. Solvent workers could help prime the pump. While construction itself was concentrated along the coasts, its effects were nationwide.

Boldness was required. The bold stroke was the National Industrial Recovery Act (N.I.R.A.) signed by the President on Jun. 16, 1933.

Chapter XIII

Naval Construction Spurs the Economy

On Jun. 13, 1933, the new president signed the National Industrial Recovery Act (N.I.R.A.). It declared, "A national emergency productive of widespread unemployment and disorganization of industry, which burdens interstate and foreign commerce, affects the public welfare, and undermines the standards of living of the American people is here by declared to exist." The policy statement continued stating that specific actions were to be taken in order to "… reduce unemployment, … [and] … rehabilitate industry …"

Its Section 202 made specific provisions for the Navy and ship construction. Describing powers given to the President in the Act that he could delegate to the Administrator, it said, "… and if in the opinion of the President it seems desirable, the construction of naval vessels with the terms and/or limits established by the London Naval Treaty and of aircraft therefore…" is authorized. Acknowledging that naval limits were still a viable issue among nations, the President was given discretion in that area.

The President could now, within limits, bypass Congress and construct warships without the specific individual authorizations required previously. In the name of domestic emergency, he had the power to authorize ships he deemed necessary to help the nation recover. It was also an aid to his foreign policy.

Thus far, Congress had surrendered one of its powers regarding the Navy – the power to authorize construction.

In the subsequent section of the Act, Congress gave the President its other power – funding. "… the President is authorized and empowered, through the Administrator or through other such agencies as he may designate or create, (1) to construct, finance, or aid in the construction or financing of any public works project included in the program pursuant to Section 202…" The method of financing was the power to float loans. Warship construction was an approved public work.

F.D.R. acted immediately. He issued an Executive Order for the construction of more than 30 ships. Some were the heavy cruisers already authorized by the law of 1929 but most were entirely new authorizations under the power of the Recovery Act. Funding of all was planned to come from the Act's inherent authority instead of the usual fight for annual appropriations and budget balancing.

Six weeks after the enactment of the new law and issuance of the Executive Order, orders were placed on Aug. 3, 1933 for two aircraft carriers, *Yorktown* (CV-5) and *Enterprise* (CV-6); one heavy cruiser, *Vincennes* (CA-44); three light cruisers of the new *Brooklyn* class, *Philadelphia* (CL-41), *Savannah* CL-42) and *Nashville* (CL-43). Three others of this class, *Phoenix* (CL-46), *Boise* (CL-47) and *Honolulu* (CL-48) were incorporated into the remaining 1929 authorization and ordered three weeks later. In addition, 20 destroyers of two classes, four of 1,800 tons and 16 of 1,450 tons and four 1,310-ton submarines were ordered.

The new carriers were the second and third, *Ranger* was the first, to be built as carriers from the keel up. Lessons learned from *Ranger* were incorporated. They were to be built in the same private yard as *Ranger* but were larger at 19,500 tons. They were faster; had greater range and could carry more fuel and ordnance. Unlike the ex-battlecruisers, they did not have 8-in. guns but carried the same 5-in, guns as the new destroyers. Like the ex-battlecruisers, however, they carried four squadrons – scout-bomber, dive-bomber, torpedo-bomber and fighter. The. U.S. was left with 3,650 tons of uncommitted carrier tonnage under the Washington Treaty limits.

The new heavy cruiser was the last of the nine ships of the 1929 authorization which cold be laid down before 1934. She would be number 17 of the 18 allowed by London. Last of a new class which differed from the *Northampton*s, she couldn't be ready before 1937. Others of the *Astoria* class were 9,950-ton "Treaty Cruisers" laid down under the Hoover administration at the urging of Vinson. They were: *New Orleans* (CA-32) – 1931, *Astoria* (CA-34) –1930, *Minneapolis* (CA-36) – 1931, *Tuscaloosa* (CA-37) – 1931, *San Francisco* (CA-38) – 1931 and *Quincy* (CA-39). The last was ordered before Hoover left office but was not started until later in 1933. They mounted nine 8-in. guns in three turrets. Building was assigned to both Navy (on each coast) and private yards. *Vincennes* (CA-44) went to a private yard in keeping with the 1929 act calling for alternate ships in private yards. Two improved versions of the earlier *Northampton*s had been laid down in 1930 and completed in 1932. These, *Portland* (CA-33) and *Indianapolis* (CA-35) were 9,800 tons. Five *Astoria*s joined the fleet in 1934; *Quincy* as seventeenth of the 18 allowed heavy cruisers was completed in 1936.

The new light cruisers, products of the compromise at London were a new type and concept unlike the older *Omaha*s. They were bigger at 9,700 tons and had their main battery in five turrets of three 6-in. guns each along the centerline. As protectors of the battleline from the destroyer charge, they were capable of engaging five targets at once beyond the range of destroyer guns or torpedoes. The latter assumption proved false during the war when the IJN surprised the Navy with the 24-in, "long lance" torpedoes of extreme range. In theory, fewer of the new *Brooklyn*s provided protection equivalent to several smaller vessels with fewer guns. It was said that the *Brooklyn*s were designed as replies to the IJN *Mogami* class of 1931 which were four 8,500-ton ships mounting 15 6-1-in. guns in five turrets. Japan regunned the *Mogami*s before the war with 8-inchers.

The new destroyer programs were important in view of the approaching block obsolescence which was going to reduce American numerical superiority in destroyers to a mere paper superiority of "iron coffins." More destroyer leaders of 1,800 tons were authorized and ordered. These were:

Porter (DD-356), *Selfridge* (DD-357), *McDougal* (DD-358), *Winslow* (DD-359), *Phelps* (DD-360), *Clark* (DD-361), *Moffett* (DD-362) and *Balch* (DD-363). They were built in private yards and completed in 1936, displacing more World War I vintage destroyers to scrap yards, back channel reserve or conversion to other duties, e.g., minesweepers, seaplane tenders or high speed transports. Sixteen 1,450 tonners with four 5-in, dual-purpose guns and 12 torpedo tubes tripled the number of new destroyers in the fleet. *Mahan* (DD-364), *Cummings* (DD-365), *Drayton* (DD-366), *Lamson* (DD-367), *Flusser* (DD-368), *Reid* (DD-369), *Case* (DD-370), *Conyngham* (DD-371), *Cassin* (DD-372), *Shaw* (DD-373), *Tucker* (DD-374), *Downes* (DD-375), *Cushing* (DD-376), *Perkins* (DD-377), S*mith* (DD-378) and *Preston* (DD-379) joined the fleet in 1936.All were to see extensive action during the war. Six were sunk. Three, *Cassin, Downes* and *Shaw* were almost destroyed at Pearl Harbor. *Shaw*'s explosion is one of the spectacular photographs of that attack. She was fitted with a new bow and returned to sea. *Cassin* and *Downes* were in drydock when bombed. Almost totaled, new hulls were built around old their old machinery and they returned to duty retaining their old hull numbers.

The concepts of the new innovators were embodied in the submarines of the 1933 program. The four of the "P" class were designed for long- range patrols and were the forerunners of the boats who took the war to Japanese waters. *Porpoise* (SS-172), *Pike* (SS-173), *Shark* (SS-174) and *Tarpon* (SS-175) were between 1,310 and 1,315 tons, had a single 3-in. gun and relied on six 21-in torpedo tubs for kills.

Vinson and Roosevelt had mastered the dilemma that had been a hurdle for SecNav Wilbur several years before. They leapt the barrier of individual authorizations by blanket authority under pubic works programming vested in the President. The obstacles of budget balancing and Treasury availability of funds each year had been overcome by a switch to deficit spending (borrowing) to prime the pump and put money in the hands of working men. By the end of 1933, the Public Works Administration (PWA) had allotted $7.5 million for naval construction.

As a stopgap measure, naval building under the Recovery Act was a start. Vinson was aware of the vicissitudes of Congress; vocal opposition by some of the public; and the limited tenure of the Act. "After expiration of two years after the date of enactment of this Act, or sooner if the President ... or the Congress shall ... declare that the emergency ... has ended, the President shall not make any further loans or grants or enter upon any new construction under this title…"

Vinson wanted something more permanent and more binding than a temporary measure tacked on to another purpose. More was needed to ensure the maintenance of an adequate under-age Navy. He knew that the upper limits were set by treaty. He also knew that the U.S. was well below those limits and age was starting to catch up with many ships. The time was propitious for converting the blanket authorizations of the National Industrial

Recovery Act into concrete blanket authorizations for the Navy, *per se*. The Congress and the public were now aware of the economic benefits of naval construction. It was time for naval construction to stand alone, away from the economic and social legislation of recovery. Vinson was ready to make his next move in 1934.

Chapter XIV

The Vinson-Trammel Act of 1934

On Jan. 8, 1934, Congressman Fred Britten, Vinson's Republican predecessor as Chairman, introduced a bill for construction of 101 ships between 1935 and 1939. The next day, a Vinson bill asked to build to the strength specified in the Treaties of Washington (1922) and London (1930). He wanted a fixed plan for building. His rationale was that such a plan did not build ships in emergency crash programs which made for later block obsolescence; it did not overtax and then under-use shipyards; it provided for orderly construction of a balanced fleet since smaller vessels taking less time to build could be scheduled to join the fleet when their larger consorts were ready. A program made for continuing employment and efficient use of facilities and thus was economical. Design changes could be incorporated from lessons learned in earlier construction. In short, Vinson wanted a balanced under-age fleet at all times.

After the usual anti-war and anti-Navy rhetoric and protests by church, women's and pacifist groups, it passed the House rather quickly. In the Senate, Park Trammel (D-Fla.) a senator since 1916 and Vinson's opposite chamber chairman, skillfully guided the bill through by a 65 to 18 vote. For this bit of work, history has added his name to the unofficial title and references cite it as "The Vinson-Trammel Act of 1934." It cleared both houses on Mar. 6 and was signed into law by F.D.R on Mar. 27, 1934.

It was a statement of policy not an authorization bill, although it did provide for ships and tonnages as replacements. It gave the President, at his discretion and timing, authority to build to treaty limits and to do it prior to treaty expirations.

The purpose of the Act was: "To establish the composition of the United States Navy with respect to the categories of vessels limited by the treaties signed at Washington, February 6, 1922 and at London, April 22, 1930, at limits prescribed by those treaties; to authorize the construction of certain naval vessels; and for other purposes."

It was thus enacted that "... the composition of the United States Navy ... is hereby established at the limits prescribed by those treaties." Also, subject to treaties, "... the President ... is hereby authorized ... prior to December 31, 1936, or as soon thereafter as he may deem advisable (in addition to the six cruisers not yet constructed under the Act approved February 13, 1929 (45 Stat. 1165), and (in addition to vessels being constructed pursuant to Executive Order Numbered 6174 of June 16, 1933), the construction of: (a) one aircraft carrier of approximately fifteen thousand tons standard displacement to replace the experimental aircraft carrier *Langley;* (b) ninety-nine thousand two hundred fifty aggregate tons of destroyers to replace over-age destroyers; (c) thirty-five thousand five hundred tons aggregate to replace over-age submarines."

At the upper limits of individual ships according to the London Treaty, this translated into more than 60 destroyers and more than 25 submarines before the end of 1936. This was a formidable undertaking for shipyards.

The President was also authorized to replace "by vessels of modern design and construction" vessels specified by type in the treaties when replacement was allowed. Aircraft were to be procured for all authorized ships. Alternating construction between private and public yards, with the exception of the carrier, was mandated. Apparently to appease the group who were blaming the "merchants of death" as being the root of arms race and wars, profits were limited to those that were "reasonable." Machinery for government audit to ensure this was set up.

Besides the specific ships that resulted from the Act, other features are worth noting.

No money was appropriated for construction. There was just a blanket authorization for building with treaty limits as the goal. It was policy. Congress was authorizing the President and directing his SecNav to submit annual budget estimates for construction. Congress, however, was on record for an under-age Navy henceforth. Implicit was the idea that keeping over-age ships, besides being uneconomical, was misleading the public and its leadership. The principle that national requirements were paramount over budget shone through the Act. It was a mandate to future legislators that the law of the land was a Navy second-to-none. An alteration of that principle would require explicit repeal of the Act.

Awarding alternate ships to Navy and private yards kept the skill of those yards high. Government yards had the primary responsibility for repair and conversion but they required new construction to keep them operating and current. Some in Congress saw that as redundant. They argued that since the government already had its own facilities, it would be best to use them exclusively instead of private yards. It was a matter of accounting techniques and the "bean counter" mentality missed the point. The real problem was in keeping shipbuilding capacity intact and enabling skilled craftsmen to maintain their skills. Alternating yards was more than a compromise. It gave the government competing yardsticks for measuring costs and values received. Government yards were kept busy and ready for fleet maintenance in war. Private yards were kept operating and available for mobilization. Alternating new ships between private and government yards was prudent.

Before looking at the ships emanating from the Act, mention must be made of subsequent Vinson Acts. These occurred after the world situation had the treaties overtaken by events. All had their genesis in the Vinson-Trammel Act and were more amendments of that Act keeping up with specific changes in the situation than new legislation. They made specific additions which adhered to the principle set down in 1934 – *the U .S. Navy will consist of modern under-age warships in such categories that make it second-to-none.* Future Vinson Acts are described in a subsequent chapter.

First let's look at the ships which came from Vinson-Trammel. It was acknowledged that six cruisers of the 1929 Cruiser Act still had not been built.

This was moot since the London Treaty limited the Navy to 18 heavy cruisers and only one more could be started and that one in 1935. Thus, the keel of *Wichita,* 10,000 tons with nine 8-in. guns in three turrets on a *Brooklyn* hull was laid down in 1935. She was commissioned in 1939. The U.S. was still 34,000 tons shy of its allowance in light cruisers. As already mentioned, the immediate effect was orders for three more *Brooklyn*s on Aug. 22, 1934. Keels for P*hoenix, Boise* and *Honolulu* were laid within a year. One went to a government yard and the others to private yards. Not as quickly since the program was to be spread out, two improved *Brooklyn*s were ordered in 1935 and laid down in 1936. At 10,000 tons they would seem to exceed the treaty limits since those laid down in 1935 used 29,100 tons leaving but 4,900 available. Thus underscores a fine point of the Vinson Act (Obviously he was getting expert advice from the new innovators on the General Board!) The treaties allowed replacement of over-age ships. In the London Treaty, vessels between 3,000 and 10,000 tons were deemed over-age after 16 years if laid down before 1920 and at 20 years if laid down later. Replacement construction could begin three years before a ship became over-age.

Two of the *Omaha*s (*Omaha* and *Milwaukee*) had been laid down in 1918 (the other eight in 1920) and were over-age in 1934. At 7,050 tons each they would release 14,100 tons for replacements. With 4,900 tons still unused after ordering the last *Brooklyn*s, 19,000 tons were available. Transfer of 1,000 tons (as per the treaty) from the destroyer category gave 20,000 tons for the two new ships. S*t. Louis* (CL-49) and *Helena* (CL-50) were thus ordered. This is a perfect illustration of the close cooperation between Vinson and the Navy planners. They made known their requirements and he came up with the means to fill them.

Another bit of tonnage legerdemain involved the new aircraft carrier. She was not to exceed 15,000 tons. After *Yorktown* and *Enterprise,* as noted, there were only 3,650 tons available for carriers. *Langley,* however, was an old ship having been laid down as a collier in 1911 and converted to a carrier in 1922. Her 11,050 tons plus the 3,650 available gave 14,700 tons for her replacement. *Wasp* (CV-7) ordered in 1935 and laid down at Bethlehem's yard in Quincy, Mass., was 14,700 tons.

With such light displacement, *Wasp* had all the bad features of *Ranger.* The Navy held to the principle of not sacrificing aircraft capacity to ship's qualities. Therefore, *Wasp* carried about as many planes as *Yorktown* but sacrificed speed, protection and radius of action in the trade off. The adverse effect of "treaty" ships was apparent in *Wasp,* as it had been in some of the earlier heavy cruisers.

The 99,250 tons of destroyers were not all used at once. The wisdom in this was two-fold and stemmed from the World War I experience. Those destroyers were all of the same design that made them easy to build. Indeed, *Ward* (DD-139) went from keel laying to launching in 17 days. While simple to build, all had the same defects and improvements could not be incorporated in subsequent designs because there were none. Just as Wilbur before, Vinson stressed the fact that an orderly program stretching over several years allowed testing of types at sea and making improvements in later designs based on experience with the concomitant advantage of avoiding block obsolescence. The program to build 99,250 tons of new destroyers was spread from 1934 to 1939. The earlier years called for as many as 15 annually steadying at eight per year. The larger numbers initially included destroyer leaders, i.e., more than 1,500 tons. Eight *Porter*s had been started under the Recovery Act and five more were needed. Others were built in multiples of four since that as the standard organization for operating destroyers. Four ships were a division, two divisions plus a leader (the larger ship had more communications and the accommodations for a squadron commander and a small staff) made a squadron.

Immediate construction for 1934 was two modified *Mahan*s, *Dunlap* (DD-384) and *Fanning* (DD-385); ten of the new 1,500-ton *Craven* class: *Gridley* (DD-380), *Craven* (DD-382), *Bagley* (DD-386), *Blue* (DD-387), *Helm* (DD-388), *Mugford* (DD-389), *Ralph Talbot* (DD-390), *Henley* (DD-391), *Patterson* (DD-392) and *Jarvis* (DD-393). Of the 12, eight were built in various Navy Yards and the others in private yards. In addition, two 1,850- ton leaders, *Somers* (DD-381) and *Warrington* (DD-383) were in the 1934 orders. These 14 used 21,700 tons of the 99,250 tons.

There were 15 in the 1935 construction. Three were more leaders of the previous class of 1,850 tons. They were *Sampson* (DD-394), *Davis* (DD-395) and *Jouett* (DD-396). The 12 ships of the *McCall* class were improved versions of the 1,500-ton *Craven*s incorporating experience into the design. They were *Benham* (DD-397), *Ellet* (DD-398), *Lang* (DD-399), *McCall* (DD-400), *Maury* (DD-401), *Mayrant (DD-402), Trippe* (DD-403), *Rhind* (DD-404), *Rowan* (DD-405), *Stack (DD-406), Sterett* (DD-407) and *Wilson* (DD-408) Their total of 23,550 tons added to that already used left 54,000 tons of Vinson-Trammel tonnage still available for the next four years.

In 1936, only 12 were laid down. This single class incorporated more improvements based on experience with those already at sea. They were 1,570 tons. Technically, they could have been in violation of the London Treaty since the leaders had already used all the allocations for ships more than 1,500 tons. That Treaty, however, was to expire at the end of 1936. In 1934, Japan had given the required two-year notice that she intended to withdraw from both treaties upon their expiration. Even though, the U.S. and Britain agreed to continue adherence to the treaties, *pro tem,* the "escalator clause" allowed building in excess of treaty limits whenever a non-party did. The U.S. applied the clause since Japan had signified her intention to build as she pleased and would not provide any information about her programs.

In late 1936, retired RAdm. Sims died in Boston. Aptly, the new class of 1,570- ton destroyers was named the *Sims* class. They were: *Sims* (DD-409), *Hughes* (DD-410), *Anderson* (DD-411), *Hammann* (DD-412), *Mustin* (DD-413), *Russell* (DD-414), *O'Brien* (DD-415), *Walke* (DD-416), *Morris* (DD-417), *Roe* (DD-418), *Wainwright* (DD-419), and *Buck* (DD-420). They used another 18,840 tons of Vinson-Trammel.

By 1937, the program was ready to settle down to an orderly eight new destroyers per year. If the *Sims* class had not exceeded the 1,500 tons envisioned in 1934, the last eight ships laid down in 1939 would have used the remainder of the 99,250 tons exactly. As it turned out, the increased size of destroyers after 1936 caused some changes in authorizations. World conditions contributed as well.

The submarine program acknowledged the particulars of submarine organization. Six boats made a division and two divisions a squadron nursed by a submarine tender. Hence, submarines were usually (but not always because those already in service were taken into account) built in multiples of six.

In 1934, six additional "P" boats were started. *Perch* (SS-176), *Pickerel* (SS-177), *Permit* (SS-178), *Plunger* (SS-179), *Pollack* (SS-180), and *Pompano* (SS-181) at 1,330 tons exceeded their 1933 sisters. They used a total of 7,980 tons. Two of the earlier (1933) "P" boats, *Shark* and *Tarpon* had been the first all-welded hull submarines in the Navy. From then on it was planned that all submarines would be welded vice the weaker riveting. Since the Portsmouth Navy Yard was not ready to shift to building welded hulls, *Plunger* and *Pollack*, products of Portsmouth, were the last submarines with riveted hulls.

The 1935 construction was six "new S" types of 1,450 tons. A feature of these was more torpedo tubes for a total of eight. These six were: *Sargo* (SS-188), *Saury* (SS-189), *Spearfish* (SS-190), *Sculpin* (SS-191), *Squalus* (SS-192) and *Swordfish* (SS-193). Their 8,850 tons left 9,970 tons to be built.

The 1938 program ate up all but 1,120 tons of the remainder. The "T" boats were still 1,450 tons but had ten torpedo tubes. *Tambor* (SS-198), *Tautog* (SS-199), *Thresher* (SS-200), *Triton* (SS-201) and *Trout* (SS-202) joined the fleet in 1940. *Tuna* (SS-203) was ready in early 1941.

All submarines of the Vinson-Trammel genre had a cruising radius in excess of 15,000 nautical miles. This was more than enough to reach the shipping lanes of Japan from Pearl Harbor. Although the Vinson-Trammel boats were insufficient in number to wage a decisive war against Japanese commerce, by 1942 they had enough sisters from later Vinson Acts to do so.

Though not specifically mentioned by the Vinson-Trammel Act, capital ships were implicit in it, calling for replacement of over-age ships. The treaties had set a "holiday" on capital ship construction, carriers excepted. No capital ships were to be begun but at the end of the "holiday" replacements for over-age ships could be started. The standard age for capital ships was 26 years. The U.S. had three battleships approaching over-age. *Arkansas* (BB-34) at 22,000 tons would be over-age in 1938. *New York* (BB-34) and *Texas (BB-35),* 27,000 tons would be over-age in 1940. Their 76,000 tons would be available for replacement construction in 1937. Since battleships were limited to 35,000 tons by treaties, and Vinson-Trammel spoke in terms of treaty limits, there would be tonnage for two new ships. *North Carolina* (BB-55) and *Washington* (BB-56), two 35,000 tonners with nine 16-in. guns were laid down in Brooklyn (1937) and Philadelphia (1938) Navy Yards respectively. They were part of Vinson-Trammel although not mentioned specifically.

The Act was an outgrowth of the President's desire to get the economy going again. When he allotted $238 million to naval construction in 1933 from PWA funds, he was doing two things. First, he was getting the shipyards back to work and spurring the economy. Second he was starting a sustained program to bring the Navy up to treaty strength. The following year, F.D.R. commented on naval construction on the occasion of his signing the "Vinson Navy Bill," "... the Bill is solely a statement by the Congress that it approves the building of our Navy up to and not beyond the strength in various types of ships authorized [by the treaties]..."

Events throughout the world changed the international situation. The "First Vinson Act" (Vinson-Trammel) set the principle; subsequent Vinson Acts would provide a "Two-Ocean Navy" second-to-none.

Chapter XV

Life in The Treaty Navy

It's time to speak of other parts of The Treaty Navy. Up to now, with a few digressions to personalities and events, the emphasis has been on ships. It has been said that a Navy, and therefore sea power, is made up of three things – men, ships and bases. Of these the most important are men, ships and bases. A look at the men of the Navy of the '20s and '30s and how they shaped the new concept of advanced bases for the war across the Pacific in the '40s will put The Treaty Navy in perspective.

While construction programs were supplying new under-age ships to the Fleet, little was being done to provide more men and officers to man them. Public works programs and deficit sending might build ships but did not produce money to pay more men. Appropriations limited the number of men serving. It also impacted on their advancement. A man was expected to do the job of his rating several ranks higher than the "Crow" he wore on his arm. It was an exception if a man made petty officer third class in less than two "hitches" of four years each. Chief petty officers were real old-timers with four or five "hashmarks." (Diagonal stripes on the lower sleeve for each four-year enlistment.)

The lowest ranking enlisted man was Seaman Apprentice. He wore a single strip around the cuff of his dress jumper. This was his rank while undergoing recruit ("boot") training. On graduation from "Boot Camp" a sailor added another stripe around his cuff and was automatically a Seaman, 2nd Class (S2/c). Those two ranks corresponded in pay to Private and Private First Class in the Marines or Army. The road to the latter rank in the Army and Corps was not as quick as in the Navy but all soldiers and Marines went from $21 to $30 a month upon finishing "Basic" or "Boot Camp." A sailor began "striking" for a specialty usually before making S1/c but usually wasn't accepted as a "striker" until he had been first class for some time. Promotion to 1/c required time in grade, an examination and a vacancy in the ship or aircraft squadron organization. (The discussion *infra* on ship's complements, manning level, etc. will show that vacancies were ever present.) All sailors wore a watch stripe around the shoulder of their jumper. Those of the fireman (engine room) branch wore a red stripe on the left shoulder of their white and blue jumpers. (Fireman 3/c received the pay of Seaman 2/c; Fireman 2/c received the pay of Seaman 1/c; and Fireman 1/c received the pay of P.O. 3/c.) Others, even those in a special branch wore the watch stripe around their right shoulder signifying the seaman branch. It was white on the blue jumper and blue on the white jumper. Petty officers, of course, did not wear a watch stripe. Their branch was depicted on which sleeve (above the elbow) they wore their "crow."

In the Navy of the '30s, there were seven "right arm" rates. They were Boatswain's Mate, Turret Captain (1/c and Chief only), Gunner's Mate,

Torpedoman's Mate, Quartermaster, Signalman and Firecontrolman. There was no Boatswain's Mate 3/c since he was a Coxswain.

There were five other branches. All were "left arm" rates. The artificer branch broke into sub-branches of an engine room force with Machinist's Mate, Water Tender or Boilermaker and Metalsmith or Molder and the other artificers of Electrician's Mate, Radioman, Carpenter's Mate, Shipfitter, Patternmaker, Printer and Painter. Some, e.g., Carpenter's Mate, Patternmaker and Painter, wore the same device below the eagle and above the inverted chevrons of their "crow" and the only way to determine their rating was by their personnel records. The commissary branch had two rates: Commissary Steward and Ship's Cook/Baker. The steward's branch did not wear inverted chevrons to indicate rank. Horizontal white bars of one for 3/c to four for chief were designations of pay grade. The emerging aviation branch had eight rates. One was restricted to Chief and First Class Petty Officers and required completion of flight training. It was Aviation Pilot (AP). Like commissioned officers similarly qualified they wore "Wings of Gold" on their left breast. Some enlisted earned their wings but retained their 2/c rating until advanced to 1/c. The other aviation ratings were: Aviation Machinist's Mate, Aviation Radioman Aviation Metalsmith, Aviation Ordnanceman, Aerographer's Mate and Photographer's Mate. For some time those with those rates with similar surface designations did not wear a special winged version of the specialty, e.g., aviation radioman.

The final branch was the special branch of Yeoman [clerk], Storekeeper, Bandmaster and Musician, and Pharmacist's Mate and Hospital Apprentice. The last were non-rated members of the Hospital Corps who wore a red cross in their left sleeve in lieu of a watch stripe.

Petty Officer ranks were Petty Officer 3/c, Petty Officer 2/c, Petty Officer 1/c and Chief Petty Officer. They were not referred to as "Petty Officer" but rather by their rank and rating, e.g., "Gunner's Mate 2/c" or "Boatswain's Mate Chief."

Promotions were slow. Many of the artificer rates required successful completion of a technical school. There was keen competition for attendance. Chief and Petty Officers 1/c were eligible for promotion to Warrant Officer (WO1) and within the Warrant ranks to Chief Warrant Officer (CWO-2 through CWO-4). It was again slow with time in grade determining selection eligibility. Also, some Warrants could advance to Limited Duty Officer (LDO) in their specialty.

Warrant specialties were: Boatswain, Gunner, Torpedoman, Electrician, Radio Electrician, Machinist, Carpenter, Ship's Clerk, Aerographer, Photographer, Pharmacist and Acting Pay Clerk.

Chief Warrant Officers ranked with but after ensigns. The rank of Midshipman came before Warrant Officers. (Cadets at West Point were not in the Army so they held no rank equivalent to their contemporaries at the Naval Academy.) When the rank of Naval Aviation Cadet (NavCad) was created in the mid'30s (see Chapter XVI on Naval Aviation) they ranked between Warrant Officer and Chief Petty Officer. The Army Air Corps put their aviation cadets in the same slot.

The officer ranks were Ensign, Lieutenant (junior grade), Lieutenant, Lieutenant Commander, Commander, Captain, Rear Admiral (lower half), Rear Admiral, Vice Admiral and Admiral. Rear Admirals of the lower half ranked with and drew the pay of an Army or Marine Corps brigadier general while upper half drew the pay of the other services two stars. Both upper and lower half wore two stars, however. Promotion to "jay gee" was about automatic after three years but from then on examinations on professional subjects equivalent to the grade to which an office was aspiring applied. Promotion above lieutenant commander was by selection of "best fitted." The last selection was to lower half rear admiral. To upper half was by seniority as vacancies occurred. This was the highest rank permanently held. Above it was temporary and went with the billet to which an officer was assigned. That was "designated" rank. Upon serving in such a billet and not being reappointed to an equivalent or higher billet, a flag officer was expected to revert to rear admiral if he was not yet eligible for retirement. As the following pay tables (after restoration of the pay cut) indicate, such was not a financial hardship.

Annual Pay (See appendix 6 for Pay Schedules): Adm. - $8,000, VAdm. - $8,000, RAdm. (Upper) - $8,000, Adm. (Lower) - $6,000, Capt. - $5,600, Cdr. - $4,500, LCdr. - $3,000, Lt. $2,400, Lt. (j.g.) - $2,000, Ens. - $1,500. Base pay increased approximately five percent for each three years of service ("fogey'). The above lists the lowest pay an officer might expect to receive when normally promoted to that grade. At 26 years a captain would make $5,600 but for over 30 years - $6,000. Likewise a commander would make $4,550 at 20 years and $4,900 at 24 years. Sea and foreign duty pay was an additional ten percent. All officers received a subsistence allowance of $18.25 per month to defer their mess bill on board ship. Married officers with dependent(s) received an increased subsistence and a rental allowance (now Basic Allowance for Quarters BAQ) in order to provide quarters for their families ashore. This varied from $40 a month for ensigns through $60 a month for lieutenant commanders and for a flag officer of the lower half - $85.50 a month. For upper half rear admirals the rental allowance was $105 per month. Flag officers in designated three- or four-star billets received an annual "Personal Cash Allowance." On this they were expected to discharge their official entertaining at home and abroad. Their aides got $15 a month extra. Officers qualified for flying or submarines, while serving in flying or submarine assignments, received an additional 50 percent of base pay for the hazards involved in such duties. (Submarine pay was initially 25 percent.)

Female nurses pay was based on years of service. They entered at $70 a month and three years later it was increased to $90 dollars a month. After 10 years they got $130 a month. Chief nurses and other supervisors got additional pay.

As noted, the number of officers was tied to the number of enlisted. The latter was a function of annual appropriations. Every year, just before the Naval Academy graduation, the Navy had to go to Congress for a one-month authority to be in excess of the number of officers allowed. This let ensigns be commissioned before vacancies were created by retirements at the end of the FY on Jun. 30.

After the nadir of "The Biggest Little Class" of 1928, with 173 graduates, restoration of funds for authorized appointments by members of Congress provided fairly steady but increasing numbers of Naval Academy graduates (with some aberrations) to the fleet each year. These were: 1929-240, 1930 – 402, 1931 – 441, 1932 – 421, 1933 – 432 (the infamous split Class), 1934 – 464, 1935 – 442, 1936 – 261, 1937 – 323, 1938 – 438, 1939 – 581, 1940 – 456 and 1941 – 399. That last Class was graduated in February *vice* June to fill billets in the expanding "Two Ocean Navy."

Lieutenants languished in grade for years. Lieutenant Commanders were approaching their mid-40s before being eligible for Commander. In many a wardroom, the rank structure of the Navy was referred to as, "Old fuds, young studs and lieutenant commanders!" It was descriptive.

Since 1921, the Battle Fleet had been stationed on the West Coast with a smaller segment, the Scouting Fleet being on the East Coast. The latter was the older battleships that were incompatible with the faster and heavier-armed newer ships in the battleline. The heavy cruisers were the Scouting Force and part of the Scouting Fleet on the East Coast. A suitable number of the numerous World War I vintage destroyers gave a semblance of balance to the East Coast Force. There was also a modicum of submarines (See Appendix 3 for Fleet organizations of 1923, 1935 and 1940.)

The seven East Coast Navy Yards were at Portsmouth, N.H., Boston, Mass., New York [Brooklyn], N.Y., Philadelphia, Penna., Washington, D.C., Norfolk, Va., and Charleston, S.C. There ships could be docked for repairs and overhaul. There were Naval Operating Bases (NOB) at Hampton Roads, Va., Key West, Fla., and New Orleans. Over the years the status of some varied. New London, Conn., was a Submarine Base and home of submarine training and several boats. Likewise, Newport, R.I., as a Naval Station (NS) was a "Navy town" with ships operating in the vicinity during the summer. It also had a Naval Training Station (NTS) or "boot camp." At NS Guantanamo Bay, Cuba, (GTMO spoken "Git Moe") there were facilities for anchoring the fleet during annual winter maneuvers when the Battle Force transited the Panama Canal. GTMO had recreational facilities for the fleet but the sailors loved going outside the fence to Guantanamo City or Caiamanera for their fleshpots and potent Cuban beer, *Hatuey*. Its label had a frowning profile of Chief Hatuey, a Carib Indian. Sailor legend said that when the "chief" turned and smiled at you with both eyes showing, you had had enough. The "one-eyed Indian" is a casualty of the Castro fence at GTMO, but it still is brewed to the Bacardi formula in Baltimore. While Pensacola on the Gulf had once been a busy base, by the '30s it was a Naval Air Station (NAS) the home of aviation training. It was known as "The Mother-in-Law of Naval Aviation" because of the number of local belles who married student aviators.

The lower part of the Caribbean was secured by the Panama Canal Zone (C.Z.) It was an Army enclave like the Philippines but the Navy based submarines and patrol planes on the NOB.

The West Coast originally had three Navy Yards plus NOBs that were really almost open roadsteads. The yards were at Puget Sound [Bremerton], Wash., and

117

Mare Island, Calif. up the bay from San Francisco. The one at Astoria, Ore., was inoperative after 1922. San Diego was a well-developed naval base with facilities for docking destroyers and submarines. Larger ships could be neither accommodated nor docked there. The big ships went to Puget Sound for docking. Destroyers and submarines of the U.S. Fleet were based in San Diego and operated from there, either in fleet or smaller maneuvers. Battleships and carriers were based on the ports of San Pedro and Long Beach of the Los Angeles Harbor. Operational conditions there were almost ideal with good weather 60 to 70 percent of the time. A breakwater at San Pedro offered protection from the outer sea. Since Los Angeles was one of the largest oil ports, savings in oil transportation costs was a determining factor in maintaining a fleet with a modest budget.

Beside bases for the ships there were also Naval Training Stations (NTS) and Naval Air Stations (NAS) in the continental limits. The latter will be described later when aviation is discussed. The "Boot Camps" were at Newport, R.I., Norfolk, Va., San Diego, Calif. and Great Lakes, Ill. The last was an admitted concession that the fleet drew many of its men from the mid-west grain belt. Lads who had never seen the ocean joined to see the world. The active status of these NTS varied over the years during the '20s and '30s.

In addition to GTMO and Coco Solo, C.Z., there were other off shore bases. Pearl Harbor, T.H., was the largest and had escaped the Washington Treaty ban on fortifications. It was not fully developed, however, and could not sustain the U.S. Fleet for any length of time. While it had dry docks, it lacked warehouses and required the importation of fuel, although the tank farm of the Tea Pot Dome scandal had now been accepted by the Navy. (See Chapter VI.) Guam was a bare bones base and nothing except a few harbor craft and an occasional seaplane tender and brood lived there. Likewise, Kiska and Dutch Harbor in Alaska were undeveloped. Subig [sic] Bay and Cavite around Manila in the Philippines were home to destroyers and submarines of the Asiatic Fleet but except for the world's largest floating dry dock (not permanent hence not a Treaty violation) the capability was meager.

The Asiatic Fleet comprised a cruiser as flagship and squadrons of four-piper destroyers and older submarines. Its commander wore four stars, however. Prestige in the Orient required it. The river gunboats of the Yangtze Patrol were based in China with occasional cruises to Manila.

Fleet routine revolved around the activities of the Battle Fleet in San Pedro. Although, most flag officers and commanding officers preferred operating four weeks at sea and returning to port for a week of upkeep, several things militated against that ideal. Underway, ships burned fuel and fuel was expensive. At anchor, they burned some fuel to keep auxiliary power going but considerably less than when at sea. To the chagrin of many flag officers and commanding officers who usually had 18 months to two years in command, operations devolved into going to sea on Monday and returning to port on Friday. Most senior officers, who had remained unmarried until they were Commanders in their early 40s, felt that the weekend in port had an adverse effect on the attitude of junior officers and the enlisted men. A tendency to view the navy as a "job" with a family life similar to civilians wasn't in keeping with the required professional dedication of a naval officer.

The annual schedule hardly varied. In the winter after Christmas, the big ships and their escorts would conduct the Fleet Problem (See Appendix 5 for a synopsis of Fleet Problems I through XXI). These usually entailed defense of the Canal before the ships transited for operations with the Scouting Fleet in the Caribbean. Often, particularly after F.D.R. and Vinson became the big advocates of the Navy, the battleships from the West Coast would proceed north along the East Coast to New York. There, the battleships, carriers and cruisers would anchor in the Hudson River and hold open house for visitors during the day. At night, searchlights would play on the clouds giving the city's citizens an awesome show. The ships would then head back for San Pedro and San Diego for a short stay in homeports. The summer meant a cruise north to Puget Sound for docking. After all the ships had had their required overhaul and refit, it was south to San Francisco for Fleet Week. En route drills at sea were conducted. Thence to home ports.

At least once a year, when the ships were on the East Coast, F.D.R. would visit and observe. He had a fondness for deep-sea fishing and obliging naval commanders would arrange such diversion in ship's boats. He preferred the new cruisers instead of the battleships. *Houston, Augusta* and *Tuscaloosa* were favorites of the President in the '30s. Because of his disability which kept him to a wheelchair (a fact discreetly avoided by news photographers) special arrangements and temporary modifications were made to the ships. Carpenters rigged ramps over the combings of vertical hatchways to allow the President access to his cabin. He usually chose a ship that was fitted with flag accommodation to take his entourage. Although the Navy was officially dry since the infamous edict of SecNav Daniels in 1914, F.D.R. made a special dispensation for himself and his guests before dinner. He liked Scotch or a dry martini.

But there were also libations without dispensations. A wooden match handed to a messmate in the Wardroom at lunch signified, "Drop by my cabin for a drink before dinner." The recipient acknowledged the arcane code and accepted the invitation by breaking the match in two. But Officers' Country was not the only place on a ship that was wet. Something could always be found in the Chief's Mess. One enterprising First Sergeant of a Marine Detachment had a regulation foot locker (issued to the top pay grades) modified by air holes in part of the bottom, thin skids on the bottom to keep it slightly off the deck for circulation, a compressor in one compartment and the remainder insulated. An electrical cord came out of the bottom and plugged into a shipboard receptacle. The improvised refrigerator held a case and a half of beer. Still, a descriptive cartoon of the era showed a sailor watching a craftsman putting miniature ships in bottles. The sailor remarks, "That's nothing. Ever try getting a bottle into a ship? "

The Public Works ploy of the Administration wasn't limited to just ships. There were requirements for public quarters for officers at various shore bases, mostly on the East Coast. There had always been sumptuous quarters for senior officers at most Navy Yards and bases but there was a dearth of adequate quarters on base

119

for the more junior officers. A basic design was drawn up for four-story apartments with two apartments per floor. There were six apartments since the top floor or attic contained a storage room for each apartment with a maid's room for each plus two common baths for the maids. There were six one-car garages in the basement. They were built in clusters in such places as Philadelphia, Norfolk, Marine Base at Quantico, Pensacola and Annapolis. The last was to accommodate junior officers attending the Naval Postgraduate School then on the grounds of the Naval Academy. An interesting debate occurred in the Congressional hearing on them. Absentee landlords who rented small apartments above their garages (formally coach houses) in Annapolis protested that providing government quarters for junior officers attending the PG school would deprive them of potential renters and thus revenues. Many of the most vocal protesters were retired or active duty officers of the Medical and Dental Corps. It would seem that the "Band of Brothers" concept wasn't all that universal. Of course, such staff at the time were not really commissioned officers. They served "with the rank of," rather than as commissioned officers of the Line.

Since no government quarters in any sizeable numbers were provided for the West Coast, one wonders whether the real estate interests and income property owners there were more successful in lobbying against quarters construction in California.

There was a shortage of suitable housing in the San Pedro-Long Beach area. This worsened when the Scouting Force cruisers were transferred there. Long Beach was preferred by Navy families. San Pedro, though the site of the fleet landings, had drawbacks which drove families elsewhere. San Pedro had a host of bars (speakeasies before Repeal), gyp joints, pawnshops and other "sailor joints" in super abundance. A common expression of the time defined the situation. "Long Beach by the sea, San Pedro by the smell." The latter was also home to a fishing fleet.

Most Navy families opted for rentals in and around Long Beach. Landlords fixed rents at the rate of the officer's housing allowance But as more arrived, rents crept up and Navy authorities hinted at moving parts of the fleet elsewhere if the practice continued. Hardship was greatest on senior enlisted who were married. Few, but some, junior officers were married.

Point Fermin, in San Pedro and close to the Officers' Landing at Cabrillo Beach, did develop an "exclusive" rental area with restrictions not allowing tenancy by anyone under Commander. When Capt. E.J. King commanded *Lexington,* he preferred to live in the exclusive Bixby Park section of Long Beach. He would come ashore in his gig on Saturday afternoon after Captain's Inspection. The gig's crew had drawn their liberty cards (a requirement for shore leave and a pawn to discipline) and on non-payday weeks he would give the coxswain a five-dollar bill "for the gig crew's dinner" with instructions to be ready to pick him up at 5 a.m. on Monday morning. The gig was secured at the landing and the $5 went a long way for a weekend liberty of the crew of four. The stern King was probably not the only captain who looked after his crew in such a manner.

The Manchurian Crisis of 1931, as noted, caused the fleet to tarry in the vicinity of Pearl Harbor after conducting war games there. The heavy cruisers of he Scouting Force temporarily remained on the West Coast at San Pedro. They subsequently returned to the East Coast.

In the fall of 1934, the new administration decided to move the Scouting Force permanently to the West Coast basing it with the battleships and carriers at San Pedro. Crowded conditions in the roadstead and the impact of the shortage of family rental units were severe.

Two incidents of that move are reflective of the situation at the time.

LCdr Jerauld Wright was the 36-year-old Gunnery Officer of *Salt Lake City* .He had been graduated with the Class of 1918 in June 1917 after war was declared. He was a bachelor and drove north to Washington, D.C., from Norfolk the weekend before the ships were to sail for the West Coast. Enjoying himself on a last fling in D.C., he failed to allow time for emergencies on the drive back to Norfolk over the less than adequate roads of the '30s. His open-top touring car ran off the road and into a ditch. He had no time to have it towed so he crawled out and hailed a passing bus. He was pier-side in Norfolk in time to see *Salt Lake City* getting underway from her anchorage. Talking the officer of the beach guard into letting him have a boat from another ship, he chased down *Salt Lake City* before she cleared the harbor and boarded her. He thus avoided a general court martial for missing ship.

Later after "Jerry" Wright retired with the four stars of Commander-in-Chief, Atlantic and Supreme Allied Commander, Atlantic, he offered a case of bourbon to the unknown officer who had saved his career. One wonders what ever happened to the touring car in the ditch?

When the ships sailed they carried the married officers leaving the wives to get the families to San Pedro. The gallant gals packed up and loaded the kids in the car to head west. Cross-country driving was an adventure in 1934 but the ladies were prepared for it. Since they all were taking the same route they devised a method of watching out for each other. A blue ribbon tied to the rear bumper signaled that the car was driven by a Navy wife. If one broke down on the way she didn't have to wait long before another Navy wife came along and recognizing the blue ribbon stopped to help. The Navy families were united in San Pedro when the ships arrived. By then the resourceful (they had to be!) ladies had rented a place and set up housekeeping.

A popular public image of "sailors" was that they were fun loving, irresponsible, drinking and carousing. This image was enhanced by Hollywood and abetted by a holier-than-thou section of Americans. Sailors were seldom welcome in the "best" homes of society. Hence, they were driven by default into some of the sleazy dives and into the hands of money-grasping sharpies, both male and female. There were sailor legends about every port where they tied up of signs saying, "Dogs and sailors keep off the grass!" Sailors didn't even get top billing. When the sailors and their payroll of the Scouting Force left Norfolk, those who instigated such an attitude had inward misgivings, albeit, not from any moral regrets. The money had moved west not to return!

But something else had moved west with the sailors. In the early '20s, initiated by the crews of *New York* and *Texas,* an annual Christmas party for orphans was held on board. With the chaplains handling the invitations but the crew making the arrangements, hundreds of children every year came aboard for a full Christmas dinner under the attendance of a sentimental sailor host, who knew what it was like to be away at Christmas. The kids left with both a full belly and a Christmas present he or she would not have had except for the Navy. The tradition accompanied the ships to the West Coast. There are many Californians, now in their 60s with fond memories of the Bluejackets who made Christmas more pleasant for kids during the Depression.

A final word on ships' manning. The entire crew needed for war was the ship's complement. It was an ideal only achieved in war. Next was the allowance. It was the level of crew that was considered as a peacetime allocation. The last was the manning level. It was a smaller number than either of the first two. It was often the minimum for the ship to get underway and operate at sea for a short time. At the time some ships were even below their manning level. The only ships kept at full allowance were submarines.

Since manning levels were always below allowances and complements, vacancies existed for promotions. Vacancies were a function of complement not manning level. But vacancies were just part of the promotion equation. Other factors entered in – total service, time in rank, conduct and proficiency marks all were assigned a multiplier before being added up to get a total score. The multipliers could be manipulated every promotion period by the BuNav personnel planners. Thus, promotions were kept within the limits of payroll appropriations. It is no wonder that "Ernie" King referred to the personnel guys as "the fixers."

An added complication to manning the ships of the Navy was the growing role of Naval Aviation. Aviation competed for officers and men from the same pool funded by Congress for the rest of the Navy.

Chapter XVI

Aviation and Aviators

Naval Aviation officially began when Lt. T.G. "Spud" Ellyson became Naval Aviator No. 1 after being taught to fly by aviation pioneer, Glenn Hammond Curtiss. Like his Classmate, Chester Nimitz, Spud Ellyson had gone to surface ships after graduation in 1905 and then to submarines. But when the call came for volunteers for aviation, it was Spud who answered. He had been working with Curtiss at North Island in San Diego. During their association, another civilian aviation pioneer had successfully flown off a flight deck rigged on the cruiser *Birmingham* (CS-2) in November 1910. Two months later he did the reverse. Eugene Ely successfully landed on a wooden platform 130 feet long and 30 feet wide rigged on the stern of armored cruiser, *Pennsylvania* (CA-4). This was in San Francisco Bay. These three events marked the start of Naval Aviation.

Naval Aviation during and immediately after World War I has been noted. The RN, however, was the first to have carriers to land planes, although the Germans utilized seaplane carriers early in the war. The world's first true aircraft carrier *was HMS Argus,* laid down in 1914 as a liner for Italy but purchased by the Admiralty. Her conversion began in 1916 and she was launched in December 1916. *HMS Furious,* a light battlecruiser converted to a seaplane carrier was converted into a true carrier after the experience with *Argus.* Both ships were flush-decked without an island structure, the last in the RN. In 1917, the RN took over the hull of a suspended Chilean battleship being built in a British yard. She was renamed *Eagle* in February 1918. A month before, the keel had been laid for the world's first carrier designed from the keel up. She was *Hermes.*

Thus, by the time the U.S. got around to her own carrier in 1919, the Brits had four in the water. The RN was to fall behind in carrier tactics and operations because of the afore-cited dominance of the Air Ministry and RAF. No such organizational encumbrances hindered the development of U.S. Naval Aviation. Its only hindrance was internal. RAdm. Moffett, ChBuAer, was fascinated with the potential of rigid lighter-than-airships. Their great flight endurance and even ability to carry heavier-than-air fighters and scouts he felt more than offset their fragility in turbulent weather. It took three fatal crashes and the life of Bill Moffett to finally drop the rigid-lighter-than-air programs but not until the advent of the Vinson Navy.

Our first carrier was *Langley* (CV-1) named after another aviation pioneer, Samuel Langley. She began life in 1912 as the fleet collier *Jupiter* (AC-3). Her collier configuration lent itself to conversion. Her turbo-electric drive was aft leaving four bunkers amidships for fitting out as pseudo-hangar space for 33 flight-ready aircraft or 55 dismantled ones Two cranes hoisted and lowered aircraft to the flight deck. That deck was flush from bow to stern, laid over the hull and supported by steel girders high above the waterline. Her silhouette earned her the nickname, "The Covered Wagon." The flight deck was 533 ft. 9 in. long and 63 ft. 11 in. wide. An elevator was amidships in the deck. In 1923, she carried VF-1 with TS-1 aircraft, single-place biplanes made by the Naval Aircraft Factory. *Langley* was the test bed for Navy carrier operations but primarily the training platform to qualify carrier pilots. Many of the carrier skippers during World War II were alumni of trial and error take offs and landings in *Langley* in the '20s. At least those who survived the errors were.

Although *Langley* added two more squadrons, usually having two fighter and one other on board varying from scouting to torpedo, she was never able to be the experimental platform for sophisticated deck handling of aircraft or tactical carrier operations. Those awaited the arrival of the big carriers, *Lexington* and *Saratoga.*

Both carriers were begat by the Washington Treaty. They were rated at 33,000 tons plus the allowed 3,000 tons for torpedo blisters and deck armor. They carried eight 8-in. guns in four turrets fore and aft of the starboard side island. A dozen 5-in. dual-purpose guns were along the gallery deck on each side both fore and aft just below the flight deck. Both ships had a distinct profile. A pronounced clipper bow led aft to the island structure. Abaft the foremast and coning tower was a tall, elongated structure housing the four consolidated funnels fitted to the uptakes of the 16 boilers. To distinguish these identical twins, the funnel structure of *Lexington* had a black band around its top. That of *Saratoga* had a broad vertical stripe down its middle. Returning plots looked down at the 888-foot long, 106-foot wide flight deck as more than ample after *Langley.* **LEX** and **SARA** in big letters at each end of the flight deck told a pilot which ship was his.

While each could carry up to 90 of the aircraft of the early '30s, many of them except the planes of the embarked squadrons were kept in a semi-assembled status suspended above the hangar deck. Four squadrons of 18 aircraft each was the usual Air Group. Initially, they carried a fighter squadron, two bomber squadrons and a torpedo bomber squadron. Extra utility aircraft were also on board.

The fighters were FB-5s, a Boeing biplane with an in-line liquid-cooled engine and fixed landing gear. There was a mix of bombers which were really fighters adapted to the bombing mission. The Navy was taking lessons in dive-bombing from their brother Naval Aviators in the Marines. One bombing squadron had F6Cs, a Curtiss-built biplane with a liquid-cooled engine and fixed landing gear. The other squadron had a mix of F3B and F4B, Boeing biplanes with fixed landing gear and an air-cooled radial engine developing more horsepower per pound of engine. The torpedo bomber was the relatively huge, three-place Martin biplane the T3M.

Until the introduction of the TBD circa 1935, all carrier aircraft were biplanes. The greater wing area gave them a slower stalling speed, a vital characteristic for carrier landings. All carrier planes were equipped with inflation devices to keep them afloat in the event of ditching at sea. To assist in spotting a plane down at sea, the top of the upper wing was painted bright yellow. Aircraft retrieved from the sea required extensive overhaul and rework but that was cheaper than buying a new one or getting it authorized from Congress.

By the mid-'30s the aircraft that had followed the Morrow Board Report were beginning to enter the fleet. The place of Naval Aviation as an element of the fleet had been assured by the Pratt-MacArthur agreement of Jan. 9, 1931. CNO and the Army Chief of Staff ended the inter-service rivalry over the responsibility for air in the services. Competitive bidding on contracts for development of designs meeting Navy needs were bringing out the best in aircraft manufacturers. Companies vied for continuing Navy orders. Certain firms were coming to the fore for particular types. Grumman started a dynasty of fighters. Boeing and Curtiss moved into the dive- and scout-bomber field. Vought specialized in observation models with interchangeability between a float for cruiser and battleship use to fixed landing gear for use on carriers or ashore. Carrier requirements of folding wings to facilitate hangar deck storage and elevator compatibility; and retractable landing gear for streamlined performance were met by airplane makers. Naval aircraft differed from those of the Army Air Corps in that carrier and ship-based float planes required sturdier airframes to withstand the shock of an arrested landing on board the carrier or the catapult-shot off a cruiser. As the later McNamara "whiz kids" were to learn there was no commonality between land-based and carrier aircraft. The laws of physics are immutable.

Flying boats or patrol planes became a separate category. Consolidated and Martin built most of these. The latter had a long lead in flying boats and seaplanes but the former's PBY, in several updates, after being first flown in 1935, became the most-produced flying boat of all time. Some are still flying.

The Army Air Corps had a different means of designating their aircraft. Types were numbered consecutively, e.g., the bomber of the mid-'30s was the B-10. It had been preceded by nine other bombers not all of which were production models accepted by the Army. A modification of a standard type added a modification letter after the basic designation. The P6E was the fifth modification of the standard Army "pursuit" biplane of the '20s. That was another Army anomaly. An overly sensitive War Department used euphemisms for words that might be offensive to the pacifist element of the public. Fighters were called pursuit planes giving them a defensive connotation. Likewise, the Army had no tanks. Tracked armored vehicles mounting a gun were called "combat cars."

Although touting itself as "The First Line of Defense" the Navy every place else called a spade a spade. It had aircraft whose mission it was to fight enemy aircraft. It called them fighters. Further, the Navy designation system was unique and utilitarian both operationally and logistically. It thoroughly identified aircraft of the same type, modification series and maker. Thus aircraft with the same performance characteristics, e.g., speed, rate of climb, range, service altitude and armament, could be readily identified for assignment to the same squadron. Likewise a squadron of the same model aircraft kept the maintenance and logistics manageable. Proper spare parts in the right quantities could be stocked. Since space on a carrier was at a premium, this made a lot of sense. The ship carried the spare parts rather than have a squadron bring them when embarked. This was an **innovation** that was to pay dividends in the coming war.

The Navy designation system was just that – a system. It was used from Mar. 19, 1923 until eliminated by the McNamara "whiz kids" in 1962 because in their quest for commonality they couldn't understand why the Air Force and Navy had different designations for the same airplane.

The Navy system basically used four characters, i.e., letter or number, to define a particular aircraft. Two additional letters either before or after the four-character designator further defined a function. A prefix before the designator, e.g., **X** indicated that the aircraft was in experimental status. A suffix at the end indicated a special purpose, e.g., **A** for the amphibious version of a flying boat.

The four characters were: a letter to indicate the type, e.g., fighter (F), bomber (B), scout (S), torpedo-bomber (T), patrol (P) or a combination like scout-bomber (SB). Next was the manufacturers sequence number. This was omitted if it was the first of that type made by a particular manufacturer. Then a letter to denote the maker. A specific letter was assigned to a manufacturer but in some cases there was duplication. The final character was a number showing the aircraft configuration sequence. This was a key in preventing the mixing of apples and oranges with the same colloquial nickname. Many Grumman fighters of its fourth fighter were called "Wildcats" but not all were the same. There being at least seven versions with improved performance and different engines along the way. (A complete list of codes for types, manufacturers and suffixes is in Appendix 7.)

An illustrative example using the Grumman family of fighters that began in 1931 and ran for 40 years in the Navy will explain the system. The first Grumman fighter, ordered in 1931 was initially XFF-1. No manufacturers sequence was used since the second character was understood in an initial version. She was a two-place biplane and the first Navy fighter with retractable landing gear. A scout version of essentially the same aircraft was SF-1. The successful trials of XFF-1 bred a requirement for a single-seat fighter and F2F-1 was born. A larger version with a longer fuselage and greater wingspan emerged as F3F-1. While the F3Fs were the backbone of carrier fighters through most of the '30s, Grumman was working on a low-wing monoplane version. It became the F4F-1 and eventually the F4F-4 became the version that was later made under wartime license by General Motors as FM-1.

The Navy wanted a twin-engined shipboard fighter and Grumman came up with the XF5F-1. This oddity was basically a wing with the nacelles of two engines forward while the fuselage extended aft from the middle of the wing. This made the pilot blind to the landing signal officer (LSO) during a carrier landing since the port engine was in the way. The XF5F was never adopted by the Navy but Grumman improved the concept to produce the F7F which through three configurations became the F7F-4N The N denoted a night fighter version. Before then however, experience of the F4Fs against the Japanese *Zero* (Japan had her own unique system of aircraft designation and zero stood for 00, the Japanese year 2000, our 1940, when the *Zero* was introduced) showed the need for a Navy fighter that could stand toe-to-toe with the *Zero*. Grumman came up with the F6F-1 that in six versions to F6F-6 was the standard fighter in the Pacific after 1943. Grumman's relation with the Navy continued through the F11F-1 that succumbed to the new designations as F-11. The latest Grumman fighter is the F-14 "Tomcat" of Libyan Sidra Gulf fame.

Names began to be attached to aircraft models. After the Marine use of the F8C-1 in the dive-bombing innovation in Nicaragua, the Navy squadrons dubbed their versions of the F8C the "Helldiver." Because of their stubby shape the FF-1s, F2Fs and F3Fs were referred to, but never officially as the Flying Barrels. The first Grumman fighter with an official name was the F4F series called the "Wildcat." The ill-starred XF5F was the "Skyrocket" but Grumman reverted to cat names with "Hellcat" (F6F), "Tigercat" (F7F), "Bearcat" (F8F), "Panther" (F9F) and the swept-wing version "Cougar" through "Tiger" (F-11) and "Tomcat" (F-14). Curtiss produced another dive-bomber, the last of the combat biplanes in the fleet and passed the "Helldiver" title to SBC-1.

When Douglas entered the naval combat field after success with civilian airliners, it tried to keep its initial in the names of its airplanes. TBD-1 that reached the fleet in 1937 was the first low-wing monoplane in the Navy carrier fleet. It carried a crew of three and was known as the "Devastator." Douglas came up with a two-seat low-wing monoplane to replace the SBCs. The "Dauntless" was to be the scout- and dive-bombing workhorse of the early days of the war. It was replaced by the larger bomb capacity SB2C that was the third Curtiss to carry the name "Helldiver."

While still in the Navy fighter business, Curtiss (it later went heavily into Army fighters) had a string with bird names: "Hawk" (F6C), "Falcon" (F8C) later "Helldiver" and "Sparrowhawk" (F9C). The last was designed to be carried inside lighter-than-airships to be launched and retrieved on a trapeze that engaged a hook on the lane's upper wing. The last real Curtiss Navy fighter had three versions under the "Goshawk" name (F11C, BFC and BF2c). Curtiss got into the observation type with the SOC "Seagull." She was a large two-seat biplane with either a single float for catapults or an interchangeable fixed landing gear for ashore. She served from 1935 through the early days of the war until replaced by Vought's "Kingfisher" (OS2U).

Vought's earlier observation planes had been "Corsair" (O2U, O3U and SU.) Consolidated's PBY strangely did not receive a name until the RAF bought some for the Fleet Air Arm in 1940. The Brits dubbed he "Catalina" a name that still is used. Another flying boat, built by Martin, was the "Mariner" (PBM).

There were other names around the fleet in the '30s. Mostly they were limited procurement models awarded to start up or maintain a manufacturer's assembly line. Two of the most notorious were Brewster's "Buffalo" (F2A) and Vought's "Vindicator" (SB2U). Both were underpowered, under-protected and under-performing. They became hand-me-downs to the Marines and were sacrificed from Midway in June 1942.

In 1934, the Navy's first designed carrier, *Ranger* (CV-4), joined the fleet. At 14,7000 tons, she displaced about 40 percent of *Lex* or *Sara*. This was not as critical as it would seem when one remembers that the ex-battlecruisers each carried four turrets with two-8-in. guns. With the attendant barbettes and ammunition, these contributed nothing to the mission of a carrier. (These were removed in 1941 and 1942 during over haul.) *Ranger*'s profile looked puny compared to the two older ships. She had a small thin island. There was no dominating structure for the stacks. In fact, the stack arrangements were similar to those used in *Langley*. Folding stacks, three each side aft, protruded several feet above the flight deck. During flight operations, they folded down out of the way. She initially carried 79 aircraft in four squadrons: fighters -F2Fs, two bombers –BGs and BFCs and one scouting – SBUs, plus command and utility planes.

Unlike *Lex* and *Sara, Ranger*'s flight and hangar decks were not integral with the hull. They were built on it as superstructure. This feature was continued in later carriers and is still current today. Two of her elevators, one abeam of the island and one forward of it, facilitated rapid spotting and clearing of the flight deck for launching and recovering aircraft. Lack of internal storage space for torpedoes made the squadron mix ultimately comprise two fighter and two scout-bomber squadrons. Although the first built as a carrier she was to prove relatively unsatisfactory for wartime service. Her lack of speed, only 29.5 knots, was a drawback. She never operated with the fast carrier task force in the Pacific. She took part in the North African landing and worked with the RN Home Fleet off the British Isles and Norway before being relegated to ferrying aircraft and giving pilots their carrier qualification training.

But the lessons learned from *Ranger* were incorporated in the next two (actually three since *Hornet* (CV-8) was a repeat of the class with *Wasp* (CV-7) coming between). *Yorktown* (CV-5) and *Enterprise* (CV-6) were 19,000 tons with a speed of 34 knots. Designed to carry 90 aircraft, they were more efficient with just 80 owing to space limitations. They had three elevators, one well forward, one just aft of the island and the third aft. At 809 feet they were 40 feet longer than *Ranger* but 80 feet shorter than the *Lexington*s. Two of the three catapults were on the hangar deck for rapid launching to either side leaving the flight deck clear for planes launching under their own power. This type of thinking was to lead to the **innovation** of rapid launching and recovery of aircraft and the rapid turn-around between strikes that were to be the hallmark of Navy carrier operations in the Pacific.

Flight deck crews were well drilled and each man thoroughly knew his job and assignment at any particular time. Colored shirts and caps strapped to their heads denoted the assignment of each member of the flight deck crew. Flight deck directors wore yellow. Plane captains, responsible for a particular aircraft, wore brown. Blue marked the handlers, "plane pushers" who were available for any assignment. Ordnance men and fuelers wore red and other colors denoted other specialties. But all worked as a team with one mission – get the planes back in the air as quickly as possible or when ordered. Flight deck spotting was an art achieved by many hours of practice and review. In general, fighters were spotted ahead. They had to be the first off to defend against enemy air and being the lightest required a shorter take off run. Next came the scouts, then the bombers and then the torpedo planes. All had their wing folded for maximum utilization of space. The yellow-shirted plane directors guided the planes forward and signaled when to unfold and lock the wings in place for take off. The pilot stamped down on the brakes; watched the Flight Deck Officer wave his flag to rev the engine. When the flag dropped, the pilot released his brakes and roared down the flight deck into the wind to take off. His airspeed was the vector sum of his aircraft speed in relation to the deck, the speed of the carrier through the water (and air) and the wind speed coming directly from the bow since the carrier had turned into the wind for launch.

Yorktown joined the fleet in the fall of 1937, 16 months after launching. She carried the standard Air group and her four squadrons were: VF-5, VB-5, VS-5 and VT-5. Until the war made rotation and replacements necessary, it was the practice to have the Air Group and Squadron numbers coincide with the hull number of the carrier. When *Enterprise* (CV-6) joined in May 1938, she carried VF-6, VB-6, VS-6 and VT-6.

Similar allocations of squadrons of squadrons were made to *Lexington* (CV-2), *Saratoga* (CV-3) and *Ranger* (CV-4). This was further carried to the point of painting the tails of all aircraft from the same carrier in that ship's "color," From Mar. 15, 1937 the carrier "colors" were: *Lexington* – lemon yellow, *Saratoga* – white, *Ranger* – willow green, *Yorktown* – insignia red, *Enterprise* – true blue. When *Wasp* was commissioned in April 1940, her color was black. Likewise the scouting squadrons of float planes assigned to battleship or cruiser divisions had distinctive tail markings. VSO-8 of Cruiser Division 8 (CruDiv-8), *Philadelphia, Brooklyn, Savannah* and *Nashville* had a double black stripe.

When war came these marking changed and eventually were eliminated. National marking also changed from those of The Treaty Navy as the red circle inside the white star inside the blue circle could be confused with the red "meatball" on Japanese aircraft and vice versa. Before the war, carrier squadrons of 18 planes were divided into six sections of three planes each. Each section had a leader and the leader and the individual planes within that section had cowling colors and positions. (Appendix 7 describes the color schemes and their meanings.)

Wasp was the last carrier ordered under Treaty limits and we have seen how *Langley*'s tonnage was traded to get *Wasp*'s 14,700 tons. Initially, she carried a fighter, a bomber and two scouting squadrons. Later it was two fighter and two scouting squadrons. Her slower speed was not up to working with the other carriers and she started the war with the British Home Fleet. She took Army P-40s to Iceland and later transported much-needed RAF fighters to Malta in early 1942. After *Yorktown* was lost at Midway in June 1942, *Wasp* went to the Pacific. She was lost near Guadalcanal to a submarine on Sept. 15, 1942 while she was covering a convoy of reinforcements for that island. Her squadron mix was one fighter, one torpedo and two scouting squadrons.

During the '20s nadir of naval construction, a proposal was made for lighter-than-air rigid airships. Congress authorized two on Jun. 24, 1926. But it was not until 1928 that contracts for what would become *USS Akron* and *USS Macon* were let to the Goodyear-Zeppelin Corp. *Akron* was christened on Aug. 8, 1931 and flew on Sept. 25, 1931. She commissioned a month later. Her homeport was NAS Lakehurst, N.J., which was the home of Navy lighter-than-air. (It was also the port for the German dirigible *Hindenburg* during its short-lived Atlantic crossings.) *Macon* was christened on Mar. 11, 1933 and flew on Apr. 21. Nine days later, *Akron* went down in bad weather off the New Jersey coast. One of her dead was RAdm. Moffett, the most senior advocate of lighter-than-air. The loss of both airships is covered in Chapter XVII.

Many tend to think of lighter-than-air in the terms of the Goodyear Blimp that appears on TV at major sports events. That is just a big gas bag with a control gondola suspended underneath for its crew and exterior engines. Dirigibles were not mere gas bags. They were huge cigar-shaped structures of lightweight interior girders covered by outer fabric. The buoyancy in the atmosphere was accomplished by the same principle wherein steel ships float in water – they displace a greater weight of fluid than they weigh. In rigid airships this was accomplished by interior gas bags filled with a lighter gas (hydrogen in foreign airships and helium in U.S.) that is less than the volume of atmosphere inside the airship. Yet, like a sea going ship, there is still atmosphere inside the airship for life support, storage and living spaces. In *Akron* and *Macon* there was even space for four aircraft.

The airships were 785 feet long and had a maximum diameter of almost 133 feet. By comparison, *Lexington* was 888 feet long with a beam of 105+ feet. They carried four F9C-s. These single-seat biplanes had fixed landing gear (able to be removed to reduce drag) and had a bracket with a hook attached to the top wing. The "hangar" was about a third of the way aft from the bow. A boom able to swivel from the horizontal inside to the vertical formed a trapeze to swing the aircraft from the inside to a suspended position beneath the airship. When the pilot who had swung down in the aircraft had his engine revved up, he released the hook; dropped a few feet and flew clear. Retrieval was more delicate since the pilot had to approach the hook; match his speed to that of the airship and then engage the hook before killing his engine. (This is now *de rigueur* with in-flight refueling except for killing the engine.) With the aircraft now hanging from the hook, the boom-trapeze was retracted into the airship. The recovered airplane was then attached to a trolley that moved it to its storage position inside the airship. The boom-trapeze was mounted along the longitudinal axis of the airship. The trolleys ran at 45-degree angles to the longitudinal.

In addition to NAS Lakehurst, a new lighter-than-air base was constructed at Sunnyvale, Calif., south of San Francisco. During debates on its authorization, one of the concerns of Congress was that it was not sufficiently inland to be beyond the range of enemy battleships. The insular mentality still pervaded.

When *Akron* went down of New Jersey, NAS Sunnyvale was renamed Moffett Field.

Shore Naval Air Stations were a necessity for The Treaty Navy. Not only were patrol planes based ashore but when the carriers were in port, their air squadrons went ashore. There they were able to operate and get in flying hours while the carrier swung on the hook.

The major air stations at this time were: NAS, Norfolk, NAS, Jacksonville, NAS, Pensacola on the East and Gulf Coasts. On the West Coast there were: NAS, North Island (on Coronado outside San Diego), and NAS, Sand Island, near Seattle. There were numerous smaller air stations and air facilities near major coastal cities for Naval Reserve squadron training. These were to increase in importance as war came closer. The offshore air stations at Coco Solo, C.Z, and Ford Island, T.H., have already been noted.

One **innovation** where the Navy came up short was in the concept of torpedo bombing. RAdm. Bradley Fiske, in the pre-World War I era claimed to have "invented" the aerial torpedo. As a self-propelled projectile through the water, a torpedo had to be launched from a tube; run a distance before it armed itself and then "steer" toward the target according to a course set into it prior to launching. The mechanism inside a torpedo was fragile and dropping from an aircraft even from a low altitude could damage the mechanism and even allow the torpedo to sink to the bottom and not run to the target. Fiske's torpedo overcame these drawbacks and the "steering" was done by pointing the launching aircraft at the target and then dropping the torpedo into the water to run to the target. The closer the torpedo was dropped to the target the shorter the run and the less chance for the target to evade. Even evasion could be a minor victory if it meant that the enemy battleline turned away as Jellicoe did from the German destroyers at Jutland.

Thus. American torpedo plane doctrine consisted of a line abreast of torpedo planes coming at a line of enemy ships on a perpendicular course. To enable the torpedo planes to get close to launch, scouting aircraft were rigged with chemical smoke canisters to generate a screen of white smoke parallel to the enemy battleline with the torpedo planes emerging from the smoke to launch. Because the chemical smoke was corrosive and because torpedoes were expensive and some of them subject to loss or damage, little actual practice was done with real smoke or live practice torpedoes. The result was poor torpedo plane performance by Naval Aviation during the war.

The Japanese, however, not only practiced but perfected their torpedo plane skills. Their doctrine was to attack not perpendicular to a target's course but to come at it from the starboard and port bows. Any turn of the target would come into the path of a torpedo. *Lexington* and *Chicago* were to be among the victims of these torpedo tactics.

As more aircraft were authorized and procured, there was a shortage of pilots to fly them. The Naval Academy Classes were providing officers for the new ships and for the planes. About 400 per year hardly filled all the needs. The program for Naval Aviation Pilots (APs), petty officers designated as Naval

Aviators was expanded to include 2/c petty officers. Many retained their regular rates, e.g., Aviation Machinists Mate when they got their wings. (There is a legend that an almost all enlisted squadron, VF-2, albeit with officers commanding and leading sections, had a sailor's white hat as its squadron insignia. Actually, the squadron dubbed itself "The Flying Chiefs" and had CPO chevrons as its squadron insignia, now called "squadron patch." Subsequently, an all officer squadron, VB-2B topped it with a "high hat" as its squadron insignia. Over the years, squadron redesignations eliminated the CPO insignia but unit genealogy has the Top Hat now with VF-14.) But even using APs wasn't enough to man all the new aircraft. Under the Aviation Cadet Act of 1935, qualified men, preferably college graduates between 20 and 28, were recruited for Navy cockpits. After 30 days at a Naval Reserve Air Station for screening they went to Pensacola for a year of flight training. Upon graduation and receiving their wings they served in the fleet for three years as Aviation Cadets. Then they were commissioned Ensigns and went to inactive duty in a Naval Reserve Squadron. Since Aviation Cadets ranked between CWOs and WOs, they weren't commissioned officers and couldn't lead flights. Pay was low and many opted for Army commissions or went with the airlines. The remedy was the Naval Aviation Reserve Act of 1939. Cadets would be Ensigns upon getting their wings. The others got backdated commissions. This provided the pilots who were to win the war in the Pacific.

Chapter XVII

Events, Public Relations and Personalities

The coming of the '30s, a full decade after World War I, brought a change in fortunes for the Navy. It was still The Treaty Navy but it was emerging from the hard years of the previous decade. Tragedies marred the horizon but there was a series of positive events that enhanced the Navy image. In addition, Hollywood developed the talking picture and discovered the Navy. Films about the Navy and Marine Corps had a positive ring. Books and magazine articles likewise were favorable. The pacifist groups were vocal but not as accepted as they had been immediately following the war.

Sen. Gerald Nye's (R-.N.D.) Committee investigating "the merchants of death" munitions makers lasted from 1934 through 1936 but only had a small group of radical devotees. It did not deter the naval construction programs of the N.R.A. or defeat the Vinson-Trammel Act. The benefits of naval revival to the economy helped the reemployed workingman while the bleeding hearts clung to their impractical ideals. The Depression had spurred recruiting for the Navy and Marine Corps. Waiting lists for enlistments were common and recruiters could arbitrarily raise standards without regard to having a quota to fill.

In the meantime, individuals began to come to the fore who would be household words during World War II. These personalities were the products of the Naval Service Culture and were to be the bedrock of victory over Japan in the '40s. Such victory was not by accident. They had been planning it since the end of World War I. Their theses (all War College students were required to write a research paper) at the War Colleges reflected forward thinking on the problems of defeating Japan or as "Pete" Ellis had put it in 1921, "In order to impose our will upon Japan, it will be necessary to ..."

Personalities were not just limited to people. Ships, too, had personalities and popular identities. These were mostly among the sailors of the Fleet but occasionally; the public became aware of individual ships and their deeds. The saga of *Lex* at Tacoma has been told. The nicknames of ships, while not common currency, were well known in their homeports on both coasts. When a ship's name appeared in the news, Americans basked in her pride. She was one of theirs. One newsreel had a standard lead-in to the weekly edition. It showed, *inter alia,* a column of battleships with bows dipping and lifting into the waves with spray splashing aside as the broad-beamed warships symbolized America's first line of defense.

The annual Army-Navy football game, before the era of football factories as prep schools for the pros, was given several columns in sports pages the final Sunday in every November. The early June editions of the newsreels regularly covered the spectacle of several hundred Midshipmen tossing their caps in the air at the Naval Academy. Americans were beginning a love affair with their Navy and its men of the Naval Service.

Events encouraged this love affair. This was especially true when triumphs emerged from tragedies.

It was Friday, Mar. 10, 1933 The Battle Force was anchored in Long Beach Harbor. About 6 p.m. there was a loud booming noise and many of the ships shuddered violently. The thoughts of those on board were that another ship had collided with theirs. All hands rushed topside. There was no sign of a collision. What had happened was ashore. An earthquake had shook the city causing severe devastation. Initially, all men ashore were ordered back on board and all ships got up steam. It was prudent to get them to sea lest an ensuing tidal wave pound them on shore. Since liberty didn't start until after Saturday morning Captain's Inspection not too many sailors were ashore. Besides the previous weekend had been payday so most of the men were broke. (Paydays were the 5th and 20th of each month. When one of these fell on a Sunday, the Paymasters, with the permission or at the direction of the CO, paid on the previous Friday or Saturday.)

The ships never did get underway. Instead the Navy answered the call for help. Parties were landed to do myriad tasks in the wrecked city. Restoration of communications was a priority so details of radiomen and portable equipment went ashore. Shore patrol assisted in keeping order and directing traffic. Marines prevented looting. Doctors and hospital corpsmen set up first aid stations to treat the injured. Medical supplies were donated, as were blankets, clothing and food. For those without shelter the ships provided a quick and handy haven. Motor whaleboats were busy taking the homeless out to the ships of the Fleet. Officers gave up their staterooms to the homeless victims mostly women and children. One cruiser was a strange sight for a few days with makeshift clotheslines rigged in various places above and below decks for drying emergency laundry. Once again, the Navy came through "to help those in peril [albeit not] on the sea."

As noted, RAdm. Moffett was a strong advocate of the lighter-than-air rigid airship. In his tenure as ChBuAer (1921-33) he pushed the development of the Navy's rigid lighter-than-air program. The successful dirigible had been a German development. In World War I, German *zeppelins* (named after the developer, Count Ferdinand Zeppelin) terrorized London and parts of the south of England with night raids on the cities. Poor weather prevented airships from playing a role in the Battle of Jutland but their potential was recognized by naval officers including Moffett. The recognized vulnerability of the German airships was their use of the volatile hydrogen to provide lift. The U.S. had a near-monopoly on the heavier, albeit lighter than the atmosphere, helium. Perhaps, that had some influence on Moffett's fascination with airships despite the fatal drawback to the advancement of airships – structural vulnerability to violent weather.

Both the U.S. and Britain received German rigid airships as war prizes. (Under the Wilson war aim of no territorial or other aggrandizement, Britain received them as prizes and the U.S. purchased them from her.) There had been several losses amongst these but the program persisted. The RN lost funding for airships

134

when the new Air Ministry and the RAF usurped British military aviation from it. The U.S. pushed on. (The Brits happily sold these "white elephants.") Lakehurst, N.J., became the site for the construction of a lighter-than-air base for the war prizes and other airships to be built in the U.S.

The first really operational Navy dirigibles were *Los Angeles* and *Shenandoah*. There was only enough helium available, in those days of limited funding, for one or the other to operate. It was transferred from ship to ship as one flew and the other sat in the huge hangar. To the public and the press, helium was a blessing since it was nonflammable. To the Navy and aircrews it seemed the opposite. The ex-German airships and those made under license in the U.S. had been designed for hydrogen and its greater lift.

On Sept. 2, 1925, over Ohio, the question of helium or hydrogen was moot. A violent storm slammed *Shenandoah* earth ward with the loss of several of her crew including LCdr. Zachary Lansdowne, her skipper. A survivor was Lt. C.E. Rosendahl who as a rear admiral was to head the Navy's blimp program during World War II.

Before the loss of *Shenandoah*, BuAer (Moffett) had conceived a new project in March 1924. The next month a design for what would become *USS Akron* and *USS Macon* was projected. A year later the BuAer proposal was formulated. Six weeks after *Shenandoah* went down, BuAer proposed the project to SecNav Wilbur on Nov. 17, 1925. Congress authorized the two airships in June 1926. After two design competitions in 1927 and 1928, a contract was awarded for both to Goodyear-Zeppelin Corporation of Ohio.

Akron preceded *Macon* by almost 18 months in christening and first flight. She was commissioned on Oct. 27, 1931 having made her first flight a month earlier. The First Lady, Mrs. Hoover, christened *Akron* on Aug. 8, 1931 and she first flew on Sept. 25. The delay in her getting into the air was caused by the manufacturer's determination that she was initially "heavier" than designed. This and sundry other things contributed to her being termed a "jinxed ship" by the press and among her detractors in both the Congress and the Navy. Not all the latter, even aviators, were sold on the idea of dirigibles.

The initial jinx story was rather ludicrous but got much attention. One of the riveters on the framework was a middle European immigrant. He clamed that he spit on each rivet before driving it home. It was his belief that the liquid spit would freeze and expand when the airship rose to high altitude. The expansion would cause the rivets to pop and thus sabotage the war machine. While the laws of physics disproved this, another factor was present. *Akron* was not designed for high altitudes. She could climb to about 10,000 feet but her operational altitude was about 3,000 to 4,000 feet. Another pre-competition assertion by two non-engineers who deemed themselves experts was that faulty material was used in the construction of the airframe. A delay for inspection by Navy engineers who disproved the faulty material claim was cited by that perennial pain-in-the-ass to the Navy, James McClinitc (D-Okla.) He, of course seized on any straw which would diminish Navy appropriations. He and other Congressmen were invited by the Navy for an orientation flight in *Akron* from

Lakehurst. Unfortunately, before *Akron* got off the ground, she was subject to violent winds at her mooring. The Congressmen had not gone on board but had front row seats to the severe damage of her lower tail fin. The flight was postponed several weeks while repairs were made. Few of the Congressmen came back to Lakehurst.

After commissioning, *Akron* did have some severe problems both mechanically and operationally. During her first 18 months her operations with the Fleet were flawed for several reasons, not the least of which as that she was a learning vehicle with no precedent for integrated fleet operations. The aircraft she was designed to carry internally for launching while in flight were slow in being made. They were modified fighters (XF9Cs) put forward as an interim solution by Cdr. Marc Mitscher of BuAer Plans Division. There was a dichotomy of thinking about the purpose of the aircraft carried. Some held they were fighters to defend the airship during her scouting mission. Others held that they were scouts to extend the radius of search of the airship and keep her out of sight of the enemy she sought. The F9Cs as fighters, albeit interim aircraft for the mission, did not have the communications equipment to be effective scouts.

Although, *Akron* did provide the training platform for her "hook-on" aircraft, she never did operate with them in her scouting mission for the Fleet. Before getting her aircraft, she did a scouting mission in the Atlantic to locate an "enemy" destroyer force for ComScoFlt. A navigation error caused her to miss her quarry. Her intended use in the Fleet Problem in 1932 on the West Coast was scrubbed because of logistical criteria. A transcontinental flight was a major problem because of lack of mooring masts across country. There were none inland except where she was built in Ohio. The West Coast had one at Camp Kearney near San Diego and one was planned at Sunnyvale south of San Francisco. Two Navy ships also had them, one on each coast. Then there was the problem of helium resupply. Other than Lakehurst and Akron, Ohio, there were no supplies available if they were needed to replace emergency expenditures. A flight to the West Coast meant crossing mountains above the normal operational altitude of *Akron.* An east-to-west flight wasn't as bad as the return flight. The higher mountains were in the west and *Akron* would reach them after losing a considerable amount of weight in fuel burned. Coming back, she would cross the mountains with much fuel still on board. Then there was the question of ground crews for handling the lines when mooring the airship to the mast. A series of draglines was necessary to guide the incoming airship to the ground. These were manhandled just as in bringing a vessel alongside.

A fatal mishap occurred at Camp Kearney on *Akron*'s initial landing there. Instead of experienced line handlers for the arrival of *Akron,* some *anus* decided that a draft of recruits from the NTS at San Diego would suffice. A sudden updraft caused *Akron* to veer back into the sky. Three recruits were jerked upward. Two lost their grips and fell to their deaths. SA Bud Cowart made himself fast to the line. It took an hour to haul him into the safety of *Akron.*

Akron's limited operational use on the West Coast did not add to her acceptance in the Fleet. One result of her missing the Fleet Problem was that the success of *Lexington* and *Saratoga* in that Problem led to the post-action report calling for more carrier construction vice airships.

Akron returned to Lakehurst for upkeep. She spent the next year-and-a-half flying from Lakehurst; working up procedures with the F9Cs and their pilots; and much to the disgust of her commanders, crews and BuAer, flying over major eastern cities to show off to the public. Still she was moving toward the day when she and her sisters (*Macon* was building but three more were planned) could fulfill their supposed destiny with the Fleet. In the meantime her second commanding officer (Rosenthal, her first had returned to sea for a normal tour) and many of her crew were detached to prepare for assignment to *Macon* then under construction. The new CO, Cdr. Frank McCord, was an experienced lighter-than-air pilot who had also been navigator of *Lexington.*

In early April 1933, *Akron* was scheduled for an extended routine operational flight that included a course to Newport, R.I., and other New England shore points to assist in calibrating Radio Direction Finding (RDF) stations. (The reader will remember that ten years earlier RDF error led to the loss of seven destroyers off California.) As was his custom from time-to-time, RAdm. Moffett opted to take part in the flight as an observer. He came up from Washington, D.C., in the afternoon of Apr. 3, and was on board for the evening take off. (Early morning or evening take offs avoided bad ground wind conditions. The fiasco which damaged the tail fin was not going to reoccur.)

The sky was overcast during lift off and even though visibility was low, and worsening, it was not deemed a problem. Even if lack of visibility delayed the RDF calibration, the extended flight would permit training exercises and engineering tests on the two- to three-day flight. Aerology forecast thundershowers with clearing. That was not seen as a problem inasmuch as *Akron* had steered around such storms before. She and all but three of the aircrew were on their last flight. She headed out to sea.

Thunderstorms were encountered with lightning flashes to either side of her course. There was a series of weather events, each minor in itself, but the cumulative result was disaster. Weather reports were spotty owing to the heavy static of the electric storm interfering with radio reception. The exact location of the storm and its movement was unknown. This absence of precise information deprived the skipper and his navigator of how best to maneuver to get behind the storm or the lesser alternative run ahead of it. Likewise, the lack of wind data, i.e., direction and force, threw dead reckoning off. The storm's air pressure caused the altimeter, which worked on the principle of an aneroid barometer to give a false reading. The control car at the bottom of he airship was almost 150 feet below the top of the airship. It was about 650 feet forward of the tail of the airship. Thus, depending on the attitude of the airship to the horizontal, the tail could be several hundred feet higher or lower than the control car where the altimeter was.

From the testimony of the senior survivor, LCdr. H.V. Wiley, the XO, it seems that McCord changed his mind about getting ahead of the storm and came to a westerly course. He misread his position from the lights below on his landfall as

Asbury Park, N.J., when he really was about 20 miles south. He again reversed to an easterly course thinking he was going to be able to elude the storm that he believed was moving east from Baltimore. At the same time *Akron* was losing altitude. To compensate, McCord tried to climb. He put the nose up thinking he still had several hundred feet below him. He didn't and the lower tail fin (the same one which had been damaged) struck the sea. Structural damage to the control surfaces doomed *Akron*. She settled on an even keel bringing the nose down to the level of the sea. When she was about 200 feet above the surface and settling, Wiley shouted, "Stand by for a crash!" *Akron* was swallowed by the sea. Having no like jackets or rubber boats on board boded ill for the crew even if they could escape from inside their cigar-shaped coffin. How many did is unknown. A passing German tanker, *MS Phoebus,* observed lights sinking into the sea and headed toward the wreck. Her boats pulled four men from the water. They were Wiley and three enlisted men. A CPO, died on board *Phoebus;* 73 others including Moffett and McCord went to a watery grave.

The news flashed from *Phoebus* to the world. *USCGC Tucker* (DD-57) relieved *Phoebus* of the survivors and a futile search went on for more. Two more lives were lost when Navy blimp J-3 went down of New Jersey searching for *Akron* survivors. *Akron* was located on the sea bottom and divers went down. They found nothing which made a substantial contribution to either the Navy or subsequent Congressional investigations. The U.S. was in the depth of the Depression. The Navy had lost an expensive toy, paid for by tax dollars. Sixty widows and dozens of their children had lost husbands and fathers. The economy measures of the prior administration had ensured that no further tax dollars would be expended. Service death benefits and widow's pensions had been slashed to save money. There was one bright spot, however, for Americans. That day, 3.2 beer had been legalized after more than a dozen years of Prohibition. Seventeen day later, *USS Macon* made her first flight. Whither goest airships in the Navy?

Macon a sister ship to *Akron* and her sleek cigar-shaped envelope was almost identical. The interior skeleton which was enclosed by the outer skin was identical in all respects to *Akron*. Both had the secondary control station in the lower tail fin. Tails fins were part of the structure bolted to the main girders in two places. They were as commodious as the fuselage of modern jet fighters and accessible from within the airship.

There had been some controversy about the new airship's name. The new Chairman of the House Naval Affairs Committee in 1930, Carl Vinson, had been a minority member of the Committee for 14 years. He was interested in having a ship named for a city in Georgia. Cruisers were named for cities and the ships of Wilbur's cruiser bill which were funded by N.R.A and other means were assigned names before Vinson succeeded to the Chairmanship. Vinson's Georgia constituents wanted a ship named for a city in their state. (*Augusta* was named for the Maine city) as Vinson came up for reelection in 1932. Two previous airships, *Los Angeles* and *Akron,* had been named for cities since airships like cruisers had the primary mission of scouting for the Fleet. Vinson's constituents were satisfied with the name, *Macon*

But there was more controversy than just the name. Who was going to be the sponsor at the christening was important to the citizens of Macon. Prestige was at stake. *Shenandoah* had been christened by Mrs. Coolidge. Another First Lady, Mrs. Hoover, had christened *Akron*. Franklin D. Roosevelt had been elected in 1932 and would be sworn into office on Mar. 4, 1933. Maconites wanted a First Lady to do the honors for their airship. RAdm. Moffett, about to retire, had in his role as advocate of the Navy's lighter-than-air rigid airship program desired that his wife christen *Macon* before he retired. She did on Mar.11, three weeks before *Akron* was to make her a widow.

It was another three months before *Macon* was commissioned. On hand to demonstrate his support for the airship program and to ride her back to Lakehurst was the new ChBuAer, RAdm. E.J. King. King had been Midshipman Battalion Commander (Today's equivalent is Brigade Commander or top "striper") in the Class of 1901. As a destroyer skipper he had been in Sims's Atlantic Torpedo Flotilla and was one of the "Band of Brothers." There was a story that when Moffett had become ChBuAer in the early '20s, he wanted King for command of *Shenandoah*. King, at the time, had opted for submarines and was commanding a submarine division as a captain. It is doubtful whether an officer of King's ambition (he made no secret early in his career of his aim to be CNO) would have felt such an assignment as career enhancing. The significance of the story is that Moffett like many others saw King as a "comer." King later, however, did follow the advice of his former mentor, Sims, and won his Wings at the age of 49 in 1927 and commanded *Lexington*. The death of Moffett caused F.D.R to search for a replacement and King was the only flag officer who could fly.

Macon entered the Fleet with many of the operational and mechanical problems faced by *Akron* either solved or reduced in magnitude. The most important one was that her F9C hook-on aircraft were available with trained aviators. *Macon* worked up to operational readiness rapidly.

The new air station for airships a Sunnyvale, Calif., had been renamed Moffett Field after the admiral's death. *Macon* was ordered there to be near the Fleet and to operate with it and develop doctrine for integrated operations. En route, she ran into storms transiting mountains through Texas canyons. Two structural beams aft in the vicinity of the tail fins snapped but were repaired.

Macon's tactical operations with the Fleet were less than spectacular. The exercises that used her in confined operational areas at her relatively low operational altitude (2,000 to 3,000 feet) had her being "shot down" by ship's anti-aircraft fire on almost a dozen occasions. The airship advocates felt that this was a misuse of an asset, which should have been doing long-range strategic searches for enemy forces at sea.

When LCdr. Wiley, the only surviving officer of the *Akron* disaster, came to Moffett Filed to take command of *Macon* in July 1934, he had one aim. It was to make *Macon* perform. The key elements in airship performance were her scouting planes. An improved RDF beacon was installed in *Macon* below her control car. Scouts could home in from a great distance out on their scouting legs. Improved radiotelephones were installed in the F9Cs giving them a greater capability to report sightings. Finally, after the planes were flown on board, their landing gear was removed and an external auxiliary fuel tank installed under the fuselage. The lack of drag of landing gear increased their speed. The extra fuel increased their range. Enemy forces could be found at sea and the airship never sighted by them.

Wiley resorted to a bit of "grandstanding" to make his point. It was not appreciated by his seniors in the fleet chain-of-command, however. Shortly after taking command "Doc" Wiley ran a long-range search problem. *New Orleans* and *Houston* were en route from Panama to Hawaii. *Houston* flew the flag of the Commander-in-Chief. Willey took *Macon* on what he told his superiors was a routine training mission. He had been tracking the two cruisers from the Canal Zone from newspaper reports filed by reporters with the President's party. *Macon* left Moffett Field on Jul. 18 under clouds which were about 1,500 feet. Clearing skies enabled him to get a navigational fix the next morning. He then altered course to intercept the cruisers where he estimated them to be. He launched his scouts. The pilots were Lt. (j.g) H.B. Miller and Lt. (j.g.) F.N. Kivette.

Lookouts on the cruisers were surprised to see F9Cs so far out to sea. Soon the decks were crowded with sailors scanning the sky. *Macon* hove into sight, retrieved her planes and then launched them again. This time the planes buzzed the decks of the ships and dropped packages of the latest newspapers plus some letters addressed to the President, a stamp collector, with *Macon*'s cachet and postmark cancellation. F.D.R. expressed appreciation and compliments on a fine performance and excellent navigation. Adm. Sellers, CINCUS, hauled Wiley on the carpet for "breach of naval protocol" and "misapplied initiative." Fortunately, Sellers took the Fleet to the Caribbean and Atlantic for the rest of the year and left Wiley and *Macon* to operate from Moffett Filed.

During this period, several crates of reinforcing parts arrived from the factory in Akron. These were to provide added strength to the structural integrity of the airframe particularly in the vicinity of the failures aft during the transit in Texas. The modifications were not considered urgent and the work proceeded routinely between flights at sea.

In February 1935, *Macon* was again engaged in exercises with the Fleet. After locating several units of the Fleet, she set course for Moffett Field while the ships headed for San Francisco. Cruising at about 2,500 feet, she ran into rainsqualls and a lowering ceiling. She could see Navy and merchant ships working against heavy seas below. In order to keep her away from the storm over land, Wiley changed course to stay over the water. About 5 p.m. *Macon* entered turbulent air and a gust pulled the control wheels from the helmsman and the elevator control man. At the same time there was a sharp report aft. It turned out to be a break in the structure holding the upper tail fin which carried away sending metal fragments into the helium gas bags diminishing lift but not dangerously – yet. The tail did drop, however, giving the airship an up attitude. The emergency action by the skipper to shed ballast combined with the vector thrust of the engines caused the airship to climb. She passed her operational altitude and helium relief valve, designed to keep her from exceeding her maximum altitude cut in venting helium and thus lift to the atmosphere.

The analogy is to that of a submarine suddenly sinking below to her crush depth who blows ballast to cause her to rise to the surface and safety. There the analogy ceases because the last thing *Macon* wanted to do was to fall to the surface which wasn't safety. But that's what happened. She hit the water stern first and started to sink

Her distress signal, "*Macon* falling…" was picked up by the ships headed for San Francisco. The next message picked up by *Richmond* was "Abandoning ship." *Richmond* was 30 miles away from the estimated crash site but the cruiser's skipper had already put all boilers on line and was headed there at flank speed. As a survivor of *Akron,* Wiley had seen to it that there were lifejackets and rubber boats on board. Thus, *Richmond* and other ships arriving in the dark and fog were able to pick up all but two of the crew of more than 80. *Macon* sank slowly by the stern as waves broke her up frame by frame. By six thirty it was all over and so was the rigid airship in the Navy. King, Vinson and the rest of the Navy hierarchy decided to put the money into patrol planes instead. When *Akron* had gone down, Vinson had said, "We've built three and lost two; you can take it from me, there won't be an more airships built." He now said, "The curtain has been rung down on lighter-than-aircraft in the Navy." The one bright spot was the successful evacuation of *Macon* and rescue of the crew.

Although the U.S. was out of the rigid airship business there was to be one final dirigible act involving the Navy. In the fall of 1935, after the loss of *Macon* Moffett Field was turned over to the Army Air Cops (returned to the Navy in early 1942) and lighter-than-air operations in the form of blimps reverted to Lakehurst. In 1936, Germany (her Zeppelin Co. as agent) and the U.S. negotiated an agreement wherein Germany could use the facilities at Lakehurst to include mooring mast, Navy ground crews to handle mooring lines and other such amenities as needed for a terminus for commercial dirigible flights from Germany to the U.S. From Jun.1, to Oct. 9, 1936, seven round trips were completed under the revocable permit. All trips were made by Germany's *Hindenburg* carrying passengers and light cargo. The permit was renewed for another series of trips after the winter. The first provided for the arrival of *Hindenburg* on May 6, 1937. As was the custom, the passengers after debarking were to be flown to Newark Airport (then New York's only airport) and then driven into New York City.

A thunderstorm had passed through Lakehurst and there was still a slight drizzle as *Hindenburg* arrived. She had passed over New York City earlier in the afternoon en route to the air station. Just after 7 p.m. in gathering twilight, she started her descent; dropped her mooring lines and was being guided toward the mooring mast. A flash of flame shot out of her stern near the top tail fin. It spread quickly to the entire airship as her hydrogen caught fire. The huge airship crumpled to the ground as fire consumed her fabric covering. Sailors of the line-handling party were quick to go to the rescue of passengers and crew. Heroic actions saved the lives of 64 passengers and crew. Thirty-three were lost. Many sailors were burned during the rescue. The charred skeleton of *Hindenburg* was the last chapter in the world of dirigibles.

After the loss of *Macon* the remainder of 1935 was routine. F.D.R. cruised in the Bahamas during March and April in *Tuscaloosa*. Aircraft from NAS, Pensacola, operating from Miami, provided airmail service to the Presidential party. At the direction of the President, *Sirius* (AK-75), an auxiliary Navy cargo ship commanded by Cdr. R.B. Carney, Jr. carried a government scientific party to the Pribilof Islands. "Mick" Carney who was to be one of the World War II luminaries and later CNO (1953-55) took part in the annual kill at the Government seal rookeries. Among the cargo of seal skins brought back was the makings of a fur coat for his "Gracie" (Mrs. Carney.)

In October an experimental P3Y-1 made a non-stop flight from NAS, Norfolk, to Coco Solo. After four days rest the plane and crew set a non-stop world's record by covering the 3,218 miles to San Francisco in an elapsed time of 34 hours 40 minutes.

A civil war in Spain, which was to be the prelude to eventual war in Europe as fascists and communists rehearsed and experimented, caused alarm for the safety of Americans abroad. A special temporary squadron, 40-T (Forty-Tare) was organized and dispatched to Spanish waters, albeit based on French ports. *Raleigh* with destroyers *Kane* (DD-235)) and *Hatfield* (DD-231) were to evacuate Americans from the Spanish war zones.

The year ended with F.D.R. embarked in *Indianapolis* and with another heavy cruiser and two destroyers, sailed to Buenos Aires for the Inter-American Conference on the Maintenance of Peace. After visiting several major South American ports, the ships returned to Charleston, S.C., on Dec. 15.

The year 1937, which was to be busy, opened on two auspicious notes. Fresh from the nadir of the *Macon* disaster and the high point of the Coco Solo flights Naval Aviation had another triumph. A patrol squadron of 12 flying boats made a non-stop flight from San Diego to Pearl Harbor overnight. It was repeated by another squadron in April. The Navy could now ferry large patrol lanes to Hawaii instead of shipping them as deck cargo on ships. Further, with tenders, patrol planes could be temporarily based on out-lying islands from Hawaii to extend search missions toward the western Pacific and Japan. Long-distance over water flights had come a long way since John Rodgers and his crew paddled the last few miles to Hawaii.

In mid-year, the eyes of the world were focused on the Navy as it searched the vast reaches of the Pacific for Amelia Earhart. She was a 39-year old aviatrix who had made the first woman's solo flight across the Atlantic in 1932. In 1935 she made a solo flight from Hawaii to California. For the latter flight, *Macon* had been placed on alert to search for her if she failed. In 1937 she was attempting an around-the-world flight in a twin-engined land plane accompanied by her navigator, Fred Noonan. On the leg between New Guinea and Howland

Island her plane was presumed down and missing since it never reached Howland, a dot on the equator due east of the Gilbert Islands (Australian Mandates) and northwest of the Phoenix Islands. Her course was south of the Caroline Islands (Japanese Mandate). Her flight path was slightly north of east almost along the equator. Japan had received the old German island possessions north of the equator at Versailles. Noonan's navigation would have had to have been off by almost 45 degrees to the north to put the flight over any Japanese Mandates. Incidentally, the Earhart aircraft was billed as a "flying laboratory."

Friday, Jul. 3, 1937, *Lexington* was in Santa Barbara and the first liberty boat had gone ashore for the long weekend. A SOS had been received at Howland Island (U.S. claimed territory) from the Earhart plane saying that she had a half hour of fuel remaining. That was the last ever heard from the aviatrix. The Navy swung into action. *Lex* picked up her liberty party and put into San Pedro to take on provisions, then down to San Diego to bring aboard her aircraft. Then she set a record for the speed run from San Diego to Hilo, T.H., where she refueled for the next 27 days of search. In the meantime, the battleship *Colorado* was in Hilo, having come from Bremerton and San Francisco with NROTC Midshipmen for their summer cruise. She had catapulted off her scout planes to Ford Island (NAS Pearl Harbor) for needed overhaul. They were in the process of tearing down the engines when the alert came to join the search for the lost aviatrix.

A patrol plane had taken off from Pearl Harbor for Howland but had to turn back because of weather. *Colorado* retrieved her planes and headed via the great circle for Howland. A Coast Guard cutter, *Itasca,* and a converted (from minesweeper) seaplane tender, *Swan* (AVP-7), were on the scene searching with the assumption that Noonan's navigation had caused the plane to overshoot Howland and then have to ditch in the sea. At 17 knots, her most efficient speed for the distance, *Colorado* was about 100 hours away from Howland. By Thursday, Jul. 8, her scout planes were searching the area southeast of Howland near the Phoenix Group. *Itasca* had searched northeast of the intended landing point and determined that any success would be in the area to the southeast.

Then-Lt. (j.g.) Bill Short was a pilot in *Colorado.* His letters home at the time are highly critical of Earhart's flight which he terms a "publicity stunt." He continues, "Even if she had been successful what would have been proven thereby except that she was the first woman to fly around the world? As it stands now she has only demonstrated once more that long flights over water in landplane are foolishly dangerous." He went on to say that the flight should never have been permitted but once it had more elaborate safeguards should have been established. He wonders why the radio station at Howland or *Itasca* didn't get a RDF fix on the plane before it went down. He then speculates that she may have been using a radio frequency too high for RDF.

Lexington meanwhile covered the 4,000-mile trip and took over the search. She remained in the area for 27 days nearly exhausting her provisions. An interesting sidelight mentioned by Bill Short is that *Colorado* refueled *Lex's* plane guard destroyers before she returned to Pearl. As we'll see later fueling at sea had fallen into disuse since the days of Nimitz and *Maumee* refueling he Queenstown-bound destroyers in 1917-18.

Amelia Earhart and Fred Noonan and their plane were never found. Their disappearance spawned myths and legends and still does. Periodically, there is a "find" on some island in the Pacific of a piece of evidence, usually wreckage, purporting to be from the plane. Two perennial myths are that she was on a spy mission and was shot/forced down by the Japanese. A derivative of that is that her mission was to ditch at sea and thus provide an excuse for the Navy to intrude into the Japanese Mandates and photograph them for eventual use when war came.

These can be debunked easily. First, the whole Navy did not take part in the search. The Fleet had returned to its West Coast ports and roadsteads after being in San Francisco for the opening dedication of the Golden Gate Bridge. *Colorado* was in Hawaii incidental to the NROTC summer cruise. She was the only ship with an aircraft scouting capability near enough to Howland to take part initially. *Lexington* was the available carrier, and a carrier was the right ship for a search mission. And she was on the West Coast. Had it been a plot, surely the Navy would have disposed its assets at Pearl vice the West Coast. Second, a photographic mission would have required more assets than the Navy had at the time. Further, pictures of ocean would be meaningless. Also, the Japanese Mandates were almost due north or northeast of Port Moresby, New Guinea, the starting point of the fatal leg. The worst navigation would be required to get the flight over the Mandates en route to Howland. It would be like flying from San Diego to Phoenix via San Francisco. The search for Amelia Earhart garnered the Navy a lot of favorable publicity but in the long run spent a lot of Navy money on a fool's errand.

There were other operational expenditures which would come under harsh press or Congressional scrutiny in this day and age. And which would have had the Navy castigated and second-guessed at every turn. One of them combined operational exercises with a moral-boosting factor.

USS Gold Star (AG-12) was a former cargo ship and psuedo-transport. She was the station ship at Guam which meant she swung on the hook or was tied to the pier most of the time. She had a regular crew and their maintenance of seagoing skills required that she exercise at sea on occasion. That exercise was the delight of the officers and dependents in the Western Pacific and "Far China Station." About three times a year, she made a trip around the Orient. The old coal-burner could barely manage 10 knots, 8 into a head wind, but she was commodious and comfortable. She would call at Yokohama for a week; and then three days in Meiik, near Nagasaki to take on coal. On to Shanghai for 10 days; five days in Hong Kong and four days in Manila. The next trip she would run the loop in reverse. Officers and men would come on board for the trip as well as their dependent wives and children. Others would be picked up en route with the provision that they pay their own way home. Upon arrival in one of the Japanese or Chinese ports, arrangements would be made for *amahs* to come on board to care for the children while their parents went shopping. For obvious reason, the cruises of *Gold Star* in the Orient were called "The Diaper Run."

The Sino-Japanese War broke out in 1937 over the Incident at the Marco Polo Bridge. Japanese invaders, supported by IJN warships occupied much of the littoral of China including most of the ports. Shanghai was one. Still the ports were open to international shipping and *Gold Star* was a commissioned vessel of the Navy. The Diaper Run stopped in Shanghai as usual.

One of the dependents who went ashore to "shop" was Thalia Massie, who we last met leaving Hawaii in a hurry in 1932. Evidently, her shopping included some libations. As she was returning to the pier to catch the launch back to the ship, she was stopped by a Japanese sentry to show her pass. This led to words, which he probably didn't understand. She was outraged at the effrontery of an oriental. Her action was to slap the sentry. That was not very wise. There is a saying that "God looks out for drunks, Americans and Marines!" This time, it as the Marines taking care of the rest not God. An alert Leatherneck on the pier rushed to Thalia before the sentry could summon his superiors. When the superiors did arrive, the Marine was able to square the situation with the Japanese and World War II was avoided for another four years.

In 1937, the flagship of the Asiatic Fleet was *USS Augusta.* She had relieved her sister ship, *Houston,* in 1933. Her CO was Capt. Chester W. Nimitz. He had relieved Capt. R.E. Ingersoll in the Puget Sound Navy Yard after Ingersoll had been in command six months. The relief was not for cause but because Ingersoll had family illness problems which would be better handled if he were not in the Western Pacific. Royal Ingersoll later put *San Francisco* in commission and made four stars during the war. Nimitz took *Augusta* out of the yard before all yard workmen had cleaned up their mess. En route to the Orient, he had the crew busy as they could be when short-handed. His return to the Asiatic Fleet after an absence of almost 30 years showed him that things hadn't changed. *Augusta* soon became the sparkling ship that *Houston* was. The secret was garbage and cheap labor. Chinese entrepreneurs would fully maintain the ship in immaculate condition throughout, including bright work and painting for a price. The price was exclusive rights to hauling off the ship's garbage. The Asiatic Fleet lived well. In April 1935, the junior officers of *Augusta* rowed a whaleboat to the liner, *SS President Lincoln* in the Whampoa River in Shanghai. Nimitz, the coxswain, was dressed in full dress frock coat, fore-and-aft hat and wore his sword. The oarsmen also were ceremoniously attired. He had turned over command and was going home.

In 1937, *Augusta* was again lying in the Whampoa, this time to show the flag and protect Americans as the Sino-Japanese War raged around the city. Unfortunately, a stray artillery shell, either Japanese or Chinese, struck the forecastle. *Augusta* lost one sailor killed and 18 wounded. These were not the last Navy casualties of 1937 in China.

Under the Sino-American Treaty of 1858, the U.S. was granted the right to protect American missionaries, businessmen and their business, travelers and other U.S. citizens in the interior of China. Extraterritoriality was also granted.

These privileges stemmed from the terms extracted from the Chinese by the British and French after their joint attack in 1857-58 on China. Although not participants with the aggressors, Russia and the U.S. demanded the same rights to protect their citizens in lawless China. The interior of China was only accessible to Occidentals through the vast waterways of China particularly the Yangtze which stretched all the way from the East China Sea west past Nanking, Hankow, up the gorges to Chungking (all spellings as of the '30s not those of the new China) and beyond. Britain and the U.S. patrolled the rivers especially the Yangtze with shallow draft, powerfully engined craft whimsically called gunboats. Their armament was two 3-in. guns and .50 and .30 caliber machine guns. rifles and side arms for landing parties.

After the war with Spain, the Navy used captured Spanish gunboats for the China river patrols. In 1926, Congress authorized and appropriated for six river gunboats for use in China (see Chapter V). They were 370 tons, 160 feet long with a 27-foot beam and drew 5 feet 3 inches of water. They were built at Kiangnan, China, and were all launched in 1927 and operating soon thereafter. One of these was *USS Panay* (PG-5).

These gunboats were used to being fired on during the Chinese civil war. They were seldom hit even when bandits or warlord armies fired from the shore. Artillery fire was ignored by the 14-knot (designed top speed which was augmented or decreased by the river flow) ships since Chinese fire control was primitive and a moving target was beyond its capability.

The last week in November 1937, Japanese forces were approaching Nanking, provisional capital of Chinese forces under Chiang Kai-shek. The Chinese notified the U.S. ambassador and he and most of the Embassy staff departed in *USS Luzon* (PG-7) on Nov. 22. Some of the staff held out for another week but finally decided to depart on *Panay*. The Ambassador notified the Japanese government on Dec. 1. On Dec. 11, *Panay* embarked the American officials and other Americans and headed up river escorting three Standard Oil barges also wanting to escape the oncoming Japanese. Two British gunboats plus other craft followed. During the first few miles, Japanese artillery fired wildly at the flotilla and hit nothing. Japanese army forces informed the IJN that some Chinese troops were fleeing Nanking in ships.

An hour before noon on Sunday, Dec. 12, *Panay* and the three barges anchored near Hoshein upstream from the capital, American colors streamed from the masts and were painted on awnings and weather decks. The sky was sunny and clear with no breeze. The crew was piped to chow and secured. Guns were secured and covered. About 1:30, three IJN bombers flew over the anchorage dropping 18 bombs. One struck *Panay* forward taking out her 3-in. gun, the pilothouse, sickbay and fire room. The CO, LCdr. J.J. Hughes was severely wounded as were several others. In the next 20 minutes, 12 dive-bombers and nine fighters made several bombing and strafing runs. By this time the ship's crew was replying with .30 caliber machine guns. Within 30 minutes all power was lost and the decks were awash. The Captain ordered, "Abandon ship!" and all hands took to the boats and headed for the reeds on the riverbank.

The planes continued to strafe the boats and the survivors as they stumbled ashore. Two of the barges were destroyed. The survivors managed to get word to the Asiatic flagship. Two days later *USS Oahu* (PR-6) and *HMS Ladybird* rescued the survivors. Two sailors and a civilian were dead, eleven officers and men seriously wounded. Lt. A.F. Anders, who had graduated from the Naval Academy ten years before, received the Navy Cross for taking charge after the captain was hit. In the tradition of the Old Navy, his son followed him to the Academy and graduated in 1955 becoming one of the first Astronauts.

The U.S. Ambassador to Japan was of the generation who "Remembered the Maine!" He felt sure that the U.S. would at least be firm in dealing with Japan. It was inconceivable that planes of the IJN (not the army) could not identify an American gunboat yet alone one that was clearly marked with U.S. Colors on a clear day. Instead, anxious to a avoid a war for which she was still not ready, the U.S. government elected to accept the Japanese claim that it was a "mistake" along with an indemnity. The parody of the Japanese apology, "So solly!" became common currency in the Fleet.

Although 1937 ended on a down-note for the Navy, there was a high note the month before. On Nov. 14 the Greek SS *Tzenny Chandris* sank off Diamond Shoals Light. One of seven patrol planes assisting in the search located the wreckage and many survivors clinging to timbers or swimming in life jackets. She guided *USCGC Mendoto* to the rescue.

In early 1938, the non-stop flights of squadrons of patrol planes continued. On Jan. 18, 1938, a squadron of 18 PBYs left San Diego and arrived in Pearl Harbor the next day. A build-up of search capability from Hawaii to the west was beginning. Another squadron of 17 planes went in September 1938 and a third of 15 in June 1939. Unfortunately it was to prove inadequate as attention shifted to the Atlantic two years later.

Disaster struck on May 23, 1939. The new submarine *Squalus* (SS-192) was conducting test dives off the Isle of Shoals off Portsmouth, N.H. She failed to surface from a test dive. A sister, *USS Sculpin* (SS-191), responded to a call for a search when *Squalus* did not report herself surfacing as scheduled. As soon as she had hit bottom, her CO, Lt. O.F. Naquin, ordered the forward marker buoy released. *Sculpin* located the buoy with the ominous message, "Submarine down here." Telephone contact was established with survivors in the forward portion of the submarine. Naquin stated that there were 32 known crewmen with him. He feared 26 were trapped in the flooded after section. Next day, submarine rescue vessel *USS Falcon* (ASR-2), a former minesweeper, arrived from New London. She established contact and lowered her McCann diving bell. It was the first use of that **innovation** in an actual rescue. In four trips to the sunken submarine which fortunately while resting on the bottom was not below her crush depth, the bell brought up 33 survivors. True to the traditions of the sea, Naquin was in the last trip.

It took almost three months for the salvage divers to get chains under the hull (they used pressure hoses to tunnel under the sub) and attach them to submerged pontoons. There was one abortive effort as the water was forced out of the

147

pontoons by compressed air to cause them to rise to the surface. *Squalus's* bow shot to the surface and slipped back. She was finally raised and towed to the Yard at Portsmouth. Investigation revealed that the main induction valve which supplied air to the diesels while surfaced failed to close. Yet the "Christmas tree" (red and green lights on the indicator board in the control room) had shown a "green board" (all secure) before Naquin ordered the dive. As a result, Electric Boat's more reliable design for the main induction valve became standard equipment thereafter.

Squalus was refitted, renamed *Sailfish* and went on to earn a Presidential Unit Citation in the war against Japan.

Although subsequent Vinson Acts (See Chapter XX) were providing ships for the future, there were requirements for ships in the Fleet at once. The four-piper destroyers of the World War I program which were laid up in the backwater were recommissioned. Fifty were to go to Britain in the destroyers for bases deal. (See Chapter XXII). Likewise, older submarines were brought back although they could not be of any service with the Fleet. The O-class of 16 boats had been launched in 1917. They were small at 500/650 tons; had no deck gun and only four 18-in. torpedo tubes. One, O-5, had been lost in 1923. Seven had been discarded. One of the eight remaining and recommissioned was O-9 (SS-70).

While engaged in a practice dive off the Isle of Shoals on Jun. 20, 1941, 0-9 failed to surface. She was down in 440 feet of water. Rescue attempts failed. Two days later services for the 32 dead were conducted at sea over the spot where 0-9 rested on the bottom.

In January 1939, the Fleet made the mass transit of the Panama Canal and proceeded to the Guantanamo-Culebra area. Fleet Problem XX was conducted in the Caribbean during February-March. On board *Houston,* the President and CNO, Adm. W.D. Leahy, observed. *Houston* returned to the West Coast; was briefly flagship of the Hawaiian Detachment until returning to Mare Island for overhaul. She departed to Manila and on Nov. 19, 1940 hoisted the flag of Adm. T.C. Hart, ComAsiaticFlt. *Houston* was to be the first "Treaty Cruiser" sunk at the end of February 1942 at Sunda Strait, Java.

During all this time, in addition to extensive coverage in the press, Americans were treated to a heavy dose of magazine articles and motion pictures about their Navy. Americans then, before television usurped their role of reading, had a multitude of weekly and monthly periodicals. These were feature magazines like: *Saturday Evening Post, Colliers, Liberty, Atlantic Monthly, Harper's Bazaar* and others that came and went. *Life* was revived as a pictorial news magazine about 1936. It was soon followed in format by *Look.* The big city newspapers had Sunday supplements and rotogravures. The latter were four or eight pages of sepia photos. Specialty magazines like *National Geographic* and *Scientific American* were fixtures in most middle-class homes.

As the Navy began to rebuild under Roosevelt, free-lance writers found the feature magazines fertile fields for articles on the new Navy. Fiction was another venue for stories about the Naval Service. John W. Thomason, a serving Marine officer who had seen action in France, regularly had short stories revolving around his protagonist, Sgt. John Houston of the "Old Breed" in China, Central American banana wars and sea duty. A standard newspaper comic strip was "Stony Craig" a Marine Gunnery Sergeant whose creator, another serving Marine, Don Dixon, used Chinese ideographs in the dialogue balloons of his Oriental characters. What the reading public did not know was that the ideographs were swear words in Chinese. Another strip was "Don Winslow." It became an evening radio serial whose 15-minutes before dinner fascinated young listeners as "Don Winslow of the Navy" with its musical theme starting "O, Columbia, the gem of the ocean..."

In June 1936, Lt. Art Ageton USN did a piece about the Navy in *National Geographic.* It covered the Navy's support of the scientific expedition to Canton Island to film the eclipse. *Shenandoah*'s record flight across country had appeared in January 1925. Also the role of Navy fliers in the Arctic expedition appeared in June 1925. Naval Aviation was the subject of *Navy Wings* (Dodd, Mead & Co. 1937) by Lt. H.B. Miller USN who we met delivering mail from *Macon* to F.D.R. *Life* devoted an entire issue to the Navy in the fall of 1940.

But the medium which was to have the most impact in giving America an appreciation for its Fleet was the movies. A first, it was not always favorable but as Hollywood realized that people would want to see their sons as wholesome products of Middle America proudly serving the Fleet, it gave them what they wanted. Cynics (and movie critics) might consider it propaganda but the public loved it.

After World War I, when the movies were still silent, the Army's recent battles in France monopolized the military movies since naval scenes were not dramatic. An exception was *What Price Glory?* about Marine Capt. Flagg (Victor MacLaughlin) and Marine Sgt. Quirt (Edmund Lowe). It was based on a play co-authored by Lawrence Stallings, a fellow officer of John Thomason, who had left a foot in France. The first real Navy theme was about the Naval Academy and it was one that would recur. In 1925, Ramon Navarro starred in *The Midshipman.* The silent film was made at the Naval Academy and filled with scenes there which were the strength of a weak plot. Some Alumni objected to Navarro in a Midshipman's uniform getting a diploma from SecNav. Midshipmen objected to a known deviate wearing their uniform. *Annapolis* was a dull repeat of *The Midshipman* The same year, an emerging Frank Capra did a combination love-triangle plot about the ill-fated S-51 and S-4 with *Submarine.* Continuing the linkage to real Navy events, *The Flying Fleet*, in 1929 was the first to depict naval aviation and the rigors of flight training. It was based on the 1925 Rodger's flight to Hawaii. It was the writing debut of physically retired Naval Aviator, Frank W. "Spig" Wead, whose Navy epics were to dominate the '30s. The aerial and carrier scenes stole the show. The same year another Annapolis saga, this time with sound, called *Annapolis Salute,* was released. Its feature, in addition to a classic shot of the Midshipmen marching on the field for the Army-Navy game, was John Wayne as a Mid in his first speaking part. *The Cockeyed World* of 1929 with MacLaughlin and Lowe was a talking sequel to

What Price Glory? The decade then opened with a John Ford attempt at submarine recruiting called *Men Without Women.* Its pre-Hay Office erotic scenes in a Shanghai bar might have had some redeeming recruiting effect but recruiting was not a problem n the Depression. The next year Ford followed with a World War I story about Q-boats (disguised armed ships deigned to entice submarine attacks on the surface) called *The Sea Beneath.* The same year another Q-boat drama, *Suicide Fleet,* featured William Boyd (Hopalong Cassidy). Frank Capra was back with the really first movie about the peacetime Navy in *Dirigible* a loose interpretation of the crash of *Shenandoah.*

In 1932, the Navy and Spig Wead came into their own with a good script and star casting. Although Wallace Berry played a drinking CPO (with a heart of gold and matchless nautical and aviation skills) which was ambivalent to acceptance by the Navy approving authority, a clean-shaven Clark Gable was the Simon-pure heir to Navy tradition. *Hell Divers* was a box office success. Not as successful because it was just another love-triangle with an incidental Navy theme was *Hell Below.* It was based on the novel, *Pig Boat,* by Edward Ellsberg, one of the salvage heroes of S-51 an S-4.

In 1933, it was back to Annapolis and *Midshipman Jack a* love story about of all things, a "turnback." The scenes in and of Bancroft Hall, the world's larges dormitory were judged to be powerful proselytization for the Academy. But the first powerful advertisement for preparedness came in 1935 with a first-class cast. Jimmy Cagney and Pat O'Brien starred in *Devil Dogs of the Air.* It was the first and only film showing that Marines were a component of Naval Aviation. Once again the aerial and carrier scenes were spectacular. A Marine landing boosted the Fleet Marine Force (FMF) concept (See Chapter XVIII) and the terse message, "The Marines are ashore and the situation is well n hand!" told it all. There were two more Academy movies that year. *Annapolis Farewell* was a sentimental turkey. *Shipmates Forever,* the second in a service trilogy, *Flirtation Walk* about West Point was the first, was an outstanding success. Crooner Dick Powell again teamed with Ruby Keeler as they did in the West Point movie and were joined by Irish tenor, Dick Foran. The first is a wise-ass Navy junior (like an "Army brat") who hates the navy and the Academy initially. The last is an ex-sailor who loves the Academy but bilges out. He dies heroically after his return to the Fleet saving Powell who is trapped in a flaming fireroom on Summer Cruise. The final scene where Powell and Keeler view Foran's grave in the Naval Academy cemetery was so moving that applications for the Academy increased that year despite anti-war protesters at the movie houses.

The third in the trilogy was the 1937, *The Singing Marine,* once again with Dick Powell. He's a Marne who has a radio audition when the Sixth Marines are being shipped to China (See Chapter XVIII). After some B-movies about Annapolis in 1937, Hollywood went all out in casting *Navy Blue and Gold.* Jimmy Stewart, Robert Young, Tom Brown and Lionel Barrymore were the male leads. Florence Rice the daughter of Grantland Rice, the sportscaster and writer, was the female interest. Barrymore was a retired naval officer in the thinly disguised role of football legend "Navy Bill" Ingrahm. The other three were the mainstays of the Navy football team with the inevitable victory over Army. The interplay of tradition and the mystique of the Academy were awesome. Another Navy movie the same year was less than awesome. *Wings Over Honolulu* a low budget production reflecting the Massie affair (See Chapter X) was more about Navy wives than about ships and airplanes. A couple of slap-stick comedies about Navy life with boy-girl themes and some music like *Follow the Fleet* (1938) and *A Girl, A Guy and A Gob* (1941) were moderate box office successes but 1937 was the real beginning of the truly Navy era in Hollywood before the war.

Submarine D-1 came out in ate 1937. Because it was a tutorial on submarine rescue technique, i.e., the Momsen Lung (an individual breathing apparatus for escape from a sunken submarine) and the McCann Diving Bell, it was released again in 1939 after the *Squalus* disaster. The public got an appreciation of just how the 33 were saved. Once again, Hollywood had put its best cast forward. George Brent, Pat O'Brien and Wayne Morris starred. The last was to become a real Navy fighter ace a few years later with seven Japs to his credit. The filmmakers were carrying a recruiting message because it sold movies. *Wings of the Navy* in 1939 was practically a documentary about flight training at Pensacola and spurred interest in the new Naval Aviation Cadet Program (See Chapter XVI). It had its preparedness message and culminated in a mass flight of PBYs to Hawaii. The taxpayer got a sense of where his dollars went.

The last three prewar movies were again high budget productions with top stars. Two were in Technicolor. *Flight Command* in 1940 starred Walter Pidgeon, Ruth Hussey and Robert Taylor. Again, a technical development, this time a bad-weather homing device, was central to the story told in black and white. After war came in 1941, the real-life Taylor won his wings and was a flight instructor at Pensacola But it was *Dive Bomber* in 1941 with Fred MacMurray, Ralph Bellamy and Errol Flynn that told the story of aviation medicine's struggle to eliminate the black-out of pilots pulling too many Gs (gravity draining blood from the brain) when pulling out of a power dive. The Flight Surgeon was Errol Flynn. It was another Spig Wead opus and it had the approval, if not the outright sponsorship of the Asst. ChBuAer, Capt. Marc Mitscher.

The final prewar movie was *To The Shores of Tripoli* with John Payne, Maureen O'Hara and Randolph Scott. Payne played a Marine junior, who hates the Corps but enlists and his father's old sergeant tries to make a man of him. One of the most vivid scenes is the actual footage of the new battleship, *North Carolina,* firing everything on board from .45 caliber pistols to 16-in. guns. The nighttime view of the ship silhouetted by the flames of the firings is one of the things that earned *North Carolina* the nickname, S*howboat.* When commissioned she was just that – a showboat.

That brings us to the last topic of this chapter – the personalities of the ships of The Treaty Navy. Among their crews, among other ships of the Fleet and to many of the people living where the Fleet was home-ported, ships had nicknames that indicated they were more than just steel monsters. Not all ships had nicknames (or at least ones which could be repeated in polite company) but a sampling of those of some of the large ones will give the reader the flavor of their personalities in The Treaty Navy.

The oldest battleship in commission after 1930 was *Arky (Arkansas). Texas* was *The Lone Star. Nevada* had been the "Cheer Up Ship" under Sims but carried no nickname later. Her sister, *Oklahoma* was *Okie. Pennsylvania* was *Pennsy. Mississippi* was *Missy* and *Idaho* was *Ida. California* was *Prune Barge, Maryland* was *Mary* and *West Virginia* was *WeeVee*. We have seen *North Carolina* as *Showboat*.

The profile of *Langley* gave her the word picture name of *Covered Wagon. Lexington* was *Lady Lex* and *Saratoga* was *Sara. Enterprise* became *The Big E*.

The cruisers tended to have fewer nicknames but there were some. *Cincinnati* was, of course, *Cinncy. Honolulu* was *The Blue Goose;* and *St. Louis* was *Lucky Lou. Pensacola* was *Little Pennsy* and her sister *Salt Lake City* was *Swayback. Chicago* was *Chi* and *Augusta* was *Augie. Louisville* was *Lady Lou* or *Big Lou. Indianapolis* answered to *Indy* among her crew while *Portland* was *Sweet Pea. Vincennes* was *Vinny. San Francisco,* to the consternation of the people of the City of St. Francis was *Frisco. Minneapolis* went by *Minnie. Wichita,* of course was *The Witch*.

Destroyers who were named for people had more personal names. A few examples will suffice. *Sims* was *Billy S.; John D. Edwards* was *Big Ed; Blue* was *Baby Blue; Rueben James* was *Rube,* etc.

Those were some of the names given to specific ships but there was another name that occasionally made the rounds of the Fleet. Before the days of "Don't ask; don't tell," every effort was made to detect and discharge homosexuals. They were relatively easy to spot once their existence was suspected on board. A pair of sailors from different divisions who regularly went ashore together and did not mix with the rest of the crew were prime candidates for suspicion of being fairies. An overt proposition on board was usually reported. The reason was simple. No sailor or skipper wanted his ship to be tagged with the damning appellation of *Queer Barge*.

Chapter XVIII

The Marines

In the days of sailing ships, Marines were part of the ship's company. Their sea-going duties did not entail the working of the ship. They had other duties which were of a combat nature. During actions between ships, Marines manned some of the guns; stationed themselves in the rigging ("fighting tops") to fire their muskets down on enemy decks, usually aiming for enemy officers; and either repulsed boarders by bayonet or answered the cry, "Away boarders!" to carry the fight to the enemy decks. Marines also formed the backbone of landing forces from ships. The function was exercised during the Revolution, War of 1812, Civil War and the war with Spain. Concomitantly, in peacetime, Marines landed from ships, usually battleships or cruisers or their sail-rigged equivalents, to restore order, quell uprisings or protect American citizens and property. Marines drifted into the role of sea-going policemen both afloat and ashore. Those were the ship's detachments. Ashore in the U.S. and her possessions, Marines also performed a security function at Navy Yards in organizations called Marine Barracks (MB). During the first few decades of the 20th Century, companies from these MBs were organized into higher echelon units usually called battalions but sometimes regiments for expeditionary duty, usually with fleet units. This was a direct result of the Roosevelt Corollary to the Monroe Doctrine, i.e., the U.S. will guarantee the payment of foreign debts of Western Hemisphere countries lest Europeans seek to intervene. There was a vocal cabal of both Navy and Army officers who thought that this function ashore could and should be taken over by the Army. Within the Navy these officers also thought that Marines on board ship were no longer needed and that the Marine Corps should be abolished.

As we have seen technology overtook events. Steam-driven ships no longer had "fighting tops." Even if they had, the breech loading, [relatively] long-range guns eliminated the tactic of closing and boarding the enemy. Marines did seem superfluous but a few visionaries, like Lejeune, saw a new and different role for "Soldiers of the Sea." The range of sailing ships had been limited only by the endurance of their crews and the extent of their provisions. Steam ships had another critical limitation. They depended on fuel to feed their boilers. For a long time this was coal but even the gradual conversion to oil made replenishment of fuel a major requirement. Coal (or oil) could be stored at bases. The RN had a string of bases around the world; the U.S. didn't. She would have to seize such bases and then defend them as well as defend bases she already had. Lejeune and his protégé, Pete Ellis, foresaw this new role for the Marines as early as 1914. They would have to take a detour to France (1918-19) before they could return and lead the Corps in this new direction.

We have noted Lejeune's approval of the Pete Ellis OpPlan 712 in 1921. The activities of Marines up to about 1930 including expeditions to the Caribbean,

Nicaragua and China have been discussed. Before going into the details of the new Marine role which evolved into perfection of amphibious warfare, we should take a look at the world-wide commitment of a force numbering less than 20,000 in the early '30s.

Marines were still in Haiti, Nicaragua and China in 1930. The brigade whom Smedley Butler took to China in 1927 came home but the Fourth Marines, an under-strength infantry regiment, remained in Shanghai. There was a Legation Guard at Peiping which although formidable was mainly a ceremonial unit. It even had a mounted detachment of "horse Marines." The violence in the two countries which occupied Hispanola was pretty much under control. Marines had left Santo Domingo in 1924 turning the *Guardia Nacional* into the *Policia Nacional* to keep Dominican leadership from thinking it was a banana republic army rather than a national constabulary. Marines were in Haiti but mostly as officers in the national organization, *Gendarmerie d'Haiti* a police force vice actual military forces. On Aug. 21, 1934 the *Gendarmerie* relieved the Marines as the 1st Marine Brigade sailed home.

Troubles in Nicaragua waxed and waned. In early 1928, Sandino's mountain headquarters of El Chipote had been located and attacked. The fortress was reduced but Sandino eluded capture and fled. He briefly hid among a guerrilla group up the Co Co River. A combined unit of Marine's from ships' detachments and *Guardia Nacional de Nicaragua* embarked upon what was to enter Marine annals as "The Co Co River Patrol." Commanded by Capt. M.A. ("Red Mike") Edson, the patrol in canoes and overland, depending on air drops for resupply, covered 400 miles in the interior compressing the rebel forces into a box and killing many of them. Once again, Sandino escaped and fled north to Mexico. "Red Mike" was to win a Medal of Honor at Guadalcanal in 1942 and retire as a major general.

More of the anti-bandit and anti-guerrilla operations in eastern Nicaragua were turned over to the *Guardia* which was officered by Marine officers and NCOs. They received the pay of their Marine Corps ranks plus the pay of higher ranks in the *Guardia* at the Nicaraguan rate of pay. As a police force, the *Guardia* (with 267 Marine officers and 2,240 enlisted Marines) could delve deeper into the populace for intelligence than could a foreign military force. In May 1930 Sandino returned from the Yucatan where he had been actively soliciting support.

Augusto Sandino had garnered a varying coterie of supporters. Much of his new support was financial but a lot of it was propagandistic. Money had come from *The Nation,* an ultra-liberal magazine published n New York City. The magazine was also filled with pro-Sandino and anti-Marine editorials. On May 30, 1930, a rally was held in Union Square in downtown Manhattan to raise funds for arms for Sandino. His main sponsor in the U.S. was the All-American Anti-Imperialist League, a fellow-traveler organization under Communist direction. *The Nation* also had a man in the enemy's camp. Their correspondent with Sandino's headquarters wrote glowing articles about interviews with the "patriot" and of his reactions against the *Guardia* and Marines.

On Mar. 31, 1931, there was a disastrous earthquake in Managua, the capital. Fire consumed much of the city. There were about 1,000 dead. Marines from the Brigade now reduced to about 1,000 officers and men, turned-to in the relief of the stricken and the rebuilding of the city.

In 1932, the *Guardia* was on its way to having the bandit and Sandino problem "well in hand." A mobile company based on Jinotega was commanded by Capt. (1st Lt. USMC) L.B. Puller. He carried the war to the bandits in a rapid series of patrols into their mountain refuge. He kept pressure on the bandits reducing their fighting effectiveness to a point that there were hardly a threat. "Chesty" Puller continued as a legend in the Corps through World War II and Korea and retired as a lieutenant general.

Although banditry was not eliminated, the U.S., in the closing days of President Hoover's administration decided on a new non-intervention policy. After the Nicaraguan election of 1932, Marines would leave. Besides roads and communications facilities, the Marines would leave an efficient *Guardia Nacional* under Marine-trained officers. Dissidents and mutineers among the *Guardia,* who had murdered some of their Marine superiors, had been tried and eliminated. Thus the Marines left on Jan. 2, 1933 and F.D.R. was sworn in on Mar. 4.

Thirteen months later, the *Jefe Director* of the *Guardia* enticed Sandino to come to Managua. Sensing that he was going to be granted a series of concessions, he swaggered in with a minor entourage expecting that "all sins are forgiven." He was not prepared for the pragmatic approach of Anastasio Somoza. The little bandit who had participated in or sanctioned the executions and mutilations of Marines and civilians for a half dozen years was disarmed and after a summary tribunal, he and his henchmen were lined up against a wall. Before the machine guns cut him down, the hero of *The Nation* wet his pants.

Several legacies from Nicaragua carried over to the eventual benefit of The Treaty Navy. Not the least of which was that it gave combat experience to the officers and NCOs who were to fight in the Pacific less than nine years later. As the World War I combat veterans moved into the upper echelons of command, they were ably replaced at the battalion and company levels by seasoned fighters from Nicaragua. Second, it was the first air-ground war ever. Scouting, resupply from the air, medical evacuation by air, and the new technique of dive-bombing gave warfare a dimension beyond that of World War I. The last item, dive-bombing, was studied by the new German war machine.

Unlike France who was preparing to fight the last war with her Maginot Line mentality or the British another Jutland, the Germans and the Marines were preparing to fight the next war. The former with her *Stuka* supported armored thrusts; the latter with amphibious assaults able to seize advanced bases for the march across the Pacific. Before looking at the development of amphibious theory and its application, we must close out the last pre-war expeditionary endeavor of the Marine Corps in China in 1937.

The beginning of the Sino-Japanese War with the incident near Peiping at the Marco Polo Bridge in 1937 attracted the attention of the U.S. The Navy was involved in protecting U.S. citizens and business interests as mentioned in the previous chapter of the *Augusta* and *Panay* incidents. With new fighting around Shanghai, the 2nd Marine Brigade headquarters with the Sixth Marines from San Diego was sent to join the Fourth Marines already there. (We have seen how Hollywood used the event to film *The Singing Marine* with Dick Powell.) In September 1937, the Brigade and regiment left San Diego on *USS Chaumont* (AP-5), an old transport. She brought them back to San Diego in April 1938 after the fighting had moved elsewhere in China.

Legend has it that the Marines painted in vertical letters below *Chaumont* on the ship's stern: "**C**hrist **H**elp **A**ll **U**nlucky **M**arines **O**n **N**avy **T**ransports." The Navy held that the **U** should have read **U**nwashed. The reason was that the PX supplies for the regiment contained several thousands cases of "pogey bait" (candy bars) but only one case of soap. The Sixth Marines became known as the "Pogey-Bait Marines." Since they had been awarded the French *fourragére* (a red and green aguillette worn around he left shoulder) along with the Fifth Marines and 6th Machine Gun Battalion in France, that decoration is still known as "The Pogey Rope."

Two other events which may or may not be inter-related but have nothing to do with amphibious warfare are worth mentioning. The Navy Personnel Act of 1916 had provided for an officer selection system for promotion. It did not provide one for the Marine Cops. Promotions from first lieutenant through colonel were based on seniority when a vacancy occurred.

Vacancies occurred through death, retirement or resignation. There was a form of selection, however, for general officer. SecNav nominated colonels to the President who with the advice and consent of the Senate approved them. The list for SecNav was prepared by the MGC *and* flag officers of the Navy designated by SecNav. In short, the Navy had a big say in who made general in the Marine Corps. When it came to a new MGC, it was an almost all-Navy choice.

There had been a long succession of Naval Academy Alumni as MGC starting with George Barnett in 1914 (Class of 1881) then John A. Lejeune in 1920 (Class of 1888), then Wendell C. Neville in 1929 (Class of 1890). When Neville died after 16 months in office, his assistant, Ben Fuller (Class of 1889) was chosen MGC. MajGen. Smedley D. Butler, not a Naval Academy graduate (or any other kind, see Chapter V) felt that he, as the senior major general had been passed over for MGC because he was not from the Academy while the senior admirals were picking one of their own. Butler retired immediately and with pique.

Butler, as in the past, was vocal. His previous public utterances, like categorizing boot-leggers as "hyphenated-Americans" or having been directed by the President to apologize to a head of a foreign government for personal remarks in public had left him in Presidential disfavor. (Butler had called Mussolini a "murderer" because the car in which he was riding struck and killed an Italian child. Butler while he may have been right he was not discreet.) Now Butler burst into print. He authored a piece called, "The Hell With the

Admirals." His vituperative blistered those he thought had done him an injustice by giving the MGC job to another Academy graduate.

Whether or not there was a cause-and-effect relationship, the Marine Corps did get its own officer promotion selection system. The climate created by the Butler tirades encouraged the new MGC to push for the long sought after selection legislation in 1934. It was passed and became effective in the term of MGC John H. Russell, Jr. (USNA 1891) who took office Mar.1, 1934. The immediate effect was that a host of superannuated captains and majors were retired before reaching the statutory age requiring retirement no matter what the rank. One wonders if Russell whose plan for the post-war officer corps had been overridden by the Neville Board (See Chapter II) felt vindicated. Companies were again commanded by younger men equal to the rigors of the job. Second lieutenants who by law were receiving the pay but not the rank of first lieutenant after five years commissioned service donned silver bars. It was a milestone for the Marine Corps.

Smedley Butler continued to be heard in retirement. His theme was that war was a racket. He said that he fought in Central America and the Caribbean for the United Fruit Company and its big shareholders. His expedition to China was merely to bail out Standard Oil. Although his remarks were welcomed by the anti-military faction and he was a darling of the isolationist press, he had no effect on The Treaty Navy.

With the withdrawal of Marines from Nicaragua and Haiti, the curtain came down on their use as colonial infantry. A new dawn was breaking. No longer required to respond to the need for expeditionary service (the short China hiatus of 1937-38 notwithstanding), the Corps could get busy with the role Lejeune had envisioned for it – *readiness.*

There had been a Marine Advanced Base Force, both in being and on paper since the turn of the century. Floating battalions had been around and used in the Caribbean before World War I. Landing exercises had been conducted at Culebra off the eastern end of Puerto Rico. The landings of Marine Detachments (MD) from warships had been a small-scale attempt at the amphibious role. But such were usually unopposed or even administrative landings. The MD, however, belonged to the ship and was under the command of the ship's CO even when ashore unless it was freed from such a command relation by higher authority. In 1916, while he was assistant Commandant, BGen. Lejeune had established a principle of command relationships in landing operations which was to play a significant part in future amphibious operations This will be discussed below.

Despite the advocacy of such zealots as Pete Ellis and his OpPlan 712, *Advanced Base Operations in Micronesia,* there were few outside the Marine Corps who believed in the efficacy of "assault from the sea." Most military minds sad it couldn't be done. For their proof they cited the bloody debacle of Gallipoli in 1915.

Gallipoli had been the brainchild of the First Lord of the Admiralty, Winston S. Churchill. While the Germans were fighting a two-front war, Britain and

France were unable to directly help their ally, Russia. Since the route through the Baltic was tactically infeasible, the southern route to the Black Sea via the Turkish Dardanelles was decided upon. A force of older (expendable?) battleships was assigned the task of forcing the straits. One modern dreadnought was attached for temporary bombardment. When the ships fighting the "forts" failed to accomplish the mission, it was decided to take the forts from the rear. A landing was to be made by troops of Great Britain and France. The most available then in the Middle East was the Australian-New Zealand Army Corps (ANZAC). The initial landings obtained a lodgment but the subsequent operations ashore were a major fiasco. Without analyzing what went wrong, conventional military wisdom concluded that amphibious operations were impossible.

Fortunately, Marines were not among those who embraced that species of conventional military wisdom. They couldn't because War Plan ORANGE for which The Treaty Navy was being built required that stepping-stones of advanced bases across the Central Pacific be seized and defended. The only approach to these stepping-stones was from the sea.

Sensing freedom from its interim role as colonial infantry of expeditionary service, senior officers as well as some relatively junior ones began acting on the thoughts and concepts that had lain dormant in the '20s. While landing exercises had been conducted in conjunction with the annual Fleet Problems they were sometimes little more than an afterthought from the Navy standpoint. Marine units other than MDs were transported in battleships, transferred to whaleboats and waded ashore. Boat officers were loathe to have coxswains let the boats touch down on a beach lest they scratch the bottom of the whaleboat. For amphibious warfare to be successful, the Navy was going to have to be disabused of the belief that it was a cardinal sin to run any craft aground. Amphibious warfare was going to require specialized ships and boats. Infantry could leap over the gunwales of a whaleboat and wade ashore. It could even take light automatic weapons across a beach that way. Artillery, tanks and trucks, vital elements in the rapid build-up of combat power from the shoreline could not be put ashore that way.

At Marine Corps schools (MCS) in Quantico, a committee started work on *Marine Corps Landing Operations* in 1931. The treatise was finished the following year but not published. On each coast there still existed the East and West Coast Expeditionary Forces but their status within the U.S. Fleet was undefined. In the meantime, at MCS, staff and students of the field grade and company grade officers courses were doing basic academic research. Their subject was an analysis of Gallipoli, not so much what went wrong but why it did. It was an update of the *dictum* attributed to Peter the Great after his first battle, "I lost but I learned how to win!" The post-mortem autopsy of Gallipoli was going to provide the guidance on how an amphibious operation should be conducted.

Two months into the academic year at MCS, the former Commandant, MCS, now the assistant to MGC Fuller and acting in his behalf suspended classes at

Quantico. The staff and students were divided into committees to study the various aspects of landing operations. Their mandate was to develop rules and doctrine on landing operations. By January 1934, they had produced, *Tentative Manual for Landing Operations.* It was a start.

It was in keeping with a recommendation Russell had made earlier. He wanted a Marine striking force, equipped, armed and trained to work as a unit of the U.S. Fleet under CINCUS. It was to be included in Fleet organization and subject to tactical employment by CINCUS. CNO, Adm. Standley, who had just succeeded Pratt, suggested that it be called Fleet Marine Force (FMF). The FMF replaced the East and West Coast Expeditionary Forces.

SecNav issued Navy Department General Order 241 on Dec. 7, 1933, eight years before the "date which will live in infamy." The MGC was to maintain a force of Marines in a state of readiness for operations with the Fleet and it was to be included in the operational force planning each fiscal year. The MGC was to designate the units and maintain them in sufficient strength appropriate to the general personnel situation of the Corps. The FMF was to be available for operations and exercises afloat or ashore as part of annual Fleet Problems. CINCUS was to command the FMF when embarked or engaged in Fleet exercises. Otherwise, command was to be retained by MGC. The CG, FMF and staff were to be designated by he MGC. At least once a year, CG FMF was to report to CINCUS for exercises or conference.

Further, a principle of command relations was restated. As alluded to earlier, Lejeune had solved such a problem with the Commander of the Atlantic Fleet regarding operations ashore in the Caribbean before World War I. Various ship's COs insisted that Marines ashore in ports and villages engaged in quelling disturbances or protecting citizens should be subject to the authority and orders of the captain of the ship standing off the port. Lejeune successfully argued that operations ashore should be conducted by the commander ashore and that once the Navy had established the Marines ashore the Navy was not to interfere with operations there. This became doctrine in FMF operations subsequently. CINCUS could designate a subordinate commander (Navy) to carry out a mission of seizing an advanced base with Marines but once command and control could be transferred ashore, the Navy officer was to pass control to the Marine commander established ashore. That way no sailor was going to be tempted to play Napoleon and second-guess the experts. Even though he was an admiral's son, John Russell was going to stick up for his Marines.

MCS remained the intellectual center of the Corps. The two officers' schools (The Basic School for new second lieutenants was still at Philadelphia) were renamed. The one for field grade officers became Senior Amphibious Warfare Course and the one for company grade was the Junior Amphibious Warfare Course. To Marines they became Senior School and Junior School. One of the first things done at MCS after the formation of the FMF was to put together a presentation team of skilled instructors to demonstrate the techniques of a specific amphibious warfare operation. These studies were professionally done scenarios of attacks on specific objectives mostly in the Pacific. They were designed for presentation at the Naval War College each year but they were also given to Junior and Senior Schools. They were classified, of course, but were called Advance Base Problems (ABP). Seven were given before war began in 1941and naturally they were suspended during the war until 1947. A list gives an indication of where Marines and the Navy were directing their thinking:

1933	APB I	Duman Quilas Bay Area, Mindanao, P.I.
1934	APB	ditto
1935	ABP II	Truk, Japanese Mandate, Caroline Islands
1936	ABP III	Palau, Japanese Mandates, Caroline Islands
1937	ABP IV	Duman Quilas, Attack, Mindanao, P.I.
1938	ABP V	Trinidad, British West Indies
1939	ABP VI	Guam, U.S. Territory, Marianas Islands
1940	ABP VII	Saipan, Japanese Mandates, Marianas Islands

The actual execution of the last two in 1944 closely followed the scripts of 1939 and 1940 updated to include equipment which had been manufactured and/or improved during the war.

Equipment was another facet of amphibious development at MCS. In 1933, the Marine Corps Equipment Board was established at Quantico. It was the first and only facility devoted to testing and developing all types of equipment for landing operations. Of course, many of its items impacted on the Navy and its ships. It had a sometimes-testy relationship with BuShips, the Navy's grand *poobah* of ship design. BuShips had a distinct proclivity for self-preservation which manifested itself in a "not-invented-here" (NIH) attitude. More than once Marines had to pull an end run on BuShips to get what Marines needed to get ashore and operate. More on these **innovations** will be discussed in Chapter XXI.

In 1938, Maj. G.C. Thomas joined the faculty of MCS. He had gone to France as a private in the 75th Company, Sixth Marines. He returned as a first lieutenant in 1919 commanding the company. He was to eventually retire at the end of 1955 with four stars. One of his other contributions to amphibious warfare was to be the operational planner and staff executor of the landing and subsequent operations on Guadalcanal.

What concerns us is his contribution in 1938 and 1939. He was assigned the billet of Schools military historian. He inherited a five-hour presentation which he expanded to seven to include a detailed analysis of Gallipoli. What happened; why it did; and what plans should have been made to prevent it happening was presented to every class at both Junior and Senior Schools. Gallipoli became a classic example of what not to do. It went further, however, by covering what must be done in future amphibious operations. Jerry Thomas inculcated those who would plan and lead future amphibious assaults in the Pacific. One of these was his able assistant in the presentation. Capt. D.M. Shoup was at Jerry Thomas's side handling slides, maps, charts, transparencies and the pointer as Jerry Thomas expounded the Do and Don't of Gallipoli. Dave Shoup was to plan the assault on Tarawa and when a regimental commander fell ill, to lead the assault regiment onto the atoll. For his 73 hours of sleepless command, he was awarded the Medal of Honor. He became the 22nd Commandant of the Marine Corps (CMC) in 1960.

The successful solution to the problem of amphibious warfare was one of the key factors in enabling the U.S. to project her fleet and land forces across the Pacific and wage war in Japanese waters. The lead in such solution was taken by the land component of The Treaty Navy.

MGC Russell did another thing which boded well for Marine Corps expansion. Though still having slightly more than 1,000 officers and 17,000 men, a Marine Corps that was going to seize advanced bases across the Pacific was going to expand enormously to do so. He remembered the drain on small unit leadership as a result of commissioning a large number of NCOs to flesh out the Corps expansion in 1917. The backbone of the Corps was experienced, professional NCOs to help the younger, less experienced officers get their feet on the ground. Hence, Russell introduced the Platoon Leaders' Class. College undergraduates would enroll for two summers of training at MCS. Upon graduation from college they would be commissioned as second lieutenants in the Reserve. Thus, a cadre of commissioned officers was available when expansion started in 1939.

Marines were among but hardly the only visionaries of The Treaty Navy.

No chapter on Marines could close without mention of the legendary GySgt. Martinez. For years he ramrodded the Sea School that turned out spit-and-polish Marines from San Diego to ships of The Treaty Navy. Yet he got into the Marine Corps by accident. Before World War I, he and his two brothers came from South America to join the Navy. In New York he became separated from them and wandering around but speaking very little English he saw a sign. As he told it, "I see this sign. It says Marines. I, Martinez, know that *marino* is sailor. I join. Then, I am thinking what a funny navy this is. They feel my muscles, give me a green suit, send me to Philadelphia and make me march. It is two weeks before I am knowing what a lucky man I am!" But it was at sea that he became a legend. For two years in a row, his 5 in. mount on a battleship had won the annual short-range battle practice. They were about to do so again when on the final round, he yanked the lanyard but it broke. Without hesitation, he used his trigger finger to trip the firing mechanism and the gun recoiled over the mechanism. The lieutenant said, "Martinez has won again!" Martinez replied, "Martinez has won but has lost his finger.!" Such were the Marines of The Treaty Navy.

Chapter XIX

London Conference of 1935 and Treaty of 1936

After the London Treaty of 1930 on naval armaments, talks on limiting other arms continued under the League of Nations at Geneva. There had been preliminary talks in 1926 and 1927 prior to the abortive Geneva Convention on Naval Arms (See Chapter VI). From Feb. 2, to Jul 21, 1932, a Conference on the Reduction and Limitations of Arms met at Geneva. There was a continuing phase of these discussions from Jan.1, to May 12, 1934. Mr. Norman Davis, with the rank of ambassador, was the American representative. Under the terms of the London Treaty of 1930, the Parties agreed to meet in 1933, "… to frame a new treaty to carry out the purpose of the present one…"

In anticipation of the agreed conference, the U.S. and Britain began preliminary talks in London with the aim of eliminating any differences beforehand and avoiding repetition of the debacle of Geneva in 1927. The talks were between the U.S. Ambassador, Robert Bingham, and the Prime Minister, Ramsay MacDonald, and his representatives. Later, Norman Davis joined the talks and it was a delicate matter for SecState Cordell Hull to soothe personalities since Davis was the real negotiator and Bingham only titular. That arrangement was necessary to avoid the impression that the U.S. had sent a delegation to London prior to the conference to align with Britain before others were invited. Eventually talks progressed to the point where it was possible to ask Japan to join the preliminary discussions. The Japanese, in addition to their ambassador in London, sent a technical delegation under VAdm. Isoroku Yamamoto. He was later to become a household word in the U.S. as the architect of the attack on Pearl Harbor. Near the end of these preliminaries in London, Japanese intent to denounce the Washington Treaty at the end of 1934 became apparent and the tone of the talks hardened.

Essentially, the preliminary talks had four phases. The first was the Anglo-American discussions for planning for preliminary conversations. These were held from Jan. 23, to Jun. 15 1934. The second phase was preliminary naval conversations between the two, also in London from Jun. 18, to Jul 19, 1934. The third phase was preliminary naval conversations, second session with the Japanese present from Oct. 19, to Dec. 19, 1934. Phase four was brought about when the Japanese Ambassador to the U.S., Hosi Saito, delivered a note to the U.S. Department of State on Saturday, Dec. 29, 1934, giving formal notice of his government's intent to terminate the Washington Treaty of 1922 on its expiration date of Dec. 31, 1936. Three days later, France made a similar denunciation stating that it had always been her intent to allow the Treaty to lapse because the ratios were not representative of France's naval prestige and importance. The Japanese move had been anticipated.

A note from the U.S. Ambassador in Tokyo, Joseph C, Grew, had cited a change in Japan since the London Conference in 1930. He stated that the pro-

Treaty admirals had been removed or forced to retire since 1930. A "Big Navy" clique was now in control and they insisted on parity. He also stated that the assassination of the Prime Minister by a group of "Young Turk" army officers had brought about a reversal of anti-military sentiment among the Japanese people.

In the U.S., Anglophobe suspicions were rising again. Hull was thinking that the British and Japanese were trying to get together. The compromise was to secure British trade rights in Japanese-controlled China in exchange for support of the Japanese demand for parity.

While the first phase of preliminary talks were about to end, Grew mentioned that the Japanese were suspicious of the Anglo-American talks because they might be detrimental to Japan. He cited the Japanese feeling about the Hoover-MacDonald talks in 1929.

President Roosevelt's note to the British Prime Minister during the second phase of the preliminary talks was delivered by Davis. Roosevelt stated that he wanted limits on naval arms; a ten-year extension of the Washington and London Treaties; and a basis of 25% reduction over the next ten years. Like his predecessors, he thought mutual reductions were the bases for relative security.

When Japan joined the third phase of discussions, Grew cabled his assessment of Japan's position on a naval race. He felt that she was more fearful of the economics of a building program where she would be out-matched, than she was hateful of the ratios.

During the third phase, Yamamoto presented Japan's desires. She wanted a "common upper limit," – no ratio of inferiority. She also wanted to eliminate or drastically reduce "offensive" ships. These, she specified as battleships, aircraft carriers and heavy cruisers. Instead of tonnage limits by categories, she wanted a global tonnage basis. It was becoming clear that she would denounce the Washington Treaty soon.

Hull wanted to be sure that denunciation occurred without any concessions to coax Japan to remain in a patched-up treaty system. He felt that denunciation without concessions would deprive her saber-rattling firebrands of any diplomatic gains. If Japan denounced, the U.S. would immediately build to Treaty limits and begin a replacement program. He so instructed his delegation.

The prospects of a conference began to wane. In a cable to be revealed to the British, Hull pointed out that while the Washington and London Treaties called for conferences, they did not say who was to call them or how they were to be called. Therefore, if no one called one, no one Party could be criticized. The American position was firm. There was going to be no compromise before Japan denounced the Treaty. Japan must go home empty-handed. There was to be no continuance of the preliminary discussions to seek an agreement lest it be inferred that the Japanese plan of radical alteration of the Treaties be accepted. The Parties should only reconvene if one of them extended an invitation under new proposals.

Just before the talks broke up, Grew reversed his assessment of Japanese intentions. He now felt that no matter what the cost, even a naval race, Japan was determined for reasons of prestige to free herself from naval inferiority. As we have seen denunciation took place on Dec. 29, 1934.

The British position through the preliminary talks had changed from that of 1930. They went back to their need for 70 not just 50 cruisers. Although they went along with the principle of tonnage reduction, they wanted to achieve it by qualitative reductions, e.g., the size of capital ships and the caliber of guns.

As the talks were obviously in jeopardy, Britain proposed a "middle course" which preserved the Washington non-fortification provisions; set qualitative limits; required a statement of intended building programs in each coming year and retained the provisions of construction notification. The discussions broke up on that note.

In 1935, Britain and Germany reached an agreement on German naval resurgence. Italian moves in East Africa against Ethiopia were of concern to Britain and her Mediterranean Fleet in particular. German naval revival was not a concern. As a matter of fact, it could be advantageous as a counterpoise to Italy and France. Thus, German offers to reach an agreement on limiting arms *vis a vis* the two nations were accepted and discussions began in mid-1935. German proposals were close to the British desires of both Geneva and the second London position. The size of battleships was to be smaller than those agreed at Washington; the larger 8-in. gun cruiser was to be eliminated; submarines were to conform to International Law; and Germany was to have a ratio of 35% of the British by categories as per the Washington and the 1930 London Treaty. France was not pleased. She felt it violated the Treaty of Versailles and was tantamount to abrogation of it. The 35% ratio was an irritant because 35% of RN tonnage of capital ships was 183,750 tons or greater than the French allowance of 175,000 tons. France had to adhere to the tonnage of Washington until 1936. Prestige of navies was more a factor in French pique than anything else. Neither Japan nor the U.S. was very concerned with the naval situation in Europe since they were concerned about each other in the Western Pacific.

After the Anglo-German Naval Agreement in the summer of 1935, further exchanges between the British government and each of the other four Parties occurred. Japan, France and Italy held that they could not consider quantitative limits as in the Washington ratios, or as extended at London and could not consider notification of intended building which would be related to the demeaning ratio system. But they would accept an invitation to consider other aspects of the "middle course." The U.S. reluctantly realized that solutions consistent with the Washington principles could not be found but agreed to attend in order to find agreement that would avoid a naval race.

The second London Naval Conference opened on Dec. 7, 1935. All the Parties to the Washington Conference including the British Dominions sent delegates.

The. U.S. delegation had three members, Ambassador Davis, CNO Adm. W.H. Standley and Under SecState William Philby. The French had their ambassador to Britain, Charles Corbin, assisted by VAdm. George Robert. British delegates were Viscount Monsell, First Lord of the Admiralty and her

Under-Secretary for Foreign Affairs, the Earl of Stanhope. Italy sent her British ambassador, Dino Grande. The Japanese had Adm. Osani Nagano, War Counsellor to the Emperor, and an ambassador without portfolio, Matsuzo Nagai.

Japan opened with her proposal for a "common upper limit" and asked that the larger navies reduce to a level below that which Japan had, regardless of respective needs and responsibilities. None of the delegates could accept this proposal and the Japanese withdrew from the Conference in January 1936.

The question of quantitative limits was strongly opposed by France and Italy and it became evident that the only way to salvage any limits would be qualitative, although the U.S. favored the combination of the two types of limitation. A vital ingredient to any new treaty was deemed to be that of exchange of information prior to construction.

Without the Japanese, a new treaty was concluded on Mar. 25, 1936 to become effective on Jan.1, 1937 or as soon as fully ratified. It was to run until Dec. 31 1942. Parties were the U.S., France and Great Britain. Two "Dominions" with no navies nor intentions of acquiring one, Union of South Africa and the Irish Free State felt that signing would require future participation in naval conferences and abstained. Italy refrained from being a Party.

The new Treaty had no quantitative limits on tonnage or numbers of ships as had the two previous treaties. It did have a naval "holiday" on building heavy cruisers, as the term was now understood. There were definitions of two categories of capital ships. A capital ship was any ship more than 10,000 tons (as per previous definition) but it was also a ship more than 8,000 tons with guns greater than 8-in. A second category was a ship less than 8,000 tons with gun smaller than 8-in. This covered capital ships of some minor navies (See Chapter II). Cruisers and destroyers were combined into the definition of *light surface vessel*. These were in sub-categories of **A, B** and **C** which were the old heavy and light cruisers and destroyers. Destroyer size was increased to 3,000 tons to include some very large destroyer leaders of France and Italy. *Auxiliary vessels* were those transports, oilers and tenders, which is the currently accepted definition. Age limits were set for the purpose of determining if a nation was increasing its navy or just replacing. Capital ship age was extended to 26 years. All others remained as in the two prior treaties.

In addition to the heavy cruiser "holiday," no 10,000-ton 6-in. cruisers were to be built for six years. The size of carriers was reduced from 27,000 to 23,000 tons and their guns from 8-in. to 6-in. Capital ships remained at 35,000 tons maximum. The size of their guns as reduced to 14-in, from 16-in., contingent upon none of the Parties to the Washington Treaty, e.g., Japan or Italy, building a ship with the larger gun. If this occurred, the Parties to the new Treaty could follow suit. There was a "zone of non-construction" in capital ships between 8,000 an 17,000 tons to make the cruiser "holiday" effective. Capital ships had to have 10-in. or greater guns to prevent construction of pseudo-capital ships that were really cruisers. The larger gun reduced speed thus ruining its utility as a cruiser.

The notification clause was a major feature. During the first third of the year, each Party had to inform the others of its annual building program in detail. No departures could be made unless invoking safeguarding clauses. Information on modification and laying down had to be given beforehand.

Safeguarding clauses were needed because there were so many non-Parties not bound, e.g., Japan, Italy, Germany and the U.S.S.R. They could, of course, become Parties. The elaborate "escalator clauses" safeguarded Parties from the non-Parties who did not observe the cruiser "holiday" and were a threat to a Party. War or other dangers to national security enabled a Party to lay down a ship not part of her announced program. The safeguards which were a necessary part of the Treaty actually emasculated it. At least the safeguards were acknowledgement of the emasculation which had occurred when Japan and Italy decided to go their own ways and the remaining Parties could not agree on quantitative limits – the heart of any arms limitation.

The London Treaty of 1936 was more form than substance and was soon overtaken by events. The ghost of naval limitations lingered on in the minds of some but naval limitation was dead. Construction continued.

The U.S. had a building program to reach treaty limits extending over several years under the Vinson-Trammel Act. The last heavy cruiser under the terms of the 1930 London Treaty could not be laid down before 1935. *Wichita* (CA-45) was laid down on Oct. 28, 1935. Also in 1935, keels were laid for three light cruisers (*Phoenix, Boise* and *Honolulu*) of 10,000 tons which were repeats of the four *Brooklyn* class of N.I.R.A. authorizations. This left two authorizations from the 15 cruisers of 1929 still to be built. The keels of the final two which were improved *Brooklyn*s (*Helena* and *St. Louis*) were laid in December of 1936 This accounted for all the 1929 program before the second London Treaty took effect. The 1930 Treaty limited destroyers to 1,500 tons. When the Treaty expired at the end of 1936, the *Sims* class then under construction or on order was modified from experience with previous classes and 70 tons added. The *Benson* class which would be the last of the "Treaty" destroyers was also increased in size. Those 24 ships were of 1,630 tons each.

On Aug. 1, 1937, the U.S. placed orders for two battleships which in effect would be replacements for aging ships and would conform to the 35,000-ton limit of second London. They were authorized by Vinson-Trammel.

On Feb. 3, 1938, SecState Hull communicated with his ambassador in Japan. "As you know persistent reports have reached us that the Japanese are building or contemplate building, ships exceeding the limits of the London Treaty of 1936." Hull told Grew that the matter had been discussed with the British and French and all agreed that identical notes, *mutatis mutandis,* should be delivered to the Japanese Government on Saturday, Feb. 5, 1938 by the respective ambassadors.

The notes which were delivered described the limits agreed to by each of the Parties to the Second London Treaty. They regretted that Japan had not been able to accept the limits. They reminded the Japanese of the right of escalation in the safeguarding clauses. They requested assurances that the persistent rumors of Japanese construction were ill founded. They asked Japan to communicate her program to the U.S. not later than Feb. 20, 1938 because of the requirements to submit her own program to the other Parties prior to the end of April. "The American Government has therefore decided that it will be necessary for it to exercise the right of escalation unless the Japanese Government can furnish the aforesaid assurances ... Should no reply be received [by Feb. 20] ... or should the reply be lacking in assurances, it will be compelled to assume that the Japanese Government is ... acquiring ... vessels not in conformity with the limits ... The American Government would thereupon be obligated in consultation with the other Naval Powers ... to resume full liberty of action."

The reply came on Feb. 12. Japan regretted that the U.S. was assuming Japanese construction on the basis of rumors. The position of Japan during the 1936 conference was reiterated and in addition to denying the alleged building, said that such was none of the business of other powers.

The fact was that in 1938, Japan was building two 67,000-ton battleships with 18-in. guns; two 29,800-ton carriers; two 8-in. cruisers of 15,200 tons and 13,800 tons; and was rearming and modernizing four recent 10,000-ton, 6-in. cruisers into 13,000 tonners with 8-in. guns plus modernizing four others to 15,000 tons.

On Mar. 31, 1938, Hull notified the ambassadors of the Parties to the 1936 Treaty, with courtesy copies to Japan and Italy via his ambassadors: "With reference to Article 25 of the Naval Treaty signed in London on March 25, 1936, I have the honor to notify ... that the Government of the United States of America finds it necessary to exercise the right of escalation ... and of effecting a departure from the limitations and restriction of the Treaty ..."

The stillborn Treaty was ready to be interred.

Chapter XX

More Vinson Acts

On May 17, 1938, the second Vinson Act was signed. In referring to the heretofore-authorized tonnages as having been in accordance the now-expired (or abrogated by invoking the escalator clause) Treaties, it increased the Navy. There would be 105,000 more tons of capital ships increasing the category to 630,000 tons. If the President wanted ships larger than 35,000 tons an additional 20,000 tons was authorized. Carrier tonnage was increased by 40,000 tons to a total of 175,000 tons. The heavy and light cruiser tonnage would be a total of 412,524 tons. Destroyer tonnage was now 228,000 tons, an increase of 38,000 tons. There would be 13,658 more tons of submarines for a new total of 81,950 tons. Significantly, specific auxiliaries were included.

How these numbers translated into specific numbers of ships, of course, depended on the size of each ship. A few examples should suffice. If capital ships were going to be held at 35,000 tons then the extra 105,000 tons would mean three new battleships. The extra 20,000 tons for the presidential option of larger ships could increase those three to 41,500+ tons. Or if the legerdemain which dropped *Langley*'s tonnage into the carrier tonnage pot and found the 14,700 tons for *Wasp* was used, judicious transfer of tonnage of over-age ships could make room for more battleships. Even though the Treaties were no longer the limits in tonnage, U.S. legislation (authorization) was dealing in tonnage as the common currency of shipbuilding.

Two more "Vinson Acts" in 1940 made it look like 1916 all over again. The war was on in Europe. The naval race was between the U.S. and Japan. The ominous possibility that Britain might be knocked out of the war and her fleet surrendered to Germany was serious. Then the U.S. would face the possibility of a showdown at sea with a victorious Axis (Japan joined the German-Italian Axis in September 1940) combining the fleets of Germany, Italy and Japan plus the conquered fleets of France and Britain but with the U.S. fleet still on the ways. There was always the question as to how the Axis would be able to man the conquered fleets. The worst-case scenario, but one which had to be taken into account, was that the conquered fleets would come complete with their crews.

It has been seen how the "China Incident" which began in July 1937 with a clash on the Marco Polo Bridge near Peiping grew into a Japanese invasion. American casualties from *Augusta* and *Panay* were the subject of accepted Japanese apologies as the U.S. played for time. Still, a sense of urgency in naval matters gripped the U.S.

By the beginning of 1938, *Ranger* and *Yorktown* were at sea. The Fleet had four carriers. *Enterprise* would join in mid-year. Seventeen of the authorized heavy cruisers were active. Number 18, *Wichita* was building. Two of the new light cruisers were in commission with the other five to join during 1938. The eight destroyers of the 1931 construction and 35 of the Recovery and Vinson-Trammel Acts were also in the Fleet. Only eleven new submarines were active.

Events in the Far East and elsewhere had led to the second Vinson Act that became law on May 17, 1938. It adhered to the principles of the 1934 Act and added tonnage above that Act. It also provided for the acquisition, conversion or construction of certain auxiliary vessels. These "acquisition" and "conversion" references were significant. The Merchant Marine Act of 1936 had provided for subsidized construction of American merchant vessels. These tankers, break-bulk cargo ships and combination passenger-cargo ships plus a few liners all had military characteristics as a condition of their subsidy. Standardized designs made for ease of follow-on construction when war broke out. (See Chapter XXI)

The second Vinson differed from the 1934 Act and previous authorizations in that it included appropriations as well as authorizations. It also authorized, if required, expansion of yard facilities and the investigation of requirements for additional air and naval bases on the coasts and in the possessions of the U.S.

The increase of 105,000 tons of capital ships raised the statutory limit from 525,000 (Vinson-Trammel had made the Washington and London limits the law of the land) to 630,000 tons. There was still tonnage available from the swap of *Arkansas, Texas* and *New York* into the two *North Carolina*s. Two 29,000-ton ships, *Nevada* and *Oklahoma,* would become over-age in 1942. The immediate action was to apply the new 105,000 tons to three new battleships. Keels of *South Dakota* (BB-57), *Indiana* (BB-58) and *Massachusetts* (BB-59) were laid in 1939. As replacement tonnage, the keel of *Alabama* (BB-60) was laid in early 1940. All were 35,000 tons near sisters to *North Carolina.*

Further anticipation of replacements for over-age ships, since *Arizona* and *Pennsylvania* would free their 66,200 tons in 1942, led to ordering *Iowa* (BB-61) and *New Jersey* (BB-62) in July 1939 and laying their keels in 1940. Since the aging ships would provide an opportunity to replace over-age tonnage in the amount of 95,200 tons, it was decided that these latest two would be larger than 35,000 tons. Thus, the first of a new 45,000-ton class with nine 16-in. guns was begun in 1940 under the second Vinson Act. The three ships of the *New Mexico* class would be over-age in 1944 so orders were placed in 1940 for two more of 45,000 tons. Keels for *Missouri* (BB-63) and *Wisconsin* (BB-64) were laid in early 1941.

A bit of legal phrase splitting kept the over-age ships around as their tonnage was converted into new ships. The Vinson-Trammel Act made the Treaties the law of the land as regards modern under-age ships. There was a dichotomy in the usage of tonnage and vessels. Because it was convenient, the criterion used was tonnage rather than specific ships. In other words, the tonnage of over-age ships, as over-age was defined in the Treaties, was assimilated into available tonnage for new construction *but* the specific over-age ships were not retired nor stricken. Of course, the over-age ships would have been stricken in the early '40s when they reached statutory over-age. War has a way of ignoring strict observance of inconvenient legislation. There is an anecdote, perhaps apocryphal, that illustrates this principle. As CNO and COMINCH, Adm. King approached his 64th birthday in November 1942; he wrote a note to F.D.R apprising him of the fact that he would be beyond the mandatory retirement age. The note supposedly came back with a handwritten, "So what, Old Top? I may send you a birthday present!" King the over-age ships stayed on to end the war.

The second Vinson Act increased carrier tonnage by 40,000 tons. The direct result was the laying of the keel for *Hornet* (CV-8) in 1939. She was a sister to the NRA carriers of 1933 at 20,000 tons She carried four squadrons, fighter, scouting, bombing and torpedo.

Cruisers were increased by 68,754 tons to 412,524 tons total. Both heavy and light cruisers were lumped together in tonnage. Since there were built or building at the time, 319,950 tons of under-age cruisers in 35 hulls, there was available 92,574 tons for new construction. In 1939, orders were let for a new type of light cruiser, dubbed an anti-aircraft cruiser because she carried 16 5-in. dual-purpose guns in twin gun houses. These ships were only 6,000 tons and the four ordered in 1939 were *Atlanta* (CL-51), *Juneau* (CL-52), *San Diego* (CL-53) and *San Juan* (CL-54). They were started in 1940 and took 24,000 tons of the new authorization. Orders were placed in the first half of 1940 and keels laid in the second half for new 10,000-ton cruisers which abandoned one of the five turrets of the *Brooklyn*s in favor of increased anti-aircraft armament. *Cleveland* (CL-55), *Columbia* (CL-56), *Montpelier* (CL-57) and *Denver* (CL-58) were the forerunners of 34 ships in what was to be the most numerous class of light cruisers ever built. The war caused nine of them to be converted to light aircraft carriers. Even this wasn't *ad hoc*. One of the types proposed in the '30s when carriers were also thought to be gun ships, was a hybrid with a combined flight deck and 6-in. guns. The "flying-off cruiser" characteristics were adapted to nine of the new *Cleveland*s. (See Chapter XXI.)

An additional 38,000 tons were authorized for new destroyers. The last of the two dozen of the first Vinson program were laid down eight per year, in 1937, 1938 and 1939. These were 1,630 tons and since they were larger than the 1,500 tons envisaged in 1934, additional tonnage had to be authorized to provide for larger ships. The second Vinson Act provided for destroyer construction in 1940. Since the *Benson* class had proved highly satisfactory, 12 more were set for construction in 1940. These *Bristol*s were slightly larger at 1,700 tons. Completion of these ships would mean that the Navy had added 109 destroyers to the Fleet since Carl Vinson assumed the Chairmanship of the House Naval Affairs Committee in 1930. Of these, 73 were Vinson-Trammel and 12 were of the second Vinson Act.

The new submarine tonnage in this Act was 13,650 tons extending the building program into 1939 and 1940. Twelve were authorized. Six of these, *Gar* (SS-206), *Grampus* (SS-207), *Grayback* (SS-208), *Grayling* (SS-209) *Grenadier* (SS-210) and *Gudgeon* (SS-211) were 1,475 tons. Work on them began in 1939. *Gato* (SS-212) *Greenling* (SS-213), *Grouper* (SS-214), *Growler* (SS-215), *Grunion* (SS-216) and *Guardfish* (SS-217) displaced 1,525 tons. Their keels were laid in 1940.

The second Vinson Act authorized aircraft construction of not less than 3,000 operable aircraft for the Fleet.

That the Act authorized construction, conversion or other acquisition of auxiliaries has been mentioned. This was most important for a fleet expected to operate from advanced bases. The Act authorized three destroyer tenders (AD) for 27,000 tons total; two submarine tenders (AS) for 18,000 tons; three large seaplane tenders (AV) for 25,000 tons; seven small seaplane tenders (AVP) for 11,500 tons; a repair ship (AR) of 9,500 tons; several mine craft and tugs; plus four oilers (AO). The last were vital to a fleet which had cut down on the size of its ships and therefore the amount of fuel they could carry. To compensate for this, the Navy was developing (again – See Chapter XXI) the technique of fueling while underway. Thus, the disadvantage of not being able to store quantities of fuel on board would offset by having another ship carry it.

A year after the second Vinson Act, Europe was at war. (See Chapter XXII.) The "phony war" ended in the spring of 1940. German arms overran Denmark and Norway. Then the *panzers,* proceeded by the *stukas* (Germany had understood the significance of Marines in Nicaragua), swept through the Lowlands, forced the evacuation of the British Expeditionary Force (BEF), minus its equipment, and crushed France. Britain was alone in the war. U-boats were loose in the Atlantic and Japan, the opportunist, pressured a defeated France for bases in Indo-China to outflank the Chinese and close supply ports and routes to China. Japan also forced the Dutch caretaker government in the Dutch East Indies into favorable oil deals to keep Japan's industrial war machine going. A Japanese move south was a real possibility and was considered inimical to American interests.

The tremendous recovery of the Navy under the guidance of Vinson was not enough. It had added, albeit not all completed, eight new battleships, four carriers, including the two NRA ships, six heavy cruisers, seven light cruisers, 85 destroyers, 46 submarines and vital auxiliaries. It had also provided aircraft. This was still insufficient if the nation was going to have to stand without allies and especially if the fleets of those defeated allies fell into enemy hands.

France fell on Jun. 10, 1940. Four days later the third Vinson Act was signed into law by the President. "Be it enacted ..., That the authorized composition of the United States Navy in under-age vessels as established by the Act of May 17, 1938 (52 Stat. 401), is hereby increased by one hundred and sixty-seven thousand [167,000] tons..."

The Act referred to the original Vinson-Trammel Act as the standard on which it and the 1938 Act were built. The President's authorization to build existed under the initial Act and was increased by this one. The Act defined over-age by category of ships. Capital ships could be 26 years. Carriers and cruisers were over age at 20. Other surface ships had 16 years and submarines were old at 13 years. The purpose was to have a fleet of under-age warships defined by law. But that did not mean that the older ships were discarded. Money was provided to modernize three older battleships, *Arkansas* was 28, *Texas* and *New York* were 26.

171

No new capital ships were authorized but an additional 79,500 tons of carriers were. Orders were placed immediately for three ships of a larger class of 27,100 tons. These were *Essex* (CV-9), *Bon Homme Richard* (CV-10) whose name was changed to *Yorktown* when CV-5 was lost at Midway, and *Intrepid* (CV-11). Keels were laid in April and December 1941.

An additional 66,500 tons of cruisers was authorized. Four heavy cruisers, *Baltimore* (CA-68), *Boston* (CA-69), *Pittsburgh* (CA-70) and *St. Paul* (CA-71) with nine 8-in. guns were ordered and laid down in late 1941. CA-70 was renamed *Canberra* and CA-71 renamed *Quincy* in honor of an Australian cruiser and CA-39 lost off Savo Island on Aug. 9, 1942. Nine more light cruisers of the *Cleveland* class were ordered for construction in 1941. Some of these became light carriers after war came.

The 21,000 tons authorized for new submarines when added to the remaining tonnage of existing authorizations allowed keels to be laid for 22 boats. All entered service in 1942.

The ink had hardly been dry on the President's signature when Vinson and the Navy were coming out with another bill for naval expansion. This new act became law just five days after the third Vinson Act on Jul. 19, 1940. Known as the "Emergency Act" it increased the third Vinson Act.

There were 385,000 tons for new capital ships in the Emergency Program. Two more 45,000-ton ships were ordered but eventually cancelled before launching. Likewise, so were a class of 58,000-ton ships mounting 12 16-in. guns but never to see service. Five were part of the Emergency Program but were cancelled in mid-1943. By that time, it was demonstratively apparent that the war against Japan as going to be won by carrier air and the strangling of the Japanese sea-lanes by long-range submarines. It was also apparent that the capital ships of the RN were not going to fall into the hands of the Axis. We would not need capital ships to fight the capital ships of Britain.

The third Vinson Act had authorized 79,500 more tons for carriers and there were 20,000 unbuilt tons from 1938. *Hornet* had used half. The three of 1941 took 81,300 of the 99,500 tons authorized. The additional 200,000 tons of the fourth Vinson Act provided tonnage for eight more 27,100-ton carriers. Orders were placed for *Kearsarge* (CV-12), *Franklin* (CV-13), *Ticonderoga* (CV-14), *Randolph* (CV-15), *Cabot* (CV-16), *Bunker Hill* (CV-17), *Oriskany* (CV-18) and *Hancock* CV-19*)*. CV-12 was renamed *Hornet;* CV-16 was renamed *Lexington* and CV-18 was renamed *Wasp*. Renaming was to honor war losses of 1942. The names of ships which were renamed for war losses were given to later carriers. Keels for the eight weren't laid for most until 1942. The keel of new *Lexington* and *Bunker Hill* were laid in mid-1941.

Destroyers had been omitted from the third Vinson Act. The U-boat menace in the Atlantic confirmed the vital need for this type of ship. The Emergency Program authorized 250,000 tons more. Thus, there were 155 destroyers under the Emergency Program. In additional 70,000 tons of submarines provided 13 more boats for the Fleet.

Chapter XXI

Innovation and Ineptitude

"What has never before been tried within the profession of arms invariably invites more opposition than support."

BGen S.L.A. Marshall USA (Ret.)

The first two years of the naval war in the Pacific for the U.S. was a matter of holding the line against a foe who had rapidly advanced his forces east and south from his main islands. It was the ships and men of The Treaty Navy who met this threat until the industrial might of the nation could turn out the weapons which would enable it to push west across the central Pacific and fight in Japanese home waters. The weapons and techniques which made this U.S. advance possible weren't spontaneous productions conceived overnight after war came in 1941. They had their roots in the thinking and planning of the doyens of The Treaty Navy.

Likewise, some of the shortcomings and failures of the early days of the war had their roots in the system imbued in the leadership of The Treaty Navy by the over-concern with the avoidance of risks or expenditures. Although lip service was given to the adage that, "You can't make an omelet without breaking eggs," few were willing to be the egg breakers and stain their escutcheon. Even the boldest of operators in the Fleet were careful not to incur the wrath of the *Poobahs* of the Bureaux.

In the long run, fortunately, necessity and logic prevailed. Even the long-cherished *dictum* that a naval craft is never intentionally run aground submitted to the logical necessity of running boats and even ships on a beach in order to project land power ashore. Over the hue and cry of many a traditionalist, particularly in BuShips, designs for ships to be intentionally run aground, and later retracted from the beach went forward.

These **innovations.** *inter alia,* ran the gamut from amphibious warfare to dive-bombing to refueling underway and more. The ineptitudes included unsatisfactory torpedoes, the lack of ability to fight at night and slavish adherence to the "not-invented-here" syndrome and more.

Amphibious warfare illustrates both **innovation** and resistance to change. The Marines were the advocates of the former; the Bureaux the protesters.

Amphibious warfare involves the projection of combat power from the sea to the shore. It further involves that combat power going from level zero at the beach to full potential with the attainment of the objective. Simplistically, the steps are determination of the objective and formulation of the mission; planning and assignment of forces. The planning must be joint, i.e., two or more services, and concurrent. Embarkation, under conditions of combat loading, i.e., first off is last on, follows. Then the forces move to the objective area. Concomitant with that is the isolation of the objective area from enemy reinforcement which would tip the balance of combat power. Then the landing zone itself must the prepared by fire – air, artillery or naval gunfire, before the troops can be put ashore. Combat power must be continuously built up until the objective is secured. There are differences among assaults on atolls, larger islands and the land masses attacked in Europe. The last were essentially land-to-land operations analogous to large river crossings. The landings were lodgments for further build-up and exploitation by follow-on armies. The landing area was isolated by air not naval superiority, *per se*. The first were assaults where, after naval forces, including air, sanitized the surrounding ocean area, the assault troops overran the entire atoll and the defenders either died or surrendered. Usually few did the latter. Atoll operations were measured in hours or even days. The second types of action, those against larger islands, were combinations of the other two. The assault forces rapidly moved to the Force Beach Head Line (FBHL) – the high ground inland the retention of which would permit the defenders to interdict the beachhead by fire. A secure beachhead, which incidentally the British never achieved at Gallipoli, provided for a logistical build-up to sustain further operations required to secure the objective and accomplish the mission, e.g., build an airfield. These were measured in weeks and sometimes months.

Marine innovators solved the tactical and logistical techniques of amphibious warfare in the classrooms of Quantico and on the beaches of Culebra, Vieques and California. These solutions revealed requirements for similar innovative solutions by the Navy. These involved, accurate, timely and responsive naval gunfire from the sea and special types of landing craft to get Marines ashore quickly with their units intact, ready to fight. The inertia to be overcome was the theory that ships can't fight forts, i.e., guns emplaced ashore; and that ships are not intentionally run aground.

The ingredients of naval gunfire were the guns afloat, a spotting party ashore, communications between both and establishment of the constantly changing position of a moving gun platform (ship) and a stationary target. Further complication occurred in the nature of the guns themselves. Naval guns were direct fire, i.e., flat trajectory weapons as opposed to land-based howitzers which were high-trajectory, indirect fire weapons although a modicum of plunging fire could be rendered by naval guns. The spotting party problem was worked out before the war by creation of units which went ashore with the troops and had maps (charts in Navy parlance) of the target areas ashore. Radios that were compatible with ship-borne equipment established the communications link required. At first, the shore sets were large and cumbersome requiring their being broken down into several man-loads for movement but as the war progressed they became more marginally manageable. The location of a moving ship relative to a stationary target was established by use of a common reference point ashore. Bearing to the reference point was initially done visually but as the war went on, radio beacons were established on shore with the landing waves. Ultimately, this evolved into establishment of a radar reflector which the ship fixed on. Suffice it to say that while the principles did not change, naval gunfire (NGF) began by crawling but by the end of the war was running full speed.

174

Marine requirements for landing craft were developed by the Equipment Board at Quantico. Unfortunately, Marines at the Board, assisted by operators in the field, were "idea men" without money to buy equipment. Appropriations for development and purchase of all vessels were in the hands of BuShips. (In 1940, the Bureau of Engineering and the Bureau of Construction and Repair were merged into the Bureau of Ships. The Construction Corps was abolished and Naval Constructors absorbed into the Line with the designation of "Engineering Duty Only." The use of BuShips to refer to the construction and design functions of the old Bureau as well as its successor is intentional since the guilty parties were the same guys in both.) Marines had their own ideas about design and the characteristics which made for a practical landing craft, amphibious tractor or tank lighter that did not fit the traditional mold of the BuShips mind set. It was a NIH situation that the Marines faced. In addition the Marines were disposed toward the products of a Gulf Coast boat builder, Andrew J. Higgins, whose "Higgins boat" was designed for the shallow waters of a bayou or swamp. Eventually, the Marine prevailed and several forms of "Higgins boats" ranging from ones capable of just handling troops who leaped over the gunwales to one with ramps suitable for vehicles. tanks and artillery were adopted. The BuShips designs for lighters not self-propelled tank landing craft were castigated by then-Sen. Harry Truman's War Investigative Committee for the Bureau's lack of knowledge of amphibious needs and wasting of five years and millions of dollars in procuring lighters that did not meet amphibious needs.

A castigated BuShips fell into line by adopting a Marine-advocated amphibious tractor. Later it was to act rapidly in converting (see *infra*) Maritime Commission ships into transports and cargo ships meeting Marine requirements.

The technique of amphibious warfare opened the whole spectrum of advance across the central Pacific to the heart of Japan to the practicality of achievement.

The other significant **innovation** attributed to the Marines was dive-bombing. While it had been initially used in Nicaragua against stationary ground targets it had potential at sea against moving target. The conventional mode of bombing, or at least that advocated by the disciples of Billy Mitchell (See Chapter V) consisted of bombers flying a straight and level flight at relatively high altitude and dropping their bomb load in a pattern set by the formation and number of aircraft in the formation. The bombs fell from each aircraft in a string landing in a straight line described by the flight path of the aircraft. In keeping with the laws of physics regarding falling objects, the bombs took a finite time to strike. The higher the drop, the longer the bombs took to strike. Since bombing required good visibility, the falling bombs were seen from the bridge of the ship/target all the way down. Further their point(s) of impact could be accurately estimated. It was not difficult for a highly maneuverable ship to avoid bombs by taking evasive action. As the coming war was to prove, high level bombing against ships underway was extremely ineffective. The target hulks that Mitchell's bombers had sunk had been moored and Mitchell had cheated on the rules for the test by coming in at a very low altitude. In practice, his planes would have been subject to ship's anti-aircraft fire had the ships been manned.

A dive-bomber, on the other hand, had the maneuvering ship in its sights from the moment it began its dive until it released its bomb. It could follow evasive turns by the target. Accuracy increased with each increment of decreasing altitude before release. The rapid change in altitude of the dive-bomber in its approach gave anti-aircraft gunners an elusive target. Further, if fighters were on the tail of the dive-bomber, shipboard gunners would have to hold their fire lest they shoot down a friendly fighter. To lessen the effect of a fighter on its tail in the dive, dive-bombers were fitted with "dive brakes." These were slotted flaps which the pilot extended during a target dive. They steadied the bomber and slowed it down to give the pilot more time to aim true. They also slowed it to the point where the faster fighter zoomed past in the dive. Hollywood (See Chapter XVIII) had already shown the public how aviation medicine had decreased the bad effect of Gs on a pilot in the pullout from a dive. Dive-bombers were potent weapons in the quiver of sea power.

Another Navy-peculiar technique was carrier deck spotting. Arrangement of flight decks for the rapid recovery and subsequent refueling, rearming and relaunching was an art. It could only be learned and improved by constant drill involving the actual flight and recovery of aircraft. It became a matter of stopwatch record. Like golfers, flight deck crews and pilots were out to beat their own time and always outdo rival carrier crews.

While experimental *Langley* with her postage stamp flight deck and minimal stowage capacity was chiefly concerned with qualifying aviators in takeoffs and landings, the bigger carriers provided platforms to develop speed and efficiency in the "ballet" which was deck spotting. It was choreography at its highest state.

It began with the initial arrangement of aircraft for a strike mission. At first light, fighters were launched to provide protection for the carrier and her consorts. The necessary air speed for take off was the vector sum of the wind over the deck and the take off speed of the aircraft which had "revved up" to maximum power before releasing its brakes for the run down the flight deck. Wind over the deck was enhanced by the ship turning directly into the wind and adding its full speed to the effect.

The lighter fighters required a shorter run and were easily airborne. The slightly heavier scouts went next and headed out on their search sectors. Immediately, the ballet began again. The strike force was readied awaiting news of discovery of enemy ships from one or more of the scouts. While the flyers waited in the Ready Room for the terse announcement over the speaker of "Pilots man your planes!" brown-shirted plane captains were sitting in the cockpits as blue-shirted plane pushers under the direction of yellow-shirted plane directors guided the aircraft into position on the flight deck as the planes emerged from the hangar deck via elevators to the flight deck. The red-shirted armorers and fuelers had already done their jobs on the hangar deck but some of the arming was done to planes which were to be the last to be airborne so that they weren't sitting idle with ordnance loaded while other planes were loaded later. The plan was synchronized to the effect that events occurred concurrently not sequentially. Not a second was wasted. When the pilots, already briefed on the mission answered the call to man their cockpits and the other aircrews took their places, the plane directors instructed them to unfold and lock their wings and summoned them forward to the launching position controlled by the Flight Deck Officer (FDO). The pilot locked his brakes, responded to the FDO's waving finger to rev his engine to maximum, returned the FDO's thumbs up with a salute indicating all was well. Then as the FDO pointed his flag forward on the flight deck, the pilot released his brakes and roared down the deck to take off. Seconds later it was repeated by another pilot.

The returning aircraft upon completion of the mission fed into a racetrack pattern around their carrier. They paralleled her on the starboard side, came left forward of her bow at a stated interval behind the plane ahead; moved down the port side; went well astern; banked left; picked up the signals of the Landing Signal Officer (LSO) and followed the directions of his paddles.

The LSO was the sole authority on landing. To ignore his signals was a cardinal sin. Further, he dictated judgment of each landing to his yeoman standing with him aft but out of sight. He critiqued each landing later in the Ready Rooms. If the paddles were straight out from his sides, the pilot was "in the groove" and could anticipate the "cut" signal of the paddle across the LSO's throat. Then the pilot killed his power and guided his aircraft to the controlled crash which was a carrier recovery. It was a successful trap when the tail hook caught one of the several wires (arresting gear pennants) athwart the after part of the flight deck. A flight deck man in heavy pads dove under the tail and disengaged the tail hook manually. A plane director guided the plane pushers or the taxiing pilot forward past the crash barrier so it could be raised for the next plane and as planned the plane was struck below by elevator or directed forward for later respotting for launch after fueling and arming. It was all part of a well-coordinated game plan.

Carrier deck spotting (and respotting) was the hallmark of Naval Aviation in The Treaty Navy. It surpassed that in any other navy. The Japanese were to learn that inferior deck spotting and aircraft handling was to cost them four carriers at Midway in June 1942. They were found with decks filled with aircraft being reamed and refueled as the U.S. aircraft struck. All four burned and eventually sank.

Another **innovation** with carriers was the divorce from the battleline and their independent use as both a scouting force through their aircraft and a strike force, again through their aircraft. Independent carrier task forces as opposed to operations tied to the battle fleet were the results of early experimentation with such operation during the '30s. Cruisers with speeds equal to the carriers, *Lexington* and *Saratoga* and later *Yorktown* and *Enterprise,* accompanied by a screen of destroyers had more freedom of action than if tied to the slower battleships. Significantly, it was such task force use that saved the carriers the fate of the battleships on Dec. 7, 1941. Two carrier task forces, each built around either *Lexington* or *Enterprise,* accompanied by cruisers and destroyer screens were operating away that day. They were returning from delivering Marine fighter squadrons to Wake and Midway Islands. The fast carrier task force of the early '40s was a product of trial and error in The Treaty Navy of the '30s.

On the deck of a large amphitheater-type room at the Naval War College, the students would refight Jutland with miniature warships moved by hand on the checker board grid. As the six columns of battleships were moved south with destroyers screening pairs of columns, the crucial moment was approaching. That crucial moment would occur when the cruisers and destroyers steaming abreast in a scouting line spotted the High Seas Fleet and signaled its course, distance and speed. The crucial moment would be followed by the signal hoist to form a battleline of the 24 battleships in six columns. Depending on the information about the enemy's dispositions, the columns would move either to port or starboard to form their battleline. Timing was critical. The course change had to be executed with precision in order to bring the four ships in each column directly behind the ones in column abeam (depending on which way the column movement was made) and to avoid colliding with the destroyers of the screen. All maneuvers were to be done in obedience to flag hoists. It was agreed by all students over the years that the maneuvers at Jutland were awkward and cumbersome. With better communications particularly radio telephone, there must be a better way.

One day, while setting up the miniature ships for a different look at the battle, a student decided to improvise. It was not really spontaneous inasmuch as he and others had given much thought to it. The screening cruisers and destroyers were placed in concentric circles around the battleships. Analysis of this during further discussion showed that such a formation placed concentrated anti-aircraft fire in the formation, not a real consideration at Jutland but one very important after World War I. Further, the formation could change direction quickly without complex maneuvers other than each ship executing a turn (not a column turn) to the new course without having to shift position. With more experimentation and analysis, it was shown that it was simpler to shift a circular formation into a battleline than to shift the old rectangular formation of parallel columns of capital ships and screens. One of the students absorbing the **innovation** was Cdr. C.W. Nimitz.

Upon graduation, Nimitz had been requested by the new CinC Battle Fleet to be his aide and tactical officer as assistant chief of staff. Nimitz reported on board *California* in which Adm. S.S. Robison flew his flag. Nimitz tried and finally succeeded in getting the Admiral and the captains of the battleships to try the circular formation. They agreed with reluctance but did find that in addition to concentrating the anti-aircraft fires of the ships it enabled the formation to remain intact and retain anti-submarine dispositions when changing course. After its initial use in 1923, it fell into disregard as new fleet commanders and skippers took over in the later years. The circular formation was to be revived and come into its own in the late '30s. There were two pertinent reasons. First, younger officers who had experienced and found it efficient were now fleeting up to higher command. But mainly, it came into being when the carrier became the centerpiece of the formation.

During the late '20s, while the carrier was coming into its own, there were still members of the "gun club" who felt that the gun was the ultimate weapon at sea. *Lexington* and *Saratoga* carried eight 8-in. guns in four twin turrets on the island to starboard. Piggy-backing on that idea, there was a project abetted by obscure terms of the London Treaty of 1930 which did not come to fruition but which led the way for the light carriers which were converted from *Cleveland* cruiser hulls when war broke out. The Treaty allowed up to 25 percent of cruiser tonnage to be devoted to ships with flight decks. In other words, some cruisers could have aircraft as well as guns. The term "flying off" cruisers was coined. This referred to those that launched aircraft with landing gear but did not recover them. The next generation in planning was for a hybrid ship which was both cruiser and carrier. A drawing board design using a modified *Brooklyn* 10,000-ton hull was fitted with three triple 6-in. turrets forward. She had a starboard island and a flight deck aft from the fore part of the island to just over the fantail. She would carry about 24 scout planes. The idea was that even if the ship had a damaged flight deck and was unable to employ her planes, she could still function as a scout in the cruiser role. Several designs from May 1930 through February 1940 were put forth. It was an idea.

When war broke out there was a critical shortage of carriers at sea although many were on the ways. The idea's time had come. The *Cleveland*s that were slightly wider *Brooklyn* hulls were adaptable to being light carriers without the three forward turrets. The flight and hangar decks could extend forward to within 50 feet of the bow. A smaller island would suffice. In this configuration about 45 aircraft could be carried. The concept which had been bandied about in the '30s became a sudden source of needed flight decks for the Fleet when desperately needed in 1942 and 1943. These new light carriers (CVL) were not like the escort carriers (CVE) built on merchant marine hulls. CVLs had a power plant to let them keep up with the fast task forces. They operated either composite groups of fighters, scouts and torpedo bombers or all fighters that provided the air cover for a group of carriers whose fighters could accompany the air strikes.

Once again, the foresight of the '30s paid off in the '40s.

The mission of the Marines was to operate with the Fleet to seize, occupy and defend advanced bases. But just what was an advanced base? Plan ORANGE initially envisaged a rush to the Philippines to prevent them from falling to the Japanese and then to use the islands as a base for the Fleet to operate in the Western Pacific. The non-fortification clause of the Washington Treaty doomed the Philippines to be defenseless. The Mandates awarded to Japan dotted the path back to the Philippines. Seizure of them could eliminate Japanese interference with a return to the Western Pacific and also provide bases as stepping-stones along the route west. An advanced base therefore was a site which initially offered nothing but on which could be *built* facilities for basing a fleet for further operations. *Built* was a key word. Building of extensive facilities takes time. The farther the supply line is extended the longer it takes to transport construction materials and supplies there.

A fleet base required dry-docking facilities, fuel storage tanks, warehouses, barracks, airfields and all the paraphernalia attendant to maintaining, repairing and resupplying ships. In a sense, ships are self-contained logistical units in that they carry with them a modicum of provisions, ammunition and fuel. When these are expended or consumed, they must be replenished. But unlike moving ground units, a ship doesn't have to be replenished every day. She can operate for some time before that is necessary. The purpose of an advanced base is to provide logistic replenishment as close to the battle area as possible. Thus, when the war moved west, new bases would have to be developed and the old ones became the backwater. Building new bases was costly in time. Abandoning old bases was costly in material. A solution would be to take the bases west with the advance of the Fleet.

When Bataan fell in April 1942, the world's largest floating dry dock was scuttled. Dewey Drydock (YFD-1) had been in the Philippines because the non-fortification clause of Washington forbade *permanent* fortifications. Those facilities for basing a fleet were considered fortifications and were forbidden. A floating dry dock, however, was not a permanent installation; nor were destroyer tenders, submarine tenders or seaplane tenders. The ships and aircraft of the Asiatic Fleet were cared for and nourished by their tenders. In addition, the Fleet Train had for years used Repair Ships (AR) which followed the Fleet and could effect major repairs and modifications just short of those which required a yard overhaul. Ammunition ships restocked depleted ship's magazines. The Fleet Train was an expandable resource. While some of it was in existence, much of it was on the planning board. Indeed, the later Vinson Acts had specifically authorized additional auxiliaries.

A case in point is the aforesaid Dewey Drydock. Her huge bulk was almost impossible to tow to the Philippines, if she was towed intact. She wasn't. She was towed there in sections that were joined on arrival. The concept was sound and the designs were saved. Several newer versions were built in sectional form and towed to the atolls of the Pacific as the war went westward. They could hold the largest warships afloat for repair of underwater battle damage or just plain bottom cleaning.

Another **innovation** in the files of BuY&D was Construction Battalions (CB). As war approached, the Navy began recruiting older men from the construction trades and giving them advanced ratings commensurate with their skills and the Navy's needs. These "Sea Bees" were the ones who built the airfields, barracks and shore facilities of the advanced bases. Sometimes they landed before the Marines had declared the atoll secured. Then they had to drop their tools and pick up their rifles to ensure that they could get on with their work. When the war moved on, the CBs loaded up their gear went on board ships and followed the Fleet. With them came the repair ships, tenders and floating dry docks to set up quickly at the new site. Through foresight of the '30s, advanced bases became mobile bases.

More must be said of the Merchant Marine Act of 1936. (See Chapter XX). Its proclaimed purpose was restoration of the America Merchant Marine to competition with other nations' merchant marine. Ship construction in American yards was subsidized, as were seamen's wages. A condition of the ship subsidy was that the ship have military conversion characteristics and be available when called upon by the government. One of the **innovators** in ship design was the New York firm of naval architects, Gibbs and Cox. They and other naval architects came up with basic designs for a series of ships called **C** (cargo) and **T** (tanker). The C-1 cargo ships were about 5,500 dead weight tons. (Merchant tonnage unlike naval tonnage is not displacement but in terms of volume. One ton is 100 cubic feet of cargo space.) The C-2 cargo ships were about 7,500 dead weight tons while the C-3 were about 8,500 dead weight tons and had an extra hold aft. The C-4 ships were combination cargo and passenger ships varying between 5,300 and 6,100 dead weight tons.

Essentially there were three T-type tankers, only two of which were suitable for Navy use, plus a Maritime Commission design. The T-1 tankers were relatively small between 1,600 and 4,000 dead weight tons. The T-2 was larger at about 16,800 dead weight tons. A T-3 version was 18,200 dead weight tons, as was the Maritime Commission tanker.

Most of the cargo versions were acquired and converted by he Navy. The civilian cargo carrying was left to the wartime Liberty and later Victory ships turned out by the thousands during the war. The C-1s became Navy cargo ships (AK) and carried break bulk cargo to forward areas. The C-2s became combat cargo ships (AKA) and were a vital part of the amphibious assaults. They carried vehicles and combat supplies for the Marines. They were fitted with many landing craft for getting the gear to the beach. The C-3s made up the bulk of the amphibious transports (APA). One APA could carry a Battalion Landing Team (BLT) of infantry, supporting artillery battery and service support elements. Their landing craft were augmented by those of the AKAs during the assault and build-up ashore. The C-4 ships became transports engaged in carrying troops overseas to ports for debarkation and were not used as assault ships. Several of the C-4s were configured as hospital ships (AH). Depending on need and availability, all versions of the Cs were found in service as repair ships, ammunition ships (AE), specialized vessels and other uses. The wisdom of having merchant ships with military characteristics paid dividends in the Pacific war.

The T-2 and Maritime Commission tankers were taken over by the Navy in droves. They were immediately converted into oilers (AO) although a few became escort carriers (CVE) as the need for more fight decks arose. But it was as oilers that the ex-tankers did yeoman service. There was a distinct difference between a tanker and a Navy oiler. A tanker took on oil at a port and delivered it to another port usually where there was a refinery. An oiler took on oil and delivered it to Navy ships underway at sea. She was fitted with pumps capable of furnishing oil to a carrier or even a destroyer while each moved through the water at a speed to discourage a submarine from wasting a torpedo. Additional equipment such as booms, blocks and tackles, and other rigging made oilers different from tankers. In turn warships were fitted with bitts and chocks to facilitate line handling during underway refueling. One of the crowning achievements of The Treaty Navy was that it revived a skill which it had allowed to die after World War I - underway refueling!

Underway refueling of the destroyers going to Ireland in World War I was accomplished in mid-Atlantic by *USS Maumee* (See Chapter I). There had been later experiments with underway refueling but the usual procedure was for ships to come alongside a tanker in a sheltered roadstead and take on oil (or coal from a collier) while both rode at anchor. Some at sea fueling wherein the fueled ship fell in astern of the oiler to be the recipient was tried. The main drawback to this method was that the distance between the ships required a long fuel line. This meant a higher- pressure pump but still the diameter of the hose made for a slow operation. Its advantage, however, in the eyes of many prudent ship handlers was that the danger of either ship colliding with the other was almost nil. The *Maumee* operation used a method known as the "riding-a-beam" or "broadside" method. This required the two ships to steam parallel to each other at a minimum distance apart. The ships were made fast to each other to prevent their veering apart during refueling. The Bernoulli effect, however, tended to bring them together if either captain was not alert in using his helm and his power in adjusting speed. The smaller ships like destroyers were more responsive to their helms and had greater power in relation to their size. Using the riding- a-beam method, *Maumee* had been able to transfer almost 32,000 gallons of fuel an hour to a destroyer alongside. The short distance between ships as opposed to the over-the-stern method permitted the use of two refueling lines and got maximum efficiency from the pumps. In 1917-18, refueling destroyers underway was a wartime fact.

The outbreak of peace brought a new attitude to The Treaty Navy. Limits on size of warships, particularly cruisers cut down the amount of fuel that could be carried. Destroyers were always fuel conscious but fueling of destroyers underway was now a given. Battleships were large enough to carry sufficient fuel for most operations and could even have some to spare for distribution to destroyers. All that was needed was perfecting the existing method to the point where larger ships could refuel from oilers while underway and in turn subsequently share their fuel with the smaller destroyers. Alas, it was not to be for almost two decades.

The problem was the tight money situation in The Treaty Navy. We've seen that one year, the annual Fleet Problem was cancelled for lack of money for fuel. (See Chapter IV.) But the real problem was faint-heartedness, for lack a better word. Money for repairs didn't exist or was extremely limited. There was danger of damage through collision while refueling underway. No captain wanted to risk causing damage to his ship in such an operation. Every skipper "had his finger on his number." (Navy parlance for covering your ass lest it reflect adversely on promotion.) BuC&R (one of the predecessors of BuShips) which controlled construction and modifications of ships, in its parsimonious wisdom took the skippers off the hook. It instructed that all equipment used for underway refueling, such as chocks, bitts, booms which held the "saddle" to support fuel lines between ships an other gear peculiar to underway refueling be removed from warships and oilers. Thus, the evil of everything from scraped paint to major damage was removed from tempting bolder ship handlers from experimenting. Underway refueling atrophied in The Treaty Navy for more than 15 years. While larger ships, e.g. battleships (See Chapter XVII on *Colorado* refueling destroyers during the Amelia Earhart episode) and sometimes carriers refueling destroyers, there was no refueling of larger combatants from oilers while underway.

But events were marching so as to make underway refueling a necessity not a luxury. The realization that the vast reaches of the Pacific would have to be crossed in any war with Japan was openly admitted after 1930. But the dominant reason concerned carrier operations. Sustained flight operations required the carrier to stream at high speed into the wind to launch and recover aircraft. The wind might not be coming from the direction of advance of the Fleet. Hence, the carrier and her consorts, particularly plane guards, (destroyers following immediately astern to pick up any flyer who crashed on launch or missed when coming aboard) had to go full speed to catch up with the formation. High speed is most uneconomical of fuel. A carrier could deplete ten percent of her bunkers in a single day of sustained flight operations. Flight operations also used much aviation fuel. If carriers were not to be tethered to their nearest fuel farm, limiting their potential, they had to refuel at sea.

CNO recognized the problems and directed CINCUS to come up with a feasible method for refueling warships from oilers as well as from each other. When the Fleet headed to the East Coast in the spring of 1939, ComBatDivOne was left behind with his flagship, *Arizona,* and units of Task Force Seven (TF-7) with instructions to develop and conduct underway refueling techniques to be used by all ships and oilers of the Fleet. The TF-7 commander resisted all the suggestions of both the staff of the Fleet Train and the experts from BuC&R to use the over-the-stern method. He was RAdm. C.W. Nimitz, late of *USS Maumee,* and he knew what he wanted and what worked. One of his tireless supporters who was willing to take his destroyer alongside anything from an oiler to a battleship was CO of USS *Mugford* (DD-389), LCdr. Arleigh Burke. Suffice it to say, these "can do" sailors were to develop the underway refueling techniques from oilers for all types of ships which was one of the key factors in victory in the Pacific. Both were to be key commanders in the war. Nimitz was Commander-in-Chief, Pacific Ocean Areas (CinCPOA) and Burke was a destroyer squadron commander. Both were to retire as CNO; Nimitz, 1945-1947 and Burke, 1955-61.

But The Treaty Navy was not all the oracle of all successful **innovation**. There were warts and blunders as well. Some have been mentioned in conjunction with the struggles for amphibious craft and the "NIH Syndrome" of those jealous of their prerogatives. Others were products of timidity when boldness was required no matter what the personal consequences. In fairness to the bold who often risked or ruined their careers, more often than not they were silenced or ignored by superiors who did not want waves made.

Torpedoes are a case in point. A torpedo is the earliest example of a self-propelled guided missile. Unlike what we think of today as a guided missile, a torpedo moves through a liquid not air. A torpedo is launched from a tube or dropped from an aircraft and immediately its motor begins to turn its propeller pushing it through the water. The motor is run by either compressed air which leaves a telltale wake of bubbles or by electricity which doesn't. The course of a torpedo which is pre-set before launching as well as its depth below water level is programmable. Its range varies with speed. The slower the speed the longer the range. A torpedo has a warhead of explosives or a dummy or practice warhead of the same weight. It can detonate on impact or as a BuOrd design intended, by magnetic influence. The latter was meant for explosion under the keel of a ship breaking its back. In short, a torpedo is an expensive and complex entity.

At one time, American battleships, cruiser, destroyers and submarines carried torpedoes. In the early days of The Treaty Navy torpedo tubes were removed from the underwater the hulls of battleships and cruisers. The weight saved was put into anti-aircraft armament. Destroyers and submarines carried the standard 21-in. torpedo. Aircraft carried one 18-in. aerial torpedo. The torpedoes in a destroyer's tubes were her full issue, one class excepted. Submarines reloaded their tubes with "fish" carried internally. PT boats came later.

In The Treaty Navy practice with live firing of torpedoes was extremely limited. There were two reasons. First, since torpedoes were expensive they were not expendable. Rules and restrictions covering torpedo firing were more concerned with the recovery of them than with the skill acquired by practicing. Second, firing a torpedo against an actual ship might either penetrate the hull or dent it by impact. That was as heinous as scrapping paint practicing underway refueling. Torpedo practice was more theoretical than practical

But the greatest injustice of all came from BuOrd. The torpedo "experts" had come up with the magnetic influence torpedo which was going to be the answer to a submariner's prayer. It wasn't. It had several flaws. It did not run at the set depth. Often it broached revealing itself to the enemy. Sometimes it boomeranged and came back to destroy the submarine. It was the greatest source of frustration to submarine commanders who risked their lives, their crew and their boat to get a hit and nothing happened. For the first 18 months of the war, submariners complained only to be met with the intransigence of the experts who defended their brainchild by blaming the shortcomings of the operators. The inept were trying to shift their ineptitude.

Eventually, the operators at (under the) sea prevailed and their recommendations solved the dilemma of torpedoes that didn't work. Before that it was NIH all over again.

Two shortcomings also had to do with torpedoes but they were shortcomings of intelligence not mechanics. The Treaty Navy intelligence people failed to determine before the war that the Japanese had the 24-in. "Long Lance" torpedo. It had a speed and range much greater than any American torpedo. This put our ships, particularly at night, at a disadvantage and created a false aura of security when maneuvering our forces in contact with the enemy. The Long Lance carried enough explosive to blow he bow off a cruiser and did so to several. The second shortcoming was not knowing that the Japanese surface ships, especially destroyers, although their cruisers still carried torpedoes, had a capability to reload their tubes. This caused more than embarrassment when it was assumed they had fired their load. The IJN put torpedoes in the water before firing guns and revealing their position.

The torpedo planes of The Treaty Navy and their tactics were also found wanting. The Devastator was the first low wing monoplane in the carrier inventory. It was slow and unable to press home an attack before being shot down. It was a patsy to fighters and vulnerable to anti-aircraft fire while skimming the surface toward a target. An early tactic of The Treaty Navy was for scout planes to lay a screen of white smoke parallel to the course of the enemy battleline and the torpedo bombers to break out of the smoke before dropping their fish. (Destroyers did something similar with bellowing black smoke from their stacks to conceal their "destroyer charge" with torpedoes.) Two things were wrong with this. The white smoke generators used chemicals which ate the tail surfaces of the smoke plane. Also U.S. torpedo planes were blinded in their run until thy emerged from the screen. U.S. torpedo-bombing techniques were not good early in the war. They cost an entire squadron and all but one of the aircrew in a futile attack at Midway.

Cautious commanders did not conduct extensive training in limited visibility. Exercises at night or in heavy weather were not routinely done in The Treaty Navy. They were in the IJN!

The final ineptitude we'll discuss has to do with fire and firefighting. Fire at sea is the most terrifying thought that a sailor can imagine. The conventional way to fight a fire is to drench it with water. Water in a ship is another disaster. That's what today would be called a "Catch-22." You're damned if you do and damned if you don't.

For years, ships had been kept in a state of superb appearance by the judicious application of paint to make them shine. A sailor learned in Boot Camp, "If it moves salute it! If it doesn't move, paint it!" Paint was the deterrent to rust. Salt air would react on paint and cause it to peel. Peeled paint exposed metal to rust. Rust was unthinkable. Hence, peeled paint on the weather-exposed surfaces of a ship was first chipped and then repainted. A chipping hammer in the hands of a seaman was as natural as a bat in the hands of Babe Ruth. The interior of a ship was another matter. It wasn't exposed to the elements all the time. Sun, wind, rain and salt spray did not act on interior paint. Salt air did but not to the extent the other elements did on the exterior. Still the solution to a drab or grimy interior bulkhead or overhead was to repaint it. Thus, without chipping, layers of paint grew up inside a ship as she grew older. There is a legend that on one of the ill-fated battleships raised from the Pearl Harbor mud and sent to the Yard at Bremerton for refit that they chipped enough weight in paint from inside her that a 5-in. gun house could be emplaced. Interior paint on older ships proved to be a lethal fire hazard for which there as no remedy. A fire from battle damage would break out and a compartment would be abandoned and sealed off by securing the watertight doors. The fire would be left to burn itself out as it starved for oxygen. No way! The flames would burn the paint on its side. The heat would be transmitted via the metal bulkhead and reach the flash point of the paint on the other side. The fires would jump into the next compartment and so on. In the matter of minutes the interior of the ship would be ablaze and the fire headed toward the magazines. Fortunately, the magazines could be protected by flooding. Interior fire was still a problem as it spread toward vital areas such as control spaces.

The other fire problem was peculiar to carriers. They were big floating garages and gasoline stations. This was compounded by torpedoes and bombs brought from protected magazines ready for loading on the planes for strikes. A gasoline fire is not responsive to pressure from fire hoses. The pressure tends to spread and splash the burning gas. The carriers of The Treaty Navy had the same high-pressure fire hoses as the rest of the Fleet. It took the loss to fire of four carriers of The Treaty Navy in 1942 before the Navy called for help from professional civilian fire fighters. The result was a combination of spray nozzles and foam to combat carrier fires. More carriers were saved from fires after 1942 than were lost in that year.

Thus, The Treaty Navy had **innovations** and ineptitude. It was fortunate that there were, on balance in importance, more of the former than the latter.

"The more you sweat in peace, the less you bleed in war."
Chinese Proverb

Chapter XXII

War and Neutrality

There were minor conflicts in the 15 years following World War I. The U.S. had been in shooting engagements in Central America and on Hispanola. Expeditions had been sent to China. All of these involved The Treaty Navy and its "colonial infantry" the Marines. These were direct applications of two of the then five American foreign policies, i.e., Monroe Doctrine and Open Door. There were other conflicts in the world as well. None of them were of more than local importance. Britain had border skirmishes in India and tribal disputes in the Middle East. One which was to have a significant influence on The Treaty Navy involved two land-locked countries of South America. The Chaco War of 1932-35 between Bolivia and Paraguay was to introduce the changed U.S. position on neutral rights. In the coming conflicts in Europe and Asia, the U.S. approach to neutrality was to be inconsistent. It was to vary from the extremes of abandonment of her traditional stand on neutral rights to blatant unneutral acts. A short explanation may suffice.

The U.S. did not have a single foreign policy during the era of The Treaty Navy. It had, in fact, a collection of five policies extending back to the first president. George Washington's admonition to avoid entangling alliances led to the nation's commitment to isolationism. Two wide oceans abetted this posture. The next in sequence of articulation was freedom of the seas and neutral rights. After the almost disastrous approach of Jefferson with an embargo on American shipping during the Napoleonic wars, the assertion of freedom of the seas and neutral rights led to the War of 1812. More than a century later this policy drew the U.S. into World War I as an "associated power" with the Allies. After the war, this kept the U.S. out of the League of Nations and the World Court. A reason, *inter alia*, was an unwillingness to support collective coercion with sanctions and/or force.

The Monroe Doctrine as a foreign policy came about when European powers were indicating further colonizing interests in the Western Hemisphere. The implication of this policy was the basis for the use of naval forces and Marines as colonial infantry from just before the turn of the century through the early '30s. The "Open Door" policy concerned China and was commerce-inspired seeking equal opportunity for trade as given to European powers, despite pious claims of the bleeding hearts of the time. The expeditions of 1927 and 1936 to China as well as the presence of U.S. gunboats on the Yangtze River were manifestations of this policy during the era of The Treaty Navy. The newest policy came with the administration of F.D. Roosevelt. It was the "Good Neighbor" policy toward the republics of the Western Hemisphere especially south of the border and in the Caribbean. Implementation of this policy took the

Marines out of Haiti and Nicaragua. The significance for The Treaty Navy was that the Marines were released from expeditionary duty and able to form the FMF (See Chapter XVIII) and prepare for the requirements of the coming war in the Pacific.

As is the purpose of an armed force, The Treaty Navy was an instrument of all five U.S. foreign policies. As war clouds gathered in Europe and Asia, the specter of the horrors of World War I reappeared. The attitude of "Never again!" was pervasive. (In view of the events of 1941-45, 1950-53, 1965-73 and 1991 plus long "peace keeping" commitments, it is worth noting that although American troops went to France in 1917, they saw no real action until June 1918. U.S. troops were in action less than six months!) A new kind of neutrality was going to keep America out of foreign wars.

Neutrality as a concept is a product of attempts to codify international (Western) behavior during times of war. Much of the body of International Law deals with rights and duties of neutrals as regards their relations to the belligerents during a declared conflict. Much of the rules concerned what was expected and allowed at sea. As concerned commerce, war was to be but a minor annoyance. In fact, neutrals should be able to profit from the needs of the belligerents. Neutrals could trade with the opposing sides without partiality. If there was partiality shown it was an unfriendly act toward the other party. The elaborate rules defined items allowed to be sold to belligerents, loans, stopping of civilian ships of either side and of neutrals for search and seizure by ships of the belligerents for disposal in prize courts. The use of submarines without restrictions upset his entire framework of rules. With war in Europe, the American mind set was more like that which led to the embargo of Jefferson than the demands of Wilson on freedom of the seas and neutral rights.

The Kellogg-Briand Peace Pact of 1928 (See Chapter VI) brought a new dimension to war and neutrality. War had been outlawed in this Pact of Paris as an instrument of national policy by all Parties. A Party who resorted to war was an outlaw and an aggressor. What were the duties of the other Parties to the Pact as regards to the aggressor? Was neutrality a tacit approval of the acts of he aggressor? Actually, it was all a matter of politics. And politics is the art of the possible or the practical as concerns the interests of individual nations.

The first test of neutrality came with the "Manchurian Incident" of 1931 (See Chapter XI). Japanese actions could be deemed an aggressive war but no war was declared. Yet technically, she was a triple outlaw in violation of the League Covenant, the Nine-Power Pact of 1922 and the Kellogg-Briand Peace Pact. But the rest of the word demurred on sanctions and the U.S. pontificated with a policy of not recognizing gains made by aggression. As we have seen, the Fleet was temporarily shifted to Hawaii as a warning to Japan.

The next event to impinge on the U.S. attitude toward neutrality was the Chaco War between Paraguay and Bolivia. The League had recommended an embargo on arms sales to only Paraguay of the two belligerents. Congress responded with a Joint Resolution on May 28, 1934 allowing the President to prohibit sales of arms to either nation. Then Curtiss-Wright Corp. got caught with its hands in the cookie jar. It sold airplanes to Bolivia under he guise that they were for commercial use. Unfortunately for Curtiss-Wright, it was found to have shipped the machine guns for the planes separately and the Attorney General prosecuted under the Congressional Resolution. The defendant held that it was unconstitutional for Congress to delegate discretionary legislative power to the President. The Supreme Court upheld the power of Congress to allow the President discretion in applying legislation in the field of foreign affairs. This was to be important in the Sino-Japanese War. At about the same time the nation was being swept by a wave of revulsion about the reasons for our entering World War I. A popular book, *The Merchants of Death* laid the causes of the war at the greed of munitions makers, financiers who lent money to the Allies and the instance of maintaining "business as usual" with Europe when such allowed Americans to put themselves in danger. The Nye Senate Investigation was the result.

The stage was set; attitudes were drawn and all that was needed was a reason to act – a reason to opt for or against neutrality in a foreign conflict.

Reasons were not long in coming. In October 1935, Italy invaded Ethiopia from Italian Somaliland. On Jul. 18, 1936, 18 Spanish military garrisons were in revolt against their government. The ensuing civil war became a proving ground for opposing European armies. Germany meanwhile had not been quiet. After consolidating his power, Hitler had withdrawn from the League; denounced the disarmament terms of Versailles; reoccupied the demilitarized Rhineland; forged the Rome-Berlin Axis; and was testing tactics in Spain while supporting the rebels. A bit later, Japan was on the move again after the July 1937 incident at the Marco Polo Bridge.

Prior to the above incident, Roosevelt had discussed the possibilities of neutrality legislation with members of Congress as it was becoming obvious that world peace was adrift. There were three main advocacies of what should be U.S. neutrality in the event of war(s). "Merchant of death" advocates wanted sweeping bans on munitions makers and related miscreants such as lenders. Congressional supremacy advocates wanted to deny presidential discretion. A third group, who were a combination of interventionists and internationalists would permit the President to decide who was the aggressor and who was the victim. Aid could be given to the "just" and withheld from the "unjust" belligerent. A complication arose when nations neglected to "declare" war and thus put themselves in *de jure* violation of Kellogg-Briand.

On Aug. 31, 1935, the President approved the Neutrality Act. It required him to proclaim the outbreak of war between two foreign *states*. Then it was unlawful to export arms or contraband to them directly or indirectly. Contraband, once easy to define had become complex as modern war became complex. It was no longer just armaments. Food and raw materials, e.g., oil, could be contraband.

When Italy invaded Ethiopia, Roosevelt proclaimed the existence of a war as it affected U.S. neutrality. U.S. citizens traveled on belligerent ships at their own risk. Arms shipments to belligerents were embargoed. The League action was feeble "moral" sanctions against Italy. They didn't work because Italy's war machine required oil; the producing nations were eager to sell it.

Subsequent Neutrality Acts placed further restrictions on American interaction with belligerents. Lending money was forbidden except for short-term trade credits, if deemed advantageous to the U.S. The loophole occurring when the recognition of the belligerency status of the Spanish rebels was an issue if the Neutrality Act was applied and was covered by a specific amendment peculiar to the case.

The last Neutrality Act before the advent of World War II was passed on May 1, 1937 for a two-year life. It was the most inclusive thus far. American ships could not carry items proclaimed by the President to belligerents. No items still owned by Americans, i.e., not paid for, could be carried by any ships to belligerents. This was the "cash and carry" provision. Americans could not travel in belligerent ships.

Italy annexed Ethiopia on May 9, 1936 before the 1937 Act came into existence. The Spanish Civil War ended in March 1939 a month before the 1937 Act expired. The "China Incident" of July 1937 had blossomed into a full-fledged war after 1937 but Roosevelt exercising the subtle discretion given him by the Acts chose not to find the existence of war between China and Japan. Trade continued with both. China had no way of interfering with U.S. ships going to Japan hence, there was no danger of the U.S. being drawn into war by that route. Likewise, since U.S. trade with China went via neutral ports, e.g., French Indo-China, Japan was not able to interdict it. It was a later embargo on exports to Japan from the U.S. that was to cause war, however. This was after Japan had cut off the Indo-China connection.

When the 1937 Act expired at the end of April 1939, in theory there were no wars in the world and no need for neutrality laws regulating Americans to preclude their actions drawing the country into war.

What then was the effect on The Treaty Navy of all this emphasis on neutrality? The most immediate effect was the establishment of a temporary squadron sent to Spanish waters on Sep. 18, 1936 to evacuate American nationals from the Spanish war areas. Squadron Forty-T (40-Tare) initially comprised *Raleigh* and the old destroyers *Hatfield* and *Kane*. The following year, it consisted of *Omaha, Claxton* and *Manley*. By 1939, the squadron was operating in the western Mediterranean and based on French ports. It then was *Trenton, Badger* and *Jacob Jones*. By 1940, it continued to operate in the western Mediterranean but "for the purpose of cultivating friendly relations and protecting American interests." Then on Oct 22, 1940, "due to the conditions prevailing in certain parts of Europe" the squadron was abolished and its ships reassigned to various unit of the Fleet.

As war clouds were gathering in early 1939, The Treaty Navy conducted its annual Fleet Problem. It took place in the Caribbean area. The scenario was in keeping with the defense- of- the- hemisphere preoccupation of the day. A revolt in an American republic (Brazil?) asked for aid from a fascist nation (Germany?). The U.S. mission was to prevent the sea-borne aid from reaching its destination in the hemisphere. In the public mind, defense was right up there with motherhood and the flag. After all, the Navy was the "The first line of defense." When the MGC had proposed adding several special battalions to the Marine Corps, he told F.D.R. that he was designating them as "Defense Battalions." The President purportedly replied, "They'll love it " Defense was sellable to the Congress and the country, particularly the isolationists.

But analysis of Fleet Problem XX reveals something different. The defenders or "good guys" only had one carrier, the small, slower *Ranger*. The "bad guys" had three carriers, *Lexington, Yorktown* and *Enterprise*. This is significant since Germany had none. Commanding the carriers for the "bad guys" was VAdm. E.J. King. "Ernie" King used his carriers aggressively to seek out and destroy *Ranger* and to attack the fleet of the "good guys." That side of the Fleet Problem was a harbinger of things to come in the Pacific in 1942. The disciples of Sims still saw a naval war in the Pacific as the destiny of The Treaty Navy.

The outbreak of war in Europe on Sept 3, 1939 (declaration by Britain and France against Germany's invasion of Poland on the 1st) brought immediate reaction from Roosevelt. He ordered the establishment of a neutrality patrol by the Navy. This extended more than 250 miles off the east coast of the Western Hemisphere. It was also beyond the capabilities of the ships, men and planes of The Treaty Navy. This tokenism of isolation was to occupy The Treaty Navy to the exclusion of all else for another year.

The day Britain declared war, one of her passenger liners, *SS Athenia,* en route to Montreal from Liverpool was sunk by a U-boat. World War II at sea was beginning where it had left off 21 years before.

On Sept. 5, 1939, concomitant with the ordering of the patrols in the Atlantic, F.D.R. issued two proclamations. One proclaimed the neutrality of the U.S.; acknowledged the existence of war; named the belligerents and forbade certain acts to be committed within the jurisdiction of the U.S. The second invoked the provisions of the Joint Resolution of Congress of May 1, 1937 which had become the since-expired Neutrality Act of 1937. Congress reconvened to enact new legislation when faced with a major war and no neutrality laws on the books. While Congress debated the 21 American Republics met in Panama to discuss ways of keeping hostile acts of belligerents out of the Western Hemisphere. They issued a declaration against belligerent hostile acts in a reasonable distance off the shores of the Western Hemisphere, Canada excluded. Thus, hemispheric trade routes were to be safe from belligerent warships. Patrols, such as the U.S. was already carrying out, were authorized.

No German, French or British warships were in Western Hemisphere ports when war broke out. Many of their merchant ships were. Germany had no effective way of interdicting the sorties of Allied ships. The RN with its ships based in Canada and the West Indies did. The orders of F.D.R. to locate, track and report all belligerent shipping in the patrol zone worked against Germany. The RN stood off ports (well outside territorial waters) known to harbor German ships. When the ships sailed, U.S. warships tracked then and broadcast, in the clear, their positions. The messages were sent to U.S. stations ashore (for plotting on F.D.R.'s situation map) but were privy to anyone who monitored them.

The queen of the German merchant marine, *SS Bremen,* was in New York. Before allowing her to sail, F.D.R. directed she be searched for weapons, hoping to delay her until the RN could come up to intercept. She slipped away, however, in a fog and reached Germany. *SS Columbus* was not so lucky. She had picked up tourists in New York in August. As war was imminent she dropped them off in Havana and headed for Vera Cruz to take on oil. In October, Hitler ordered her home. The patrols of The Treaty Navy were on their toes. *Columbus* was shadowed by destroyers. Then *Tuscaloosa* took up the watch. Her broadcasts brought a British cruiser and the skipper of *Columbus* scuttled his ship.

The debate on a new neutrality law concerned two factions. One was isolationists who wanted a "storm cellar neutrality" eliminating all chances of American involvement in Europe's war. Interventionists felt that a blanket embargo would reward Germany and not be in the best interests of the U.S. and world peace. Best interests of the U.S. included worldwide trade with those parts of the British Commonwealth not in Europe. A compromise was reached.

The Act became law on Nov. 4, 1939. It allowed the President to proclaim a war zone around Europe forbidden to American ships. For the first time since the Chaco War, "merchants of death" were allowed to export arms to belligerents, albeit, under licensing controls. Such exports had to be "cash-and-carry" and that included commodities other than weapons. Americans could not travel on belligerent ships. U.S. merchantmen could not be armed. Aircraft were considered vessels. Replenishment of belligerent vessels was prohibited in the U.S. Armed merchantmen and submarines were proscribed from those ports. Other provisions forbade loans, fund raising and recruiting in the U.S.

The Neutrality Act of 1939 was adequate for the "phony war" of 1939 through April 1940. Then, Hitler suddenly invaded Norway and Denmark causing F.D.R. to extend the war zone. In May, the *blitzkrieg* rolled through the Lowlands and France. France was out of the war by June. Italy came into the war in time for the kill against France. Britain was alone in the war with the manpower of an army which had left its equipment on the beach at Dunkirk. The RN stood between invasion as the *Luftwaffe* pounded England and the RAF. If Britain fell, loss of her fleet to Germany would bode ill for the Western Hemisphere. The Old Guard of The Treaty Navy who held that if you could beat the RN battleships you could beat anyone might have their thesis tested. Germany had four capital ships plus two "pocket battleships" (*Graf Spee* was scuttled in 1939 off Montevideo after a battle with three British cruisers) of 12,000 tons with 11-in. guns. She had six more on the drawing board. Italy had four battleships. There was a question mark about the disposition of the seven French battleships after June 1940 but they could potentially be added to the Axis fleet. The real question was what would be the disposition of the 15 British battleships if Britain were conquered by Germany. The Axis in 1940 had a potential of 30+ battleships against 17 U.S. in mid-1940. The war had changed suddenly and could change even more. It was not a repeat of 1917 with no physical threat to the Americas. There was a vested U.S. interest in keeping Britain in the war. The approach to neutrality became more unneutral.

The Navy had been selectively calling individuals of the Naval Reserve to active duty to man the ships, especially those of the Atlantic Neutrality Patrol since war broke out. In the summer of 1940 after the debacle in Europe, debate began on the first peacetime draft. On Sept. 1, 1940, the Selective Service and Training Act became law. Draftees were limited to one year of active duty for training and were not to serve outside the U.S. or her possessions. The Army called its Reserve officers to train draftees and the President federalized the National Guards of the States. The expansion of the Army was limited by its ability to build facilities and new camps. The Navy and Marine Corps continued to accept volunteers only despite the Navy's difficulties manning the new vessels entering service as well as the old destroyers which had been laid up at San Diego and Philadelphia. There was more than just elitism involved. It took more than a year to train a competent seaman to be of use at sea. Further, the ships of the Navy as well as Marines served in places other than U.S. possessions. Compliance with the law would disrupt the availability of crews for "duty at sea and on foreign service."

The two Vinson Acts on "Increase of the Navy" of 1940 have been noted (See Chapter XX). The additional tonnage for capital ships was a reflection of the tilt in balance to the Axis in capital ships which would occur with the defeat of Britain and the annexation of the RN by Hitler and gang. An addition to this equation which also had to be reckoned with was the 12 Japanese capital ships when she joined the Axis in September 1940.

In July 1940, the RN attempted to limit the equation by serving an ultimatum to a French force of four battleships and attendant vessels in port at Mers-el-Kebir, near Oran, North Africa, to recant the terms of the French surrender and come over to the remaining Allies (various "Free" governments not recognizing the surrender of their homelands). The French admiral refused and the RN bombarded the ships of its former ally.

Other French ships posed a problem for The Treaty Navy. A carrier and cruiser lay at Martinique in the West Indies. The carrier *Bèarn* carried a deck load of 50 SBCs, purchased by France before her fall. to be carried to Europe by *Bèarn*. The ships and aircraft could be potential additions to the German war machine. In addition, Martinique could be a foothold in the hemisphere for German submarine replenishment or a base for subversive agents of the Axis.

The Treaty Navy planned an operation to seize Martinique, by force if negotiations failed, and remove the threat, real or imagined, which it posed. A task force of two carriers, *Ranger* and *Wasp,* screened by four new destroyers, including *Billy S.* would provide air support. The Fifth Marines and its supporting artillery and logistical units embarked in three transports. The bombardment group, if necessary, was *Texas, Vincennes, Chester* and *Memphis* plus 14 old destroyers. After the Marines had seized a lodgment, a regiment of the Army's 1st Infantry Division was to land administratively for further operations or occupation. Since draftees were not yet out of the training camps, Regular Army could be used outside the U.S. It was a formidable force.

Although the U.S. negotiator tried to convince the French admiral that capitulation in face of overwhelming force was not a disgrace, the admiral refused. Finally, a *modus vendi* was reached and the French agreed to inform the U.S. four days before any ship movements were to take place and also permit reconnaissance flights over the island. In turn, the U.S. would supply the islands with food paid for from frozen French assets.

Contingency plans were made for further preemptive seizure by The Treaty Navy. Neutral Portugal owned the Azores in mid-Atlantic. They were a potential target for German seizure and use as a submarine base. They also had potential as a U.S. base for her far-reaching patrols. Lack of sufficient, suitable bases in the Caribbean for ships and aircraft of the patrol was becoming an acute problem for The Treaty Navy as it strained to keep up with operational commitments in the Atlantic which impinged on training its new ships and their crews for war.

Another unneutral act, "hostile" in the mind of Hitler, was to ease the base problem in the hemisphere. In a *quid pro quo,* it was to help a problem of the RN which had lost many destroyers in the fighting off Norway and later in evacuating the BEF from the continent in the "strategic retreat" from Dunkirk. The loss of destroyers was aggravated by an increased need against the U-boats which were threatening to cut Britain's import lifeline. U-boats with longer ranges than those of the earlier war were able to move their hunting grounds farther west in the Atlantic. Convoys had to be protected all the way across not just in the approaches to the British Isles. This time, the RN did not have bases in the geographical southern part of Ireland which was now the neutral Irish Free State.

The composition of the RN of capital ships and cruisers to protect its lifelines from surface raiders was the wrong mix for protection against U-boat. The U-boats were threatening starvation for the "tight little island." The best weapon against a U-boat was a destroyer, especially in convoying merchant ships. The Treaty Navy, thanks to the emergency program of 1917, had the largest destroyer force in the world, albeit aging. Further, it was having problems manning all the new destroyers and other ships coming down the ways in 1940. The old destroyers had been recommissioned but were a drain on manpower and on resources for upkeep. The new Prime Minister, Winston S. Churchill, who had replaced Neville Chamberlain after France fell, had a modicum of acquaintance with naval matters having been First Lord of the Admiralty before 1914 and through 1915. He also held the same portfolio at the outbreak of the war in 1939. He assessed the destroyer situation in The Treaty Navy and deemed many of the older ones were "surplus " to U.S. needs. This was a nice euphemism for "We need them more than you do!"

Churchill started a long correspondence with Roosevelt on the "surplus" destroyers. Roosevelt's naval advisers were against transfer, sale or other give-away of vessels of the U. S. Navy, although such had been done before on individual ship bases to friendly governments. Roosevelt saw that they might be amenable if it meant gaining base rights on British possessions in the Western Hemisphere. Churchill was against "selling off parts of the Empire." Eventually, agreement was reached. It took some legal sleight-of-hand by both parties.

The 1939 Neutrality Act did not embargo arms sales or ship transfers, provided ships didn't leave U.S. ports to initiate operations. International Law doesn't ban neutrals, private firms or citizens, from selling warships or other arms to belligerents. Building or fitting out ships is prohibited, however. Before the Pact of Paris, International Law did not allow the direct transfer of arms to a belligerent. And prior to the destroyer request the U.S. had traded some equipment, e.g., the French SBCs, back to the manufacturer who sold them on a cash-and-carry basis. Now the U.S. was dropping the subterfuge and dealing directly on the warships in a straight deal between a neutral and a belligerent .The U.S. Attorney General ruled it legal since Germany, a Party to the Pact of Paris, had violated her treaty obligation by resorting to war. Viewed in its entirety under International Law, the U.S. action was not a violation of the law of neutrality.

The transfer of 50 destroyers to the RN was done by Executive Agreement on Sept. 2, 1940 in response to a British note of the same date offering air and naval base rights in Newfoundland, Bermuda and other British islands in the Caribbean. U.S. crews spruced up the destroyers, provisioned them with ammunition, spare parts and victuals, before sailing them to Halifax, Nova Scotia. The first increment arrived just as a transport brought in British crews. With minimum ceremony, the U.S. crews decommissioned them and marched off the dock to entrain for home. A cadre of officers and men remained to assist in transition and indoctrination.

Earlier in 1940, CINCUS, Adm. J.O. "Joe" Richardson, had conducted Fleet Problem XXI. It was to be a realistic exercise using a Plan ORANGE scenario and to take place in the Pacific. Joe Richardson had participated in Fleet Problem XX flying his flag in *Enterprise.* He was determined to have an exercise free from artificial constraints imposed by monetary or safety restrictions. Heretofore, all training since World War I had been characterized by two overriding considerations. These had been individual safety and the conservation of government property and funds. These blacked out all other considerations in operational training. Joe Richardson ran an operation from the beginning of April until mid-May 1940 that stretched the endurance of ships and their crews; taxed the imagination and ingenuity of commanders and commanding officers of ships; utilized improved concepts of organization like task forces and task groups; conducted underway refueling; and despite near collisions ran night exercises.

Fleet Problem XXI was scheduled to end May 9, 1940 while the Fleet was in Hawaiian waters. Return to West Coast bases was to occur on May 17. The German *blitzkrieg* had begun the day before the Problem was over. CINCUS had been alerted that the Fleet might be ordered to remain in Hawaii since

Italy's entry into the war was anticipated. The alert presumed a short delay in return to West Coast ports.

The "short delay" was originally to be two weeks. During that time the situation in Europe was fluid and bleak for the Allies. The Lowlands had been overrun; the BEF was retreating toward the beach at Dunkirk and France was reeling. Two weeks was hardly enough time for F.D.R. to sort out the situation. It had ominous overtones worldwide. The loss of the Netherlands put the status of the Dutch East Indies in question. Likewise, French Indo-China was a question mark if France fell. The resources and raw materials of both Asian regions were coveted by Japan. Indo-China was the rice bowl of the Orient. The oil of the Indies was vital for industrialized Japan both for peace and war. If England fell, Hong Kong and Singapore wee ripe for plucking. From the standpoint of international chess, the presence of the U.S. Fleet in Hawaii was a major move in deterring Japanese adventurism from moving south. As will be seen, the Japanese thought so too.

From the viewpoint of Joe Richardson, keeping his ships and men in Hawaii was an administrative and tactical nightmare. The end of Fleet Problem XXI did not mean the end of training because Problems were usually followed by gunnery competition and engineering evaluation. Then ships would be docked for bottom cleaning and upkeep. While dry docks were available in Pearl Harbor, they were unable to service the Fleet on a timely basis even working three shifts. Customarily, enlistments expired during the summer and usually transfers were effected then. Such detachments were made from the ships's bases on the West Coast. Replacements would be joined after the ships returned to their bases. If training was going to continue, targets would have to be towed out to Hawaii. This would take almost a month to organize and execute. A change in duration of stay in Hawaii could cause the Fleet heading east to pass its targets being towed west. There was insufficient mobilization and training ammunition in Hawaii to supply the Fleet. The Navy's two ammunition ships could not satisfy the need quickly. Oil was insufficient in Hawaii to keep the ships steaming. That in the disputed storage tank farm (See Chapter IV) was war reserve stocks. And, of course, families were waiting on the West Coast for the return of the Fleet from Fleet Problem XXI.

Joe Richardson made his views known to CNO, Adm. "Betty" Stark. He even went back to Washington to appeal to the President. He protested the conflicting directives he was getting from the Bureaux. BuNav (Personnel) was telling him to return men whose enlistments were expiring on one hand but admonishing him not to relieve anyone until a qualified replacement was on board. Aviator replacements had to be carrier-qualified but aviators ordered to Pensacola as instructors were to be detached on a priority basis to alleviate the instructor shortage there. BuShips was adamant about attention to ship's upkeep schedule. It seemed like the left hand didn't know what the right hand was doing. In the end Joe Richardson's protests for his ships and his men were to cost him his command.

While the officers and men of the U.S. Fleet languished in the lush trade winds of tropical Hawaii, the action was in the harsh waters of the Atlantic.

After the reelection of Roosevelt for a third term in November 1940, "Betty" Stark, on his own initiative put together four alternate strategic plans for the U.S. They were: a) Defense of the hemisphere with little influence on the European war; b) Concentrate on a Pacific offensive and a defensive Atlantic posture; c) Assist Britain actively in both oceans and d) Build an offensive capability in the Atlantic while defending in the Pacific. In the phonetic alphabet of the time they were Able, Baker, Cast and Dog. Stark advocated Plan Dog which became Europe First. Its implementation would mean escorting convoys in the Atlantic; basing ships and aircraft in the British Isles; possible seizure of the Azores and Cape Verde Islands; and U.S. task forces to the Mediterranean and Singapore. It would mean bringing the Fleet to the Atlantic where the war was. He felt that victory over Germany, however, could not be won by naval action alone. Europe would have to be reclaimed by land.

U.S. naval observers under RAdm. R.L. Ghormley had been sent to London after the fall of France. Their mission was to consult with and plan mutual operations with the British if the U.S. joined the war. They were not authorized to commit the U.S. to any course of action. Stark informed Ghormley of his advocacy of Plan Dog. With the direct approval of Roosevelt, Stark appointed a new commander of the Patrol Force in early 1941. VAdm. King who had earned his way back out of the Navy's doghouse took over. He had reverted to two stars and been shelved to the General Board before coming back as ComAirLant. King started of with a notice to all subordinates (See Appendix 10) stating that he was fed up with the usual practice of playing it safe and covering your ass by telling subordinates more than just *what, when* and *why* (the last only if it contributed to the understanding of execution). There was no place in his Navy to tell subordinates *how.*If they had to be told *how*, they were useless and should be relieved. A new look was emerging. First, Joe Richardson and Fleet Problem XXI and now Ernie King and the Patrol Force. Things were looking up in The Treaty Navy.

The year 1941 started off positively. Stark directed the Navy to prepare to escort convoys in the western Atlantic by April. The Naval Academy Class was graduated in February (early) to man the new ships. A Support Force was organized to facilitate convoying. New-construction destroyers built on the East Coast were retained in the Atlantic. The Atlantic Fleet was recreated and Ernie King got a fourth star to command it. The Neutrality Patrol terminated and ships under went upkeep and stripped for action. Training was again stressed. The Marines upgraded the FMF units on each coast to the status of divisions with maneuver elements (infantry), fire support (artillery and tanks) and logistical support units. The 1st Division (1stMarDiv) had three infantry regiments, First, Fifth and Seventh plus the Eleventh Marines as artillery. They were on the East Coast and training in Puerto Rico and GTMO. The 2ndMarDiv was in San Diego with Second, Sixth and Eighth Marines as infantry and Tenth Marines, artillery. When the Martinique and Azores contingencies were reactivated the 1stMarDiv was earmarked for the operations and began rehearsals.

There was one down note at the beginning of the year. CINCUS was still in Hawaii with the Fleet, albeit, making waves to return the ships to the West Coast. He went further and advised the President that the Fleet was not ready for war and by sitting at Pearl Harbor, it was not improving. It was announced that on Jan. 31, 1941, Richardson would be relieved as CINCUS before his two-year tour was up. His replacement would be Adm. H.E. Kimmel who "fleeted up" from ComCruBatFor. The progression was not the normal one of "going through the chairs" nor was the timing. It as obvious throughout the Fleet that Joe Richardson had stepped on the toes of the State Dept. weenies who were playing chess with the Fleet as a deterrent to Japan. Since F.D.R. was his own SecState, Richardson had stepped on the toes of the President. The new CINCUS was more docile and pliant to the White House view.

Kimmel never gained the affection that Richardson had among the officers and men of the Fleet. They regarded him a pseudo-martinet of the prewar school of The Treaty Navy who "kept their finger on their number." When Kimmel decreed that all officers going ashore in mufti would wear hats, the junior officers dubbed their fedoras, "kimmels." It is significant that after the war when Kimmel was trying o get his name cleared and his four-star rank restored, none of the CNOs or senior Fleet commanders, who were junior and middle grade officers in The Treaty Navy spoke out for him.

In the meantime, the new Atlantic Fleet was augmented by major units from Hawaii. In early May, ships left Pearl Harbor for what appeared to be routine exercises at sea. When the COs opened their sealed orders they found that they were heading for the Canal and transit to the Atlantic. Fortunately, some of them had made return trips to the West Coast since their departure for Fleet Problem XXI in the spring of 1940. These visits for upkeep and provisions were referred to in the Fleet as "love boat trips" because of the conjugal connotations. Joe Richardson took care of the men (and their women) of The Treaty Navy.

The transfers to the Atlantic were in several increments during May 1941. The passage through the Canal was usually made at night to maintain secrecy. *Yorktown, Mississippi, Idaho, New Mexico, Brooklyn, Philadelphia, Nashville* and *Savannah* with two squadrons (19 ships) of destroyers made the trip to the new Atlantic Fleet.

They were needed as the Azores and Martinique seizures were again being considered with the 1stMarDiv in assault. More transfers would have been made had not the Japanese moved south to French Indo-China.

British-American naval discussions were continuing as Lend-Lease eased the British financial pinch and freed Britain from the cash provision of "cash-and-carry." U.S. merchantmen, however, were not sailing into the restricted waters of the eastern Atlantic. Japanese moves in the Western Pacific engendered a British request for an American force based at Singapore. F.D.R. declined because he was not willing to expose the Navy to attack there. British ships coming to North America for war cargoes did not travel empty. Britain still exported what she could to obtain hard cash. Products bearing the label "Britain Delivers the Goods" were available in the U.S. Many prudes of the Prohibition Era questioned why Britain was producing and exporting whisky when she should have been producing for war. Little did they realize that the best Scotch was eight- years old or older and had been made long before the war!

Iceland and Greenland belonged to Denmark. They were sparsely inhabited but strategically located in the North Atlantic. British troops had occupied Iceland with the approval of the Free Danish Government-in-Exile in London. Churchill was anxious to redeploy his troops to gainful military duties in North Africa. He asked Roosevelt for a U.S. garrison. F.D.R. concurred but a problem arose. Draftees could not be used outside U.S. possessions. To field Army troops for Iceland would require stripping units of non-draftees to form a force. Marines, however, were volunteers and used to expeditionary duty. The 1stMarDiv which was the Atlantic Fleet's FMF was committed to the Azores and/or Martinique contingency plan. Thus, like the ships in May, Marines were shifted from the Pacific to the Atlantic. The 1st Marine Brigade (1stMarBde) was formed around the Sixth Marines from San Diego to include the 2nd Battalion, Tenth Marines (2/10) as artillery plus supporting units. The Brigade left San Diego in secrecy on May 31, 1941. Rumor had the three transports en route to Martinique, the Azores or other exotic tropical destination in the Caribbean. They went through the Canal and docked in Charleston, S.C., in mid-June. They sailed for Reykjavik with orders from CNO – TASK: IN COOPERATION WITH THE BRITISH GARRISON, DEFEND ICELAND AGAINST HOSTILE ATTACK The convoy now of four transports, two cargo ships and an oiler (all of the ships save *Orizaba* (AP-24) were recent conversions/acquisitions from the merchant fleet) moved north escorted by *Arkansas, New York, Brooklyn, Nashville* and 13 destroyers. Arrival and debarkation were uneventful. The conditions in Iceland were bleak. The Marines were to be relieved eventually by Army troops but in the meantime they set up their tents tactically, i.e., in an irregular pattern to avoid loss to strafing aircraft. That was the initiative of the commander of the Headquarters Battalion, Maj. Dave Shoup.

Iceland became a terminus of U.S. convoy escorts when the Navy began escorting U.S. ships to Iceland as well as any Allied ships who wished to avail themselves of U.S. protection in the passage through the western Atlantic. U.S. escorts would sortie from Argentia, Newfoundland, one of the bases acquired for destroyers, and meet the convoy. It would proceed under U.S. protection to a Mid-Ocean Meeting Point (MOMP) where Allied escorts would take over. The U.S. escorts and other U.S. ships would break off and proceed to Iceland. U.S. escorts from Iceland would pick up Allied convoys at the MOMP and take them west to North America.

Patrol planes worked from Iceland based on their tenders. To provide fighter cover, *Wasp* ferried a squadron of Army Air Corps P-40 fighters which flew off to Iceland.

Despite Hitler's determination not to provoke U.S. forces by attacking U.S. ships, U-boat captains were adverse to his prohibitions. This was especially true when U.S. ships tracked them and reported them to the RN for attack. On Sept. 4, 1941, *Greer* (DD-145) sighted a U-boat which dove. *Greer* did not intend to attack since she was not escorting U.S. ships but did report it. The report was picked up by the RN and the U-boat was attacked. Whether out of pique or self-preservation, the U-boat commander fired a spread of "fish" at *Greer*. (In fairness to the U-boat skipper, it should be realized that *Greer* was a World War I destroyer and thus had the same ship silhouette as the 50 destroyers transferred to the RN a year before.) A week later, the incident that had been reported in the press without reference to the preliminaries prior to the firing of the torpedoes, elicited a presidential speech which the press called a "shoot on sight" order. The Treaty Navy was in a shooting war.

A month before, F.D.R. and Churchill had met in Argentia. Roosevelt had boarded the Presidential Yacht, *Potomac,* in Washington for a "fishing trip" off New England. After being observed fishing, he secretly boarded *Augusta* leaving a stand-in to fish from *Potomac. Augusta* and escorts proceeded to Argentia where Churchill arrived in *HMS Prince of Wales.* That new RN battleship had survived the battle with *Bismarck* when *HMS Hood* had been sunk. *Prince of Wales* was to go down off Malaya four months later.

Roosevelt and Churchill firmed up American assistance in the Battle of the Atlantic. The British proposal for a U.S. force in Singapore was turned down which set the table for *Prince of Wales*'s ill-fated mission. Churchill returned via Iceland where he reviewed the 1stMarBde and was fascinated by a "delightful tune," *The Marine Hymn. USS Mayrant* (DD-402) accompanied *Prince of Wales* part of the way home. Serving in the destroyer was Ens. Franklin D. Roosevelt, Jr. All four Roosevelt sons were on active duty. Two were in the Navy, one in the Army Air Corps and the eldest was a Marine raider captain.

As part of hemisphere defense, ships of The Treaty Navy ventured into the South Atlantic. RAdm. Jonas Ingram was sent to Recife, Brazil, to establish cordial relations and a base for U.S. warships and patrol planes. U-boats, raiders and German blockade-runners had been active in the South Atlantic off the West Coast of Africa. In addition, there was a suspicion that mother ships were resupplying U-boats. The presence of many German and Italian immigrants in South America made sympathies of local governments questionable at the time. The South Atlantic detachment consisted of *Omaha, Milwaukee, Memphis* and *Cincinnati* plus four of the 1,850-ton *Somers* class destroyer leaders. These ships, *Somers, Jouett, Davis* and *Warrington* at this time were still configured with 5-in. guns in twin gun houses which were not rated as dual-purpose. Inasmuch as the threat of Axis air was nil in the South-Atlantic, they were adequate for the task.

There arose in November 1941 a situation unique to naval annals of the 20th Century. It was ultimately settled after litigation in 1947. It is probably the last time prize money will ever be awarded to the U.S. Navy.

Omaha and *Somers* were in company patrolling between Africa and Brazil when smoke appeared on the horizon. The ship flew the American flag and had "*Willmoto* Philadelphia" on her stern. Her appearance, however, did not correspond to that name in the recognition book. She was ordered to heave to and receive a boarding party from the cruiser. They found her to be the German *MV Odenwald*. The boarders thwarted the scuttling which the Germans had attempted. She was taken to Puerto Rico by a prize crew. Her seizure was made under a 19th Century bit of International Law that suspicious vessels off Africa could be apprehended by warships of any nation as suspected slavers. That sufficed for the boarding episode; the subsequent action of seizure was made under the right of salvage since her crew had attempted to scuttle and abandon her. Her salvage value was put at $3,000,000. Each member of the "official" boarding and salvage party got $3,000. Crewmembers of *Omaha and Somers* who were not aboard *Odenwald* got two months pay and allowances.

Before returning to the actions in the North Atlantic and the disastrous month of October 1941, a look must be had at the last pure vestige of The Treaty Navy. While new recruits and officers of the Naval Reserve were the crews of older ships and experienced old hands were transferred to be the cadres of new construction the Asiatic Fleet remained intact and in place.

Houston had replaced *Augusta* as flagship in November 1940. Adm. T.C. Hart flew his flag in her but had a headquarters ashore in Manila. The Asiatic Fleet was pretty much operating in the waters around the Philippines and based at Cavite in Manila Bay and at Olongapo in Subic Bay. *Marblehead* was part of the Fleet. A new addition was the late carrier and now seaplane tender, *Langley* (AV-3). She cared for a brood of 32 PBYs assisted by two AVDs. There were five of the "Bird" class minesweepers which had been built to sweep the North Sea Mine Barrage of 1918. A "Bird" served as a small seaplane tender and another as salvage vessel.

There were three divisions of four destroyers each in DesRon29. They were all old four-pipers which had been on the "China Station" it seemed forever. Capt. H.V. Wiley of *Macon* (See Chapter XVII) flew his pennant in the thirteenth DD, *Paul Jones*. *Black Hawk* (AD-9) was their tender. The best potential punch for offensive action of the Fleet lay in the 32 submarines of ComSubAsiaticFlt. Six of these were "old S-boats" and the rest were fleet boats of Vinson programs. Among them was the raised and refitted *Sailfish* formerly *Squalus*. The submarines were "mothered" by the old tenders, *Canopus* (AS-9) and *Holland* (AS-3). Three of the remaining five river gunboats joined three other old gunboats as the Inshore Patrol in the Philippines The other two were still in China. *Wake* was at Shanghai and *Tutuila* upriver at Chungking where she was bombed by the Japanese in late July 1941. The Asiatic Fleet was the final gesture of The Treaty Navy and was about to see action as such.

One other element of The Treaty Navy must be mentioned. In November, the Fourth Marines boarded a liner in Shanghai and sailed to Manila. Events the previous month in the North Atlantic presaged the imminence of war. All thought it would come there.

The U.S. Navy had been escorting convoys to and from the MOMP since late summer. On Oct. 17, *Kearny* (DD-432) was in a night attack on a convoy by U-boats which sank six ships including a tanker that burned brightly illuminating

Kearny who had backed engines and stopped to avoid collision with a RN corvette. A torpedo found *Kearny* on her starboard side. It killed all in a fireroom. But the new "gold platers" of The Treaty Navy were tough and well designed. The crew under LCdr. A.L. Danis carried out their damage control duties with perfection. Steam from the other fireroom enabled the listing destroyer to proceed to Iceland for repairs, attending to her wounded and burying her dead. "Tony" Danis had survived the crash of *Macon.*

On the night of Oct. 29, *USS Salinas* (AO-19) was in a returning convoy after emptying her tanks in Iceland. She had the unenviable position at the head of the outboard column in the convoy escorted by U.S. destroyers. She caught a fish but her capable crew was equal to the occasion and she reached St. Johns, Newfoundland, on Nov. 3, in company with escorts sent out from Argentia. All hands were intact.

Halloween was to be a night of dirty tricks for The Treaty Navy and as had been the case since American-British cooperation had started in the Atlantic, no treats.

The old four-piper *Rueben James* (DD-245) was patrolling on the port beam of a convoy shepherded by five U.S. destroyers heading to the MOMP. They were about 600 miles west of Ireland when a torpedo struck *Rube* on her port side. It ignited the forward magazine and blew off the entire fore part of the ship aft to the fourth stack. The stern floated for about five minutes before diving to the bottom. As she went down, depth charges which had not been set on SAFE in the rapidity of the events, exploded killing some survivors in the water. Of the ship's company of 160, 45 were rescued. No officers survived. The Treaty Navy had lost it second ship to an "undeclared" enemy. Before war was declared it was to lose more.

Friction had heated up with Japan when the U.S. froze Japanese assets and embargoed oil and scrap metal exports to her in the summer of 1941. Japanese saber rattling pointed to her moving south to the wealth of the Dutch East Indies with feints or forays at the Philippines and Malaya en route. The President had been appealing to the Japanese for peaceful settlements of difference stemming from the "China Incident" of 1937. Japan responded by sending a special negotiator to Washington to work with he Ambassador there in reaching a mutual accord. They were due to see the SecState at 1 p.m. on Sunday Dec. 7. Because Hawaii was five-and-half hours behind the U.S. East Coast, that would have been 7:30 a.m. there.

Saturday night before the titular end of the era of The Treaty Navy, its ships were spread over the oceans of the world. Unfortunately, many were concentrated in one place.

In the South Atlantic were *Milwaukee, Omaha, Cincinnati* and *Memphis* with attendant destroyers and patrol planes. On the other coast of South America, *Richmond* was off Peru and *Trenton* south of Panama.

Eight of the battleships were in the North Atlantic. These were: *New Mexico, Idaho, Mississippi, Arkansas, New York, Texas, Washington* and *North Carolina.* Four of the seven carriers were there too. *Yorktown* had joined from the Pacific during the summer; *Hornet* had been commissioned at Norfolk in October and was under going shakedown. *Ranger* and *Wasp* had been in the Atlantic a while. Heavy and light cruisers had joined from the Pacific to supplement the Atlantic Fleet. The nine "Treaty cruisers" were: *Wichita, Augusta, Tuscaloosa, Vincennes, Quincy, Brooklyn, Savannah, Nashville* and *Philadelphia.* Old four-pipers and the newer destroyers were also amply employed in the Atlantic.

On the China Station, the Asiatic Fleet had dispersed a bit. A destroyer division and all but two of the submarines, S-36 an S–39 were at Cavite and Olongapo as were the submarine tenders and *Langley. Houston* was at Ilolio. DesRon 29 with two DesDiv had gone south to Borneo. DesDiv 58 was with *Marblehead* at Tarakan while DesDiv 57 was at Balikpapan. *Boise* had arrived with a convoy two days earlier and was at Cebu. *William B. Preston* (AVD-7) was at Davao with four PBYs.

Louisville was en route from Tarakan to Pearl Harbor escorting *SS President Coolidge* and a freighter. *Pensacola* had left Pearl Harbor on Nov. 29, with a convoy to Manila and was to be diverted on Dec. 7, to Brisbane, Australia. At sea, south of Oahu, *Minneapolis* was conducting gunnery practice.

Two Task Forces were at sea. TF-12 with *Lexington, Chicago, Portland, Astoria* and destroyers *Porter, Flusser, Drayton, Lamson* and *Mahan* was en route to Midway to fly off VMSB-231. Adm. Kimmel directed this force to abort the delivery of the aircraft and join *Indianapolis* which had been detached to conduct a simulated bombardment and landing exercise with five new DMSs on Johnston Island. The other, TF-8, flying the flag of VAdm. W.F. Halsey, Jr. had just flown off the ill-fated VMF-221 to Wake Island. Halsey's ships were: *Enterprise, Northampton Chester* and *Salt Lake City.* His destroyers of DesRon 6 were: *Balch, Gridley, Craven, McCall, Maury, Dunlap, Fanning, Benham* and *Ellet.*

Colorado was in overhaul at Puget Sound Navy Yard. *Concord* and *Sara* were on the West Coast.

The liberty sections of the rest of the Pacific Fleet were whooping it up on a Saturday night of a payday weekend in Honolulu, Pearl City and on Waikiki. A recommissioned four-piper, *USS Ward* (DD-139) was off the submarine nets at the entrance to Pearl Harbor. *Ward* had been launched 17 days after keel laying in 1918 (See Chapter XIV). Coming into Pearl Harbor was *USS Antares* (AKS-3) towing an empty steel barge.

The ships of the Pacific Fleet were moored in Middle Loch off Pearl City; nested in threes and fours in East Loch; along Battleship Row on the east of Ford Island; or tied to the piers of the Naval Station. Three, *Pennsylvania* and destroyers *Cassin* and *Downes* were in dry dock together. *Helm* was preparing to move to West Loch in the morning.

Going clockwise from the entrance to Middle Loch to the west of Pearl City the dispositions were thus: old four pipers now minelayers, *Ramsay, Gamble* and *Montgomery* were nested. Next came sister ships shunted to minesweeping –mine laying, *Trever, Breese, Zane, Perry* and *Wasmuth.* Repair ship *Medusa* lay in mid-channel with *Curtiss* (AV-4) swinging on the hook to starboard. Off to the east was Ford Island with seaplane tender, *Tangier,* tied to the bollards. Astern of her was the ex-battleship, *Utah,* now doing duty as a planked-over target ship with a flat deck like a carrier. Ahead of her off Ford Island were *Raleigh* and *Detroit.* In East Loch north of Ford Island and east of Pearl City were nests of destroyers. They started with *Dale, Monaghan, Farragut* and *Alywin.* Next were: *Henley, Patterson* and *Ralph Talbot* Tender *Whitney* mothered *Selfridge, Case, Tucker, Reid, Conyngham. Blue* stood alone, as did *Phoenix* off Aiea. Astern of *Whitney* was tender *Dobbin*'s brood of *Phelps, MacDonough, Worden, Hull* and *Dewey.* To *Dobbin*'s starboard the hospital ship *Solace* was alone and to her starboard were four-pipers, *Allen* and *Chew.* Coming down Battleship Row from abaft were *Nevada, Arizona* with repair ship *Vestal* outboard, then *Tennessee* with Wee*Vee* outboard, ahead were *Maryland* with *Okie* outboard, *Neosho* (AO-23) was alone and ahead of her was *Prune Barge.* The small seaplane tender *Avocet* was tied to Ford Island closest to egress from Pearl Harbor. In the Southeast Loch of the Naval Station was sub tender, *Pelias,* then tied to finger piers the submarines, *Narwhal, Gudgeon, Dolphin, Tautog* and AVDs, *Thornton* and *Hulbert.* Survey ship *Sumner* with storeship, *Castor* were next at Merry Point. *Bagley* was at the west end of the Loch before coming to berths at the Naval Station. In the first set of berths were destroyers, *Cummings* and *Schley.* Behind them were *St. Louis* and *Honolulu* nested with *Blue Goose* being outboard. Across from her was *Frisco* The next berth held DMs *Preble, Tracy, Pruitt, Sicard* and DMS *Grebe.. New Orleans* was astern of them. The berth to port had *Rigel* (AR-11) with oiler, *Rampano,* aft of her. The little seaplane tender *Swan* had a berth to herself, the next one was vacant and then the destroyers *Jarvis* and *Mugford* were berthed ahead of transport *Argonne* and gunboat *Sacramento.* Rounding the corner to Ten Ten Dock one came to *Helena* with *Ogalala* outboard of her. Proceeding toward the dry docks, there was *Cachalot* then *Pennsy* with *Cassin* and *Downes* forward of her in the dock. The next two dry docks were empty but *Shaw* was in floating dry dock YFD-2. Hospital Point was the last promontory before the channel egress from Pearl Harbor. The infamous oil tank farm of Tea Pot Dome (Se Chapter V) lay behind it on the Naval Station.

The cast of characters was assembled. Before Colors the next morning the curtain was to go up on the nadir of The Treaty Navy. But it was to rise again and fulfill its destiny in the Pacific for which it was created.

PART IV

Epilogue

Chapter XXIII

The Treaty Navy Holds the Line

Japan's Ambassador, Kichisaburo Nomura, and the Special Envoy, Saburo Kurusu, asked to call on SecState Hull at 1 p.m. on Sunday, Dec. 7, 1941 in Washington. That was 7:30 a.m. in Hawaii. At 7:30 Washington time, i.e., five-and-a-half hours earlier, the Navy crypto-center, which had been deciphering the Japanese diplomatic codes for some time, broke the last of a 14-part Japanese message to Nomura and Kurusu. It was hand-carried to CNO, the White House and State Department. The final part of it was a rejection of U.S. proposals for solutions to problems which had come to a head with the freezing of Japanese assets and the embargoes. (See Chapter XXII.) It appeared that Kurusu and Nomura were requesting the meeting with Hull to sever negotiations.

The Japanese Embassy was having a problem getting the message typed for delivery. A regular typist was not allowed to see the message so it was being "hunt and pecked" by an official with clearance but no typing skills. Realizing that they were going to be late the envoys called the State Department for a 45-minute postponement. It was granted.

Earlier, an Army intercept of a plain language message instructing the Japanese envoys to request their appointment with Cordell Hull for exactly 1 p.m. on Sunday alerted a colonel to the possibility of the audience coinciding with a surprise dawn attack in the Pacific. Dawn would be west of Hawaii and closer to Guam, the Philippines of Malaya.

At 6:30 a.m. in Hawaii, *Antares* reported a periscope sighting to *Ward*. The submarine nets opened for *Antares* and two midget subs followed her into Pearl Harbor. Another was not so lucky. *Ward* attacked, fired upon and depth charged her. *Ward* relayed this to 14th Naval District.

A half hour later, an Army radar station on the north shore of Oahu stayed on the air beyond its scheduled shut down of 7 a.m. The operator detected and reported a large flight of aircraft coming from the north. He was told that they were probably B-17s expected that morning from the mainland. The Army had even paid a local radio station to broadcast during the night to guide the Flying Fortresses to Hawaii. That same broadcast was used by IJN carrier planes as a beacon.

In Washington, both Navy and Army duty officers were reluctant to send any warnings to commanders in the Pacific without specific authorization from CNO Stark or Army Chief of Staff Gen, Marshall. The latter was on his morning canter unavailable before going to his office later than usual on Sunday. Stark felt that enough "war warnings" had been sent to the Pacific and another would be like crying "wolf." In any event, both Stark and Marshall would have given their priority of warning to the Philippines. Beneath it all was the worry that a war warning stemming from the message broken by crypto people would tip off the Japs that we were reading their mail. MAGIC, the code word for our tapping into their messages was a close-held secret.

Eighteen minutes before the attack, a floatplane from a Japanese cruiser looked down on Pearl Harbor and reported that all was serene and the U.S. Fleet moored where expected by Japanese intelligence. The attackers had rehearsed on mock-ups and had memorized charts. The first wave came through Koli Koli Pass. Some peeled off to attack Schofield Barracks and Wheeler Field. The rest headed for the ships in Pearl Harbor and Army planes at adjacent Hickam Field. A separate attack hit the patrol plane base at Kaneohe "over the Pali" on the windward side of Oahu.

The first bombs dropped at 7:53 a.m. Hawaii time. That was 23 minutes after the originally scheduled appointment of Kurusu and Nomura with Hull. Although they presented their ultimatum after the actual act of the attack, they had tried to obey their instructions as to timing but failed to do so because of clerical ineptness.

The initial wave of dive- and torpedo-bombers of the IJN ripped The Treaty Navy asunder. An era was over.

Crews and ships bands were standing by for Morning Colors when the bombs fell. A message was telephoned to Adm. Kimmel's headquarters, "Enemy air raid – not drill." Five minutes after the first bomb, a broadcast hit the United States, "Air raid, Pearl Harbor – This is no drill." War had come to the United States where everyone had least expected it.

In the first 30 minutes four separate torpedo attacks hit the ships at Pearl Harbor. The first by a dozen planes went straight for the battleships. So did the second that may have been three tardy ones of the first attack. Then a single plane dropped her fish at *Helena* at Ten Ten Dock. The fourth attack of four planes hit the other side of Ford Island from Battleship Row. That was where the carriers usually tied up. All dropped torpedoes adapted for the shoal water of Pearl Harbor. Dive-bombers sowed death along Battleship Row then strafed after releasing their load. *Arizona,* penultimate ship in Battleship Row, took a bomb which penetrated a forward magazine. The explosion broke her in two forward and toppled her conning tower and foremast toward the bow. She settled quickly to the bottom with almost 1,000 of her trapped crew in her. Beside the fatal bomb hit which killed her skipper, Capt. Franklin Van Valkenburgh, and RAdm. Isaac Kidd who flew his flag in her, she was hit repeatedly. Flames from burning oil fed a billowing cloud of smoke which hung above Pearl Harbor.

Oklahoma, outboard of *Maryland* had taken torpedoes and capsized. Torpedoes had holed *WeeVee* and she was settling. Likewise, *Prune Barge* was sinking into the mud. She had been anticipating a below decks inspection on Monday and her watertight doors were left open. *Tennessee,* inboard of *West Virginia,* was protected from torpedoes but bombs found her and started fires.

Fragments from one bomb wounded Capt. Bennion on the bridge of *West Virginia*. He continued to direct damage control efforts to contain the fires and supervised the excellent work of counter-flooding by the damage control parties he had trained. *WeeVee* settled to the bottom on an even keel. Capt. Bennion succumbed to his wounds on the deck of his ship. *Tennessee* was damaged but her power plant was intact. She was unable to sortie since she was wedged in by sunken *West Virginia*. *Maryland* was lucky and took fewest hits but she was moored inside capsized *Okie* and hemmed in aft by *Tennessee* and *West Virginia*. *Neosho* ahead of her was able to get underway by backing down and then coming clear of settling *Prune Barge* ahead of her. The most significant ship to slip her cables and get underway was *Nevada*. The senior officer on board was LCdr. F.J. Thomas, a recalled Reserve officer who had been graduated from the Naval Academy in 1925. The officer of the deck who got her AA batteries in action was Ens. J.K. Taussig, Jr. who had graduated the previous February. He was the son of the officer who had taken the first destroyers to Ireland in 1917. (See Chapter I.) *Nevada* was last in line on Battleship Row. During the fist 90 minutes of the attack she took a torpedo forward and several bomb hits. LCdr. Thomas, as acting CO, decided to stand out to sea. He backed down and then went ahead past the burning battlewagons toward Hospital Point before making the turn to port to go down the channel. Dive-bombers concentrated on her as she sortied. She was heavily damaged but underway. The Senior Officer Present Afloat (SOPA), however, feared she might be sunk blocking the channel. He ordered her beached on Hospital Point which she was. The channel was clear.

On the north side of Ford Island away from Battleship Row, Japanese torpedo- and dive-bombers were busy as well. Target ship *Utah*, with her planked over hull was mistaken for a carrier and took several torpedoes causing her to turn turtle and leave her bottom pointing skyward barely above water. She was the scene of several rescues as sailors with acetylene torches opened her bottom to save entrapped crewmen. *Raleigh* ahead of *Utah* took a torpedo in the fireroom and in a later attack a bomb went through her exploding on the harbor bottom. Excellent damage control saved her to fight another day. She also claimed several Japs shot down. Torpedoes and bombs missed *Detroit* astern of *Raleigh*. *Monaghan* having the alert duty had been ordered to support *Ward* after the report of the attack on a submarine. She got underway a half-hour after the first attack and headed out. En route she sighted and rammed one of the midgets which had followed *Antares* in. She also shot down a Jap which crashed into *Curtiss*.

Phoenix and several destroyers were able to get underway and stand outside the Harbor. At the Naval Station, there were more fireworks. *Shaw* in the floating dry dock took a hit which blew off her bow in a spectacular explosion. *Helena* was hit amidships by a torpedo which passed under *Ogalala* blowing a hole in the latter. *Ogalala* was towed aft of the cruiser and moored to the dock but she turned over. Both ships were later repaired and returned to service. In dry dock, *Pennsy* took several hits but was not severely damaged. Forward of her, *Cassin* and *Downes* were wrecked when bomb explosions knocked them off the keel blocks. They were not deemed "totaled" by the Navy and their machinery, guns and other vitals were returned to the U.S. and hulls built around them. They retained their names and numbers.

The IJN did not get away scot-free. It lost several midgets sub and a fair number of aircraft shot down or failed to return to the carriers. While the toll among ships and crews was the center of attention in the press, a considerable loss of combat power occurred in destruction on the ground of Navy and Army Air Corps aircraft. In addition, six SBDs from *Enterprise* were shot down by trigger-happy gunners on Ford Island as they attempted to land after the attack. But almost half of the battleships of The Treaty Navy lay in the mud of Pearl Harbor or beached at Hospital Point. *Arizona* was gone forever, albeit is still in commission as the grave of her crew. *Oklahoma* had her masts on the harbor bed with her bottom protruding above water. She was raised but sank when being towed to the West Coast. The others would be raised, modernized and fit to fight again.

Two bright spots, if there were any, were that no carriers were in Pearl Harbor that fateful morning. They and the cruisers and destroyer of The Treaty Navy would hold the line until ships of the later Vinson Acts and other war construction could "impose our will upon Japan." The second bright spot was that the IJN failed to hit the oil tanks which were filled to capacity. The Fleet, or its remnants, had fuel to fight.

The two carrier task forces remained at sea until after the attack. There was an attempt to relieve Wake Island by a force centered around *Saratoga* which had sped from the West Coast. The relief was recalled at the last minute because of refueling problems. Rerouting of the Manila convoy has been mentioned. Fault finding for the disaster began immediately. Heads had to roll. A game of musical chairs at the top of the old Treaty Navy began.

Before looking at the cast of characters in that game, a glance at Navy rank structure is in order. Most officers in The Treaty Navy were Naval Academy graduates. Practically all of the flag officers came from the pre-World War I graduates of the Academy. All graduates of the same Class held the same initial date of rank. This was in order of merit at graduation. Dates of rank changed with promotion but the relative precedence remained the same. The selection system of 1916 provided for departure from that Class-Standing precedence. An example might suffice. When a Class came up for selection to commander on the basis of "best fitted," an officer whose academic prowess had earned him a top spot in his Class might not have cut the mustard in the Fleet. His Classmates junior to him might have performed better in the Fleet as their fitness reports so indicated. The officer who had been higher academically, might be "passed over" i.e., not selected and his peers would be promoted and hence be senior to him. If a later selection board deemed him fit for promotion, he would advance in rank but still be junior to those he once preceded. The lineal precedence would obtain all the way to the highest *permanent* rank of rear admiral of the upper half. The two ranks above, i.e., vice admiral (three stars) and admiral (four stars) were "designated ranks" and filled not by selection board decision but by decision of the Commander-in-Chief on the recommendation of SecNav who passed on that of CNO. Once a flag officer left a billet designated for more than two stars and did not get another one or one higher, he reverted to his permanent rank of two stars and filled a billet appropriate to that rank. It was understood and accepted by the officers but not always by their ladies. An example of the latter is when MGC Barnett reverted to brigadier general in 1919. (See Chapter XVIII)

Another example of the up and down effect was that of Ernie King. As Commander, Aircraft, Battle Force, in the late '30s he was a vice admiral. When he left that assignment, he went back to rear admiral and assignment to the General Board. He felt his career was over. Among some, in and out of the Navy, he had the reputation, deserved or not, of being a drinker and "a lady's man" (these days it would be termed "womanizer") at least he was known as "fanny pincher" among the junior officers' ladies. We have seen how King was returned from the oblivion of the General Board to command the Atlantic Patrol Force with three stars and then the new Atlantic Fleet (CinCLant) with a fourth star. He was to move ahead again after Pearl Harbor. As he was wont to say, "When things get tough, they send for the sonavabitches!"

King had been graduated from the Academy in 1901. Therefore, he was '01. He was number 4 of 67 graduates and commander of the Midshipman battalion (now a Brigade). A look at some of the others and their Classes will put things in perspective.

At the time of Pearl Harbor, CNO was Adm. H.R. Stark '03 (30 of 50); former CINCUS was Adm. J.O. Richardson '02 (5 of 59); current CINCUS was Adm. H.E. Kimmel '04 (13 of 62); ComBatFor was VAdm. W.S. Pye '01 (32 0f 67) a DesDiv Commander at Honda Point (See Chapter V); ComAirBatFor was VAdm. W.F. Halsey, Jr. '04 (43 of 62) and ChBuNav was RAdm. C.W. Nimitz '05 (7 0f 114).

The initial moves made King CINCUS which he promptly made COMINCH to replace the poorly verbalized CINCUS. Pye became the interim Commander Pacific Fleet (CinCPac) Kimmel's other designation; Richardson remained in the "created" billet in Washington as an adviser; and Nimitz became CinCPac. He arrived in Pearl on Christmas day and assumed command and his four stars on the first of the year. One of the first things the new COMINCH did before the new CinCPac left Washington was to draw a line on the chart from Midway to Samoa, Fiji and Brisbane. Nimitz and the remnants of The Treaty Navy were to hold that line at all costs.

After the attack on Pearl Harbor, the Japanese blows came where they had originally been expected. Japan caught the U.S. Army Air Corps on the ground in the Philippines. This occurred hours after the attack at Pearl Harbor should have alerted LtGen. Douglas MacArthur to take steps for dispersal. Japanese strategy had taken out the Fleet meant to be a deterrent to its freedom of action in the Western Pacific and it had destroyed MacArthur's airpower there. The fall of the Philippines was assured and Tommy Hart '97 (13 of 47) sent his ships south to the Dutch East Indies. The Asiatic Fleet of The Treaty Navy girded for battle. Its first losses were to be: *Bittern* (AM-20) bombed and sunk in Cavite, *Sealion* bombed and wrecked in dry dock in Cavite then destroyed by the Navy; *Penguin* (AVP-6) bombed and sunk in Guam; *Robert L. Barnes* (AG-27) captured at Guam; and *Wake* (PR-3) captured at Shanghai. The Asiatic Fleet was to suffer 23 more losses through May as Malaya, the Dutch East Indies and the Philippines fell.

The Japanese advanced on several axes. Troops from the Chinese mainland attacked and took Hong Kong in two weeks. An invasion fleet put troops ashore at Lingayen Gulf in northern Luzon to sweep down the valley toward Manila. Another landing was made on the Malayan Peninsula for the drive to Singapore. The RN had sent a force originally to be composed of two capital ships, a carrier and destroyers to Singapore to protect that bastion. The carrier, *HMS Indomitable* ripped her bottom on an uncharted rock thus depriving *Prince of Wales* and the old battlecruiser, *Repulse,* of air cover. Both ships and a destroyer succumbed to IJN land-based torpedo bombers off Malaya on Dec. 10, 1941.

U.S. submarines immediately went to sea from Cavite to stalk the Japanese invasion flotilla for Luzon and to conduct unrestricted submarine warfare in the East and South China seas. While their torpedo accuracy was less than spectacular, they were to learn that even when they hit, the unreliable torpedoes failed to explode.

Adm. Hart sent most of his surface combat units south to Java and Australia. Some destroyers were already in Borneo at Tarakan and Balikpapan with the tender, *Black Hawk.* The seaplane tenders and their surviving PBYs were also sent south. Tommy Hart shifted his flag south when MacArthur declared Manila an Open City and moved the Army west to the Bataan Peninsula. The submarines which had been operating from Manila Bay tended by *Canopus* (AS-9) had to submerge alongside during daylight and surface for servicing at night. When Manila was declared an Open City by MacArthur, Hart shifted *Canopus* to Bataan, leaving behind torpedoes and other submarine provisions at Cavite. This was caused by the sudden decision of MacArthur to evacuate Manila and the failure to notify the Navy. Tommy Hart left in *Shark* the day after Christmas.

Previously, Hart had organized TF-5 under RAdm. W.A. Glassford '06 (21 of 116) in *Houston* to leave the Philippines for Balikpapen. TF-5 included: "borrowed" *Boise,* oilers, *Trinity* and *Pecos,* and the old *Covered Wagon,* now tending seaplanes.

Things moved swiftly in January and February of 1942. IJN air and sea power supported the advances of land forces against U.S., British and Dutch troops who lacked such support. *Boise* struck an uncharted shoal in Sape Strait and had to retire to Columbo, thence Bombay and home to Mare Island for repairs. When *Canopus* could no longer tend to the needs of submarines because of air attacks on Mariveles, the submarines moved to western Australia with tenders *Holland* and *Otus.* S-36 ran aground and was scuttled in Makasser Strait on Jan. 20. *Shark* was overdue and presumed lost in March. *Perch* was lost without a trace in April operating in the shallow waters of the Malay Barrier. The Japanese were not hospitable to survivors of U.S. submarines.

The Asiatic Fleet was committed by Washington to the defense of the Dutch East Indies when it became apparent that it could do nothing to save the Philippines except run in and evacuate personnel. *Trout* (SS-202) brought ammunition into Bataan and took out the gold of the Filipino treasury.

A bold strike by U.S. destroyers on Jan. 24 caught a group of transports by surprise at night. The destroyers got in among the ships off Balikpapan and with torpedoes and gunfire sank four and damaged another. No U.S. ships were lost.

The heavy units, including *Houston, Langley* and some destroyers went as far as Darwin in northern Australia for replenishment. A support base had been established there.

In mid-January, the Combined Chiefs of Staff (set up by Roosevelt and Churchill soon after the Pearl Harbor attack) established the American, British, Dutch and Australian (ABDA) command. It was charged with the defense of the area north of Australia, through the middle of New Guinea, to north of the Philippines then west to the Asian mainland of China, south along Southeast Asia, across the Malay Peninsula, north to Burma and then south through the Indian Ocean and then east to Australia. Its supreme commander was British Field Marshal Wavell. Tommy Hart had the naval component. The Asiatic Fleet thus continued in existence until the end of January when Glassford was promoted to vice admiral and command of U.S. Naval Forces in the Southwest Pacific. It replaced the Asiatic Fleet although the latter was not formerly abolished.

On Feb. 4, a combined striking force of two Dutch and two U.S. cruisers, *Houston* and *Marblehead,* flanked by four U.S. and four Dutch destroyers came under attack by IJN land-based bombes. *Marblehead* was heavily damaged and afire. Her rudder jammed left and the ship began to list. Damage control parties freed her rudder in time to dodge another attack. She had to leave the force and make her way back to Tjilatjap in Java, steering by engines with a damaged rudder. After jury-rigged repairs in Java, she wended her way home through the Indian Ocean, around Africa and up the South Atlantic to the yard at Brooklyn. She was lost to further action with the Asiatic Fleet but was to be its only major survivor.

A bold Japanese carrier strike on Feb.19 caught Darwin by surprise. *Peary* was sunk. Meanwhile ABDA surface forces were mixing it up with the IJN in Badung Strait southeast of Bali.

Stewart, J.D. Edwards, Parrott and *Pillsbury* took part in an ill-planned, uncoordinated night attack on destroyer-escorted transports in Badung Strait on Feb 20. The Dutch admiral committed his forces in phases and thus piecemeal. The result was that the U.S. "tin cans" expended most of their remaining precious torpedoes and ran their material readiness to almost zero. A period of upkeep was vital. *Stewart* was placed in a private floating dry dock in Surabaya. The docking was inept because of the flight of skilled native labor to the hills.

211

Motion of the dry dock caused *Stewart* to slip off the keel blocks and become a helpless hulk.

Java was about to fall. The RN senior officer decided to exercise his option and withdraw his ships from ABDA and so informed the Dutch admiral. The Dutchman was irate and asked VAdm. Glassford what his intentions were. Glassford said that he was under the orders of the Dutch admiral but would prefer to evacuate his remaining units to Australia. The Dutchman replied that he didn't give a damn what the Brits did but Glassford was ordered to save the American ships. Not many were saved, however.

Air cover was a major problem for the defense of Java and the ABDA ships. There were flyable P-40s in Australia and in theory they could be flown from there to Java via crude airstrips en route. Alas, the skills of the Army aviators weren't up to it and few aircraft made it all the way. Many crashed or were disabled before they got to Java. It was decided to ship both flyable and crated planes to Java, The former were the most needed and readiest for action. *Langley* took on 32 P-40s and their pilots in Darwin and made a dash toward Tjilatjap in southern Java. In the afternoon of Feb. 27, *Covered Wagon* was caught by IJN carrier planes. She was sunk. *Edsall* and *Whipple* picked up survivors and later transferred them to *Pecos* (AO-6).

On the last day of February three separate remnants of the ABDA sortied from ports in northern Java seeking to break out to the south. *Ford, Paul Jones, Alden* and *J.D. Edwards* left Surababya after dark, slipped through Bali Strait and made it to safety. *Pope* escorting wounded *HMS Exeter*, one of the victors over *Graf Spee,* and a RN destroyer left to head west and cut through Sundra Strait at the western end of Java. They were diverted north by Japanese warships and after a running battle, *Pope* was the last to be sunk. *Houston* left Batavia with *HMAS Perth* trying to escape via Sundra Strait. *Houston*'s number three turret was out of action from a previous engagement and the two ships lacked escorts. They ran into Nip transports disembarking troops and equipment, a cruiser skipper's dream. The guns of both ships were having a field day until IJN cruisers and destroyers arrived. The odds were insurmountable and both *Perth* and *Houston* went down firing. Survivors were picked up in the water by the Japs or captured after they swam ashore. Prisoners of the Japanese wondered what ever happened to the Geneva Convention on the humane treatment of POWs. It didn't seem to have a Japanese translation.

An interesting footnote to Japanese treatment of POWs concerns the crew of one of the submarines lost from the Asiatic Fleet. She was "overdue and presume lost." There was no word of survivors, if any. The crew was initially presumed missing and after a suitable interval was declared dead. The "widow" of one of the officers remarried. He was another submariner who had been a Plebe at the Academy when her first husband was a First Classman. It was a typical Enoch Aden situation when the war was over. The "dead" submariners were found alive, if not well. The joyous reunion of the dead with his widow was short lived. He died in a hunting accident a few months later. He was 42.

212

The saga of the Asiatic Fleet was no quite over. *Pecos* and *Edsall* were sunk by bombs south of Java on Mar. 1. *Pillsbury* was not heard of again after that same day. In her dry dock trap, *Stewart* was subject to demolition charges to destroy her. Unfortunately, they weren't completely successful and she was floated and repaired by the Japanese to serve the IJN as P-102. On the brighter side, *Parrott* and *Whipple* made good their escape from Tjilatjap to Australia. There were still units of the Asiatic Fleet in the Philippines after the Dutch East Indies fell.

When Bataan surrendered in early April 1942, *Finch* (AM-9) was destroyed by her crew. Old *Canopus* shed her camouflage of netting and foliage and backed into the stream. Explosive charges set by her crew sent her to the bottom. The floating dry dock, *Dewey,* was also scuttled, as was *Napa* (AT-32). Corregidor held out for another month sealing the harbor of Manila from the Japanese. Before all U.S. forces surrendered on May 10, the final scuttlings took place. *Quail* (AM-15), *Tanager* (AM-5), *Mindanao* (PR-8), *Oahu* (PR-6), *Genesee* (ATO-55) and *Pigeon* (ARS-9) went down. Only *Luzon* (PR-7) remained to be captured. The disappearance of *Asheville* (PG-21) closed out the "Far China Station" of The Treaty Navy when she was stricken from the Navy list on May 8.

In the meantime, things were busy in the rest of the Pacific. *Yorktown* had come back from the Atlantic, as had many destroyers to escort the new carrier task forces. *Hornet,* too, had come west and she, under her first skipper, Capt. Marc Mitscher, was to have a special mission.

There had been an abortive mission to relieve the siege of Wake Island early in December 1941. TF-14 of *Sara, Astoria, Minnie* and *Frisco* with accompanying destroyers under command of RAdm. Frank Jack Fletcher, '06 (26 of 116), a non-flyer, sailed for Wake. RAdm. A.W. "Jake" Fitch '06 (110 0f 116), the most experienced flag officer with wings, flew his flag in *Saratoga* but was junior to Fletcher. The latter who was to be known as "Fueling Frank" began to establish that sobriquet by delaying the relief a day in order to top off the destroyers. The delay caused Pye to recall the ships and Wake Island fell adding another saga of sacrifice to the annals of the Marine Corps.

Fletcher shifted his flag to *Yorktown* when she transited the Canal. His first task was to cover a convoy reinforcing Samoa with Marines. On Jan. 11, 1942, *Sara* was torpedoed by a sub and went to Bremerton for modernization and repair. The former consisted of removing the eight 8-in. guns and turrets and replacing them with twin gun houses with 5-in. dual- purpose guns as in the new battleships. Radar was also installed. *Lex* had had her 8-in. guns removed earlier at Pearl but no 5-in. guns replaced them.

Japan was expanding her defense perimeter to retain what she had gotten quickly after the attack on Hawaii. The British and Australian Mandates in the Gilbert Islands and Bismarck Archipelago were easily overrun since they were hardly defended. The lifeline to Australia from the West Coast and Panama Canal was threatened if further Japanese moves occurred. Rabaul, in the

Bismarcks, was being developed by the Japs as a staging base for moves southeast and south.

There was fear that an amphibious thrust from either the Marshalls or Truk would be made at Samoa. To forestall this, Halsey, flying his flag in *Enterprise,* with RAdm. R.A. Spruance '07 (25 of 208) and cruisers, *Northampton, Salt Lake City* and *Chester* made up TF-8. They conducted a carrier raid on Wotje, Maloela and Kwajalein in the Marshalls. Spruances's cruisers bombarded the first two atolls as well. At the same time, Fletcher commanding TF-17 in *Yorktown* with *Louisville* and *St. Louis* hit the southern Marshalls at Jaluit, Mili and Makin. These early February carrier raids were no roaring successes but they did show that The Treaty Navy was holding the line and hitting back.

Lexington, Minneapolis, Indianapolis, San Francisco and *Pensacola* plus five destroyers were dispatched to attack Rabaul before the IJN could become established there. On Feb. 21, the force was detected by a Jap flying boat which was shot down. Its report brought a flock of bombers to attack the task force. *Lex* scrambled a combat air patrol (CAP) of F4F Wildcats. Lt. E.H. "Butch" O'Hare '37 (256 of 323) earned a Medal of Honor for shooting down five. When he was killed flying a F6F-6N off *Enterprise* more than two years later, the airport in Chicago, his hometown, was named for him.

With its discovery, the mission to Rabaul was scrubbed. At the same time, Halsey's *Enterprise* force was bombing and bombarding Wake. Then in the first week in March, he moved within 1,000 miles of Japan to strike Marcus Island. While none of these diversions deterred the IJN carriers and the Japanese army from their conquests, they were providing the U.S. Navy and its carrier forces with experience and combat. The Japanese, in the meantime had landed on the northeastern tip of New Guinea and seized the small ports of Lae and Salamaua. This posed a springboard to advances east over the Owen Stanley Mountains to Port Moresby on the southern coast of New Guinea across from Australia. The task forces of *Lexington* and *Yorktown* teamed up for an American version of Pearl Harbor, albeit, in miniature. The two carriers launched aircraft from the Coral Sea, south of New Guinea. The attackers flew over the Owen Stanley Range and through a 7,500-foot pass. Losing only one of the 104 plans engaged, they had a "field day" surprising the warships and "Marus' (Jap merchant ships had Maru in all their names) in the harbors. *Lex* returned to Pearl while *Yorktown* went to Tongatabu near Fiji.

After completing her shakedown and work up, *Hornet* took on a strange deck load at Alameda NAS in San Francisco Bay. Early in January, the kernel of an idea to bomb Japan had taken root. There were no bases close enough and to send carriers within range of their own aircraft was to expose them to Japanese land-based air. It was proposed to use Army Air Corps twin-engined B-25 Mitchell bombers from a carrier but they would continue on to China after bombing Japan. The carrier would retire east when the launch was done. Army pilots had flown fighters off a carrier to Iceland in 1941 so it was a matter of training them in short field takeoffs. This was done in Florida and they flew to Alameda to be hoisted aboard *Hornet.* They filled the flight deck aft of the island. The carrier's planes were stowed on the hangar deck, some in dismantled condition. *Hornet* sailed on Apr. 2, 1942 with *Vincennes, Nashville and* four destroyers. Oiler, *Cimarron,* accompanied. The rendezvous with Halsey occurred west of the 180th meridian at 39 degrees north on Apr. 13. TF-16 had *Enterprise* and *Hornet,* the latter with 16 B-25s, *Northampton, Salt Lake City, Vincennes* and *Nashville* under Spruance; DesRon 6 of DesDiv 12, *Balch, Benham, Ellet, Fanning* and DesDiv 22 of *Grayson, Gwin, Meredith* and *Monnsen.* Oilers, *Sabine* and *Cimarron* rounded out the all Treaty Navy strike force. Although detection caused the B-25s to launch 200 miles early, the surprise of the attack was a success and the ships returned to Pearl Harbor on Apr. 25. The IJN revised its estimates on what was an adequate outer perimeter defense. U.S. crypto people read it in the message traffic.

The first Japanese move was to be toward Port Moresby on the south side of New Guinea, an ominous threat to Australia. Land-based air was in Rabaul, where two invasion forces staged. One force was to seize Tulagi in the Solomon Islands, a weakly defended British possession. The second was destined for Port Moresby. A carrier striking force of two of the six carriers which bombed Pearl Harbor was escorted by two heavy cruisers and six destroyers. A covering force of four heavy cruisers and the light carrier *Shoho,* plus light cruisers and a seaplane carrier completed the IJN forces. The chitchat from the assembly of such a force alerted the code breakers.

A U.S.- Australian force was put together under Fletcher. He flew his flag in *Yorktown* with *Minneapolis, New Orleans, Astoria, Chester* and *Portland.* The destroyer screen was *Phelps, Dewey, Farragut, Alywin* and *Monaghan.* A support group under RAdm. J.G. Crace RN had two Australian cruisers plus *Chicago* and two U.S. destroyers, *Perkins* and *Walke.* Jake Fitch was in tactical command of the carrier group when *Lexington* and her force joined. Fitch flew his flag in *Lexington* with a destroyer screen of *Morris, Anderson, Hammann* and *Russell. Sims* and *Worden* escorted oilers, *Neosho* and *Tippecanoe.* The Treaty Navy came to play.

And play they did; but not without loss. The enemy's seaplane base on Tulagi was shot up by *Yorktown* aircraft as the two opposing carrier units sought each other. Scouts from *Lex* found the covering group with *Shoho* and *Lex*'s dive-bombers were able to send, "Scratch one flattop!" Then ensued the first sea battle wherein the opposing forces engaged without the ships ever seeing each other. It began when the Japs found and sank *Sims* and *Neosho* on May 7, 1942. The scouts of each carrier force found the other. Attacking flights passed en route to their targets. All four carriers sustained damage from air attacks. *Yorktown* took bomb hits inflicting structural damage but she was able to continue to launch and recover. *Lex* took bomb and torpedo hits rupturing internal fuel lines. A chance spark from a generator ignited volatile AVGAS vapors and fire spread beyond control. She was abandoned and sunk by U.S. destroyers lest she be a beacon in the night for the IJN.

The Port Moresby invasion force turned back. They still celebrate May 8 in Australia as Battle of the Coral Sea Day, the day Australia was saved from invasion. Badly damaged *Shokaku* and lesser hurt *Zuikaku* but without most of her air group, limped back to Japan. They were to be absent from the next move of the IJN. *Yorktown* with the survivors of her task force headed back to Pearl. They were needed to thwart the next move of the IJN. *Chicago* and *Perkins,* however, went to Sydney. There they were unsuccessfully attacked by four midget subs in the harbor. One of the subs is now mounted as a trophy at the Australian War Memorial Museum, Canberra.

The next IJN move was to be against Midway Island, about 1,000 miles west-northwest of Hawaii. Adm. Yamamoto, the planner of the Pearl Harbor strike was to lead the IJN in an invasion of the island with the hope of drawing the U.S. Fleet out for a showdown battle. His Combined Fleet had four components plus diversionary strike and occupation forces to Alaska and the Aleutians. The Advance Expeditionary Force was 16 I-class submarines deployed to discover the U.S. sortie from Pearl and harass it. The carrier striking force had four of the six carriers that had made the Pearl Harbor raid, two cruisers, two battleships and a screen of 12 destroyers., all supported by five oilers. The occupation force of 12 transports carried about 5,000 troops covered by two battleships, eight cruisers and 19 destroyers. It had a support group of oilers and seaplane carriers. His main body was under his personal command. Yamamoto flew his flag in the new giant battleship, *Yamato,* one of seven in the main body. It also had a light carrier, two light cruisers and a screen of 12 destroyers.

The Northern Areas Force was intended to entice forces north and away from Midway by air strikes against Dutch Harbor and then occupy Kiska and Attu-Adak. It had two light carriers, three heavy and two light cruisers, a dozen destroyers, four transports, three cargo ships and three oilers. Six submarines acted as scouts. Its operations were to precede the initial air strikes on Midway. Dutch Harbor was hit on Jun. 1.

Nimitz knew when and where Yamamoto was coming. *Yorktown* with her consorts limped into Pearl on May 27, for an estimated three months of repair. She was docked and the workmen swarmed on and in an around-the-clock operation had her ready for sea in less than three days. Halsey's task force, which after the Tokyo raid had been sent south too late for the Battle of the Coral Sea, had returned to Pearl where he was hospitalized for a skin disorder. Spruance was named, by Nimitz, to Halsey's command. *Enterprise* and *Hornet* with TF-16 left Pearl before the IJN subs were in place to observe. It had *New Orleans, Minneapolis, Vincennes, Northampton, Pensacola* all Treaty Navy ships and the new light cruiser *Atlanta.* Its destroyer screen was, *Phelps, Worden, Monaghan, Alywin, Balch, Conyngham, Benham, Ellet* and *Maury, Dewey* and *Monssen* escorted *Cimarron* and *Platte.*

Fletcher's TF-17 left Pearl as soon as *Yorktown* was ready. It was again prior to the Jap subs being in position. TF-17 had *Astoria* and *Portland* screened by *Hammann, Hughes, Morris, Anderson, Russell* and *Gwin.*

Aware of Yamamoto's plan, Nimitz put his task forces northeast of where he thought the Japanese carriers would launch against Midway, Poised undetected

216

on their left flank, he had the opportunity to inflict the maximum punishment on the Jap carriers. He did.

The air attack on Midway was destructive but not fatal. High- level counter-raids on the carriers were ineffectual. Thus, undaunted the Nips opted for another Midway strike. Prudently, the Jap carrier commander was searching for U.S. carriers which could be around. In accordance with IJN doctrine, floatplanes from the cruisers and battleships did this. One was delayed by mechanical problems. She was the one that found a U.S. carrier. Her late report caught the Japanese in a dilemma. They were rearming for a second strike on Midway and expected to launch before the first strike returned thus clearing their decks to recover aircraft. The second strike was armed for ground targets not for ship attacks. A change in armament to torpedoes and armor-piercing bombs would delay the strike against the U.S. carriers and would compound vulnerability as the first strike returned. Unknown to the Japanese there were three U.S. carriers. They were soon to find out. In response to a PBY sighting, Spruance had projected the position of the IJN carriers. Almost unfortunately, they changed course to recover aircraft into the wind and were not where predicted when the U.S. three-carrier aircraft strike arrived. Besides, the U.S. strike was not coordinated nor directed by an airborne commander. Still, luck held. The ill-fated TBDs arrived first. They came in low and slow drawing the Combat Air Patrol (CAP) down to the water. While successful in defending against the Devastators by shooting 38 out of 42 down, the Zeros were out of position when the six squadrons (the SBDs of the VSs as well of those of the VBs could dive-bomb) arrived. Caught with their decks filled with aircraft being refueled and bombs and torpedoes exposed, *Kaga, Akagi* and *Soryu* were soon flaming wrecks. *Hiryu* bringing up the rear of the diamond formation was hit but escaped *pro tem.* She was able to launch planes to attack U.S. carriers and they picked out *Yorktown.*

Yorktown was hurt and previous damage, hastily repaired, did not help her situation. After a gallant damage control battle, she was abandoned for fear of capsizing. Then a skeleton force returned to salvage her as she came back on an even keel. A tug was coming from Pearl. Things looked bright and *Hammann* stood alongside assisting. But on Jun. 6, I-168 slipped through the destroyer screen and fired a spread of four torpedoes. One missed, two went under *Hammann* and into *Yorktown.* The other broke *Hammann* in half. Meanwhile, the second strikes from *Enterprise* and *Hornet* had sent *Hiryu* to join the other three. The cruiser, *Mikuma,* after a collision with her sister, *Mogami,* had crippled her, was sunk by aircraft. *Mogami* went back to Japan for a year of repair. Deprived of his air striking power, Yamamoto withdrew his forces to the Inland Sea, In four days, June 4-7; The Treaty Navy had held the line and turned the tide toward eventual victory. Before 1942 was over, The Treaty Navy was to be plunged into another battle to hold the line and to be bloodied.

Before the Battle of Midway had been joined, Nimitz responded to the threat to Alaska by forming TF-8 under RAdm. R.A. Theobald '07 (9 of 208). It was all surface ships with air search vested in PBYs based on tenders, *Williamson*

(AVD-2), Gillis (AVD-12) and *Casco* (AVP-12). Theobald's flagship was *Nashville* and he had *Indianapolis, Louisville, St. Louis* and *Honolulu* screened by DesDiv 11 of *Gridley, McCall, Gilmer* and *Humphreys*. He put together a destroyer striking group of *Case, Reid, Brooks, Sands, Kane, Dent, Talbot, King* and *Waters*. Six "old S boats" were his submarine group, S-18, S-23, S-27, S-28, S-34 and S-35. Weather precluded surface actions when the enemy could not be located. Air strikes by both sides were inhibited by weather but the Japanese benefited from the clearer skies over land targets and bombed Dutch Harbor and other bases. When the weather cleared Japanese troops were discovered occupying Kiska and Attu.

Both sides went into naval hibernation for the summer but U.S. submarines were active trying to sever the Japanese lifeline from the Dutch East Indies to her south. Japan may have conquered the oil of the Indies but she was going to be hard pressed to use it. Defective U.S. torpedoes, however, were helping her and frustrating U.S. submarine crews.

Intelligence revealed that the Japanese had crossed from Tulagi in the Solomons and were building an airfield on Guadalcanal to its south. The body of water separating them was going to earn the name "Iron Bottom Sound" before the year was out.

A Japanese air base on Guadalcanal could extend long-range air attacks south to Espiritu Santo and even Noumea with the possibility of Japanese amphibious attacks to take and hold those way stations on the route to Australia. Even Samoa farther east could be threatened. While the overall Allied strategic plan was pointing toward an invasion of North Africa in late fall, the new situation in the South Pacific was deemed an emergency requiring immediate counter-action. King was foremost on the Joint Chiefs of Staff (JCS) in pushing the case for the Guadalcanal operation. Clearly, an amphibious landing by U.S. forces on Guadalcanal and Tulagi was required. The siphoning off of ground and shipping assets from North Africa was out of the question. Warships, excluding destroyers, however, could be available for what the Army, including its Air Corps deemed the sideshow in the Pacific. Marines were an integral part of the Naval Service so Guadalcanal could be a Navy show, albeit, on a shoestring compared with North Africa.

The 1stMarDiv was en route to New Zealand less its Seventh Marines in Samoa as that territory's defense force. Sufficient shipping could be assembled to lift the 1stMarDiv, naval construction battalions (CBs) and Marine air units to mount an attack on Guadalcanal and Tulagi before the Japanese became too strong. The race was on!

Almost every warship, capital ships excepted, of the prewar Treaty Navy was to take part in the several battles around and for Guadalcanal, which raged for more than five months. Four of the five carriers, less *Ranger,* participated. Two were sunk and the others heavily damaged. Sixteen of the remaining 17 prewar heavy cruisers took part. *Augusta* was the exception. Five were lost and two had bows blown off by the "long lance" torpedoes. Others were badly shot up. One of the *Brooklyn* class light cruisers was heavily damaged by gunfire. None of the

7,050-ton scout cruisers, however, took part. The toll among destroyers was 13 sunk and a score or more damaged.

For those for whom a box score is important, the IJN lost 134,840 tons of warships to the U.S.N. loss of 116,250 tons. (Does not include the loss of 10,570-ton *HMAS Canberra.*) The IJN lost two battleships, a carrier, three heavy cruisers, a light cruiser, 11 destroyers and six submarines. U.S. losses were two carriers, five heavy cruisers, two light cruisers (6,000-ton antiaircraft cruisers not really part of The Treaty Navy,) 14 destroyers and no submarines.

The 1stMarDiv was reinforced by the Second Marines from 2ndMarDiv to compensate for the missing Seventh Marines, plus the 1st Raider Battalion and the 1st Parachute Battalion. The Guadalcanal transport Group consisted of four Transport Divisions (TransDiv) each with three attack transports (APA) and an attack cargo ship (AKA). The landing on Guadalcanal was almost without opposition and the airfield was quickly over run. The TransDiv for Tulagi was augmented by four small transports converted from four-piper destroyers (APD). The fighting for Tulagi, Florida Island and adjacent islets was severe but they were taken and unlike Guadalcanal were not reinforced by the Japanese after the US. landing.

TF-61 was the expeditionary force of now-VAdm. Fletcher. "Fueling Frank" had *Saratoga, Enterprise* and *Wasp.* He had *North Carolina.* His cruisers were, *New Orleans, Minneapolis, Portland, San Francisco, Salt Lake City* and the new *Atlanta.* Sixteen destroyers were the screen and five oilers nursed his "habit."

The Amphibious Task Force (ATF) was commanded by RAdm. R.K. "Kelly" Turner '08 (5 of 210) recently come from duty as Ernie King's planner. He had an escort group of three RAN cruisers and *Chicago* plus nine U.S. destroyers. His fire support group was *Astoria, Quincy* and *Vincennes* plus six destroyers and new light cruiser, *San Juan.* Five old four-pipers converted to minecraft (DMS) were his sweeping force.

After a delay in New Zealand where Marine supplies and equipment had to be reloaded from commercial to combat load, first off is last on, the various components sailed. The landings took place on Aug. 7, 1942, the first of many more amphibious operations of the U.S.N. in the Pacific. Initially all went well until the bombers showed up. *George F. Elliott* (AP-13) was hit and set afire. *Jarvis* (DD-393) was hit but her crew kept her afloat and she was sent to Noumea *sans* escort for repairs.

Fueling Frank was anxious to get his carriers out of the vicinity where they could be subjected to air attack from Rabaul. Turner was reluctant to keep the transports off the beaches without air cover. Much Marine gear was still in the transports. On the second night of the landings, an IJN force of cruisers and destroyers roared in just before midnight and in a gun action, punctuated with torpedoes sank *Astoria, Quincy, Vincennes* and *HMAS Canberra.* Ill-fated *Jarvis* was lost with all hands to aircraft the next day. It was just the beginning of the actions which would earn Iron Bottom Sound its name.

The Japanese decided that they must win back Guadalcanal from the Marines. The only way they could do that was to reinforce their meager garrison on the island and drive the Marines into the sea. Since the Americans from Henderson Field, named for Maj. Lofton Henderson '26 (169 0f 456) killed at Midway, the IJN exploited its superiority in night tactics. Under the cover of bombardment ships which shelled the Marines and Henderson Field at night, destroyers and barges landed Japanese reinforcements. The Marines were short of everything from food to heavy equipment since Turner had pulled his transports. Gradually, supplies trickled back to Guadalcanal as APDs and other ships ran the danger of Iron Bottom Sound. Marines for their part held against Japanese attacks and retained Henderson Field.

In the air and sea battles around Guadalcanal, The Treaty Navy was stretched taut but held and rebounded to win. During the last week of August in an air-sea battle east of the Solomons, *Enterprise* was damaged and had to leave the area. Her Air Group flew to Henderson Field. Next damaged was *Sara* once more the victim of a submarine torpedo and she retired, leaving her Air Group to beef up Henderson Field.

Hornet now joined, escorted by *North Carolina*. She and *Wasp* were in company when another submarine counted coup. *Wasp* was hit and burned. When the fires raged out of control, she was abandoned and sunk. Then *North Carolina* caught a "fish" and although still seaworthy, retired for repairs. September was a rough month ashore and afloat for the U.S.

On the night of Oct. 11-12, an IJN bombardment group came down "the Slot" (U.S. nickname for the path between the northern islands of the Solomons chain from Rabaul.) This was the nightly "Tokyo Express" but this one was screening troop reinforcements. TF-64 under RAdm. Norman Scott '11 (173 of 193) was looking for a fight with *San Francisco, Salt Lake City, Boise* and *Helena*. His destroyers were, *Farenholt, Buchanan, Laffey, Duncan* and *McCalla*. In the melee which followed off Cape Esperance, the Japanese lost a cruiser and four destroyers but the reinforcements were landed. *Boise* was damaged and went stateside for repairs. *Duncan* was sunk.

Toward the end of October, the opposing carriers were back in the fight. RAdm. T.C. Kinkaid '08 (136 0f 201) led TF-16 in *Enterprise* with *South Dakota* and *Portland* and new cruiser, *San Juan*. His eight destroyers were, *Porter, Mahan, Cushing, Preston, Smith, Maury, Conyngham* and *Shaw*. The last back from repairs. TF-17 had *Hornet, Northampton, Pensacola* and new cruisers, *San Diego* and *Juneau* plus six "tin cans" *Morris, Anderson, Hughes, Mustin, Russell* and *Barton*. TF-63 under RAdm. W.A. Lee '08 (106 of 201) in *Washington* with *San Francisco, Helena*, new cruiser *Atlanta* and six Treaty Navy destroyers was operating separately and did not engage. The two carrier forces were opposed by four IJN carriers, four battleships, eight heavy cruisers, two light cruisers and 29 destroyers.

Once again, like Coral Sea and Midway, it was a battle where the opposing fleets never saw each other. It was aircraft against ships. During the attacks on *Enterprise, South Dakota* claimed downing 32 enemy planes. Losses among the Jap air groups were heavy. Two of their carriers were badly damaged and incapable of flight operations. An IJN submarine torpedoed and sank *Porter*. A bomb damaged *Enterprise* but her planes joined Henderson Field fliers. *Hornet* was hit and burning. She was abandoned and U.S. destroyers vainly tired to sink her but the defective torpedoes either missed or failed to explode. She was left as a hulk and the IJN swept through the area. Their torpedoes finished *Hornet* at close range. Thus ended the Oct. 26-27 Battle of Santa Cruz.

November was to be the last month of sea battles off Guadalcanal. There were three.

While Japanese ships were bringing in troops almost every night, Marine ground reinforcements were nil. The assault forces for Tulagi had been redeployed to Guadalcanal but replacements for casualties weren't made. The Seventh Marines, heavy artillery and an Army regiment were earmarked for arrival in early November and Kelly Turner assembled a strong escort force to get them to Guadalcanal. They arrived but Japanese units were reinforcing there too. The IJN was also shelling hell out of Henderson Field and the 1stMarDiv nightly, assuming that the U.S. Navy went home when the sun went down and its air cover left. RAdm. D.J. Callaghan '11 (39 0f 193) put together a scratch force of cruisers and destroyers to derail the "Tokyo Express." His flagship was *San Francisco* which he had recently commanded as a captain after having been Naval Aide to F.D.R. He had *Portland, Helena,* new light cruisers, *Atlanta* and *Juneau* plus destroyers, *Cushing, Laffey, Sterett, O'Bannon, Barton, Monssen, Aaron Ward* and *Fletcher.* Not all his ships had radar. On Friday the 13th, an hour after midnight, Dan Callaghan ran into an IJN forces of two battleships, a light cruiser and 11 destroyers intent on shelling Henderson Field. Both sides were surprised but the Americans fired first. Then the "long lances" filled the water. Heavy caliber shells filled the sky. *Atlanta* was the first to go but Callaghan "took on the big ones," *Hiei,* a battleship was hit again and again. So was *San Francisco.* Her bridge was wrecked killing her skipper, Capt. Cassin Young '16 (174 of 177) and Callaghan. LCdr. Bruce McCandless '32 (267 of 421) took over and saved the ship earning a Medal of Honor. He was the son of a commodore ('05) who ran the recommissioning of the old destroyers at San Diego and the father of future astronaut ('58). The toll among the destroyers was *Cushing, Laffey, Barton* and *Monssen* sunk with the others hit. The next morning an IJN sub broke *Juneau*'s back with a torpedo taking most of her crew to the bottom. Lost were RAdm. Norman Scott and five brothers from Iowa– the Sullivans.

Kincaid was in the area next morning with hastily repaired *Enterprise.* Her planes found and sank *Hiei.* But that night the IJN was back with troop reinforcements and shells for Henderson Field. RAdm. "Ching Chong" Lee decided to deal himself a hand with *Washington* and *South Dakota* plus a pick-up screen of *Walke, Benham, Gwin* and *Preston.* In the meantime on the 14th, U.S. aircraft from Henderson Field and *Enterprise* found seven IJN transports attempting to land troops on Guadalcanal. To the delight of U.S. destroyer survivors bobbing in the water, the planes avenged the loss of their ships.

That night the Tokyo Express bombardment group was the battleship survivor of two nights before, *Kirishima*, two heavy and two light cruisers and nine destroyers. In derailing the Tokyo Express, Lee lost *Walke, Preston* and *Benham* with *South Dakota* damaged. *Kirishima* was put out of action to be finished of by air the next day. The Marines, now reinforced were moving forward against the Jap troops who were now isolated from resupply.

There was one more night action to go and this was similar to the opening one in August. The IJN was still trying, with little success, however to bolster the troops on the island. The last night of November they tried to get seven destroyers into Guadalcanal carrying troops. Another scratched together cruiser and destroyer force was sent to intercept. These were *Minneapolis, New Orleans, Pensacola, Northampton* and *Honolulu* with *Fletcher, Drayton, Maury, Perkins, Lamson* and *Lardner.* The Battle of Tassafaronga was a disaster for The Treaty Navy. The "long lance" had a field day. *Northampton* was sunk. *New Orleans* took one forward and lost her bow back to her bridge Likewise, *Minneapolis* lost part of her bow too. Both staggered to Tulagi where under netting and foliage they made temporary repairs for the long voyage home and a year in the yard. The skipper of *Minnie* was Capt. C.E. Rosendahl '14 (53 of 154), a survivor of *Shenandoah* (See Chapter V). IJN loss was a destroyer.

The 1stMarDiv was relieved by the 2ndMarDiv and the Army Americal Division. Guadalcanal was secured by the end of January 1943. On Jan. 2, TF-18 was operating off the Rennell Islands. Only three of its ships were from The Treaty Navy, *Wichita, Chicago* and *Louisville.* There were three new light cruisers of the *Cleveland* class, two "jeep" carriers and eight new destroyers. IJN torpedo planes found the formation at night. Flares were dropped and *Chicago* was torpedoed. She sank the next day. Two more Treaty Navy ships were to be sunk in later battles as the Navy climbed up "The Slot" in the Solomons. *Helena* was torpedoed and sunk in Kula Gulf in July 1943, A week later, *Gwin* was sunk. By that time, the newer ships of the later Vinson Programs were joining the Fleet and carrying the war to Japanese waters. Ironically, the last ship sunk during the war was from The Treaty Navy. On Jul. 30, 1945, *Indianapolis* was steaming alone in the Philippine Sea. An IJN submarine sent a torpedo into her and she sank. In the rush to victory that accompanied the two atomic bombs on Japan, the loss of the cruiser went unnoticed for several days. In that time sharks and the elements had claimed more of her crew. It was she, however, who carried one of the bombs to Tinian for delivery to Japan.

There was a penultimate hurrah for ships of The Treaty Navy. Raised from the mud of Pearl Harbor, refitted and modernized but still too slow to keep up with the fast carrier task forces, four old battleships plus another "oldie" who had not been at Pearl, crossed the T of an IJN battleship force in Surigao Strait in the Philippines on Oct. 25, 1945. *California, West Virginia* and *Maryland* joined by *Mississippi* fired their big guns in anger at IJN battleships. Also present were *Boise, Phoenix, Minneapolis, Portland* and *Louisville.*

The final moment of glory for The Treaty Navy came on Sept. 2, 1945 in Tokyo Bay as the Japanese delegates came on board *Missouri* to surrender. The Treaty Navy had held the line in 1942 until the new ships, unfettered by Treaty restrictions, and the **innovations** sought in vain prior to Pearl Harbor being attacked, had given survivors and heirs of The Treaty Navy the means to "impose our will upon Japan [by projecting] our fleet an land forces across the Pacific and wage[ing] war in Japanese waters."

Lest the reader wonder why no mention is made of events in the Atlantic after the attack on Pearl Harbor, it must be remembered that the author's contention is that The Treaty Navy was the product of thinking of those who foresaw Japan as the enemy. The concept for the Pacific was a naval offensive. It was for such a victory that the concept of The Treaty Navy was born *after the* imposition of limits on naval construction and base fortifications were made in 1922. The European-Atlantic war was a naval defensive of convoys and protection of sea lanes. It was not a projection of sea power *per se,* albeit, the Navy brought land power to Europe.

Chapter XXIV

Reflections

A myth is that the genesis of Arms Limitation Treaties and hence The Treaty Navy was political. After all SecState Charles Evans Hughes strove to have the Washington Conference of 1921-22 composed of diplomats vice military and naval officers. His delegation, except for technical advisers, had no military. Those of the other nations wisely did not so limit themselves. While that may make it seem that the basis for calling of the Conference and the acceptances of the invitation by other nations was political, the reason for the Conference was economic not political.

The political side was to induce others to reduce naval expenditures so there was no requirement to spend and compete. The opening statement of Hughes (See Chapter III) makes clear the economic basis of naval limits. Attempting to "do it on the cheap" set the tone for the entire Treaty Navy until Vinson and F.D.R. turned it around with deficit spending to face up to the gathering threat of Japanese naval power in the Western Pacific.

It has been said that the most expensive thing a nation can have is a second-rate armed force. The national attitude of trying to get something for nothing almost prevailed. In this case the "something" was peace and national security. With that, of course, goes economic well-being and prosperity. Short-ranged fiscal achievements, e.g., minimal annual naval expenditures, sacrificed the future of long-range economic welfare.

Such has been and is currently the approach of the attorneys and accountants who manipulate government on the basis of "evidence" and other tangibles which exculpate them if the element of chance favors the short end of the odds. True leaders and statesman, however, rely on experience and professional judgment of enemy capabilities and are willing to stake their lives and those of others on it.

This approach was not confined just to the era of The Treaty Navy between the World Wars. Since the end of World War II we have had "the bigger bang for a buck" theory and later that of "cost effectiveness." Each has attempted to treat national security as a balance sheet entry.

The Eisenhower-Dulles" bigger bang" theory postulated a smaller armed force leaving every potential international problem to be solved by the singularity of our nuclear arsenal. That was not unlike the assumption at Washington in 1921 that the capital ship tonnage was the yardstick of naval power. The McNamara "cost-effectiveness" approach was a "bean counter" quantification of "What will it cost to do it?" The true professional, on the other hand, wants to know, "What will it cost **not** to do it?"

While capital ships were the most tangible expression of costs, the most expensive item of a navy is manpower. Men must be trained and that takes time. A trained man is worth more than a recruit. Yet, The Treaty Navy was training and then losing valuable men because of low pay, slow promotions and inadequately maintained ships. Congress and the public might perceive that the personal strength of The Treaty Navy held at a constant figure (actually not constant but the number allowed by appropriations) but it really was the product of turnovers being replaced by lower-paid recruits. As to pay, there was not any raise during the entire era of The Treaty Navy. From 1922 to 1942, the only change in pay was the 15% cut of the early '30s. The cut was restored but never reimbursed.

When the author was a Midshipman, there were black plaques with gold letters on the bulkheads of Luce Hall, the Seamanship and Navigation Building. They had inspirational quotes like *"'Damn the torpedoes, full speed ahead' – Farragut"* One particularly remembered had been amended. It originally said, *"The price of good navigation is constant vigilance."* A Midshipman, obviously of The Treaty Navy era had scratched through *"constant vigilance"* with chalk and substituted, *"more than $125 a month!"* Ensigns were not overpaid.

In a way, the Washington Treaty and subsequent conference and Treaties were mixed blessings. The mistaken notion that capital ships were the criteria did two things - one good and one bad. The good was that the U.S. not only divested itself of older and expensive capital ships but it also did not acquire the new (and more expensive) ones it had on the ways or drawing boards. Their expensive upkeep would have deprived The Treaty Navy of more vital types given a parsimonious Congress. The bad thing was that it inculcated into the minds of Congress and the public that capital ships were the end-all-be-all of naval power. An academic, writing long after The Treaty Navy era reflected on the requests by the Navy for various types of ships. In keeping with the mind-set of amateurs, he termed it a scramble by the various "fleet factions" to have something for everybody The "battleship guys" wanted theirs; the "cruiser guys" wanted theirs; the "flyboys" wanted something, etc. Besides having no understanding of the concept of a balanced fleet, he acquainted it with the present Navy of "communities" i.e., nukie-pukies, aviators (of several varieties, e.g., fighters, heavy or light attack, patrol planes etc.) surface warriors, SEALS, amphibs, *et al.*

The Treaty Navy was **one** Navy not a hodge-podge. Doc Wiley and Tony Danis went from airships back to destroyers. Rosendahl went back to command a cruiser from airships and then returned to lighter-than-air as a flag officer. Pratt, King and Halsey started in the destroyer flotilla of Sims. Pratt went n to battleships; King to submarines and aviation; and Halsey to aviation. Nimitz started in submarines, commanded a cruiser and then a battleship division. Tommy Hart was a submariner who served in cruisers and commanded a battleship. Kelly Turner, an aviator, became the supreme amphib. All served the Navy not a community.

Another Treaty drawback was the unrealistic influence on the size of ships. Using tonnage as criterion for design left no room for improvement or incorporating new requirements. The "bean counter" mentality of economics again came to the fore. While the rules of economics are changeable (the old story of the economics professor who asked the same questions on the final exam for 30 years only changing the answers); the laws of physics are immutable. Only so much armor, ammunition, anti-craft, fuel, machinery, provisions and men can be crammed into a hull of finite tonnage. The "Treaty Cruisers" provide one example.

At 10,000 tons (the first ones came in just more than 9,500) trade-offs had to be made in order to up-grade their air defense capability when that became necessary. Thus, their torpedo tubes were removed. The IJN, having denounced the Treaties, had no such constraints. Destroyers are another example. It was found that the 1,500-ton limit was a bit to small for a modern destroyer. Thus, new ships were commissioned without racks for depth charges. Cognizant of the "escalator clause" in the Treaties, the designers provided for their addition for war.

The most significant example of lack of practical naval thinking being used in determining tonnage is that of the 135,000 tons of carriers agreed to by the U.S. diplomats a Washington in 1922. The dominance of economics once more came into play. Two battlecruisers were saved vice spending money to build from the keel up. This was strictly "doing it on the cheap." These ships were 33,000 tons in their new configuration. The Treaty allowed 3,000 tons of non-chargeable displacement for torpedo blisters and protection. In a bit of design double-talk, these 3,000 tons were subtracted to rate them at 30,000 tons for Treaty purposes. Actually, the 3,000 tons became "extra" to 33,000 tons upon commissioning but the fiction was that they were "30,000 tons." This left 75,000 tons for future carriers (after *Langley* was retired or converted.) *Ranger,* the first carrier designed and built from keel up was 14,500 tons. If she proved satisfactory; four more could be built of that size. She did not. Although, she carried as many planes as the larger carriers, her size was insufficient for a power plant able to make more than 29.5 knots. While this speed was enough to keep up with the slower battleships, experience with *Lex* and *Sara* had shown that a carrier had to do 33+ knots to be effective. A ship able to do so had to be a third larger than *Ranger.*

Yorktown and *Enterprise* were built at 19,000 tons. *Ranger*'s war contribution was nil. This illustrates how the "bean counter" mentality, when given dominance can produce "the most expensive thing ... a second-rate armed force."

The annual Fleet Problems were artificial and usually had a canned scenario. The overriding emphasis was on "safety" an euphemism for "don't have any damage because we haven't put money in the budget for repairs" restricted the ingenuity of commanders in planning and execution. Since a senior commander seldom had more than one opportunity to show his mettle at a specific level of command, the conventional wisdom was to play it safe and opt for the conservative approach. A bold, radical approach by an officer "auditioning for higher command" would most likely be derided by the nay-sayers as being merely luck in having pulled it off. The "way to promotion and pay" was to be able to successfully apply gamesmanship to demonstrate the ability to

226

administer the maneuvering of large fleet formations without endangering ships or men.

Until the watershed of 1930, Fleet Problems were no more than variations of Jutland. It wasn't until *Lex* and *Sara* joined that innovations began t appear. The value of carriers not tied to the battleline began to be appreciated. King's carrier tactics in Fleet Problem XX (1939) in the Caribbean were **innovative** and prophetic. Richardson's departures from the restrictions of the goddess of safety for Fleet Problem XXI (1940) in the Pacific was a refreshing break from the past. These had their roots in the earlier Fleet Problem successes of Pratt (IX) and Yarnell's 1932 attack on Pearl Harbor by carrier air.

The value of these innovative Fleet Problems was its effect on the thinking of the more junior officers involved. They saw the potential of tactics which could be applied when there was an abundance of means. As wartime leaders, once the ships of the later Vinson Acts came on line, they could operate unfettered by the conservative approaches of The Treaty Navy. They had been brought up in The Treaty Navy but their thinking was to the future. They learned to think big and were prepared to use the tools when they became available. Those who didn't eventually fell by the wayside. It was those who were able to make the transition from the administration of The Treaty Navy to the operations of the victorious Navy of 1943-45 who succeeded. Both had been raised in The Treaty Navy but only the latter excelled.

A point made in the 1930 London Treaty was that unrestricted submarine warfare was banned in perpetuity not just for the life of the Treaty. Yet, one of the first things done when Pearl Harbor was bombed was to signal Fleet submarines, "Commence unrestricted submarine warfare against Japan immediately." Was this a blatant violation of a solemn obligations made by the U.S.? The answer is legally and technically, no. In International Law there are two rules of customary law. One is *pacta sunt servanda* [treaties must be observed]. It is a basic but not inviolate rule. Standing with this and tacitly understood in every treaty is *clausula rebus sic stantibus.* It holds that when the state of things which are essential to the treaty have under gone material change, the treaty has ceased to exist. When Germany launched unrestricted submarine warfare sinking *Athenia* on the first day of the war in 1939, the terms of the London Treaty were no longer binding on the Parties (U.S. and Britain while Japan's denunciation made her further participation moot.) The "escalator clause" applied in a different manner. Japan's joining the Axis brought her into the act and she was subject to unrestricted submarine warfare. That the visionaries in the Navy foresaw this and built submarines able to take commerce warfare across the Pacific is all to their credit.

There has been a dual theme on these pages. The first is that the so-called controversy between the "battleship admirals" and the "carrier admirals" was mere myth. The author contends that this was more a matter of factions who beheld different enemies. One saw Britain as a threat at sea. Thus, capital ships should be built to stand toe-to-toe with the RN, This was pure Mahan and his fleet-in-being *dictum* to force a decision and then conduct the *guerre de course* to cripple the enemy's sea commerce. In Mahan's time, Britain was the most dependent on trade by sea. After his death, Japan's move to industrialization was to make her insular position dependent on trade, particularly imports.

The scare in 1940 that the RN would fall into the hands of the Axis temporarily revived battleship building but that was laid to rest after the U.S. entered the war against Japan.

The second group was those who realized the potential of the new weapons of aviation and submarines and who saw Japan as the enemy not Britain. Of these, the Anglophile Sims was the most vocal and had a following in the naval service. Ellis, Pratt, King, Halsey and others all had come under the Sims mystique. Sims had a close association with Theodore Roosevelt. In fact, it was closer than T.R. had with his erstwhile neighbor at Oyster Bay on Long Island, A.T. Mahan. Whether Sims was protégé or mentor to T.R. in naval thinking is immaterial. The fact that Sims influenced a generation of officers who were to make their mark on The Treaty Navy and its composition is germane. Sims, in retirement, lived and was writing during the development of The Treaty Navy and its philosophy that Japan was the enemy to be beaten in a naval war.

These are my contentions about The Treaty Navy. Academics, accountants and attorneys may counter with "there is no evidence to prove" such. I feel that that phrase, "there is no evidence..." has been the basis for more irresponsible conclusions and recommendations in our history than anything else. In 1941, all "evidence" pointed to a Japanese move south to the Malay Barrier. Her *capability* to attack to the east first was disregarded by the "experts." Fortunately, then we were blessed with leaders who made their decisions on experience and professional judgment of enemy capabilities not his intentions in most cases. .

My contentions and conclusions therefore are not made on "evidence" *per se* but on experience, analysis and professional judgment based on knowledge of the era involved. It is not a matter of life or death so I merely stake my reputation on my judgments.

It may not be too late to reassess the proper use of "The Peace Dividend" for the long term vice short-term benefit. There are still those out there who don't like us.

This is especially true since we no longer live in a world of strictly Western Civilization. It is a multi-cultural melee now. We fought and beat one non-Western Culture with The Treaty Navy. We must be ready to meet and beat others who don't recognize or play by our "rules." The Treaty Navy provides the experience to avoid (as Yogi Berra says) *"déjà vu all over again!"*

God and the soldier all men adore
In time of danger and not before
When the danger is past and all things righted
God is forgotten and the old soldier slighted

John F. Kennedy
January 20, 1961

Appendix 1

The Color and Rainbow Plans

From about the turn of the century until the late '30s, U.S. contingency plans for war or other operations against a foreign nation were labeled by COLORs to identify the opponent. U.S. was always BLUE. These plans were revised and updated as conditions changed: BLACK-Germany; ORANGE-Japan; RED-Great. Britain; CRIMSON-Canada; SCARLET-Australia; GARNET-New Zealand; RUBY-India; GOLD-France; SILVER-Italy, OLIVE-Spain; GREEN-Mexico; PURPLE-U.S.S.R.; BROWN-East Indies; LEMON-Portugal; CITRON-Brazil; YELLOW-China; INDIGO-Iceland; EMERALD-Eire; GRAY-Azores; TAN-Cuba; VIOLET-China Intervention; WHITE-Contingency for U.S. domestic emergency.

As crises developed in the world, it became apparent that the COLOR Plans, which were predicated, on one-on-one confrontations with a single enemy were no longer germane. Future involvement in conflict(s) would be against a coalition of enemies and with the U.S. acting alone or with allies. Since some of the players of the COLOR Plans were members of the combinations which were possible, the new plans were called The RAINBOW Plans. There were basically five in the following simplified recaps:

RAINBOW 1 – Prevent violation of the Monroe Doctrine; protect the U.S., her possessions and sea trade. Acting without allies, the U.S. would preserve the Western Hemisphere with a strategic defense in the Pacific along the Alaska-Hawaii-Panama line. When the situation in the Atlantic was sorted out, the Fleet would be concentrated in the Pacific for action against Japan.

RAINBOW 2 – Carry out RAINBOW 1 but acting with allies (Britain and France) devote minimal attention to Europe and the Atlantic and sustain the interests of the democratic powers by offensive action across the Pacific.

RAINBOW 3 – Acting without allies, after assuring hemisphere defense, project naval forces west to secure control of the Western Pacific.

RAINBOW 4 – U.S., without allies, to ensure hemisphere defense by sending task forces and troops to South America and the eastern Atlantic. A strategic defensive to be maintained in the Pacific until the Atlantic situation freed naval forces for offensive action against Japan.

RAINBOW 5 – To accomplish RAINBOWS 1 and 4, the U.S acting with allies, British Empire and France, ultimately would send forces to Europe or Africa to defeat Germany, Italy or both. Maintain a strategic defensive in the Pacific until success in Europe permitted transfer of major naval forces to the Pacific for an offensive against Japan.

All five plans contained the element of eventual offensive naval operations across the Pacific against Japan; therefore ORANGE the *raison d' être* of The Treaty Navy.

Appendix 2

Hull Designations and Name Sources

Ship categories were given a two or three-letter designation followed by a [hull] number. If reassigned to another category, a ship usually retained her name but acquired a new designation and hull number within that designation. There were exceptions. When collier, *Jupiter* (AC-3) was converted to a carrier she became *Langley* (CV-1) but when she was converted to a seaplane tender she was AV-3. Designators and name sources are:

BB Battleships – named for states (Exception *Kearsarge* (BB-5)

CC Battlecruisers – named for U.S. victories and victorious U.S. warships of yore

CA Heavy cruisers – named for U.S. cities

CL Light cruisers – named for U.S. cities

CV Aircraft carriers – names came with the converted battlecruisers,

DD Destroyers – named for SecNavs, Navy and Marine Corps heroes, deceased flag officers. After 1930 many were converted to other duties retaining their names:

> **DM** Destroyer minelayer   **DMS** Destroyer minesweeper
>
> **APD** High speed transport   **AVD** Light seaplane tender

SS Submarines – named or marine life, SS-1 through SS-159 had a letter and number,

CM Minelayers – many were conversions retaining original civilian names

AM Minesweepers. Forty-one ("Bird Class") built for the 1918 sweeping of the Mine Barrage. Fifteen were reclassified:

> **AVP** Light seaplane tenders (9)   **ASR** Submarine rescue vessels (6)

PG Gunboats – named for smaller U.S. cities

PR River gunboats – named for U.S. island possessions

Auxiliaries

Should not be confused with the older term "combat auxiliary" (warships other than capital ships to about 1930). Ships of the Fleet Train, armed and manned by Navy crews, they kept the Fleet fit to fight.

AV Seaplane tenders – named for U.S. bays and inlets.

AVP Smaller seaplane tenders – named for bays and inlets

AD Destroyer tenders – named for American regions; e.g., *Dixie*

AS Submarine tenders – named for submarine pioneers

AR Repair ships – named for artisans of mythology

AO Oilers – named for American rivers

AE Ammunition ships- named for explosives or volcanoes

AF Storeships (refrigerated) – named for stars

AK Cargo ships – named for stars

AKA Attack cargo ships – named for counties

AP Transports – named for deceased Marine General Officers

APA Attack transports – named for counties

AH Hospital ships – given soothing names, e.g., *Solace*

AT Ocean-going tugs – named for Indian tribes

AG Miscellaneous vessels from Presidential yacht to target ships, no name source

YN Net tenders –named for trees

IX Unclassified vessels, e.g., hulks, relics and receiving ships

That was the orderliness of designations in The Treaty Navy. It was a comfortable and understood system and when learned it was simple. When it came to naming ships, The Treaty Navy had a lot of class.

APPENDIX 3

FLEET ORGANIZATION 1923, 1935, 1939
ORGANIZATION TABLE I
September 1923
THE UNITED STATES FLEET
Seattle (Flagship)
BATTLE FLEET (Pacific)
California (Flagship)
BATTLESHIP DIVISIONS
New Mexico (Flagship)

DIVISION THREE	DIVISION FOUR	DIVISION FIVE
New York	*Arizona*	*New Mexico*
Texas	*Pennsylvania*	*Tennessee*
Oklahoma	*Mississippi*	*Maryland*
Nevada	*Idaho*	*California*

DESTROYER SQUADRONS
Melville (Flagship ComDesRons)
Altair, Rigel (tenders)
SQUADRON ELEVEN
Delphy (Squadron leader)

DIVISION 31	DIVISION 32	DIVISION 33
Chauncey	*Stoddert*	*William Jones*
Fuller	*Reno*	*Woodbury*
Percival	*Farquhar*	*S.P. Lee*
John Francis Burns	*Thompson*	*Nicholas*
Farragut	*Kennedy*	*Young*
Somers	*Paul Hamilton*	*Zeilin*

SQUADRON TWELVE
McDermott (Squadron leader)

DIVISION 34	DIVISION 35	DIVISION 36
Yarborough	*Selfridge*	*Hull*
Lavallette	*Marcus*	*MacDonough*
Sloat	*Mervine*	*Sumner*
Wood	*Chase*	*Corry*
Shirk	*Robert Smith*	*Melvin*
Kidder	*Mullany*	*Farenholt*

AIRCRAFT SQUADRONS, BATTLE FLEET
Aroostook (aircraft tender and flagship)
Garnet (aircraft tender)
Langley (to relieve *Aroostook*)
Air Units
VO-1,VO-2,VO-3,VTB-2, VF-1, VF-2, VF-3
SUBMARINE DIVISION, PACIFIC
Beaver (flagship)

DIVISION NINE (Pearl Harbor)	DIVISION FOURTEEN (Pearl Harbor
R-1,R-2,R-3, R-4, R-5, R-6, R-7, R-8, R-10	R-11, R-12, R-13, R-16, R-17, R-18, R-19, R-20
DIVISION SIXTEEN (*Beaver* tender)	DIVISION SEVENTEEN (*Canopus* tender)
S-30,S-31, S-32, S-33, S-34, S-35	S-36, S-37, S-38, S-39

FLEET BASE FORCE (Pacific)
Procyon (Flagship)
MINE SQUADRON TWO

DIVISION TWO	DIVISION FOUR
Ludlow *Burns*	*Tanager* *Whippoorwill*

231

TRAIN

Brant	Pinola	Artic
Partridge	Cuyama	Relief
Kingfisher	Kanawha	Jason
Tern	Neches	Sonoma
	Prometheus	

SCOUTING FLEET (Atlantic)

Wyoming (flagship)

BATTLESHIP DIVISIONS

DIVISION TWO

| Wyoming | Arkansas | Florida | Utah |

DESTROYER SQUADRONS

Bridgeport, Denebola (tenders)

SQUADRON NINE

Sharkey (squadron leader)

DIVISION TWENTY-FIVE	DIVISION TWENTY-SIX	DIVISION TWENTY-SEVEN
Toucey	Worden	Chas. Ausburn
Breck	Flusser	Osborne
Isherwood	Dale	Coghlan
Case	Converse	Preston
Lardner	Reid	Lamson
Putnam	Billingsley	Bruce

SQUADRON FOURTEEN

DIVISION FORTY	DIVISION FORTY-ONE	DIVISION FORTY-TWO
Hatfield	MacFarland	Sands
Brooks	J.K. Paulding	Williamson
Gilmer	Overton	Rueben James
Fox	Sturtevant	Bainbridge
Kane	Childs	Goff
Humphreys	King	Barry

AIRCRAFT SQUADRONS SCOUTING FLEET

Wright (flagship and aircraft tender)   Sandpiper (aircraft tender)

VS-1, VTB1, Kite-balloon Sqdn-1

TRAIN

Bobolink	Virego	Proteus	Robin
Bridge	Contocook	Rail	Teal
Rappahannock	Vestal	Brazos	Mercy

CONTROL FORCE (Atlantic)

Savannah (flagship)

SUBMARINE DIVISIONS ATLANTIC

Savannah (flagship)

DIVISION ONE	DIVISION TWO	DIVISION THREE
R-21, R-23, R-24, R-25, R-26, R-27	R-9, R-22, S-1, S-3	S-19, S-20
DIVISION FOUR	DIVISION EIGHT	DIVISION TEN
S-10, S-11, S -12, S-13,	O-1, O-2,O-4, O-5, O-6	O-11, O-12, O-13,
S-28, S-49, S-50, S-51	O-7, O-8, O-9,O –10	O-14, O-15, O-16
	DIVISION ELEVEN	
	S-21, S-24 S-25, S-26, S-27,	

MINE SQUADRON ONE

Shawmut (flagship

DIVISION ONE	DIVISION THREE
Mahan	Lark
Maury	Mallard

232

ASIATIC FLEET

Huron (flagship)

Ashville		*Scramenbto*

Yangtze Patrol

Isabel

Elcano

Villalobos		*Palos*
Monocacy		

South China Patrol

Helena　　　　　　　　*Pampanga*

DESTROYER SQUADRON

Black Hawk (tender)

Stewart (Squadron leader)

DIVISION THIRTY-EIGHT	DIVISION FORTY-THREE	DIVISION FORTY-FIVE
Smith Thompson	*Pope*	*Hulbert*
Barker	*Peary*	*Noa*
Tracy	*Pillsbury*	*Wm. B Preston*
Borie	*John D. Ford*	*Preble*
John D .Edwards	*Truxtun*	*Sicard*
Whipple	*Paul Jones*	*Pruitt*

SUBMARINE DIVISIONS

Rainbow (flagship)

DIVISION TWELVE	DIVISION EIGHTEEN
S-4, S-6, S-7, S-8, S-9	*S-2, S-14, S-15, S-16, S-17*

MINE DETACHMENT

Rizal	*Hart*	*Finch*	*Bittern*

ASIATIC FLEET – AUXILARIES

Abarenda	*General Alava*	*Pecos*

NAVAL FORCES, EUROPE

Pittsburgh (flagship)

DESTROYER DETACHMENT

Parrott	*Edsall*	*MacLeish*	*Simpson*
Bulmer	*McCormick*	*Lawrence*	*Litchfield*

AT CONSTANTINOPLE

Scorpion

SPECIAL SERVCE SQUADRON

Rochester (flagship)	*Cleveland*	*Denver*	*Tacoma*

NAVAL TRANSPORTATION SERVICE

Argonne	*Vega*	*Ramapo*
Chaumont	*Kittery*	*Sapelo*
Henderson	*Beaufort*	*Trinity*
Capella	*Newport News*	*Pyro*
Gold Star	*Orion*	*Nitro*
Sirius	*Patoka*	

ORGANIZATION TABLE II

Mobilization Plan predicated on ratification of Treaty for Limitation of Armament

UNITED STATES FLEET

Seattle (flagship)

BATTLE FLEET

California (flagship)

BATTLESIP DIVISIONS

New Mexico (flagship)

DIVISION THREE	DIVISION FOUR	DIVISION FIVE
New York	*Arizona*	*New Mexico*
Texas	*Nevada*	*Idaho*
Oklahoma	*Mississippi*	*Tennessee*
California	*Pennsylvania*	*Maryland*

233

LIGHT CRUISER DIVISION
DIVISION TWO

Richmond	*Omaha*	*Milwaukee*	*Cincinnati*

DESTROYERS SQUADRONS
Charleston (Flagship ComDesRons)
Altair, Melville, Rigel (tenders)
SQUADRON FOUR
Welles (Squadron leader)

DIVISION TEN	DIVISION ELEVEN	DIVISION TWELVE
Wickes	*Tarbell*	*Rathburne*
Philip	*Yarnall*	*Talbot*
Evans	*Upshur*	*Waters*
Buchanan	*Greer*	*Dent*
Aaron Ward	*Elliott*	*Dorsey*
	Roper	*Lea*

SQUADRON FIVE
Aulick (quadroon leader)

DIVISION THIRTEEN	DIVISION FOURTEEN	DIVISION FIFTEEN
Lamberton	*Tatnall*	*Boggs*
Radford	*Badger*	*Kilty*
Montgomery	*Twiggs*	*Kennison*
Breese	*Barrett*	*Ward*
Gamble	*Jacob Jones*	*Claxton*
Ramsay		*Hamilton*

SQUADRON SIX
Turner (Squadron Leader)

DIVIION SIXTEEN	DIVISION SEVENTEEN	DIVISION EIGHTEEN
Schley	*Crane*	*MacKenzie*
Champlin	*Palmer*	*Renshaw*
Mugford	*Thatcher*	*O'Bannon*
Chew	*Walker*	*Hogan*
Hazelwood	*Crosby*	*Howard*
Williams		*Stansbury*

SQUADRON TEN
Turner (Squadron leader)

DIVISION TWENTY-EIGHT	DIVISION TWENTY-NINE	DIVISION THIRTY
Laub	*Bailey*	*Sinclair*
McLanahan	*Thornton*	*McCawley*
Edwards	*Morris*	*Moody*
Greene	*Tingey*	*Henshaw*
Ballard	*Swasey*	*Meyer*
Shubrick	*Meade*	*Doyen*

SQUADRON ELEVEN
Delphy (Squadron leader)

DIVISION THIRTY-ONE	DIVISION THIRTY-TWO	DIVISION THIRTY-THREE
Chauncey	*Stoddert*	*William Jones*
Fuller	*Reno*	*Woodbury*
Percival	*Farquhar*	*S.P. Lee*
John Francis Burns	*Thompson*	*Nicholas*
Farragut	*Kennedy*	*Young*
Somers	*Paul Hamilton*	*Zeilin*

SQUADRON TWELVE

McDermut (Squadron leader)

DIVISION THIRTY-FOUR	DIVISION THIRTY-FIVE	DIVISION THIRTY-SIX
Yarborough	*Selfridge*	*Hull*
La Vallette	*Marcus*	*MacDonough*
Sloat	*Mervine*	*Farenholt*
Wood	*Chase*	*Sumner*
Shirk	*Robert Smith*	*Corry*
Kidder	*Mullany*	*Melvin*

Note: Less divisions detailed to the Asiatic Fleet to maintain a total of three divisions and a Squadron leader on that station.

SUBMARINE DIVISIONS, PACIFIC

Tenders: *Canopus, Beaver, Bushnell* and *Holland* (when completed)

Divisions 3, 9, 14, 16, 17, 19

AIR SQUADRONS

Langley Flagship ComAirRons), *Gannet,* (tender), *Saratoga* (when completed)

SCOUTING FLEET

Wyoming (flagship)

DIVISION ONE	DIVISION TWO
Florida Utah North Dakota	*Wyoming Arkansas Delaware*

LIGHT CRUISER DIVISION

DIVISION ONE	DIVISION TWO	DIVISION THREE
Birmingham	*Concord*	*Marblehead*
Chester	*Trenton*	*Raleigh*
Salem	*Memphis*	*Detroit*

DESTROYER SQUADRONS

Rochester (Flagship ComDesRons)

SQUADRON ONE

Dickerson (Squadron leader)

DIVISION ONE	DIVISION TWO	DVISION THREE
Downes	*O'Brien*	*Cassin*
Duncan	*Nicholson*	*Cumming*
Alyvin	*Winslow*	*Tucker*
Parker	*McDougal*	*Conynham*
Benham	*Cushing*	*Porter*
Balch	*Ericsson*	*Wainwright*

SQUADRON TWO

Leary (Squadron leader)

DIVISION FOUR	DIVISION FIVE	DIVISION SIX
Shaw	*Wadsworth*	*Little*
Sampson	*Manley*	*Kimberly*
Rowan	*Craven*	*Sigourney*
Davis	*Gwin*	*Gregory*
Allen	*Conner*	*Stringham*
Wilkes	*Stockton*	*Caldwell*

SQUADRON THREE

Schenck (Squadron leader)

DIVISION SEVEN	DIVISION EIGHT	DIVISION NINE
Dyer	*McKean*	*Meredith*
Colhoun	*Harding*	*Bush*
Stevens	*Gridley*	*Cowell*
McKee	*Fairfax*	*Maddox*
Robinson	*Taylor*	*Foote*
Ringgold	*Bell*	*Kalk*

SQUADRON SEVEN
Dallas (Squadron leader)

DIVISION NINETEEN	DIVISION TWENTY	DIVISION TWENTY-ONE
Hopewell	*Dahlgren*	*Abel P. Upshur*
Thomas	*Goldsborough*	*Hunt*
Blakeley	*Semmes*	*Welborn C. Wood*
Abbott	*Satterlee*	*Geo. E. Badger*
Bagley	*Mason*	*Branch*
Clemson		*Herndon*

SQUADRON EIGHT
Herbert (Squadron leader)

DIVISION TWENTY-TWO	DIVISION TWENTY-THREE	DIVISION TWENT-FOUR
Breckinridge	*Hale*	*Belknap*
Barney	*Crowninshield*	*McCook*
Blakley	*Tillman*	*McCalla*
Biddle	*Ellis*	*Rodgers*
Dupont	*Cole*	*Osmond Ingram*
Bernadou	*J. Fred Talbot*	*Bancroft*

SQUADRON NINE
Sharkey (Squadron Leader)

DIVISION TWENTY-FIVE	DIVISION TWENTY-SIX	DIVISION TWENTY-SEVEN
Putnam	*Billlingsley*	*Chas. Ausburne*
Toucey	*Worden*	*Osborne*
Breeck	*Flusser*	*Coghlan*
Sherwood	*Dale*	*Preston*
Case	*Converse*	*Lamson*
Lardner	*Reid*	*Bruce*

SQUADRON THIRTEEN
Stewart (Squadron leader)

DIVISION THIRTY-SEVEN	DIVISION THIRTY-EIGHT	DIVISION THIRTY-NINE
Chandler	*Smith Thomson*	*Parrott*
Southard	*Barker*	*Edsall*
Hovey	*Tracy*	*MacLeish*
Long	*Borie*	*Simpson*
Broome	*John D. Edwards*	*Bulmer*
Alden	*Whipple*	*McCormick*

SQUADRON FOURTEEN
*Hopkins (*Squadron leader

DIVISION FORTY	DIVISION ORTY-ONE	DIVISION FORTY-TWO
Hatfield	*McFarland*	*Sands*
Brooks	*James K. Paulding*	*Williamson*
Gilmer	*Overton*	*Rueben James*
Fox	*Sturtevant*	*Bainbridge*
Kane	*Childs*	*Goff*
Humphreys	*King*	*Barry*

SQUADRN FIFTEEN
Lawrence (Squadron leader)

DIVISION FORTY-THREE	DIVISION FORTY-FOUR	DIVISION FORTY-FIVE
Paul Jones	*Litchfield*	*Hulbert*
Pope	*Zane*	*Noa*
Peary	*Wasmuth*	*William B. Preston*
Pillsbury	*Trever*	*Preble*
Ford	*Perry*	*Sicard*
Truxton	*Decatur*	*Pruitt*

Note: Less divisions detailed to the Asiatic Fleet to maintain a total of three divisions and a Squadron leader on that station

SUBMARINE DIVISIONS, PACIFIC
Tenders: *Canopus, Beaver, Bushnell* and *Holland* (when complete)
Divisions 3, 9,14,16, 17, 19
AIR SQUADRONS
Wright (Flagship, ComAirRons), Tenders:: *Teal, Sandpiper, Lexington* (when completed)
CONTROL FORCE
Pittsburgh (Flagship)
CRUISER DVISIONS

DIVISION ONE		DIVISION TWO	
Huntington	*Pueblo*	*Pittsburgh*	*Missoula*
Frederick	*St. Louis*	*Charlotte*	*Huron* (On Asiatic Station)

MINE SQUADRON ONE
Shawmut (Flagship)
San Francisco

DIVISION ONE		DIVISION THREE		DIVISION FIVE	
Murray	*Maury*	*Chewink*	*Mallard*	*Cormorant*	*Grebe*
Israel	*Lansdale*	*Curlew*	*Quail*	*Swan*	*Woodcock*
Luce	*Mahan*	*Lark*		*Red Wing*	*Owl*

SUBMARINE DIVISIONS, ATLANTIC
Tenders: *Savannah, Fulton, Camden* DIVISIONS 1, 2, 4, 5, 6, 7, 8, 10, 15
FLEET BASE FORCE
Procyon (Flagship)
MINE SQUADRON TWO
Aroostook (Flagship)

DIVISION TWO		DIVISION FOUR		DIVISION SIX	
Stribling	*Ingraham*	*Seagull*	*Thrush*	*Oriole*	*Sanderlng*
Ludlow	*Burns*	*Tanager*	*Whippoorwill*	*Penguin*	*Pigeon*
Anthony	*Sproston*	*Lapwing*	*Pelican*	*Eider*	*Turkey*

DESTROYER SQUADRON
Tender: *Buffalo*
SQUADRON ZERO
Jenkins (Squadron leader)

DIVISION ZERO 1	DIVISION ZER0 2	DIVISION ZERO 3
Ammen	*Jouett*	*Perkins*
Beale	*Mayrant*	*Roe*
Burrows	*McCall*	*Sterett*
Drayton	*Monaghan*	*Terry*
Fanning	*Patterson*	*Trippe*
Henley	*Paulding*	*Walke*
Jarvis		*Warrington*

TRAIN
Vessels of the Train
ASIATIC FLEET
Note: On mobilization, Asiatic Fleet comes under command of CinCUS as a task fleet
Huron (Flagship)
Sacramento Ashville

YANGTSE PATROL			MINE DETACHMENT-DIVISION SEVEN		
Isabel	*Elcano*	*Palos*	*Rizal*	*Hart*	*Heron*
Monocacy	*Pigeon*	*Penguin*	*Finch*	*Avocet*	*Bittern*

SOUTH CHINA PATROL
Helena Pampanga
DESTROYER SQUADRON
Tender, leader and three divisions as assigned from Battle Fleet and Scouting Fleet.

SUBMARINE DIVISIONS
Tender: *Rainbow* (Flagship ComSubDiv)

DIVISION TWELVE	DIVISION EIGHTEEN
S-4, S-6, S-7, S-8, S-9	*S-2, S-14, S-15, S-16, S-17*

Note: When *Colorado* **and** *West Virginia* **are commissioned and** *Delaware* **and** *North Dakota*
are scrapped, the battleship divisions will be reorganized as follows:

DIVISION ONE	DIVISION TWO	DIVISION THREE
Wyoming	*New York*	*Arizona*
Arkansas	*Texas*	*Oklahoma*
Utah	*Florida*	*Nevada*
		Pennsylvania

DIVISION FOUR	DIVISION FIVE
New Mexico	*West Virginia*
Idaho	*Maryland*
Tennessee	*Colorado*
Mississippi	*California*

NAVAL FORCES NOT UNDER CinCUS
SPECIAL SERVICE SQUADRON

CRUISER DIVISION ONE	CRUISER DIVISION TWO
Cleveland Denver Tacoma	*Galveston Chattanooga Des Moines*

April 1935

UNITED STATES FLEET
Pennsylvania (Flagship) 4 VOS
BATTLE FORCE, U.S. FLEET
California (Flagship) 4VOS
BATTLESHIPS, BATTLE FORCE
West Virginia (Flagship)

BATTLESHIP DIVISION 1, VO-1B – 9VOS		BATTLESHIP DIVISION 3, VO-3B – 9 VOS	
Texas	*New York*	*New Mexico*	*Mississippi*
Oklahoma		*Idaho*	
BATTLESHIP DIVISION 2 , VO-2B – 9 VOS		BATTLESHIP DIVISION 4, VO-B – 9 VOS	
Arizona	*Pennsylvania*	*West Virginia*	*Colorado*
Nevada	*Tennessee*	*Maryland*	*California*

CRUISERS, BATTLE FORCE
Richmond (Flagship)

CRUISER DIVISION 2, VS-5B – 6 VSO		CRUISER DIVISION 3, VS-6B – 8 VSO	
Richmond	*Marblehead*	*Concord*	*Omaha*
Memphis		*Cincinnati*	*Milwaukee*

DESTROYERS, BATTLE FORCE
Detroit (Flagship) 2 VSO
Tenders: *Melville, Altair, Rigel* (San Diego with reserve DDs), Mobile targets: *Lamberton, Boggs*
DESTROYER FLOTILLA 2
DESTROYER SQUADRON 2
Decatur (Flagship)

DESTROYER DIVISION 4	DESTROYER DIVISION 5	DESTROYER DIVISION 6
Wickes	*Aaron Ward*	*Roper*
Philip	*Buchanan*	*Dorsey*
Evans	*Crownenshield*	*Lea*
Twiggs	*Hale*	*Elliot*

DESTROYER SQUADRON 4
Borie (Flagship)

DESTROYER DIVISION 10	DESTROYER DIVISION 11	DESTROYER DIVISION 12
Alden	*Perry*	*MacLeish*
Broome	*Trever*	*Simpson*
Pruitt	*Wasmuth*	*McCormick*
Sicard	*Zane*	*Truxtun*

DESTROYER DIVISION 16
Tracy   Dahlgren   Preble

ROTATING DESTRPYER SQUADRON 20

Chandler	*Dent*	*Waters*
Hovey	*Rathburne*	*Litchfield*
Long	*Talbot*	*Barry*

AIRCRAFT, BATLE FORCE
Saratoga (Flagship)
CARRIER DIVISION 1

Saratoga VF-6B, 18 VF, 1 VS; VB-2B, 18VBF, 1; VS-2B, 18 VS; VT-2B, 18 VT; 3 VOS, 1 VS
Lexington VF-2B, 18 VF, 1 VS; VF-5B, 18 VF, 1 VS; VB-1B, 18 VB; VS-3B, 18 VS; 3 VOS, 2 VJ
Ranger VF-3B, 18 VF, 1 VS; VB-3B, 18 VB; VB-5B, 18VBF, 1 VS; VS-1B 18 VS; 3 VOS, 2VJ
Langley 3 VOS

MINECRAFT, BATTLE FORCE
Oglala (Flagship)
MINE SQUADRON 1

MINE DIVISION 1		MINE DIVISION 2	
Gamble	*Ramsay*	*Lark*	*Quail*
Montgomery	*Breese*	*Tanager*	*Whippoorwill*

SCOUTING FORCE, U.S. FLEET
Indianapolis – 4 VSO (Flagship)
CRUISERS SCOUTING FORCE
Chicago – 4 VSO (Flagship)   *Vestal* (Repair ship)

CRUISER DIVISION 4 VS-9S, 16 VSO		CRUISER DIVISION 5 VS-10S, 12 VSO	
Chester	*Northampton*	*Chicago*	*Portland*
Pensacola	*Salt Lake City*	*Houston*	

CRUISER DIVISION 6 VS-11S, 12 VSO		CRUISER DIVISION 7 VS-12S, 12 VSO	
Louisville	*Indianapolis*	*Tuscaloosa*	*Minneapolis*
New Orleans	*San Francisco*	*Astoria*	

EXPERIMENTAL DIVISION 1
Semmes
SUBMARINE SQUADRON 3 (Coco Solo)
SUBMARINE DIVIION 5
S-10, S-11, S-12, S-13, S-48, Mallard (rescue vessel
SUBMARINE SQUADRON 4 (Peal Harbor)
Tenders: *Beaver, Keosanqua, Seagull,* Rescue vessel: *Widgeon*

SUBMARINE DIVISION 7	SUBMARINE DIVISION 8	SUBMARINE DIVISION 9
S-1, S-18, S-21, S-22, S-23	*S-24, S-25, S-26, S-27,S-28*	*S-30, S-31, S-32, S-33, S-34,*
Argonaut	*S-29*	*S-35*

SUBMARINE DIVISION 11
S-42, S-43, S-44, S-45, S-46, S-47
SUBMARINE DIVISION 12
Tender: *Holland,* Rescue vessel: *Ortolan*

Barracuda	*Bass*	*Bonita*	*Cachalot*
Cuttlefish	*Narwhal*	*Nautilus*	*Dolphin*

BASE FORCE, U.S. FLEET
Argonne (Flagship)
TRAIN, BASE FORCE

Utah	*Kingfisher*	*Pinola*	*Kalmia*	*Bobolink*	*Tern*
Cuyama	*Kanawha*	*Robin*	*Vireo*	*Neches*	*Relief*
Rail	*Bridge*	*Artic*	*Sonoma*	*Brant*	*Brazos*
ARD-1	*Grebe*	*Medusa*	*Partridge*	*Kalmia*	

AIRCRAFT, BASE FORCE
Wright 2 VOS (Flagship) Sandpiper, Gannet

Wright   VP-7F, 6VPB; VP-9F, 6VPB;VJ-1F, 8VM, 2VR;VJ-2F, 6VM, 1VR; 1 VOS

FAB, Coco Solo   *Teal, Lapwing,* VP-2F, 12VPB;VP-3F, 12VPBVP-5F, 12 VPB; 2 VF, 2 VR, 2VJ

FAB, Pearl Harbor   *Pelican, Avocet, Swan,* VP-1F, 12VPB; VP-4F, 12 VPB; VP-6F, 12 VPM,
VP-8F, 6 VPB; VP10F, 6 VPM; 2VF, 1 VR, 2 VJ

AIRCRAFT, FLEET MAINE FORCE

AIRCRAFT ONE (Quantico)   AIRCRAFT TWO (San Diego)

VO-7M, 12 VS;   VO-9M , 2VS;   VB-4M, 12 VB,   VO-8M, 12 Vs

VF-9M 14 VF, 1 VS   VJ-6M, 4 VM, 4 VR   VJ-7M, 3 M, 3 VR

ASIATIC FLEET
Augusta 4 VSO (Flagship)   *Asheville,   Isabel   Sacramento   Tulsa*

YANGTZE PATROL   SOUTH CHINA PATROL

Luzon   Tutuila   Panay   Guam   Monocacy   Palos   Mindanao

DETROYERS, ASIATIC FLEET
DESTROYER SQUADRON 5

Paul Jones (Flagship)   *Black Hawk* (tender)

DESTROYER DIVISION 13	DESTROYER DIVISION 14	DESTROYER DIVISION 15
Smith Thompson	*Parrott*	*Pope*
Barker	*Edsall*	*Peary*
J.D. Edwards	*Bulmer*	*Pillsbury*
Whipple	*Stewart*	*John D. Ford*

SUBMARINE, ASIATIC FLEET
SUBMARINE SQUADRON 5

Canopus (Flagship)

SUBMARINE DIVISION 10

S-36, S-37, S-38, S-39, S-40, S-41, Pigeon (rescue vessel)

MINECRAFT, ASIATIC FLEET
MINE DIVISION 3

Finch   *Bittern*

AIRCRAFT DETACHMENT, ASIATIC FLEET
Heron 2 VJ (tender)

SPECIAL SERVICE SQUADRON
Trenton 2 VO   *Taylor*   *Claxton*

NAVAL TRNSPOTATION SERVICE
Chaumont   Vega   Salinas   Henderson   Sirius   Ramapo   Nitro

October 1939

UNITED STATES FLEET
Pennsylvania (Flagship)

BATTLE FORCE, U.S. FLEET
California (Flagship)

BATTLESHIP, BATTLE FORCE

BATTLESHIP DIVISION 1 VO-1, 9VOS	BATTLESHIP DIVISION 2 Vo-2, 9 VOS
Arizona	*Tennessee*
Nevada	*Oklahoma*
Pennsylvania	*California*

BATTLESHIP DIVISION 3 VO-3, 9VOS
Idaho
Mississippi
New Mexico

BATTLESHIP DIVISION 4 VO-4, 9 VOS
West Virginia
Colorado
Maryland

CRUISERS BATTLE FORCE
Honolulu (Flagship)

CRUISER DIVISION 3
VCS-3 10 VSO
Concord   Cincinnati
Milwaukee   Omaha
Trenton with Sqdron 40-T

CRUISER DIVISION 8
VCS-8, 16 VSO
Philadelphia   Brooklyn
Savannah   Nashville

CRUISER DIVISION 9
VCS-9, 20 VSO
Helena   Honolulu
Boise   Phoenix
St. Louis

DESTROYERS, BATTLE FORCE
Detroit 2 VSO (Flagship)
DESTROYER FLOTILLA 1
Detroit 2 VS (Flagship) *Dobbin* (tender – DesRon 1 & 3), *Whitney* (tender DesRon 2 & 9)
DESTROYER SQUADRON 1
Phelps (Flagship)

DESTROYER DIVISION 1
Dewey   Hull
MacDonough Worden

DESTROYER DIVISION 2
Alywin   Dale
Farragut   Monaghan

DESTROYER SQUADRON 2
Porter (Flagship)

DESTROYER DIVISION 3
Drayton   Flusser
Lamson   Mahan

DESTROYER DIVISION 4
Cushing   Perkins
Preston   Smith

DESTROYER SQUADRON 3
Clark (Flagship)

DESTROYER DIVISION 5
Cassin   Conyngham
Downes   Reid

DESTROYER DDIVISION 6
Case   Shaw
Cummings   Tucker

DESTROYER SQUADRON 9
McDougal (Flagship)

DESTROYER DIVISION 17
Somers   Winslow
Warrington

DESTROYER DIVISION 18
Sampson   Davis
Jouett

DESTROYER FLOTILLA 2
Detroit (Flagship) *Altair* (tender DesRon 4 & 6) *Melville* (tender DesRon 7,8,12 & DesDiv 19)
DESTROYER SUADRON 4
Selfridge (Flagship)

DESTROYER DIVISION 7
Henley   Helm
Blue   Bagley

DESTROYER DIVISION 8
Mugford   Ralph Talbot
Jarvis   Patterson

DESTROYER SUADRON 6
Balch (Flagship)

DESTROYER DIVISION 11
Gridley   Craven
Maury   McCall

DESTROYER DIVISION 12
Dunlap   Benham
Fanning   Ellet

DESTROYER SQUADRON 7
Moffett (Flagship)

DESTROYER DIVISION 24
Perry   Wasmuth
Zane   Trever

DESTROYER DIVISION 28
Southhard   Chandler
Hovey   Long

DESTROYER SQUADRON 8
Winslow (Flagship)

DESTROYER DIVISION 9
Lang   Sterett   Wilson

DESTROYER DIVISION 10
Mayrant   Rowan

DESTROYER SQUADRON 12
Moffett (Flagship)

DESTROYER DIVISION 25
Anderson *Hammann*
Hughes *Sims*

DESTROYER DIVISION 26
Mustin

DESTROYER SQUADRON 31
MacLeish (Flagship)

DESTROYER DIVISION 62
McCormick *Overton*
Sturevant *Bainbridge*

DESTROYER DIVISION 63
Lawrence *Sands*
King *Humphreys*

DESTROYER SQUADRON 32
Lea (Flagship)

DESTROYER DIVISION 64
Twiggs *Wickes*
Philip *Evans*

DESTROYER DIVISION 65
Crowninshield *Hale*
Aaron Ward *Buchanan*

DESTROYER DIVISION 19
Rathburne Talbot Dent Waters

AIRCRAFT, BATTLE FORCE
Yorktown (Flagship)
CARRIER DIVISION 1
Lexington VB-2, 18 VSB; VF-2, 18 VF,1 VSB, 2 VM, VS-2, 18 VSB; VT-2, 18 VTB; 3 VSO
Saratoga VB-3, 18 VSB; VF-3, 18 VF, 1VSB, 2 VM; VS-3, 18 VSB, VT-3, 18 VTB; 3 VSO
CARRIER DIVISION 2
Yorktown VB-5, 18 VB; VF-5, 18 VF, 1 VSB, 2 VM; VS-5, 18 VSB; VT-5, 18 VTB; 3 VSO
Enterprise VB-6, 18 VB; VF-6, 18 VF, 1 VSB, 2 VM; VS-6, 18 VSB, VT-6, 18 VTB; 3 vSO

MINECRAFT, BATTE FORCE, U.S. FLEET
Ogalala (Flagship)

MINE DIVISION 1
Pruitt *Preble*
Sicard *Tracy*

MINE DIVISION 2
Tanager *Quail*
Lark *Whippoorwill*

MINE DIVISION 5
Montgomery *Ramsay*
Gamble *Breese*

SCOUTING FORCE, U.S. FLEET
Indianapolis (Flagship)
CRUISERS, SCOUTING FORCE
Chicago (Flagship

CRUISER DIVISION 4
Northampton *Houston*
Pensacola *Salt Lake City*

CRUISER DIVISION 5
Chicago *Chester*
Louisville *Portland*

CRUISER DIVISION 6
Minneapolis *Astoria*
New Orleans *Indianapolis*

AIRCRAFT, SCOUTING FORCE
Memphis 3 VSO, 1 VJ, (Flagship)
PATROL WING ONE (San Diego)
Tenders: *Wright* (temp Pearl Harbor) *Pelican, Avocet,* 2 VSO, 1 VJ, 2 VM
VP-11, 12 VPB; VP-12, 12 VPB; VP-13, 12 VPB (temp. Pearl Harbor
PATROL WING TWO (Pearl Harbor)
Tenders: *Langley* (temp. Cavite), *Childs, Swan,* 4 VF, 2 VSO, 1 VJR, 4 VJ, 2 VM
VP-21m 12 VPB (tenp. Cavite); VP-22, 12 VPB; VP-23, 12 VTB; VP-24, 12 VPB; VP25, 12 VPB
PATROL WING THREE (Coco Solo)
Tenders: Lapwing , *Sandpiper* 2 VF, 3 VSO, 2 VJR, 2 VM
VP-31, 12 VPB; VP-332, 12 VPB; VP-33, 12 VPB
PARTROL WING FOUR (Seattle)
Tenders: *Williamson Teal,* NAS Stka, 1 VJ, 2 VF, 2 VM
VP-41, 6 VPB; VP-2, 6 VPB; VP-42, 6 VPB; VP-44, 6 VPB; VP-45, 6 VPB
PATROL WING FIV (Norfolk)
Tenders: *Gannet, Thrush, Owl, Patoka*
VP-51, 12 VPB; VP-52, 9 VPB; VP-53, 12 VPB; VP-4, 12 VPB

242

SUBMARINE FORCE. U.S. FLEET
Richmond 2 VSO (Flagship), *Litchfield* (*Tactical flagship*)
SUBMARINE BASE, NEW LONDON
SUBMARINE SQUADRON 2

SUBMARINE DIVISION 4 1	SUBMARINE DIVISION 8	EXPERIMENTAL. DIVISION
Falcon (rescue vessel) *R-2*	*S-21 S-24, S-25 S-26 S-29*	*Semmes* *S-20* *S-22*
R-4 -10 R-11 R-13 R-14	*S-29 S-30* (Comm. in reserve)	

SUBMARINE BASE, COCO SOLO
SUBMARINE DIVISION 11
S-42 S-43 -44 S-45 S-46 S-47 Mallard (rescue vessel)

SUBMARINE BASE, PEARL HARBOR
SUBMARINE SQUADRN 4
Tenders: *Keosanqua Seagull* Rescue vessel: *Widgeon*

SUBMARINE DIVISION 7		SUBMARINE DIVISION 12	SUBMARINE DIVISION 13	
S-18	*S-23*	*Dolphin*	*Narwhal*	*Shark* *Cachalot*
S-34	*S-35*	*Nautilus*	*Argonaut*	*Cuttlefish* *Plunger*
				Pollack *Pompano*

SUBMARINE SQUADRON 6

SUBMARINE DIVISION 15			SUBMARINE DIVISION 16		
Snapper	*Salmon*	*Seal*	*Sargo*	*Saury*	*Sculpin*
Skipjack	*Stingray*	*Sturgeon*	*Spearfish*	*Squalus*	*Swordfish*

Experimental Division 2
S-27   *S-28*

ATLANTIC SQUADRON, U.S.FLEET
New York (Flagship)
Ranger VB-4 18 VSB; VF-4, 18 VF, 1 VSB, 2 VM, VS-41, 18 VSB; VS-42, 18 VSB: 3 VSO

BATTLESHIP DIVISION 5		CRUISER DIVISION 7 VSC-7, 20 VS		
New York	*Arkansas*	*Wichita*	*Quincy*	*San Fancisco*
Texas	*Wyoming*	*Tuscaloosa*	*Vincennes*	

DESTROYERS, ATLANTIC SQUADRON, U.S. FLEET
DESTROYER SQUADRON 19
Decatur (Flagship)

DESTROYER DIVISION 21		DESTROYER DIVISION 22	
Hopkins	*Barry*	*Leary*	*Schenck*
Goff	*Rueben James*	*Fairfax*	*Manley*
DESTROYER DIVISION 27		DESTROYER DIVISION 29	
Borie	*Broome*	*Badger*	*Jacob Jones*
Simpson	*Truxtun*	*Herbert*	*Dickerson*

DESTROYER DIVISION 29
Roper Hamilton Babbitt Claxton
DESTROYER SQUADRON 30
Gilmer (Flagship)

DESTROYER DIVISION 60		DESTROYER DIVISION 61	
Ellis	*Dupont*	*Greer*	*Tarbell*
Bernadou	*Cole*	*Yarnall*	*Upshur*

DESTROYER SQUADRON 41
Dallas (Flagship)

DESTROYER DIVISION 82		DESTROYER DIVISION 66	
Hatfield	*Fox*	*Breckenridge*	*Barney*
Brooks	*Kane*	*Blakeley*	*Biddle*

BASE FORCE, U.S. FLEET
Argonne (Flagship) *Rigel* Tender with out-of-commission destroyers in San Diego
Utility Wing
VJ-1, 10 VJ, 10 VJR; VJ-2, 10 VJ, 10 VJR; VJ-3, 2 VJ 4 VJR, 6 VM

243

TRAIN, BASE FORCE
Argonne (Flagship)

Antares	*ARD-1*	*Arctic*	*Algorma*	*Bobolink*	*Brant*	*Brazos*
Bridge	*Cimarron*	*Cuyama*	*Grebe*	*Kalmia*	*Rail*	*Medusa*
Kanawha	*Neches*	*Neosho*	*Partridge*	*Pinola*	*Relief*	*Robin*
Kingfisher	*Sonoma*	*Tern*	*Turkey*	*Utah*	*Vestal*	*Vireo*

MOBILE TARGET DIVISION 1
Dorsey   Elliot   Lamberton   Boggs

AIRCRAFT FLEET MARINE FORCE
AIRCRAFT ONE (Quantico
VMB-1, 18 VSB; VMF-1, 19 VF, 1 VSB; VMS-1, 18 VSB; VMJ-1 4 VM, 4 VR,! VJR:VMB-3, 6 VJ, 3, 1 VJR; (St. Thomas, V.I.)
AIRCRAFT TWO San Diego
VMB-2, 18 VSB; VMF-2, 18 VF, 1 VSB, VMS-2, 18 VSB; VMJ-2, 5 VM, 3 VR, 1 VJR

ASIATIC FLEET
Augusta 4 VSO (Flagship)
Marblehead 2 VSO *Asheville   Isabel   Tulsa*

YANGTZE PATROL	SOUTH CHNA PATROL
Guam Luzon Oahu Tutuila	*Mindanao*

DESTROYERS, ASATIC FLEET
DESTROYER SQUADRON 8
Paul Jones (Squadron leader) *Black Hawk* (tender

DESTROYER DIVISION 13	DESTROYER DIVISION 14	DESTROYER DIVISION 15	
Alden	*Barker*	*Bulmer*	*Edsall*	*John D. Ford*	*Peary*
J.D. Edwards	*Whipple*	*Parrott*	*Stewart*	*Pillsbury*	*Pope*

SUBMARINES, ASIATIC FLEET
SUBMARINE SQUARO 5
Canopus (tender) *Pigeon* (rescue vessel)

SUBMARINE DIVISION 10	SUBMARINE DIVISION 14		
S-36 S-37 S-38 S-39 Si40 S-41	*Perch*	*Porpoise*	*Pike*
	Tarpon	*Pickerel*	*Permit*

TRAN, ASIATIC FLEET
MINE DIVISION 3
Finch   Bittern

AIRCRAFT DETACHMENT
Heron 3 VJ (tender)

AUXILIARIES
Pecos   Napa

SPECIAL SERVICE SQUADRON
Charleston   Erie   J.F. Talbott   Tattnall

SQUADRON 40-T (European waters under CNO)
Trenton (Flagship)
Dickerson   Herbert

NAVAL TRANSPORTATION SERVICE

Capella	*Chaumont*	*Henderson*	*Nitro*	*Pyro*	*Vega*
Salinas	*Sirius*	*Rampano*	*Trinity*		

Note: Not all ships were actually in place as of the date of October 1939, e.g., none of SubDiv 16 had reported to CinCUS. As a matter of fact *Squalus* had sunk during sea trial off Portsmouth, N.H., in May. She was raised, recommissioned as *Sailfish* and joined SubDiv16 in 1940

Appendix 4

Ships Sacrificed to the Treaties

Scrapped by the Washington Treaty of 1922

U.S. Navy: Built (From 20 to 13 years of age): *Maine, Missouri, Ohio, Virginia, Nebraska, Georgia, New Jersey, Rhode Island, Connecticut, Louisiana, Vermont, Kansas, Minnesota, New Hampshire, South Carolina, Michigan*
Building: *Washington, South Dakota, Indiana, Montana, North Carolina, Iowa, Massachusetts, Constitution, Constellation, Ranger, United States.* Scrapped after replacements commissioned in 1923: *Delaware, North Dakota*
Royal Navy: Built (From 16 to 7 years of age*): Commonwealth, Agamemnon, Dreadnought, Bellerophon, St. Vincent, Inflexible, Superb, Neptune, Hercules, Indomitable, Temeraire, New Zealand, Lion, Princess Royal, Conqueror, Monarch, Orion, Australia, Agincourt, Erin. Building*: Four ships not yet given names. In 1925, upon completion of two new 35,000-ton ships allowed*: King George V, Ajax, Centurion, Thunderer*
France: None until 1930: *Jean Bart, Courbet*
Italy: None until 1931: *Dante Alighieri*
Imperial Japanese Navy: Built (From 20 to 11 years of age): *Hizen, Mikasa, Kashima, Katori, Satsuma, Aki, Settsu, Ikoma, Ibuki, Krama.* Building: *Kaga*, Tosa Takao* and eight ships projected but not laid down. (*When *Amagi* was lost on the ways during the 1923 earthquake, *Kaga* was saved to be a carrier agreed upon in the Treaty.)
U.S. ships scrapped, stricken or demilitarized after 1930: *Florida, Utah* (target ship), *Wyoming* (training ship), *Denver, Des Moines, Chattanooga, Galveston, Cleveland, St. Louis, Pueblo, Frederick, Huron, Charlotte, Missoula, Charleston, Pittsburgh*
Four-pipers of 1917 Emergency Destroyer Program stricken in 1930: *Maury, Mahan, Hart, Ludlow, Burns, McDermut, McCawley, Moody, Henshaw, Meyer, Doyen, Sharkey, Toucey, Breck, Case, Isherwood, Lardner, Putnam, Worden, Flusser, Dale, Converse, Reid, Billingsley Chas. Ausburn, Osborne, Percival, J.F. Burns, Farragut, Somers, Reno, Farquhar, Thompson, Kennedy Wm. Jones, Paul Hamilton, Zeilin, Yarborough, La Vallette, Wood, Shirk, Kidder, Selfridge, Mervine, Chase, Robert Smith, Mullany, Coghlan, Preston, Lamson, Bruce, Hull, MacDonough, Farenholt, Sumner, Corry, Melvin, Rizal,*
Old destroyers of 1898-1914 and 33 of the 1917 program stricken 1934-1937 to provide tonnage for the Vinson programs: *Caldwell, Gwin, Kimberly, Dyer, Stevens, McKee, Harding, Gridley, Taylor, Bell, Stribling, Murray, Israel, Luce, Lansdale, Champlain, Mugford, Hazelwood, Ingrahm, Radford, Meredith, Bush, Anthony, Preston, Renshaw, O'Bannon, J.K. Paulding, Turner, Morris, Tingey, Sinclair, Stoddert, Sloat, Marcus, Paulding, Drayton, Roe, Terry, Perkins, Sterett, McCall, Burrows, Mayrant, Warrington, Monaghan, Trippe, Walke, Ammen, Patterson, Fanning, Jarvis, Henley, Beale, Jouett, Jenkins, Cassin, Cummings, Downes, Duncan, Alywin, Parker, Benham, Balch, O'Brien, Nicholson, Winslow, McDougal, Cushing, Ericsson, Tucker, Conygham, Porter, Wadsworth, Wainwright, Sampson, Rowan, Davis, Wilkes, Shaw*
Many of the names were given to new construction and some names even continued in The Treaty Navy. *Smith Thompson* was damaged in a collision with *Whipple* on Apr. 14, 1936. She was beyond repair and scuttled off Subic Bay, P.I.

Appendix 5

Fleet Problems I-XXI 1923-1940

Annual Fleet Problems were part of The Treaty Navy. They served two purposes. First they assembled the entire Fleet, foreign detachments excepted, at least once a year to examine strategy; to exercises tactics; and ship handling of large, complex formations. Second, they gave senior commanders, who were "auditioning" for higher command, an opportunity to demonstrate their prowess. In an economy-minded Navy, many restrictions applied to the exercises. Safety was paramount. Neither ships nor men could be put at risk. Death or injuries during a Problem would be fodder for the anti-Navy factions. Damage, however slight, to ships would divert money from an already impoverished Navy budget. Shortage of money for fuel kept high speeds, which burned fuels uneconomically, from being used for realistic maneuvering.

There were political dimensions as well. Care had to be taken in devising scenarios. The mission of the Navy was advertised, at home and abroad, as being defensive. Offensive-based scenarios could not be developed. The "bad guys" always had to be the attackers. The "good guys" had to be the defenders and it would be poor public relations when the "good guys" lost. As would be expected, the significant Problems were those where the attackers succeeded. From these unscheduled successes progress was made in the development of Fleet doctrine. Another political artificiality was that the "aggressor" had to be a notional but fictional entity. It would be bad for foreign relations to single out any real nation as a potential opponent. The opposing forces were identified by color but supposedly, there was not a correlation between the colors of the Problems an those of the COLOR PLANS. The friendly forces ("good guys") were usually BLUE but in some Problems they were WHITE or PURPLE. The "bad guys" or attackers were usually BLACK but ORANGE did make an appearance.

The strategic aspects of the Problems led to several artificialities. These mainly stemmed from the lack of a potent air capability in the 20s. Battleships with only float scout aircraft were dubbed carriers and their paucity of aircraft became squadrons to conduct attacks on targets ashore or at sea. Likewise a single ship or a small group might represent a larger formation. This caused commanders to react to notional rather than actual opposing strength.

Rather than belabor each Fleet Problem, *ad nauseam,* a brief sketch of each is given but only those with real significance to The Treaty Navy in its coming war at sea with Japan are described in, albeit short, detail.

Fleet Problems

A Fleet Problem scheduled for 1922 was cancelled because of lack of money for fuel.

I - February 1923 - took place in the Bay of Panama to test defenses of the Panama Canal. It was characterized by the breakdown of older ships and poor submarine performance. Its purpose was to give commanders experience in reacting to an attack on the Canal. Unfortunately for the BLUE commander, "squadrons" from BLACK's "slow carriers" (BBs) penetrated to the Canal and were ruled as having destroyed some locks. The good side was that the potential of carrier air was recognized by the forward thinkers.

II, III & IV – January 1924 – These were three seemingly successive but not really sequential Problems of the BLUES against the BLACKS. Again the focus was the Panama Canal The initial section of the three had the BLACK forces simulating an advance west across the Pacific. The second Problem which followed immediately entailed once again testing the defenses of the Canal and the feasibility of it being used for wartime transit. BLUE steamed toward the Canal and transit to the Caribbean.

246

BLACK, with *Langley*, attacked the Canal Zone. The attacks of her aircraft on the Canal were beaten off and BLUE successfully transited and engaged BLACK on the Atlantic side. BLUE immediately proceeded to Culebra, P.R to land Marines to seize an advance base (simulated westward movement across the Pacific from Hawaii?) to meet a hostile fleet advancing. Several conclusions were drawn from the three Problems. The Canal was vulnerable to air and ground attack from enemy landings in Central America. Amphibious forces lacked specialized equipment and assault shipping to get heavy weapon and equipment ashore on a hostile beach. But what drew public attention was the "Coontz Report" on fleet deficiencies.

V – March 1925 – The Pacific Fleet as BLACK simulated seizing and occupying an undefended anchorage on the West Coast. Further training included screening operations including submarines and experimenting with fueling operations from battleships to destroyers at sea. After the completion, the Fleet headed for Hawaii thence "down under" to Australia and New Zealand.

VI – February 1926 – Off the Pacific Cast of Central America focused on training in convoy escort.

VII – March 1927 – in the Caribbean also concerned convoying and submarines against convoys.

VIII – April 1928 – in the Pacific, vicinity of Hawaii. It did not involve a fleet concentration but was mainly a scouting problem. As such it showed the need for more cruisers. The enemy forces were labeled ORANGE.

IX – January 1929 – on the Pacific side of the Canal. It included the two new carriers, *Lexington* and *Saratoga*, one with each opposing force. BLACK was the main Battle Feet with the mission of assaulting the Canal from the Pacific side. BLUE was the Scouting Force which transited the Canal to defend on the Pacific side. BLACK's *Saratoga* with a small escort made a wide end run to the south away from the Battle Force surprise the defenders. It set the tone for independent carrier operations in the future.

X – March 1930 – was a Fleet concentration in West Indies waters pitting the Scouting Force against the defending Battle Fleet. Aircraft from attacking *Lexington* were ruled to have crippled the Battle Fleet's battleships

XI – April 1930 – was an immediate continuation of **X.** *Lexington's* aircraft caught opposing *Saratoga* with her decks filled with aircraft awaiting orders to launch. The latter was deemed destroyed. As a result of the recent Fleet Problem, planners began to conceive a task organization built around the striking power of a carrier escorted by fast cruisers and destroyers. Further, improvements in aircraft design as well as increased armor for the carriers were recognized as needed but were precluded by lack of funding.

XII – February 1931 – had similar objectives to the Problems of the previous year but involved defense of a longer coast line on the Pacific side of Central America. BLACK was to attempt a landing to establish air bases to project attacks on the Canal. Defending WHITE was built around a task force of the two new carriers since the scenario had the bulk of White's Battle Fleet hypothetically defending in the Atlantic against another potential attacker. Aircraft from the two carriers won the day against the attackers but in their enthusiasm of attacking were delayed in returnng to their decks until after dark. Capt. E.J. King of *Lexington*, like her namesake in a similar situation 13 years later, "Let there be light" with is searchlights to guide the pilots home. It was the first major night landing on board a carrier and thankfully there were no mishaps to mar the event and allow critics to howl. In this Problem, the airship, *Los Angeles,* took part with no significant impact.

XIII – March 1932- was the defense of Hawaii from attack by carrier aircraft. Its preliminary in February was portent of things to come. *Lexington* and *Saratoga* with two destroyer divisions left the West Coast for Hawaiian waters. Commanded by RAdm. Harry Yarnell, the two carriers hid in squalls north of Oahu and launched and recovered their aircraft which successfully attacked on a Sunday morning. Despite the weather the strike was recovered without loss. *Lexington* then made a speed run back to the West Coast to join with the Scouting Force around from the Atlantic for the phase wherein the BLACK of the Scouting Force would defend Hawaii from invasion. The operations of the carriers in both phases demonstrated a need for more of them. Also significant was the retention of the Scouting Force in the Pacific as a deterrent to Japanese aggression on the Asian mainland.

XIV – January & February 1933 – was initially a BLACK (Scouting Force) attack on Oahu by carrier air. It "conquered" Oahu despite defense by coast artillery and Army Air Corps. BLACK with the two new carriers then threatened the California coast. BLUE, the Battle Fleet defended. Almost every major fleet unit except those undergoing modernization participated. BLACK sent one carrier force to attack San Francisco and the other to hit the San Pedro-San Diego complexes. He also formed a decoy force of cruisers. The lighter BLACK forces were thwarted. The BLACK commander was deemed to have used his carriers ineptly and thus failed his "audition" for higher command

XV – May 1934 – involved an attack on and defense of the Canal for the transit of the ships in the Pacific to effect a concentration with those in the Atlantic n the Caribbean. Patrol plane squadrons from the West Coast and Panama, as well as the airship *Macon,* took part. The climax was an amphibious assault of Culebra, P.R., by Marines.

XVI – May & June 1935 – in the North Pacific off Alaska was the largest exercise to date. *Ranger* and several new heavy cruisers had joined the Fleet. Much of the initial operation was shrouded in secrecy but it involved an expeditionary force to seize and defend an advanced naval base. Secrecy was lifted when a patrol plane from one of the squadrons flying from Midway was lost with all hands. Commanders were displaying more boldness inasmuch as four destroyers were damaged in collisions during high speed maneuvering.

XVII – May 1936 – involved larger forces than **XVI** but did not include a fleet engagement. It took place in the eastern Pacific off the Canal. It featured submarine operations and submarine countermeasures, extended patrol plane and surface scouting. Carrier air struck shore targets. Air operations were becoming more significant.

XVIII – April 1937- was again in the North Pacific initially with a shift to Hawaiian waters. Hawaii was to hold for a week with small naval forces against an invading BLACK force. The latter succeeded in taking the Big Island and established an advance base to allow its fleet to attack Oahu. None of these repeated Problems in the Pacific deterred Japanese ambitions since they invaded China a few months later.

XIX – April 1938 – was in two phases. The first took place in Hawaiian waters and was almost a repeat of Yarnell's 1932 attack on Oahu. RAdm. E.J. King was ComCarDiv 1 (*Saratoga* and *Lexington*) and he planned to attack from the north and south. Unfortunately, an epidemic on board forced *Lexington* to abort to Pearl. King flying his flag in *Saratoga* moved to the northwest of Oahu and hid in a squall system moving east. He was hidden from patrolling aircraft based in Hawaii. After thee days of hiding, he launched a successful attack on Pearl and recovered all his planes. He was then given command of PURPLE forces for the second phase, an attack on San Francisco by carrier air against a defending BLACK fleet. He left Pearl with his carriers and escorts and his deceptive course toward San Diego got him in position undiscovered and he launched a successful attack on Mare Island Naval Yard. Ernie King was making a name for himself as a carrier tactician.

XX – February-March 1939 – for the first time in several years, the Problem returned to the Caribbean and off the northeast coast of South America. With war clouds gathering in rope and Hitler bloodlessly devoured much of central Europe, the scenario was to defend against a European power's invasion of South America (Brazil?). Defense of the Canal was also a key element. The "star" of the Problem was King, who again used his carriers aggressively in eliminating the opponent's carriers and patrol planes. He did the latter by sinking the tenders both by air and destroyer attacks. A key observer of the Problem was the Commander-in-Chief, President Roosevelt.

XXI – April- May 1940 – took place in the Pacific in the vicinity of Hawaii, the scenario had a realistic ORANGE setting although the opposing forces were again designated WHITE and BLACK. There was little doubt about the identity of BLACK. There were two phases. In the second phase, WHITE was redesignated MAROON and BLACK was PURPLE. CINCUS, Adm. J.O. Richardson, was both Chef Umpire to decide the outcome of tactical operations between opponents but also the driving force behind the demand for realism. He wanted warships underway to be able to refuel from oilers thus allowing larger ships to continue being sources of fuel for the "small boys;" he wanted high speed maneuvering and encouraged boldness in ship handling and changing station; Formation keeping at night during "darken ship" was demanded. Night actions were part of a Problem for the first time, albeit, there had been sporadic exercise of night tactics in smaller training exercises. At the end of the Problem, the entire Fleet pulled liberty in Hawaii. By then, France and the Lowlands had been invaded by Hitler. F.D.R ordered the Fleet to remain in Hawaii. Except for some of it redeployed to the Atlantic when Britain stood alone, most of the Fleet was at Pearl for a year and a half. It was supposed to be a deterrent to Japanese aggression n the Western Pacific but as in 1932, that didn't work.

.

Appendix 6

Pay Scales

Annual Pay and Allowances of Commissioned Officers
Adm. $8,000   RAdm. (upper half) $8,000
VAdm. 8,000   RAdm. (lower half) 6,000
Personal Cash Allowances: Adm - $2,500   Vdm. - $500

	Under 3	Over 3	Over 5	Over 6	Over 7	Over 9	Over 10	Over 12
Capt.	$ 3,500	3,675		3,850		4,025		4,200
Capt. (Staff)	4,000	4,200		4,400		4,600		4,800
Cdr.	3,000	3,150		3,300		3,450		3,600
Cdr. (Staff0	3,500	3,675		3,950		4,025		4,200
LCdr. (under 14)	2,400	2,520		2,640		2,760		2,880
LCdr. (appt. above Ens)	3,000	3,150		3,300		3,450		3,600
Lieut.	2,000	2,100		2,200	2,640	2,760		2,880
Lieut (appt above Ens)	2,400	2,520		2,640		2,760		2,880
Lieut. (j.g.)	1,500	2,100		2,200		2,300	2,760	2,880
Ens.	1,500	1,575	2,100	2,200		2,300		2,400
Midn.	780							
CWO								
Comm. Lees 10 yrs	2,000	2,100		2,200		2,300		2,400
After 10 yrs comm..							2,760	2,880

	Over 15	Over 17	Over 18	Over 21	Over 24	Over 26	Over 27	Over 30
Capt.	$ 4,375		4,550	4,727	4,900	5,600	5,800	6,000
Capt. (Staff0	5,000		5,200	5,400	5,600			
Cdr.	3,750		3,900	4,725	4,900		5,073	5,750
Cdr. (Staff)	4,375		4,550					
LCdr.	3,600		3,750	4,050	4,900		5,075	5,250
Lieut.	3,000	3,750	3,900	4,050	4,200		4,360	4,500
Lieut. (j.g.)	3,000		3,120	3,240	3,360		3,480	3,600
Ens.	2,500		2,600	2,700	2,800		2,900	3,000
CWO								
After 10 yrr comm.	3,000		3,120	3,240	3,360		3,480	3,600
After 20 yrs comm.				4,050	4,200		4,350	4,500

Warrant Officers
1-6 yrs service - $, 1,836 ; 7-12 yrs service - $2,016; After 12 yrs service -$2,268
Female Nurses
1-3 yrs - $840; 4-6 yrs.- 1,080; -9 yrs. 1,380; after 10 yrs. 1,550
Additional allowances to Pay as nurses: Supt. Nurse Corps - $2,500; Asst. Supt., Directors;
Asst Directors -$1,500; Chief Nurse - $600

Rental and Subsistence

All officers and Nurses received a Subsistence Allowance of $219 a year For those with dependents, Warrant Officers and Nurses excepted this was doubled to $438. Certain Captains, Commanders (less Staff) and Lieutenant Commanders received $657.Rental allowance varied by rank and years of service as well as status of being with or without dependents. Officers living in government quarters with dependents forfeited their rental allowance. Officers without dependents either living in government quarters or stationed on board ship also forfeited their rental allowance. All flag officers without dependents received $960 rental allowance. Those with dependents received $1,262 except for rear admirals, lower half who got $1,062. Most Captains and Commanders got $1,440. Lieutenant Commanders got $1,400 while Lieutenants got $960, "Jay Gees" got $720, Ensigns $ 480.

Longevity for Naval Academy Graduates

Officers who had been graduated from the Naval Academy in the Class of 1916 or earlier received   credit for pay purposes for their time at the Academy as Midshipmen. This was changed when in 1913, a delegation of civilian professors at the Academy , who were Civil Service grade employees, petitioned Congress for step increases in pay for the years they had spent acquiring an education. They argued that Midshipmen were getting government credit for going to school so why shouldn't they? Congress in its parsimonious wisdom rejected their claim and eliminated their argument by doing away with longevity credit for Midshipmen, henceforth except that the Midshipmen then at the Academy were grand-fathered in. The dichotomy of Congressional rationale remains until this day. Anyone not graduating from the Academy who takes further federal service including enlisting gets longevity credit for time spent as a Midshipman. Likewise, a graduate who later resigns or retires (dual compensation regulations applies in most cases to the latter) and takes federal employment including Civil Service also gets credit for Naval Academy service.

Monthly Pay of Enlisted men

	Under 4	Over 4	Over 8	Over 12	Over 16
CPO (Perm appt.)	$ 126.00	136.60	144.90	151.20	157.50
CPO (Acting appt.)	96.00	108.90	113.85	118.80	123.75
P.O 1/c, Off Stew 1/c, Off Cook 1/c	84.00	92.40	96.60	100.80	105.00
P.O 2/c, Off Stew 2/c, off cook 2/c, Mus 1/c	72.00	79.20	82.80	86.40	90.00
P.O. 3/c, F 1/c Off Stew 3/c, Off cook 3/c	60.00	66.00	69.00	72.00	75.00
NR 1/c , F 2/c, Mess Attd 1/c	54.00	59.40	62.10	64.80	67.50
NR 2/c, F 3/c, Mess Attd, 2/c	36.00	39.60	41.40	43.20	45.00
NR 3/c Mess Attd 3/c	21.00	23.10	24.15	25.20	26.25

Officers assigned duty involving flying received an additional 50% of base pay. Officers qualified in submarines received an additional 25% when so assigned.
Enlisted Allowances and Special Pay

Awards of the Medal of Honor, Distinguished Service Medal, Distinguished Flying Cross or Navy Cross (the Naval Service had no other awards, albeit, some Marines were awarded the Army's Silver Star Commendation for World War I, which became the Silver Star medal circa 1932), merited $2 a month.

Crew's messmen got $5 per month.

Gun Captains got $2 to $5 a month based on proficiency. Gun Pointers and Gun Director Pointers got $2 to $5 a month based on proficiency at short-range battle practice. Gun range finder operators got $5 a month based on proficiency.

Mail clerks got $10 to $30 a month per size of ship.

Expert Riflemen (Navy and Marines) got $3 a month. Sharpshooters got $1 per month.

Divers, depending on qualification, got $10 to $30 per month.

Those assigned to duty involving flying got an additional 50% of their base pay.

Submariners received pay based on the number of dives per month. This varied for unqualified men from $5 to $10 a month. Those qualified in submarines received from $20 to a maximum of $30 a month.

Everyone in the Naval Service paid 20¢ per month to the Navy Hospital Fund to finance medical care.

Marines received the same pay as their equivalent pay grades in the Navy. There were two variations. Since Marines did not have an officer selection system, second lieutenants did not move to first lieutenant after three years as ensigns did to j.g., hence, at the end of five years, second lieutenants received first lieutenant's (j.g.) pay (See pay tables). Also, seamen upon graduation from "boot camp" were advanced to Seaman 2/c at $36 per month. Marine Privates upon graduation from "boot camp" got $30 a month. Like the Navy of the era, the Marines had seven enlisted pay grades. These were Private, Private First Class (PFC), Corporal (CPL) and Sergeant for the four lowest grades. Above that were Staff Non-Commissioned Officers (SNCO). These ranks wore the three chevrons of a sergeant but with either the rounded "rockers" below for those of the "line" or straight bars across for those of the staff, e.g., communicators, aviation mechanics or even cooks. The rockers or bars started with one and moved to three. The equivalent ranks (*staff in italics*) were: Platoon Sergeant, S*taff Sergeant, Chief Cook;* Gunnery Sergeant, *Technical Sergeant, Supply Sergeant;* Sergeant Major, First Sergeant, Master Gunnery Sergeant, *Master Technical Sergeant, Quartermaster Sergeant, Paymaster Sergeant.*

All enlisted received an additional 10% of base pay for sea and foreign service.

All enlisted received quarters, afloat or ashore, as well as messing. Pay was checked for time lost by unauthorized absence or sickness "due to own misconduct."

For almost all of the era, no "government employees" paid federal income tax.

Appendix 7

Naval Aircraft Designations and Markings

Aircraft of The Treaty Navy were designated systematically. The system was unique to the Naval Service and came into use on Mar. 29, 1922. It endured for 40 years, well past the era of The Treaty Navy. It was superceded on Sept. 18, 1962 when Secretary of Defense (SecDef) R.S. McNamara and his "whiz kids" in their quest for commonality decreed that all military aircraft should be designated the same way regardless of maker or modifications.

The 1922 Navy system had four elements and provided for special status or class prefixes and special purpose suffixes. The elements were:

Type or Class – Letter(s) signifying the type of aircraft, e.g., **F** for Fighting, **B** for Bombing, etc.

Manufacturers type sequence – A number indicating the number of the type produced by a manufacturer. The number **1** was omitted since it was understood.

Manufacturer – A letter was assigned to each manufacturer (after The Treaty Navy, the numbers of aircraft makers exceeded the alphabet). This was important to logisticians because it let aircraft from the same manufacturer be assigned to Air Groups regardless of type. Thus, where the same manufacturer made a fighter and a bomber, many of the parts were interchangeable. Also, parts could be stocked aboard ship on the basis of who made the plane.

Aircraft configuration sequence – A number preceded by a dash which indicated changes made to models during subsequent production.

A common prefix was **X** for experimental. A common suffix was **A** for amphibious version.

Type designations were: **B** – Bombing, **BF** - Bombing-Fighting, **F** – Fighting, **O** – Observation, **OS** - Observation-Scouting, **S** – Scouting, **SB** - Scouting-Bombing, **SO** Scouting-Observation, **P** – Patrol, **PB** - Patrol Bombing, **PT** Patrol-Torpedo, **TB** Torpedo-Bombing, **J** - Utility, **JR** - Utility-Transport, **R** - Transport (multi-engine), **G** - Transport (single-engine), **N** – Training, **M** - Miscellaneous. In addition the letters **V** (for heavier than air) and **Z** (for lighter than air) were used to identify squadrons. VF-1 was "Fighting Squadron One," or simply "Fighting One." A Marine squadron added the letter **M**, e.g., VMF-.1

Manufacturer's Symbols in The Treaty Navy were: **A** - Brewster, **B** – Boeing, **C** – Curtiss, **D** – Douglas, **E** – Bellanca, **F** – Grumman, **G** -Bell (*nee* Great Lakes), **H** - Hall American, **J** - North American, **K** - Kinner also Keystone, **L** – Loening, **M** – Martin **N** - Naval Aircraft Factory, **O** – Lockheed, **P** - Pitcairn Autogiro, **Q** – Stinson, **R** - Stout also Ford, **S** - Sikorsky and Stearman, **T** – Northrop, **U** -Chance-Vought, **W** – Waco, **Y** - Consolidated

Thus, the F3F-2 was the third fighter made by Grumman in the second configuration.

Aircraft Markings

Naval aircraft were most colorful in the markings on the upper wings, tails and light gray fuselage. The National Insignia of a large blue circle with a white star inside with its five points tangent to the circle and a red circle inside the star inside the star tangent to the five inner points of the star were on the tops and bottoms of the aircraft's wings for a total of four. The tops of the wings were painted chrome yellow for identification if downed at sea. A varied colored Vee ran from the center of the leading edge aft. The underside of the lower wing (single wing in monoplanes) had in large block letters, "U.S. NAVY."

A squadron consisted of 18 planes of six sections of three planes each. Each section had a leader. Each section also had a distinctive color: 1 - Insignia Red, 2 – White, 3- True Blue, 4 - Black, 5 – Willow Green and 6 – Lemon Yellow. Planes were numbered in sequence with 1 to 3 in Section 1 and 16 to 18 in Section 6. The leader of each section had the entire cowl painted in the section's color. It also had a leader's band around the fuselage aft of the cockpit. Perpendicular to this band was the identification of the squadron, its type and the number of the plane in the squadron, e.g., 1-F-1. On the section leader the letter was the center of the leader stripe. The other planes had no leader stripe but their cowls were painted in the section colors thus: second plane in the section – upper half of the cowl; third plane – lower half of the cowl. Squadron insignia was on both sides of the fuselage forward of the cockpit.

Carrier aircraft had solid painted tails indicating their carrier. *Lexington* was Lemon Yellow; *Saratoga* was White; *Ranger* was Willow Green; *Yorktown* was Insignia Red; *Enterprise* was True Blue and *Wasp* was Black. Observation squadrons assigned to BatDivs or CruDivs had similar markings but they tails were usually stripes of two or more colors. The aircraft assigned to the flag officer commanding the ship division had its fuselage painted blue. It was his flying "barge."

A practiced eye could tell a lot about Naval aircraft from their markings.

Appendix 8

Shipboard Routine

Daily life on board ships of The Treaty Navy varied according to the type of ship. Four-hour watches were in addition to performing drills and ship's work. The "black gang" stood their watches over the machinery of the ship. Deck watches were lookouts, helmsmen, boat crews and on the navigation and signal bridges. Watches began with midnight to 4 a.m. "Dog watches" were two-hour stints dividing up the 4 p.m. to 8 p.m. period. This allowed a progression of the watch schedule every day so no one was permanently on the "mid-watch (midnight to 4 a.m.) It was custom to relieve the watch 15 minutes early. The following routines are given in Navy time, i.e., a 24-hour system vice a.m. and p.m. (Pipe call in *italics*.)

DAILY ROUTINE IN PORT

0440   Call cooks of the watch.
0445   Call police petty officers, boatswain's mates, buglers and hammock stowers.
0500   Reveille; *Up hammocks,* serve coffee, *Smoking lamp is lighted.*
0515   Police petty officers report deck clear of hammocks.
0520   *Sweepers,* sweep down before decks are wet.
0525   Off shoes and socks; or don boots, get out wash-deck gear.
0530   Turn-to; smoking lamp out; execute morning orders; clear lower decks; station men to turn off anchor, boom and gangway lights at sunrise; scrub clothes.
0600   Knock off scrubbing clothes; trice up lines.
0645   Remove gun covers and hatch cloths (clement weather only.)
0700   Up all hammocks (late watch sleepers.)
0715   *Mess gear; Smoking lamp lighted;* publish uniform of the day.
0730   Breakfast.
0800   Colors.
0815   Turn-to; smoking lamp out; deck and gun bright work.
0830   Sick call.
0845   Retreat from turn-to; sweep down; clear up deck for quarters.
0910   Officers' call; divisions fall in for muster.
0915   Quarters for muster and inspection; physical and day's drills.
1130   Retreat from drill; *Down scrubbed clothes;* sweep down; *Smoking lamp lighted*; Mast for reports and requests.
1145   *Mess gear.*
1200   Dinner.
1230   Band call; concert until 1300.
1300   Turn-to; smoking lamp out; *Sweepers; Down aired bedding.*
1330   Drill call.
1430   Retreat from drill; turn-to.
1600   Knock off work; sweep down; *Smoking lamp lighted.*
1630   Lay aft the liberty party.
1730   Clear up decks.
1745   *Mess gear.*
1800   Supper. Call guard of the day and band (5 min. before sunset; station detail to turn on standing lights at sunset.)
1830   Turn-to; *Sweepers;* wet down decks for scrubbing clothes.
1930   *Hammocks;* no smoking below main deck.
2000   Muster anchor watch; searchlight drills if ordered.

2030 Trice up clotheslines.
2055 First call; smoking lamp out.
2100 Tattoo; pipe down; silence; muster and set first anchor watch.
2105 Taps.

DAILY ROUTINE AT SEA

0200 Relieve wheel and lookouts.
0340 Call watch section.
0400 Relieve the watch; muster watch section and lifeboat crew; *Smoking lamp is lighted;* call cooks. Details at running lights to turn of at sunrise; relieve and station masthead lookouts.
0500 Reveille; coffee.
0530 Turn-to; smoking lamp out; execute morning orders.
0600 Relieve wheel and lookouts; trice up clotheslines.
0700 Up all hammocks.
0715 *Mess gear; Smoking lamp lighted.*
0730 Breakfast; shift to uniform of the day.
0800 Relieve the watch; muster lifeboat's crew.
0815 Turn-to; smoking lamp out; bright work.
0830 Sick call.
0845 Knock off bright work; sweep down; clear up decks for quarters.
0910 Officers' call; divisions fall in for quarters.
0915 Quarters for muster and inspection; physical and day's drill.
1000 Relieve the wheel and lookouts.
1030 Retreat from drill; sweep down.
1145 *Mess gear.*
1200 Dinner.
1230 Relieve the watch; band call.
1315 Drill call.
1400 Relieve the wheel and lookouts.
1415 Retreat from drill; *Sweepers;* turn-to.
1530 Down washed clothes.
1600 Relieve the watch; muster lifeboat's crew.
1630 *Sweepers;* knock off ship's work; *Smoking lamp lighted;* turn on running lights at sunset (Follow SOPA); station lookouts; muster lifeboat's crew; inspect lifeboat.
1730 Clear up decks.
1745 *Mess gear.*
1800 Supper; relieve the wheel and lookouts.
1830 Turn-to; *Sweepers;* wet down the decks for scrubbing clothes.
1900 Band concert for crew until 2000.
2000 Relieve the wheel and lookouts; muster lifeboat's crew; all lights out except standing lights, lights in officers' quarters and CPO Mess.
2100 Tattoo; silence about the decks; smoking lamp out; lights out in CPO Mess.
2105 Taps.
2200 Lights out in officer's quarters.
2400 Relieve the watch. Muster lifeboat's crew.

Both in port and at sea, Sundays and National Holidays provided for a less stringent routine. There were no drills but routine watches were maintained. In lieu of arduous scrub downs and cleaning, the drill was to "titivate ship."

256

Each man received a bucket of fresh water daily for washing, shaving and laundry. The larger ships had laundries for officers. These were manned by "volunteers" who worked at night. It was a sought-after job since a *sub rosa,* but tolerated by COs and XOs, moonlighting ploy was to do the crew's laundry for $1 a man per month. Each week, the division would deliver a mattress cover filled with laundry which was returned rough-dry. It was a lucrative enterprise even after expenses for supplies were deducted. Officers, of course, paid for their laundry. The MarDet on larger ships had their own small steam pressers for their uniforms. Marines were not above accepting pressing work, for a fee, from sailors. There were many cottage industries aboard ship. Barbering, haircut inasmuch as beards were not allowed, was done in ship's barbershops at 15¢ for the men and 25¢ for the officers.

Most ships were "good feeders." The Officer of the Deck (OD) ate every meal (brought to him on a tray to the bridge) and said it was "sufficient as to quality and quantity." If you like beans for breakfast, you got them Wednesday and Saturday. Congress mandated that bread be a day old when served.

Most of the older ships did not have fresh-water showers but newer ones did. As the older ones were refitted, showers were installed. Fresh water was valuable with priorities going to the boilers, cooking and finally the crew. A shipboard shower was: wetting down and turning off the water; soaping up; turning on the water briefly to rinse. Sanitary facilities were primitive. The *head* (Navy term for toilet) had a trough on a bulkhead with flowing seawater vented to the overboard discharge. This was the urinal. Across from it on the opposite bulkhead was a lower trough with pairs of smooth buttocks-shaped slats. These were the "thrones" and running seawater kept them flushed. Officers and CPO amenities were only slightly better.

Smaller ships, like destroyers and submarines, had laundry and other services provided by the tenders. Shipboard life in The Treaty Navy was austere.

After World War I, there was a change in uniforms worn by officers. The high-neck tunic gave way to a double-breasted blue jacket with gold buttons. Rank was still worn on the sleeves in the form of gold stripes. A white shirt and black tie was worn with it. For summer or tropical wear, a high collar single-breasted gold-buttoned tunic with shoulder boards indicating rank was worn. The new cap had a wider crown. Aviation officers had a forest green version of the blues which they wore when ashore working with aircraft. Chiefs wore a single-breasted buttoned jacket in both blue and white with trousers to match. The CPO anchor device was worn on the cover of "The Hat" with no contrasting background. Enlisted had two sets of blues or whites, dress and undress. The blue trousers had a 13-button flap in front in lieu of a fly front as in the whites. Undress jumpers had plain collars draping over the back. A blue collar draping over the back with three narrow white stripes and two stars in the corners were on both blue and white dress jumpers. Both had blue knitted cuffs. There were two pieces of headgear. A white "dixie cup" cap was worn with both blues and whites except in winter when a flat blue cap was worn. (The latter was a casualty of the automobile age of the '60s. Too many hitch-hiking sailors were unseen victims of drivers at night.) The tight-fitting uniforms had no usable pockets. Sailors stuck their cigarette packs in their socks and a folded billfold was the outside of a "sandwich" over the top of the trousers but hidden by the overlap of the jumper. Many "salts" invested in a tailor made set of blues, usually with a bell-bottom to the trousers for liberty. An embroidered multi-colored dragon on the underside of the jumper cuff was the sign of an old "China hand." Another bit of decoration was the ribbon of the blue flat hat. It had either the name of the ship in which a sailor served or U.S. Navy if he wasn't in a ship

Appendix 9

CincCLant on Command

On Jan. 21, 1941, Adm. E.J King issued a circular letter to his subordinates in the newly formed Atlantic Fleet. Ernie King addressed the attitude problems which had crept into The Treaty Navy in the 20 years of its being dominated by thrift, discouragement of risk, lest it incur costs, and the fear of failure. It could well have saved the micromanagers of Vietnam, the Gulf War and all the national fiascos in between from their inept blundering.

Subject: Exercise of Command - Excess of detail in Orders and Instructions

1. I have been concerned for many years over the increasing tendency - now grown almost to "standard practice" of flag officers and other group commanders to issue orders or instructions in which their subordinates are told "how" as well as "what" to do to such an extent and in such detail that the "Custom of the service" has virtually become the antithesis of the essential element of command-"initiative of the subordinate."

2. We are preparing for - and are now close to - those active operations (commonly called war) which require the exercise and the utilization of the full powers and capabilities of every officer in command status. There will be neither time nor opportunity to do more than prescribe the several tasks of the several subordinates (to say *"what"* perhaps "when" and "where" and usually, for their intelligent cooperation, "why"); leaving to them - expecting and requiring them - the capacity to perform the assigned tasks (to do the *"how"*).

3. If subordinates are deprived - as they are now - of that training and experience which will enable them to act "on their own" - if they do not know, by constant practice, how to exercise "initiative of the subordinates" - if they are reluctant (afraid) to act because they are accustomed to detailed orders and instructions - if they are not habituated to think, to judge, to decide and to act for themselves in their several echelons of command - we shall be in sorry case when the time of "active operations" arrives.

258

4. The reasons for the current state of affairs - how did we get this way - are many but amongst most of them are four which need mention; first, the "anxiety" of seniors that everything in their commands shall be conducted so correctly and go so smoothly, that none may comment unfavorably; second, those energetic activities of staffs which lead to infringement of (not to say interference with) the functions for which lower echelons exist; third, the consequent "anxiety" of subordinates lest their exercise of initiative, even in legitimate spheres, should result in their doing something which may prejudice their selection for promotion; fourth, the habit on the one hand and the expectation on the other of "nursing" and "being nursed" which lead respectively to that violation of command principles known as "orders to obey orders" and to the admission of incapacity or confusion evidenced by "request instructions."

5. Let us consider certain facts: first, submarines operating submerged are constantly confronted with situations requiring the *correct* exercise of judgment, decision and action; second, planes, whether operating singly or in company, are even more called upon to act; third, surface ships entering or leaving port, making a landfall steaming in thick weather, etc. can and do meet such situations while "acting singly" and as well, the problems involved in maneuvering in formations and dispositions. Yet, these same people - proven competent to do these things without benefit of "advice" from higher up - are when grown in years and experience to be echelon commanders, all too often not made full use of in conducting the affairs administrative and operative of their several echelons - echelons which exist for the purpose of facilitating command.

6. It is essential to extend the knowledge and practice of initiative of the subordinate in principle and in application until they are universal in the exercise of command

throughout all echelons of command. Henceforth, we must see to it that full use is made of the echelons of command – whether administrative (type) or operative (task) by habitually framing orders and instructions to echelon commanders so as to tell them "what to do" but not "how to do it" unless particular circumstances so *demand.*

7. The corollaries of paragraph 6 are:
    (a)   adopt the premise that the echelon commanders are competent in their several command echelons unless and until they prove themselves otherwise;
    (b)   teach them that they are not only *expected* to be competent but it is *required* of them to be compete;
    (c)   train them – by guidance and supervision – to exercise foresight, to think, to judge, to decide and to act for themselves;
    (d)   stop "nursing" them
    (e)   finally, train ourselves to be satisfied with "acceptable solutions" even when they are not "staff solutions" or other particular solutions that we ourselves prefer.

E.J. King
Admiral USN

Where are the Ernie Kings now when we need them?

Appendix 10

Fifty Destroyers for Bases

By Executive Order of Sept. 2, 1940, President Roosevelt traded 50 U.S. destroyers for 99-year leases on British North American possessions for use as bases. The ships were:

DD-70 *USS Conway – HMS Lewes*
DD-72 *USS Connor – HMS Leeds*
DD-73 *USS Stockton – HMS Ludlow*
DD-75 *USS Wickes – HMCS Montgomery*
DD-76 *USS Philip – HMS Lancaster*
DD-78 *USS Evans – HMCS Mansfield*
DD-81 *USS Sigourney – HNMS Newport*
DD-88 *USS Robinson – HMS Newmarket*
DD-89 *USS Ringgold – HMS Newark*
DD-93 *USS Fairfax – HMCS Richmond –* Soviet *Zhivuchi*
DD-108 *USS Williams – HMCS St. Clair*
DD-127 *USS Twiggs – HMCS Leamington –* Soviet *Zhguchi*
DD-131 *USS Buchanan – HMS Campbelton* lost St. Nazaire 1942
DD-132 *USS Aaron Ward – HMS Castleton*
DD-133 *USS Hale – HMCS Caldwell*
DD-134 *USS Crowninshield – HMCS Chelsea -* Soviet *Derzki*
DD-135 *USS Tillman – HMS Wells*
DD-140 *USS Claxton – HNMS Salisbury*
DD-143 *USS Yarnell – HNMS Lincoln –* Soviet *Druzni*
DD-162 *USS Thatcher – HMCS Niagara*
DD-167 *USS Cowell – HMS Brighton –* Soviet *Zharki*
DD-168 *USS Maddox – HMS Georgetown –* Soviet *Zhostki*
DD-169 *USS Foote – HNMS Roxburgh –* Soviet *Dbltoini*
DD-170 *USS Kalk – HMCS Hamilton*
DD-175 *USS Mackenzie – HMCS Annapolis*
DD-181 *USS Hopewell – HNMS Bath* lost Aug. 19, 1941
DD-182 *USS Thomas – HNMS St. Albans –* Soviet *Dostonini*
DD-183 *USS Haraden – HMCS Columbia*
DD-184 *USS Abbot – HMS Charleston*
DD-185 *USS Doran – HMS St. Marys*
DD-190 *USS Satterlee – HMS Belmont* lost Jan. 31, 1942
DD-191 *USS Mason –* HMS *Broadwater* lost Oct. 18, 1941
DD-193 *USS Abel P. Upshur – HMS Clare*
DD-194 *USS Hunt – HMS Broadway*
DD-195 *USS Welborn C. Wood – HMS Chesterfield*
DD-197 *USS Branch – HMS Beverly* lost Apr. 11, 1943
DD-198 *USS Herndon – HMS Churchill –* Soviet *Deiatenyi*
DD-252 *USS McCook – HMCS St. Croix* lost Sept. 20, 1943
DD-253 *USS McCalla – HNMS Stanlet* lost Feb. 19, 1941
DD-254 *USS Rodgers – HMS Sherwood*
DD-256 *USS Bancroft – HMCS* St. *Francis* lost May 14, 1945
DD-257 *USS Welles – HMS Scamerob* lost Dc. 15, 1940
DD-258 *USS Aulick – HMS Burnham*
DD-263 *USS Laub – HMS Burwell*
DD-264 *USS McLanahan – HMS Bradford*
DD-265 *USS Edwards – HMCS Buxton*
DD-268 *USS Shubrick – HMS Ripley*
DD-269 *USS Bailey – HMS Reading*
DD-273 *USS Swasey – HMS Rockingham* lost Sept. 27, 1944

At the direction of Prime Minister Churchill, the RN names of the destroyers were names of cities and towns common to both Britain and the U.S.

Some were manned by Canadian crews and by crews from the Free governments of Occupied Countries, e.g., the Netherlands.

Several were given to U.S.S.R. as tonnage-in-kind for war reparations from the surrendered Italian fleet in 1943; USS *Milwaukee* (CL-5) became the Soviet *Murmansk* in April 1944 under the same conditions.

Appendix 11

Ship Losses of The Treaty Navy

Dec. 12, 1937   *Panay* (PR-5) Yangtze River –Air attack
Oct. 31, 1941   *Rueben James* No. Atlantic – submarine
Dec. 7, 1941   *Arizona* (BB-39) Pearl Harbor – Air attack
                          Oklahoma (BB-37) Pearl Harbor – Air attack
                          Utah (AG-16) Pearl Harbor – Air attack
Dec. 8, 1941   *Wake* (PR-3) Shanghai – Captured
                          Penguin (AVP-6) Guam – Air attack
Dec. 10, 1941   *Sealion* (SS-195) Cavite – Air attack
                          Bittern (AM-36) Cavite – Air attack
Dec. 12, 1941   *Robert L. Barnes* (AG-27) Guam – Captured
Jan. 20, 1942   S-36 (SS-141) Makasser Strait – Grounded
Jan. 23, 1942   *Neches* (AO-5) Off Hawaii- Submarine
Jan. 24, 1942   S-26 (SS-131) Panama – Collision
Feb. 18, 1942   *Truxton* (DD-229) Newfoundland – Wrecked in storm
                          Pollux (AKS-2) Newfoundland – Wrecked in storm
Feb. 19, 1942   *Peary* (DD-226) Darwin –Air attack
Feb. 27, 1942   *Langley* (AV-3) South of Java – Air attack
Feb. 28, 1942   *Jacob Jones* (DD-130) Off New Jersey – Submarine
                          Houston (CA-30) Sundra Strait – Gunfire
Mar. 1, 1942   *Pecos* (AO-6) South of Java – Air attack
                          Edsall (DD-219) South of Java – Gunfire
                          Pillsbury (DD-227) Bali Strait – Gunfire
                          Pope (DD-225) Bali Strait – Gunfire and air attack
Mar 2, 1942   *Stewart* (DD-224) Surabaya – Scuttled (IJN P-102)
Mar.3, 1942   *Asheville* (PG-21) South of Java – Gunfire
Mar.18, 1942   *Shark* (SS-174) East China Sea – Overdue
Apr 3, 1942   *Pigeon* (ARS-9) Corregidor – Air attack
Apr.4, 1942   *Tanager* (AM-5) Corregidor – Air attack
Apr.8, 1942   *Napa* (AT-32) Bataan – Scuttled
Apr.10, 1942   *Dewey Drydock (*YFD-1) Bataan – Scuttled
                          Canopus (AS-9) Bataan – Scuttled
                          Finch (AM-9) Corregidor – Air attack
Apr.11, 1942   *Perch* (SS-176) Java – Overdue
Apr. 26, 1942   *Sturtevant* (DD-240) Off Florida – Mine
May 2, 1942   *Mindanao* (PR-8) Corregidor – Air attack
May 4, 1942   *Oahu* (PR-6) Corregidor – Gunfire
May 5, 1942   *Luzon* (PR-7) Corregidor – Captured
                          Quail (AM-15) Corregidor – Gunfire
                          Genesse (ATO-55) Corregidor – Scuttled
May 7, 1942   *Sims* (DD-409) Coral Sea – Air attack
                          Neosho (AO-23) Coral Sea – Air attack
May 8, 1942   *Lexington* (CV-2) Coral Sea – Air attack
Jun.6, 1942   *Hammann* (DD-412) Midway – Submarine
Jun.7, 1942   *Yorktown* (CV-5) Midway – Submarine
                          Gannet (AVP-8) Off Bermuda – Submarine
Jun. 19, 1942   S-27 (SS-132) Amchitka Island – Grounded
Aug. 4, 1942   *Tucker* (DD-374) Espiritu Santo – Mine
Aug. 8, 1942   *George F. Elliot* (AP-13) Guadalcanal – Air attack
                          Jarvis (DD-393) Guadalcanal – Air attack
Aug. 9, 1942   *Astoria* (CA-34) Savo Island – Gunfire and torpedo
                          Quincy (CA-39) Savo Island – Gunfire and torpedo

	Vincennes (CA-44) Savo Island – Gunfire and torpedo
Aug.18, 1942	S-39 (SS-144) Rossell Island – Grounded
Aug.22, 1942	*Ingraham* (DD-444) Atlantic – Collision
	Blue (DD-387) Guadalcanal – Torpedo
Sep. 5, 1942	*Colhoun* (APD-2) Guadalcanal – Gunfire
	Gregory (APD-3) Guadalcanal – Gunfire
	Little (APD-4) Guadalcanal – Gunfire
Sep.15, 1942	*O'Brien* (DD-415) South of Solomons – Submarine
	Wasp (CV-7) Solomons – Submarine
Oct.5, 1942	*Grunion* (SS-216) Pacific – Overdue
Oct.12, 1942	*Duncan* (DD-485) Cape Esperance – Gunfire
Oct.15, 1942	*Meredith* (DD-434) Solomons – Air attack
Oct.26, 1942	*Hornet* (CV-8) Santa Cruz – Air attack
	Porter (DD-356) Santa Cruz – Air attack
Nov.12, 1942	*Erie* (PG-50) Curacao – Submarine
Nov.13, 1942	*Monssen* (DD-436) Guadalcanal – Gunfire
	Cushing (DD-376) Guadalcanal – Gunfire
	Laffey (DD-459) Guadalcanal – Gunfire
Nov.15, 1942	*Benham* (DD-397) Guadalcanal – Torpedo
	Preston (DD-379) Guadalcanal – Gunfire
	Walke (DD-416) Guadalcanal – Gunfire and torpedo
Nov.29, 1942	*Wasmuth* (DMS-15) Aleutians – Foundered
Nov.30, 1942	*Northampton* (CA-26) Tassafaronga – Torpedo
Jan. 1, 1943	*Rescuer* (ARS-18) Aleutians – Grounded
Jan.10, 1943	*Argonaut* (SS-166) Southwest Pacific – Overdue
Jan.12, 1943	*Worden* (DD-353) Amchitka Island – Grounded
Jan.30, 1943	*Chicago* (CA-29) Rennell Island – Air attack
Feb. 1, 1943	*DeHaven* (DD-469) Savo Island – Air attack
Apr. 7, 1943	*Aaron Ward* (DD-483) Guadalcanal – Air attack
	Kanawha (AO-1) Guadalcanal – Air attack
Jun.12, 1943	R-12 (SS-89) U.S Coast – Overdue
	Amberjack (SS-219) Pacific – Overdue
	Grampus (SS-207) Pacific – Overdue
Jun.28, 1943	*Redwing* (ARS-4) Mediterranean – Mine
Jul. 5, 1943	*Strong* (DD-467) New Georgia – Torpedo
Jul. 6, 1943	*Helena* (CL-50) Kula Gulf – Torpedo
Jul. 7, 1943	*Maddox* (DD-622) Sicily – Air attack
Jul.13 1943	*Gwin* DD-433) Kollombangara – Gunfire
Jul.22, 1943	*Triton* (SS-201) Pacific – Overdue
Aug.15, 1943	*Pickerel* (SS-177) Pacific – Overdue
Sep.11, 1943	*Rowan* (DD-405) Off Italy – Air attack
Sep.14, 1943	*Grenadier* (SS-210) Pacific – Overdue
Oct. 3, 1943	*Henley* (DD-391) South Pacific – Torpedo
Oct. 9, 1943	*Buck* (DD-420) Salerno Gulf - Submarine
Oct.10, 1943	*Chevalier (*DD-451) Vella LaVella – Torpedo
Oct.13, 1943	*Bristol* (DD-453) Mediterranean – Submarine
Oct.27, 1943	*Runner* (SS-275) Pacific – Overdue
Nov. 1, 1943	*Borie* (DD-215) North Atlantic – Rammed U-boat
Nov.17, 1943	*McKean* (APD-5) Bougainville – Air attack
Nov.18, 1943	*Sculpin* (SS-191) Truk- Depth charge
Nov.29, 1943	*Perkins* (DD-377) New Guinea – Collision
Dec. 2, 1943	*Wahoo* (SS-238) Pacific – Overdue
Dec.24, 1943	*Dorado* (SS-248) Pacific – Overdue
	Leary (DD-158) North Atlantic – Submarine
	Grayling (SS-209) Pacific – Overdue
Dec.27, 1943	*Brownson* (DD-518) Cape Gloucester – Air attack

Jan. 1, 1944   *Turner* (DD-648) Sandy Hook – Explosion
Jan. 5, 1944   *Pompano* (SS-181) Pacific – Overdue
Feb. 8, 1943   S-44 (SS-155) Pacific – Overdue
Feb.12, 1944   *Macaw* (ARS-11) Midway Island – Grounded
Mar.14, 1944   *Corvina* (SS-226) Pacific – Overdue
Mar.22, 1944   *Scorpion* (SS-278) Pacific – Overdue
Apr.20, 1944   *Lansdale* (DD-426) Mediterranean – Air attack
May 2, 1944   *Parrott* (DD-218) Norfolk – Collision
Jun. 4, 1944   S-28 (SS-133) Hawaii – Accident
Jun. 5, 1944   *Osprey* (AM-56) English Channel – Mine
Jun. 6, 1944   *Corry* (DD-463) Normandy - Mine
Jun. 7, 1944   *Glennon* (DD-620) Normandy - Mine
Jun.20, 1944   *Grayback* (SS-208) Pacific - Overdue
Jul.22, 1944   *Trout* (SS-202) Pacific – Overdue
               Tublibee (SS-284) Pacific – Overdue
Sep. 6, 1944   *Robalo* (SS-273) Pacific – Overdue
Sep.12, 1944   *Noa* (APD-24) Pacific – Collision
               Gudgeon (SS-211) Pacific – Overdue
Sep.13, 1944   *Warrington* (DD-383) Atlantic – Hurricane
Sep.14, 1944   *Perry* (DMS-17 Palau) – Mine
Sep.19, 1944   *Flier* (SS-250) Pacific – Operational loss
Sep.17, 1944   *Montgomery* (DM-17) Ngulu Lagoon – Mine
Oct.23, 1944   *Herring* (SS-233) Pacific – Overdue
Oct.24, 1944   *Darter* (SS-237 Leyte – Stranded on a rock
Oct.25, 1944   *Hoel* (DD-533) Leyte Gulf – Gunfire
               Johnston (DD-557) Leyte Gulf – Gunfire
Dec. 7, 1944   *Ward* (APD-16) Leyte – Air attack
               Mahan (DD-364) Leyte – Air attack
Dec.11, 1944   *Reid* (DD-369) Ormoc Bay – Air attack
Dec.17, 1944   *Hull* (DD-350) Off Luzon – Typhoon
               Monaghan (DD-354) Off Luzon – Typhoon
               Spence (DD-512) Off Luzon – Typhoon
Dec.28, 1944   *Seawolf* (SS-197) Pacific – Overdue
Jan. 2, 1945   *Harder* (SS-257) Pacific – Overdue
               Growler (SS-215) Pacific - Overdue
Jan. 6, 1945   *Hovey* (DMS-11) Lingayen Gulf – Air attack
               Long (DMS-12) Lingayen Gulf – Air attack
Jan 7, 1945   *Palmer* (DMS-5) Lingayen Gulf – Air attack
Feb.18, 1945   *Gamble* (DM-15) Iwo Jima – Air attack
Mar.26, 1945   *Halligan* (DD-584) Okinawa - Mine
Mar.27, 1945   *Albacore* (SS-218) Pacific - Overdue
Apr. 5, 1945   *Thornton* (AVD-11) Okinawa – Collision
               *Dickerson (*APD-21) Okinawa – Air attack
Apr. 6, 1945   *Bush* (DD-529) Okinawa – *Kamikaze*
               Emmons (DMS-22) – *Kamikaze*
Apr.12, 1945   *Scamp* (SS-277) Pacific – Overdue
Apr.16, 1945   *Pringle* (DD-477) Okinawa – *Kamikaze*
May 4, 1945   *Morrison* (DD-560) Okinawa – *Kamikaze*
               Luce (DD-522) Okinawa – *Kamikaze*
               Swordfish (SS-193) Pacific - Overdue
May18, 1945   *Longshaw* (DD-559) Okinawa – *Kamikaze*
May25, 1945   *Bates* (APD-47) Okinawa – *Kamikaze*
Jun.10, 1945   *William D. Porter* (DD-579) Okinawa – *Kamikaze*
Jun.16, 1945   *Twiggs* (DD-591) Okinawa – Torpedo
Jun. 21, 1945 *Barry* (APD-29) Okinawa – *Kamikaze*
Jul. 5, 1945   *Trigger* (SS-237) Pacific – Overdue

Jul.30, 1945	*Indianapolis* (CA-35) Philippine Sea – Submarine
Aug.4, 1945	*Snook* (SS-279) Pacific – Overdue
Aug.11, 1945	*Bonefish* (SS-223) Pacific – Overdue

Not all surviving ships of The Treaty Navy were discarded after the war and sent to the breakers to be made into razor blades. Nine are preserved as memorials. Six light cruisers were sold to South American countries. There were 43 of the later destroyers sold to Taiwan, Greece, Italy, Japan, Turkey, Brazil, Spain, Peru and Argentina. But a few were destined for an honorable burial at sea as a result of the two A–tests at Bikini Atoll in the summer of 1946. Many survived the bombing but were later scuttled at sea or like *Nevada* two years later sunk by 16-in., 6-in. guns and aerial torpedoes.

War Memorials

Alabama (BB-60) and *Drum* (SS-228) – Mobile Bay, Ala.; *Cavalla* (SS-244) – Galveston, Texas; *Ling* (SS-244) – Hackensack, N.J.; *Massachusetts* (BB-59) and *Lionfish* (SS-298) – Fall River, Mass.; *North Carolina* (BB-55) – Wilmington, N.C.; *Silversides* (SS-236) – Evanston, Ill.; *Texas* (BB-35) – San Jacinto, Texas, and *Missouri* (BB-63) – Honolulu, Hawaii. There are other ships memorials but these are those of The Treaty Navy.

Light Cruisers to South America

Brooklyn (CL-40) to Chile as *O'Higgins*; *Philadelphia* (CL-41) to Brazil as *Barroso; Nashville* (CL-43) to Chile as *Capitan Prat; Phoenix* (CL—46) to Argentina as *General Belgrano* (sunk by a RN submarine in the 1982 Falklands War); *Boise* (CL-47) to Argentina as *9 De Julio;* and *St. Louis* (CL-49) to Brazil as *Tamandare*.

Target Ships at Bikini

Saratoga (CV-3), *Arkansas* (BB-33), *New York* (BB-34), *Nevada* (BB-36), *Pensacola* (CA-24), *Salt Lake City* (CA-25), *Lamson* (DD-367), *Mugford* (DD-389), *Ralph Talbot* (DD-390), *Mayrant* (DD-402), *Trippe* (DD-403), *Rhind* (DD-404), *Stack* (DD-406), *Wilson* (DD-408), *Hughes* (DD-410), *Anderson* (DD-411), *Mustin* (DD-413), *Roe* (DD-418), *Skipjack* (SS-184), *Searaven* (SS-196), and *Tuna* (SS-203).

The "Mothball" Fleet

"What goes around comes around!" There was one final folly of the "bean counter mentality." It was tantamount to the complacency after World War I when the U.S. had more than 300 destroyers (of the same age) and therefore didn't need to build any more. The ships built during World War II were basically all of the same age and state of the art. It was decided to preserve them for future emergencies. They were "mothballed," describing their preservation in dehumidified status with "cocoons" of plastic keeping them in a non-rusting state. Of course, the hulls, weapons and machinery were preserved for a good number of years – *so was the technology.* Unfortunately, progress in technology was rapid and like Rip Van Winkle, the sleeping ships of the victorious Navy were left behind. No money was spent on keeping them current since the Congress and public were lulled into a false sense of security.

Communications equipment, on board, still used vacuum tubes in the radios when transistors were becoming state-of-the art (not to mention later microchips). Fire control computers were still bulky mechanical devices when electronics were becoming the wave of the present. Mechanical computers weren't fast enough to generate a solution against speedy jets. The mighty hulls in "mothballs" were becoming obsolete every day. What was worse was that this was not realized and a false sense of security developed. Like their valiant crews, the ships of World War II were getting old. To depend on either to fight a future war was foolish.

Vinson's vision for a Navy of modern under-age ships was betrayed, *pro tem.*

266

Bibliographical Essay

Since my purpose is to tell the story of The Treaty Navy for the reader, not to provide a road map for scholars to do further research, I have dispensed with a formal bibliography. Instead, I use this essay to give the more serious reader some background material for further insight into The Treaty Navy. There is a dearth of material on the subject *per se.* This volume is the only one I know of that covers the topic as an entity. Many other works, particularly about naval operations in World War II or biographies of the U.S. naval leaders of that struggle, allude in preface or in passing to the existence of a Naval Service prior to World War II but only as background to the story of that war.

My interest in naval heritage, especially the portion I cover herein, was piqued by several of my professors at the Naval Academy, *inter alia,* Bill Russell, Ned Potter, Paolo Coletta, Jim Cutting, Allen Blow Cook and Bill Jefferies. My M.A, thesis at Catholic University of America (International Law – 1971) was on the legality of poison gas which lead to my first book, *Poison Gas – The Myths versus Reality* (Westport: Greenwood Press, 1999). My thesis at the University of Nevada (Journalism – 1981) was on the press as a historical resource. Hence the first publication that I invite the reader's attention to is a newspaper.

The New York Times, particularly during the period covered in this volume, is a national newspaper of record. It is easily accessed through *The New York Times Index.* Annual volumes of the *Index* devote a complete topical heading to **Navy** with numerous sub-topics such as: Appropriations, Construction, specific ships by name as well as individuals. Most good libraries have copies of all editions of the newspaper on microfilm so the reader can look up and even follow a contemporary story on The Treaty Navy. Although most other newspapers which now have indices of their own, did not have them during the '20s and '30s, reference to the date of a particular event in *The Times* can steer the reader to when to find it in another newspaper. Another newspaper that provides useful information about The Treaty Navy, especially the debates on authorizations and appropriations is the *Congressional Record.*

The Annual Report of the Secretary of the Navy is a good source for major chronology as well as technical data on personnel, maneuvers, policy, projections of future employment and other information. It also contains reports of each of the Bureaux. More informal information including pay scales can be found in the annual *Navy Register* put out during the period by the Navy. A wealth of information on ships and officers of the Naval Service can be found in the quarterly *Navy Directory* issued by the Bureau of Navigation. It lists all officers, Navy and Marine Corps, on active duty. It has an index to specific vessels including their mailing address, home yard and homeport. The entire wardroom roster, by ship, is listed. A complete listing of the Shore Establishment with its major stations and their smaller tenants gives an idea as to the enormity of the Navy's infrastructure. Short "biographies" of every ship in The Treaty Navy can be found in the Navy Department, Naval History Division's multi-volume work: *Dictionary of American Naval Fighting Ships.* This project started after World War II with alphabetical volumes does list all of the ships in The Treaty Navy. Some newer ships with names at the beginning of the alphabet had, perforce, to be included in later supplements. Information on Naval Academy Classes during the period of The Treaty Navy can be gleaned from the U.S. Naval Academy Alumni Association's annual *Register of Alumni.* Any edition prior to 1995 since that is the last year graduates were listed by order of graduation is germane. Later volumes are more alphabetical Class directories..

There are many readable works and biographies which can give the reader a broad flavor of the era of The Treaty Navy and the war for which it was built and which it fought. Thomas A. Bailey's *A Diplomatic History of the American People Ninth Edition* (Englewood Cliffs, N.J.: Prentice-Hall, 1974) gives a good overview of the United States on the international scene during the first half of the century. A must for any serous student of American naval activity during the 20th Century are the 15 volumes of Samuel E. Morrison's *History of United States Naval Operations in World War II* (Boston: Little Brown and Company 1947-1962). Although written before the secret of our reading the Japanese codes was revealed, the work gives an excellent account of the Naval Service in World War II. Anyone not versed in the theory of naval warfare advocated by RAdm. Alfred T. Mahan might want to read his *The Influence of Sea Power on History* (New York Sagamore Press, 1957). A good short biographical sketch of Adm. William S. Sims can be found in *Makers of Naval Tradition* (Boston: Ginn and Company, 1943) by Carroll S. Alden and Ralph Earle. Paolo E. Coletta edited a two-volume collection *American Secretaries of the Navy* (Annapolis: Naval Institute Press 1980). His second volume contains capsule biographies of the Secretaries during The Treaty Navy.

A work that shows that in 1921 there were strategic thinkers anticipating a naval war with Japan in the Pacific is Major Earl H. Ellis's Operation Plan 721, *Advanced Base Operations in Micronesia.* His mentor, John A. Lejeune in *The Reminiscences of a Marine* (Philadelphia: Dorrance and Company, 1932) gives an account of the Marine Corps during his tenure as MGC. A view of naval thinking on "the other side of the pond" is the theme of retired Capt. Stephen Roskill RN. His *Naval Policy Between the Wars - The Period of Anglo-American Antagonism 1919-1929* (New York: Walker and Company, 1968) recounts the British view on naval armaments. Gerald E. Wheeler in *Admiral William Veazie Pratt USN* (Washington: Naval History Division, 1974) gives much of the credit for healing the Anglo-American rift to his subject. Although the biography provides background on the initial years of The Treaty Navy it is a "puff piece" on a participant whom many of his subordinates considered more of a political opportunist than naval professional. The volume omits some significant episodes of his tenure, e.g., the Massie Affair. A better insight into the pre World War II Naval Service can be found in VAdm. George C. Dyer's *On the Treadmill to Pearl Harbor,* (same publisher), the memoirs of Adm. J.O. Richardson. George Dyer, a naval professional was Adm. Richardson's Flag Lieutenant. Another biography replete with good background on the era and its innovations and innovators is E.B. Potter's *Nimitz* (Annapolis: Naval Institute Press, 1976). Since Naval Aviation really found itself during the time of The Treaty Navy and came of age in World War II, a history of Naval Aviation in its beginnings is a must. Such a work is *History of United States Naval Aviation* (New Haven: Yale University Press, 1949). This work by Archibald D. Turnbull and Clifford L. Lord traces he bumpy rise of Naval Aviation during the '20s and '30s. Another work on the foibles of Naval Aviation during the period is by Richard K. Smith. His *The Airships Akron and Macon* (Annapolis: Naval Institute Press, 1965) tells of the fatal fascination some aviation advocates had with rigid airships.

A reminder in these days of global commitments of our forces to "peace keeping" is Maj. (later LtGen.) Julian C. Smith's, *A Review of the Organization and Operations of the* Guardia Nacional de Nicaragua (Washington, USMC, undated). He tells of the efforts of Marines to keep peace in Nicaragua. The story of Marine innovators and their struggle against the "conventional wisdom" of military experts is the thesis of Jeter A. Isley and Phillip A. Crowl. Their *The U.S. Marines and Amphibious War* (Princeton: Princeton University Press, 1951) tells that the Marine Corps foresaw that its mission was to enable The Treaty Navy to "wage war in Japanese waters." Some of the best descriptions of the Marine Corps between the wars are found in the chapters on that time in *Soldiers of the Sea* (Annapolis: U.S. Naval Institute, 1962) by Col. Robert D. Heinl USMC (Ret.)

I have saved for the end of this essay a litany of those items some (not I) feel are the *sine qua non* of a written work – the official documents. Good background on the early troubles with Japan as well as on the roots of The Treaty Navy can be found in *The Papers of Theodore Roosevelt*. I found them on microfilm and not catalogued by topic but chronologically. They are voluminous but worth reading.

For the exact wording of naval legislation I refer the reader to *U.S. Statutes at Large* the various volumes from 1916 to 1941. In all look for the title "Increase of the Navy." In the early '30s also consult "National Industrial Recovery Act."

Papers Relating to the Foreign Relations of the United States [by year and/or country] (Washington: Government Printing Office) list most of the correspondence with our ambassadors, delegations plus other diplomatic matters. *The Department of State Conference Series* details, *inter alia*, the various naval limitations conferences. U.S. Department of State's *Treaties of theUnited States* is a source for the naval limitation treaty texts.

Since my coverage of the affair of William B. Shearer is relatively extensive, I refer the interested reader to two documents on the subject. The first is *Records of the Conference for the Limitations of Naval Armaments, Held at Geneva, Switzerland, from June 20 to August 4, 1927, 79th Congress, 1st Session, Senate Document No. 55* (Washington: Government Printing Office, 1928.) The other is: *U.S. Senate, Subcommittee on Naval Affairs, Genera Conference, Alleged activities at, by William B. Shearer:* Senate Resolution 114, 71st Congress, 2nd Session (Washington: Government Printing Office, 1929.)

The full terms of the "Destroyers for Bases" deal can be found in U.S. Department of State Executive Agreement Series No 181, *Naval and Air Bases – Arrangement between the United States of America and Great Britain* (Washington: Government Printing Office, 1940). Samuel D. Roseman's editing of the 13 volumes of The *Public Papers and Addresses of Franklin D. Roosevelt* (New York: Russell and Russell, 1938-1950) is a good source for many of F.D.R.'s views on The Treaty Navy.

Finally for those skeptics who still wonder if American unrestricted submarine warfare wasn't a violation of a treaty obligation in perpetuity, I invite them to: Oppenheim, L. (Lauterpacht, H, (ed.) *International Law Vol. 2, Disputes, War and Neutrality* 7th Ed. (New York: David McKay Company, 1952.)

INDEX

275

277

278

THE AUTHOR

Wes Hammond, a 1951 graduate of the U.S. Naval Academy, retired from the U.S. Marine Corps in 1975. In addition to a B.S. from the Naval Academy, he has a M.A. (International Law) from the Catholic University of America and a M.A. (Journalism) from the University of Nevada.

During more than a quarter of a century of active duty, he was wounded in action as an infantry platoon leader in Korea; twice, he was a tactics instructor at the Marine Corps Basic School in Quantico, Va.; commanded a company in an infantry battalion afloat in the Mediterranean; was aide-de-camp to MajGen. D.M. Shoup (later 22n Commandant of the Marine Crops) on Okinawa, where Wes met and married Miss Donna M. Selby of Brighton, Colorado. He deployed with the forces afloat for the Cuban Missile Crisis. He commanded the 2nd Battalion, Fourth Marines ("The Magnificent Bastards") in Vietnam until wounded in action and evacuated. He returned to duty as Plans Officer of the 3rd Marine Division until wounded again. Then he was Head, Command Dept., Marine Corps Command & Staff College in Quantico. There he taught Research and Writing; Command and Staff Organization and a future concept of amphibious operations called "Sea Base." He was transferred to Hawaii and promoted to colonel and assigned as Protocol Officer and Aide to Commander-in-Chief, Pacific, Adm. John S. McCain, Jr. USN. He retired from Camp Pendleton, Calif., and returned to Reno, Nevada.

While on active duty (1964-67) he was Editor & Publisher of the *Marine Corps Gazette,* the professional journal of the Marine Corps Association. Eight years after retiring from the Marine Corps, he moved to Annapolis, Md., to be editor of *Shipmate,* the monthly magazine of the U.S. Naval Academy Alumni Association. After a dozen years there, he again retired and returned to Reno.

He is the author of more than 50 articles in professional military journals as well as popular publications. His *Poison Gas – The Myths versus Reality* (Greenwood Press, Westport Conn. 1999) is a plea for common sense lest we be held hostage to fear of the unknown.

The Hammonds make their home in Reno but travel extensively. They have three children and seven grandchildren. A collaborator in this volume was LtCol. James W. Hammond, III USMC, who while still a Midshipman at the U.S. Naval Academy, traced down the answers to many queries from his father by searching the stacks of the Nimitz Library at the Academy.

ISBN 1552128768

55674480R00163

Made in the USA
Middletown, DE
17 July 2019